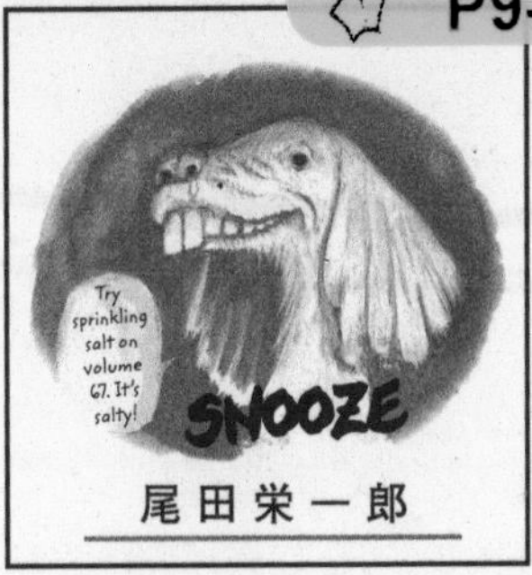
Try sprinkling salt on volume 67. It's salty!
SNOOZE
尾田栄一郎

Snooze. What the heck is "snooze"? Somehow this weird little word has permeated our society. *Snooze*. If I had to conjure up an image of the word devoid of context, it would be this illustration. Okay, here comes volume 67. Don't snooze on it!!

-Eiichiro Oda, 2012

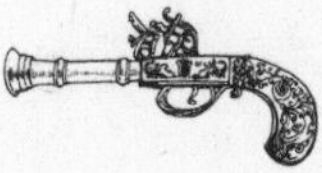

Eiichiro Oda began his manga career at the age of 17, when his one-shot cowboy manga **Wanted!** won second place in the coveted Tezuka manga awards. Oda went on to work as an assistant to some of the biggest manga artists in the industry, including Nobuhiro Watsuki, before winning the Hop Step Award for new artists. His pirate adventure **One Piece**, which debuted in **Weekly Shonen Jump** in 1997, quickly became one of the most popular manga in Japan.

ONE PIECE VOL. 67
NEW WORLD PART 7

SHONEN JUMP Manga Edition

STORY AND ART BY EIICHIRO ODA

Translation/Stephen Paul
Touch-up Art & Lettering/Vanessa Satone
Design/Fawn Lau
Editor/Alexis Kirsch

ONE PIECE © 1997 by Eiichiro Oda. All rights reserved.
First published in Japan in 1997 by SHUEISHA Inc., Tokyo.
English translation rights arranged by SHUEISHA Inc.

The rights of the author(s) of the work(s) in this publication to be so
identified have been asserted in accordance with the Copyright, Designs
and Patents Act 1988. A CIP catalogue record for this book is available
from the British Library.

The stories, characters and incidents mentioned in this publication are
entirely fictional.

Printed in the U.S.A.

Published by VIZ Media, LLC
P.O. Box 77010
San Francisco, CA 94107

10 9 8 7 6 5 4 3 2 1
First printing, June 2013

www.viz.com

THE WORLD'S MOST POPULAR MANGA
SHONEN JUMP
www.shonenjump.com

ONE PIECE

Vol. 67 COOL FIGHT

STORY AND ART BY

EIICHIRO ODA

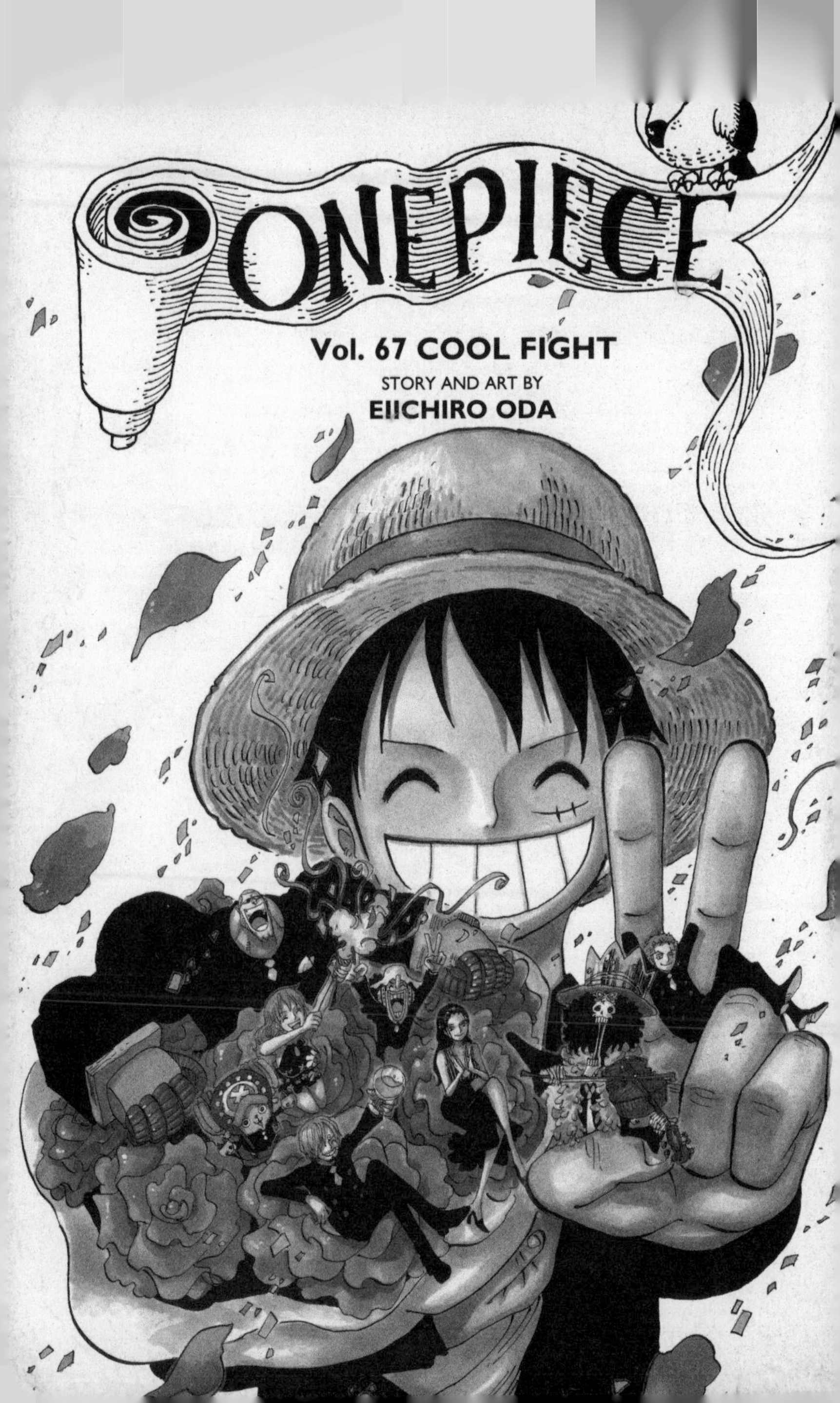

The Straw Hat Crew

Monkey D. Luffy

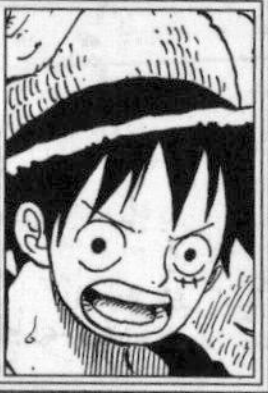

A young man who dreams of becoming the Pirate King. After training with Rayleigh, he and his crew head for the New World!

Captain, Bounty: 400 million berries

Roronoa Zolo

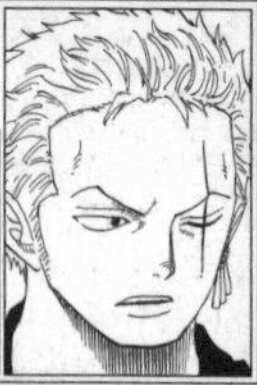

He swallowed his pride and asked to be trained by Mihawk on Gloom Island before reuniting with the rest of the crew.

Fighter, Bounty: 120 million berries

Tony Tony Chopper

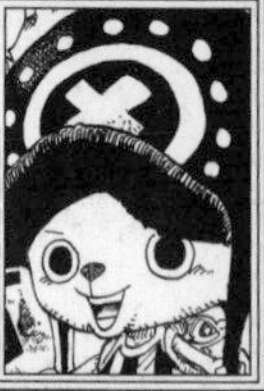

After researching powerful medicine in Birdie Kingdom, he reunites with the rest of the crew.

Ship's Doctor, Bounty: 50 berries

Nami

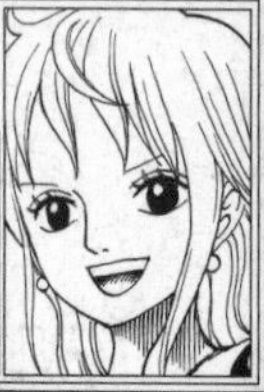

She studied the weather of the New World on the small Sky Island Weatheria, a place where weather is studied as a science.

Navigator, Bounty: 16 million berries

Nico Robin

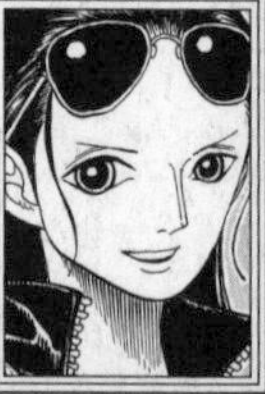

She spent her time in Baltigo with the leader of the Revolutionary Army: Luffy's father, Dragon.

Archeologist, Bounty: 80 million berries

Usopp

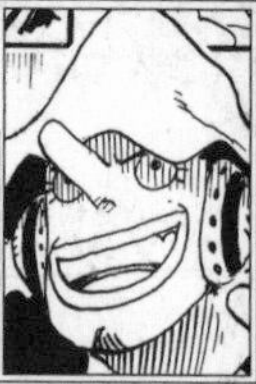

He trained under Heracles at the Bowin Islands to become the King of Snipers.

Sniper, Bounty: 30 million berries

Franky

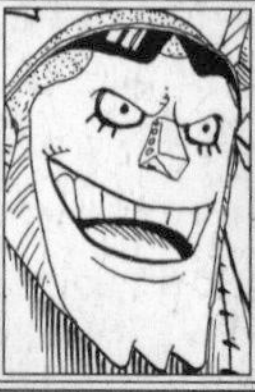

He modified himself in Future Land Baldimore and turned himself into Armored Franky before reuniting with the rest of the crew.

Shipwright, Bounty: 44 million berries

Sanji

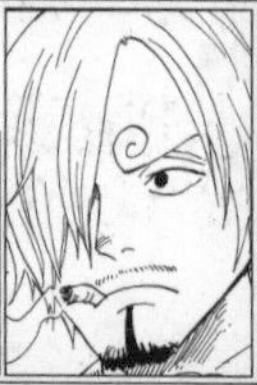

After fighting the New Kama Karate masters in the Kamabakka Kingdom, he returned to the crew.

Cook, Bounty: 77 million berries

Brook

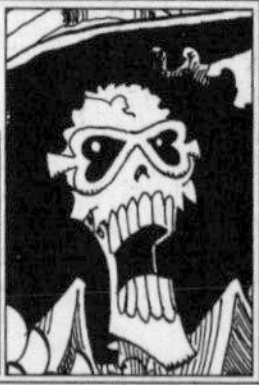

After being captured and used as a freak show by the Longarm Tribe, he became a famous rock star called "Soul King" Brook.

Musician, Bounty: 33 million berries

The story of ONE PIECE 1»67

Shanks

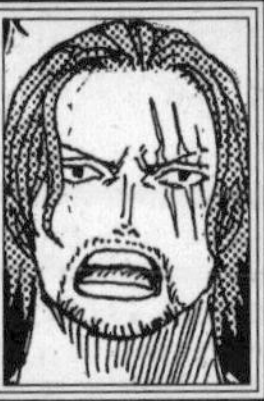

One of the Four Emperors. He continues to wait for Luffy in the second half of the Grand Line, called the New World.

Captain of the Red-Haired Pirates

Naval G-5: 5th Branch of the Naval Grand Line Forces

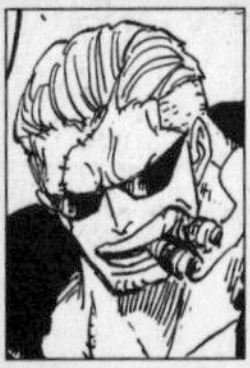

White Chase Smoker

G-5 Vice Admiral

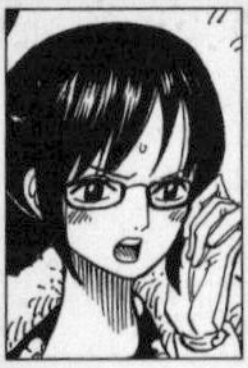

Tashigi

G-5 Captain

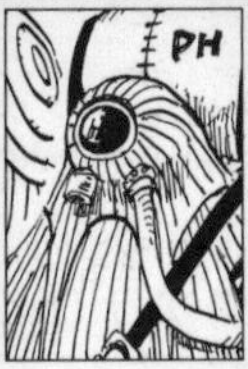
PH

?

?

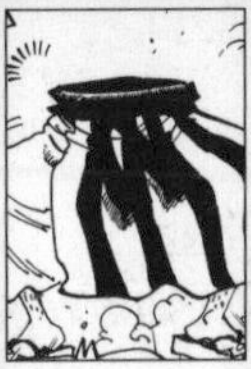

?

?

Story

Having finished their two years of training, the Straw Hat crew reunites on the Sabaody Archipelago. They set sail more determined than ever to reach the New World!

The *Thousand Sunny* takes them to Fish-Man Island, 30,000 feet below the sea, where the Fish-Men hold a deep hatred for mankind. Captain Hody of the New Fish-Man Pirates announces his intent to take over the kingdom! Luffy's crew rescues Princess Shirahoshi, who wants peace with the humans, and they stop Hody's scheme. Now the island is ready to walk forward into the future...

After saying their goodbyes to Shirahoshi, the Straw Hats set off for the New World. Up on the surface, they receive an emergency signal and land on an island...guarded by a dragon! And what's up with the guy who's just a pair of legs?!

Vol. 67
Cool Fight

CONTENTS

Chapter 657:
SEVERED HEAD

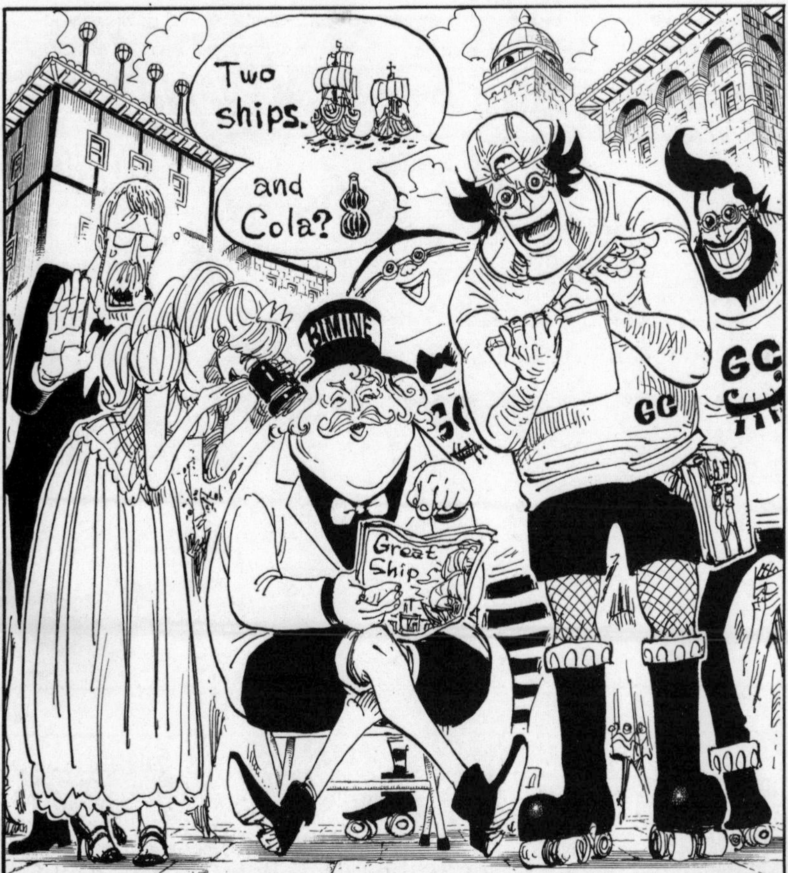

Two ships.
and Cola?
BIMINE
Great Ship
GC
GC

DECKS OF THE WORLD, VOL. 39: "GOURMET TOWN PUCCI—FOR SHIP BUYING, REPAIRS AND DISMANTLING, SEE THE ZAMBAI UNION"

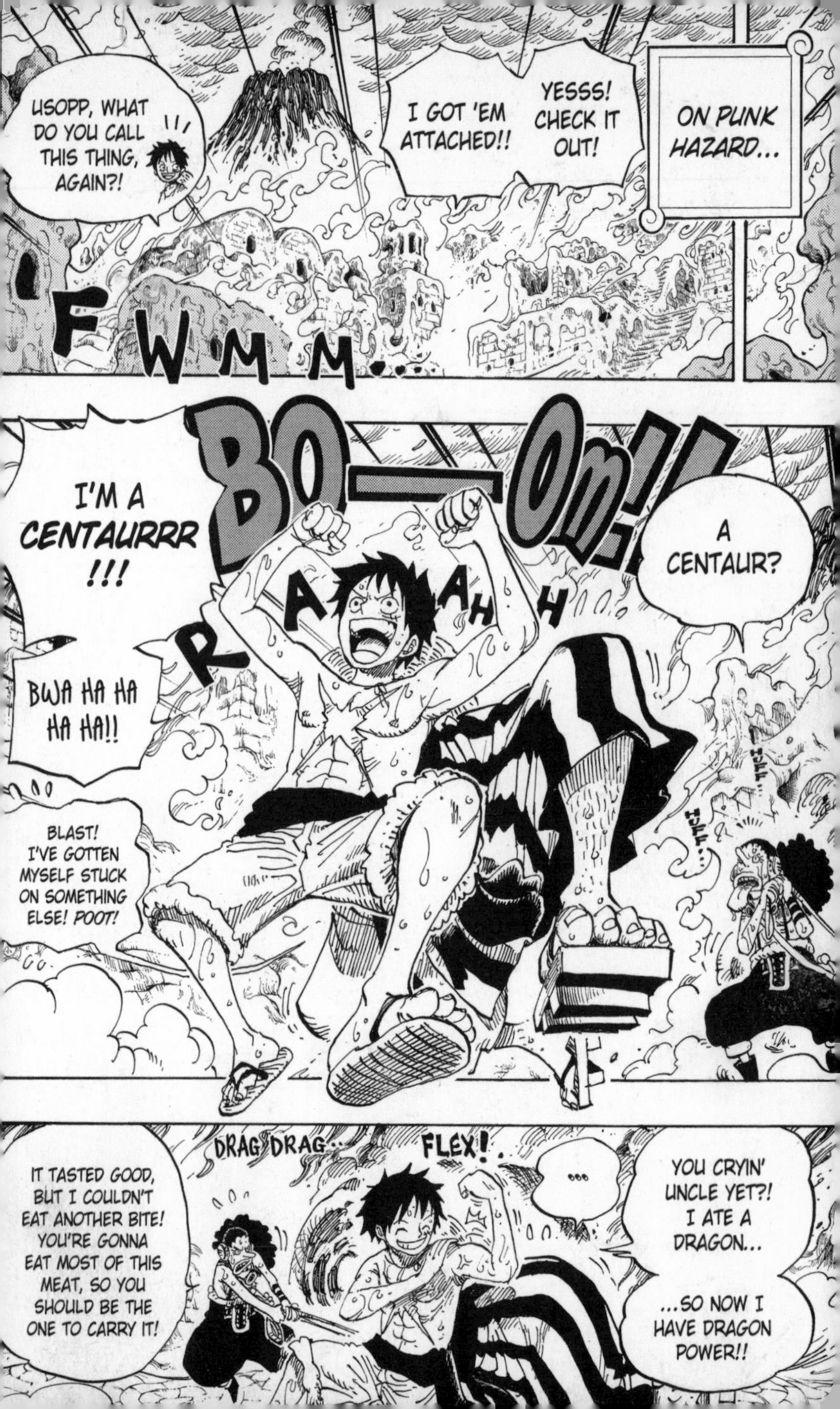

ON PUNK HAZARD...
YESSS! CHECK IT OUT!
I GOT 'EM ATTACHED!!
USOPP, WHAT DO YOU CALL THIS THING, AGAIN?!
FWMM...
A CENTAUR?
BO—OM!!
I'M A CENTAURRR!!!
RAAHH
BWA HA HA HA HA!!
HUFF... HUFF...
BLAST! I'VE GOTTEN MYSELF STUCK ON SOMETHING ELSE! POOT!
YOU CRYIN' UNCLE YET?! I ATE A DRAGON...
...SO NOW I HAVE DRAGON POWER!!
...
FLEX!
DRAG DRAG...
IT TASTED GOOD, BUT I COULDN'T EAT ANOTHER BITE! YOU'RE GONNA EAT MOST OF THIS MEAT, SO YOU SHOULD BE THE ONE TO CARRY IT!

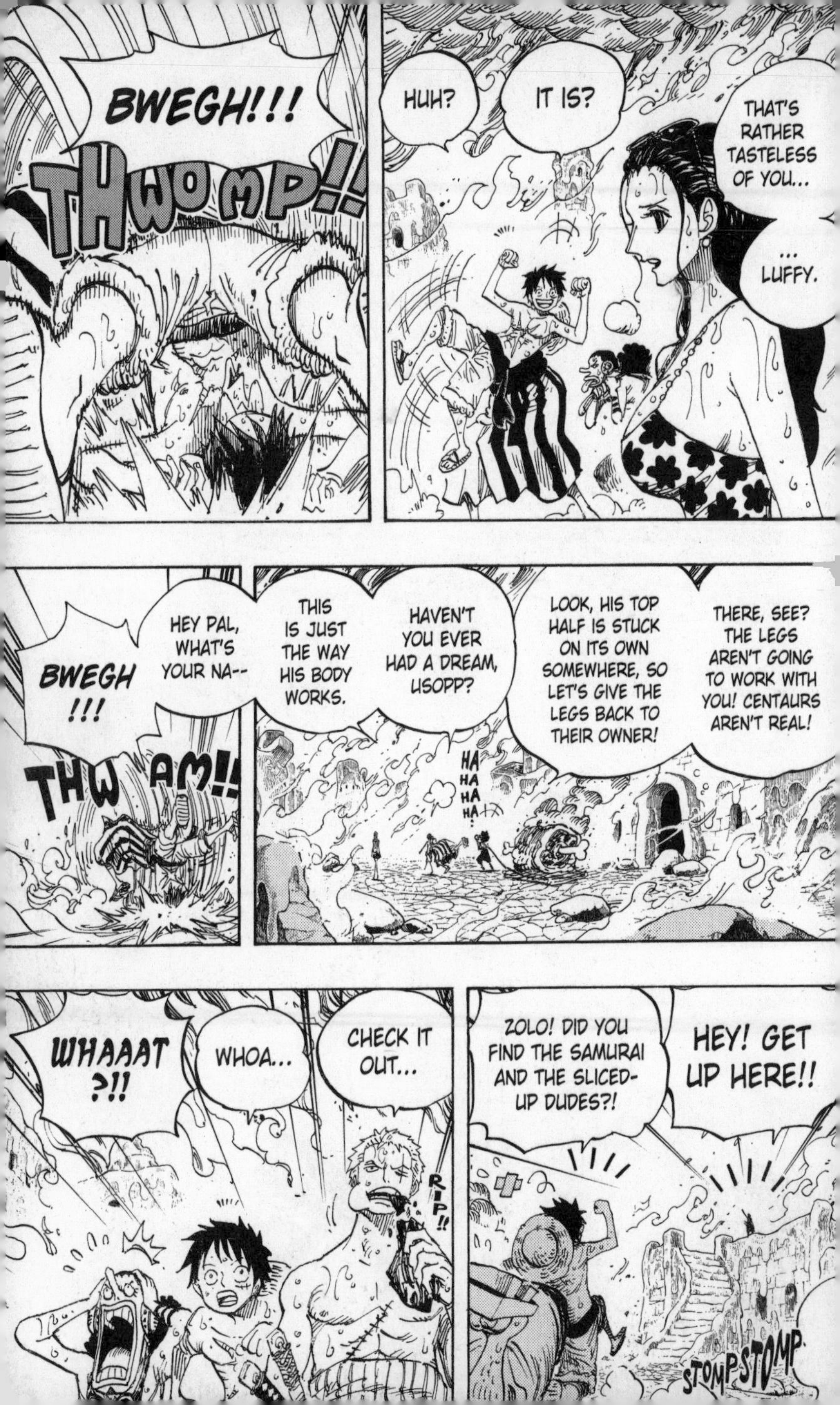
THAT'S RATHER TASTELESS OF YOU...
... LUFFY.
IT IS?
HUH?
BWEGH!!!
THWOMP!!
THERE, SEE? THE LEGS AREN'T GOING TO WORK WITH YOU! CENTAURS AREN'T REAL!
LOOK, HIS TOP HALF IS STUCK ON ITS OWN SOMEWHERE, SO LET'S GIVE THE LEGS BACK TO THEIR OWNER!
HAVEN'T YOU EVER HAD A DREAM, USOPP?
THIS IS JUST THE WAY HIS BODY WORKS.
HA HA HA HA
HEY PAL, WHAT'S YOUR NA--
BWEGH !!!
THWAM!!
HEY! GET UP HERE!!
ZOLO! DID YOU FIND THE SAMURAI AND THE SLICED-UP DUDES?!
STOMP STOMP
CHECK IT OUT...
RIP!!
WHOA...
WHAAAT ?!!

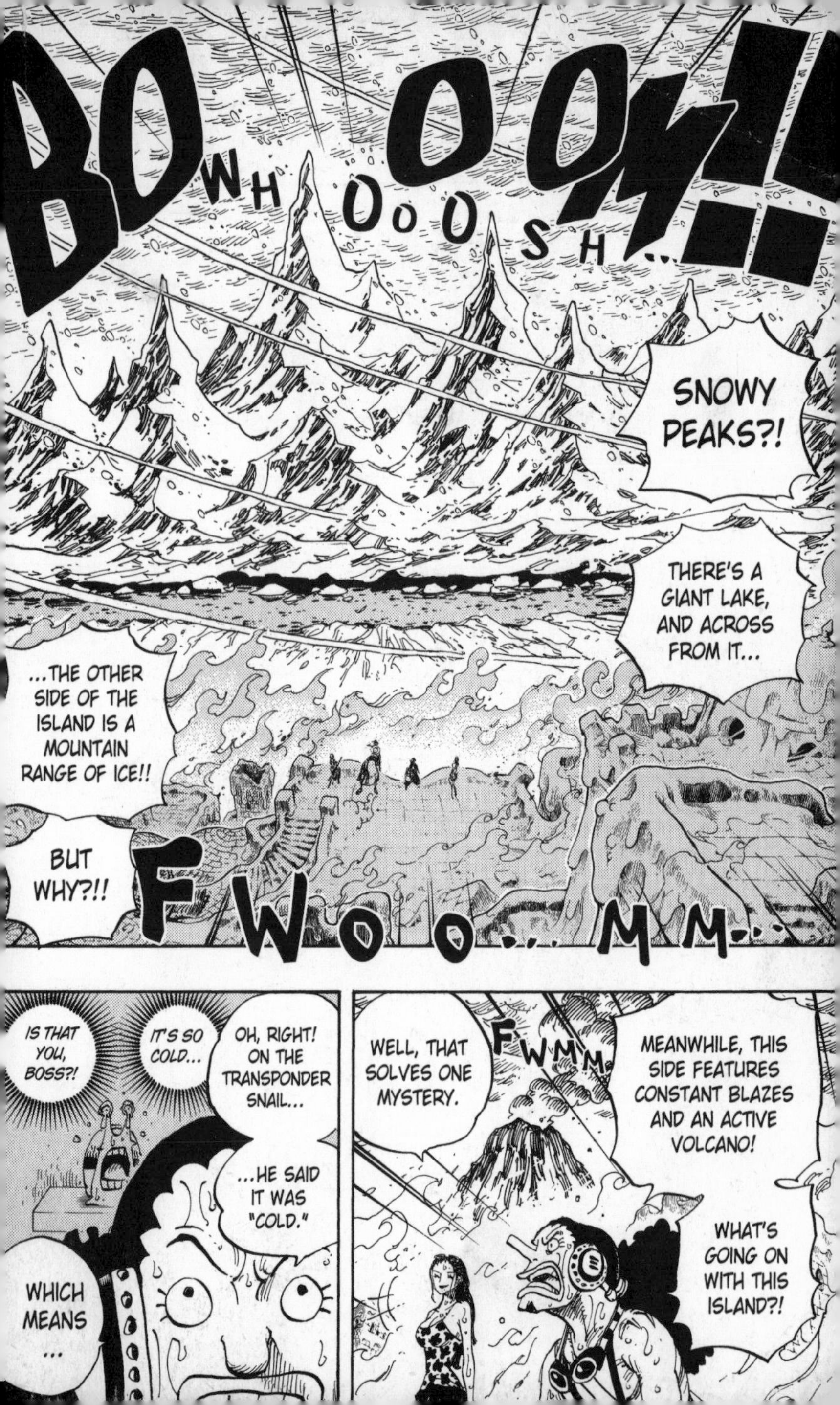
BOOOM!!
WHOOOSH...
SNOWY PEAKS?!
THERE'S A GIANT LAKE, AND ACROSS FROM IT...
...THE OTHER SIDE OF THE ISLAND IS A MOUNTAIN RANGE OF ICE!!
BUT WHY?!!
FWOO... MM...
MEANWHILE, THIS SIDE FEATURES CONSTANT BLAZES AND AN ACTIVE VOLCANO!
FWMM
WELL, THAT SOLVES ONE MYSTERY.
WHAT'S GOING ON WITH THIS ISLAND?!
OH, RIGHT! ON THE TRANSPONDER SNAIL...
IT'S SO COLD...
IS THAT YOU, BOSS?!
...HE SAID IT WAS "COLD."
WHICH MEANS ...

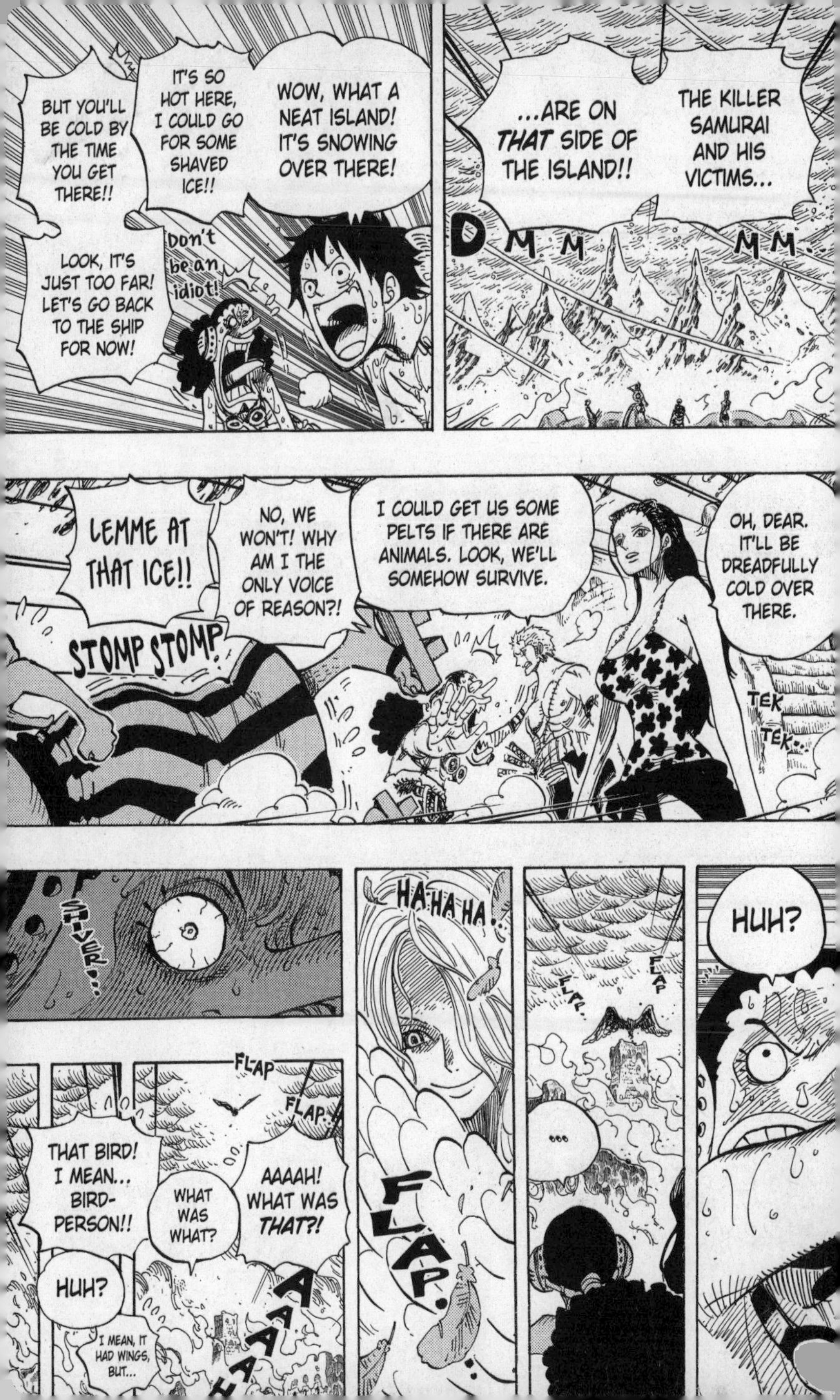
THE KILLER SAMURAI AND HIS VICTIMS...
...ARE ON *THAT* SIDE OF THE ISLAND!!
DMM MM...
WOW, WHAT A NEAT ISLAND! IT'S SNOWING OVER THERE!
IT'S SO HOT HERE, I COULD GO FOR SOME SHAVED ICE!!
BUT YOU'LL BE COLD BY THE TIME YOU GET THERE!!
Don't be an idiot!
LOOK, IT'S JUST TOO FAR! LET'S GO BACK TO THE SHIP FOR NOW!
OH, DEAR. IT'LL BE DREADFULLY COLD OVER THERE.
TEK TEK...
I COULD GET US SOME PELTS IF THERE ARE ANIMALS. LOOK, WE'LL SOMEHOW SURVIVE.
NO, WE WON'T! WHY AM I THE ONLY VOICE OF REASON?!
LEMME AT THAT ICE!!
STOMP STOMP
HUH?
FLAP FLAP
...
HA HA HA...
FLAP.
SHIVER...
FLAP FLAP
AAAAH! WHAT WAS *THAT*?!
WHAT WAS WHAT?
THAT BIRD! I MEAN... BIRD-PERSON!!
HUH?
I MEAN, IT HAD WINGS, BUT...
AAAAH

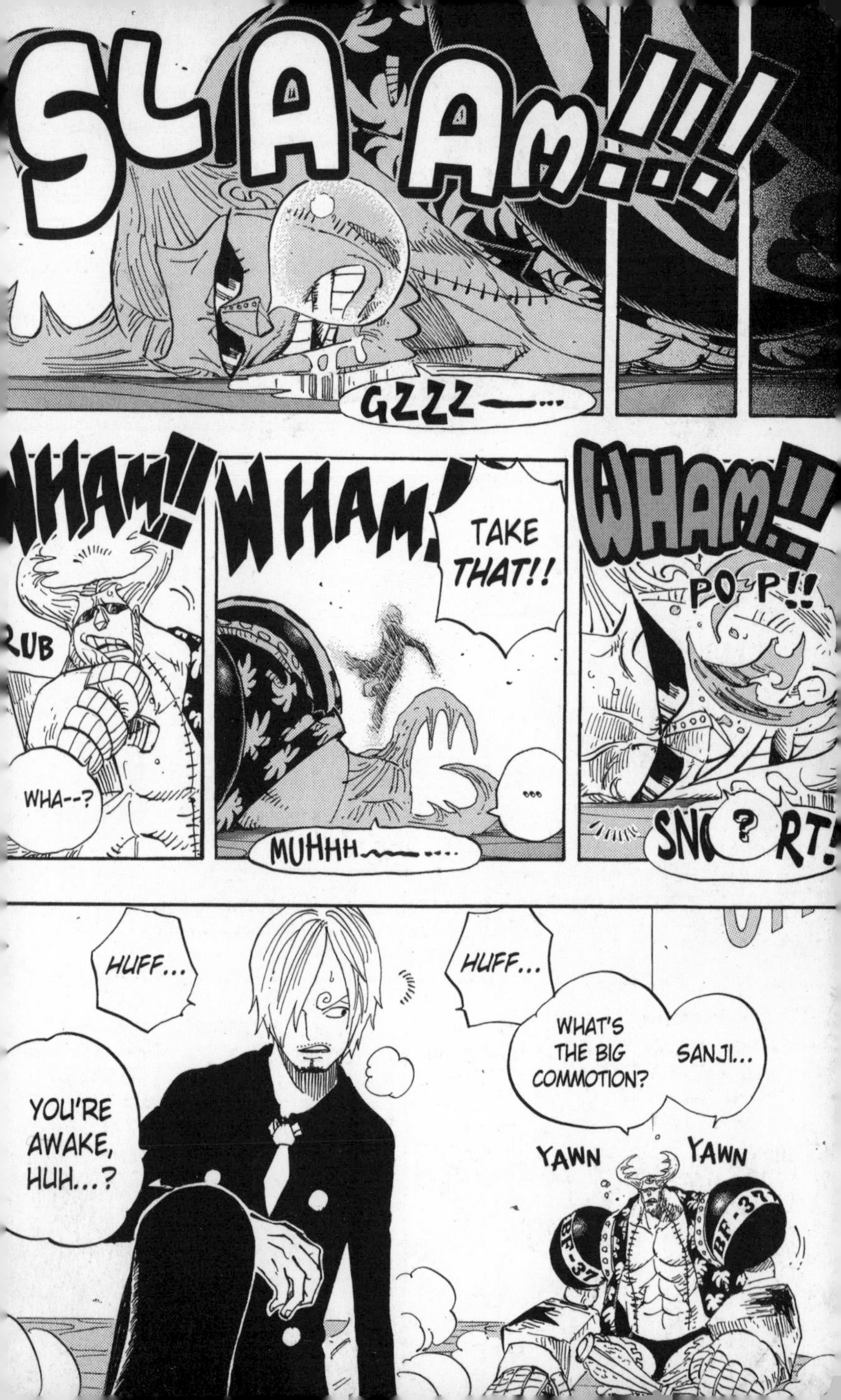
SLAM!!!
GZZZ—...
WHAM!!
POP!!
?
SN RT!
WHAM!
TAKE THAT!!
...
MUHHH—....
WHAM!!
RUB
WHA--?
HUFF...
SANJI...
WHAT'S THE BIG COMMOTION?
YAWN
YAWN
HUFF...
YOU'RE AWAKE, HUH...?

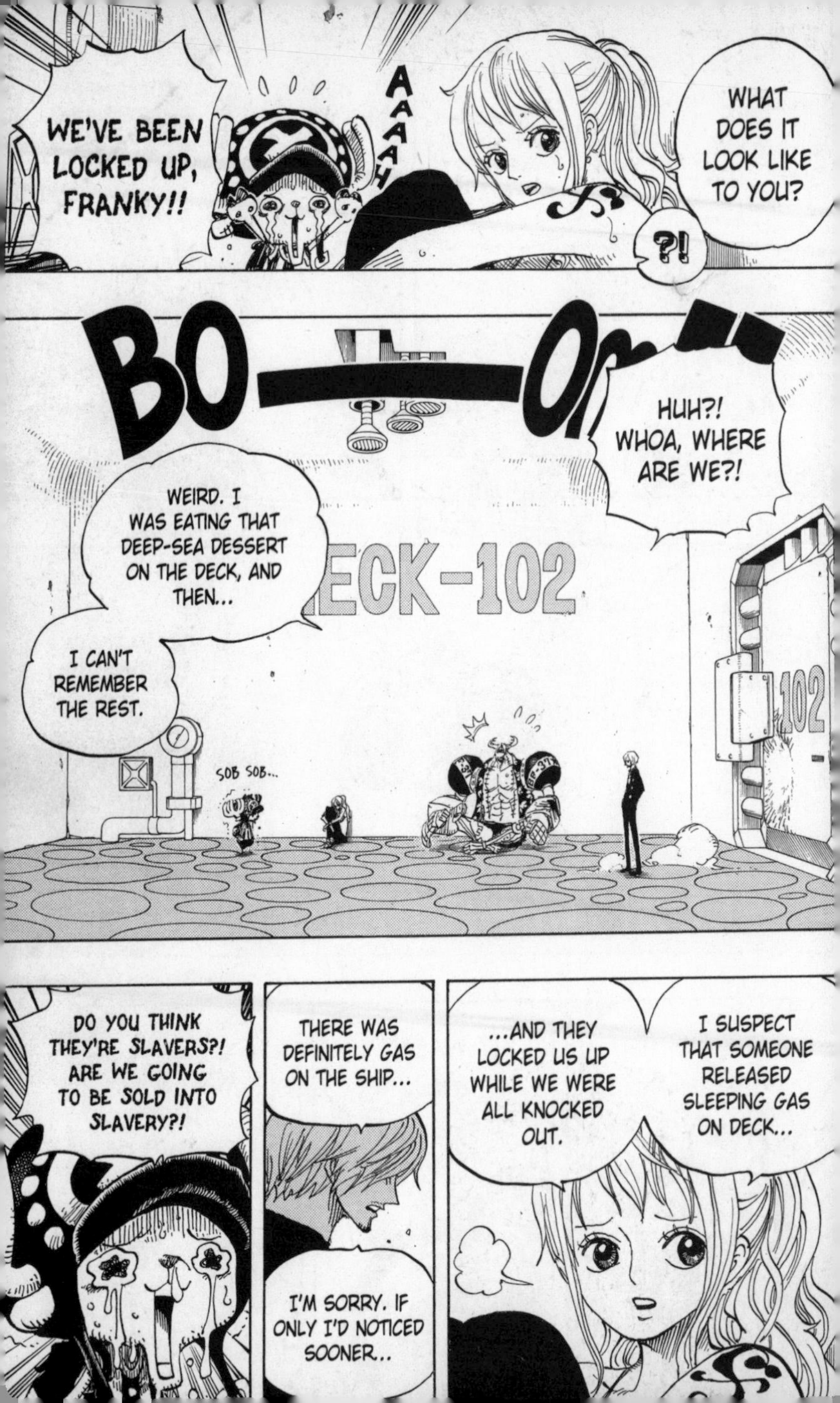
WHAT DOES IT LOOK LIKE TO YOU?
?!
AAAAH
WE'VE BEEN LOCKED UP, FRANKY!!
BO——ON
HUH?! WHOA, WHERE ARE WE?!
ECK-102
102
WEIRD. I WAS EATING THAT DEEP-SEA DESSERT ON THE DECK, AND THEN...
I CAN'T REMEMBER THE REST.
SOB SOB...
I SUSPECT THAT SOMEONE RELEASED SLEEPING GAS ON DECK...
...AND THEY LOCKED US UP WHILE WE WERE ALL KNOCKED OUT.
THERE WAS DEFINITELY GAS ON THE SHIP...
I'M SORRY. IF ONLY I'D NOTICED SOONER..
DO YOU THINK THEY'RE SLAVERS?! ARE WE GOING TO BE SOLD INTO SLAVERY?!

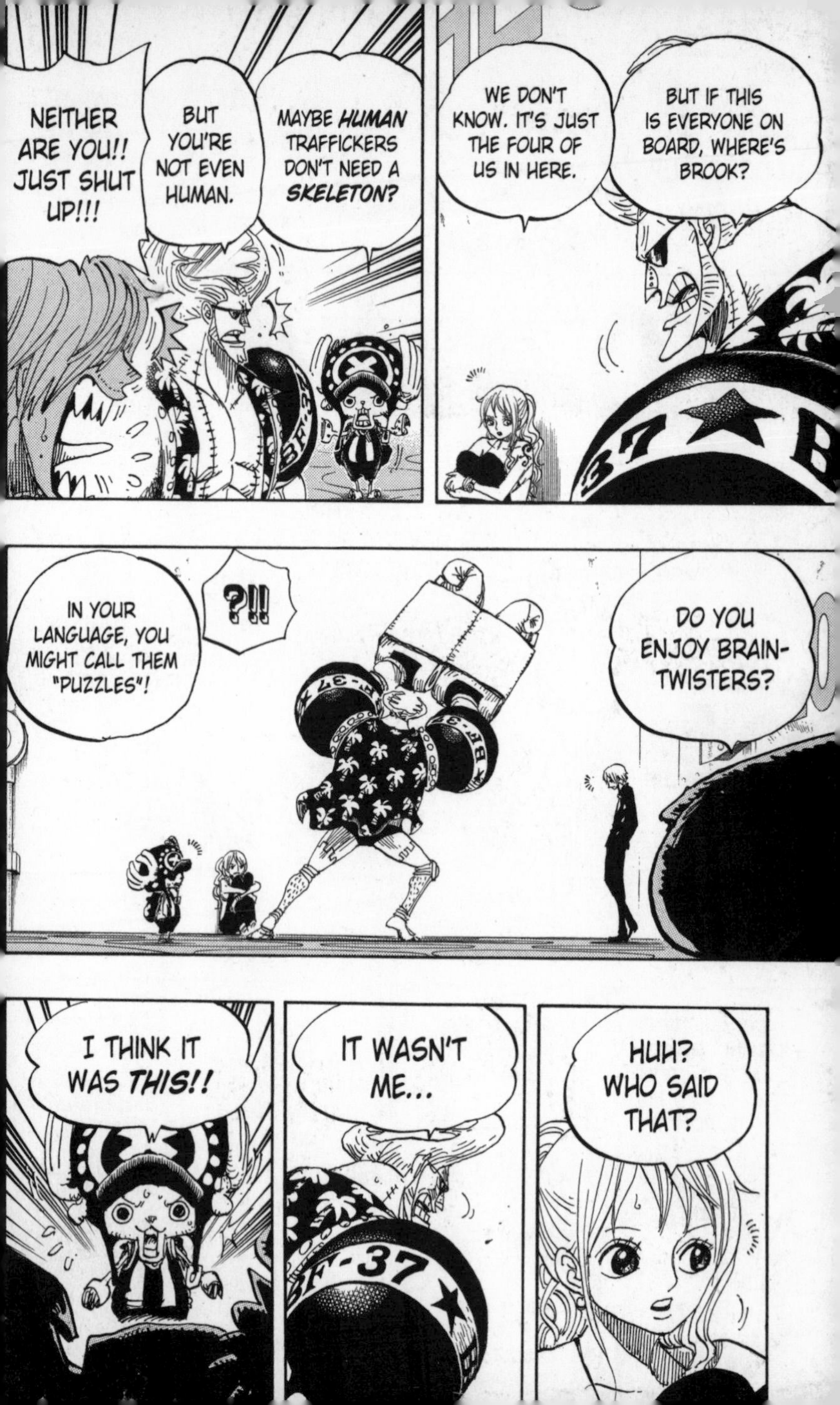
BUT IF THIS IS EVERYONE ON BOARD, WHERE'S BROOK?
WE DON'T KNOW. IT'S JUST THE FOUR OF US IN HERE.
MAYBE *HUMAN* TRAFFICKERS DON'T NEED A *SKELETON?*
BUT YOU'RE NOT EVEN HUMAN.
NEITHER ARE YOU!! JUST SHUT UP!!!
DO YOU ENJOY BRAIN-TWISTERS?
?!!
IN YOUR LANGUAGE, YOU MIGHT CALL THEM "PUZZLES"!
HUH? WHO SAID THAT?
IT WASN'T ME...
I THINK IT WAS *THIS!!*

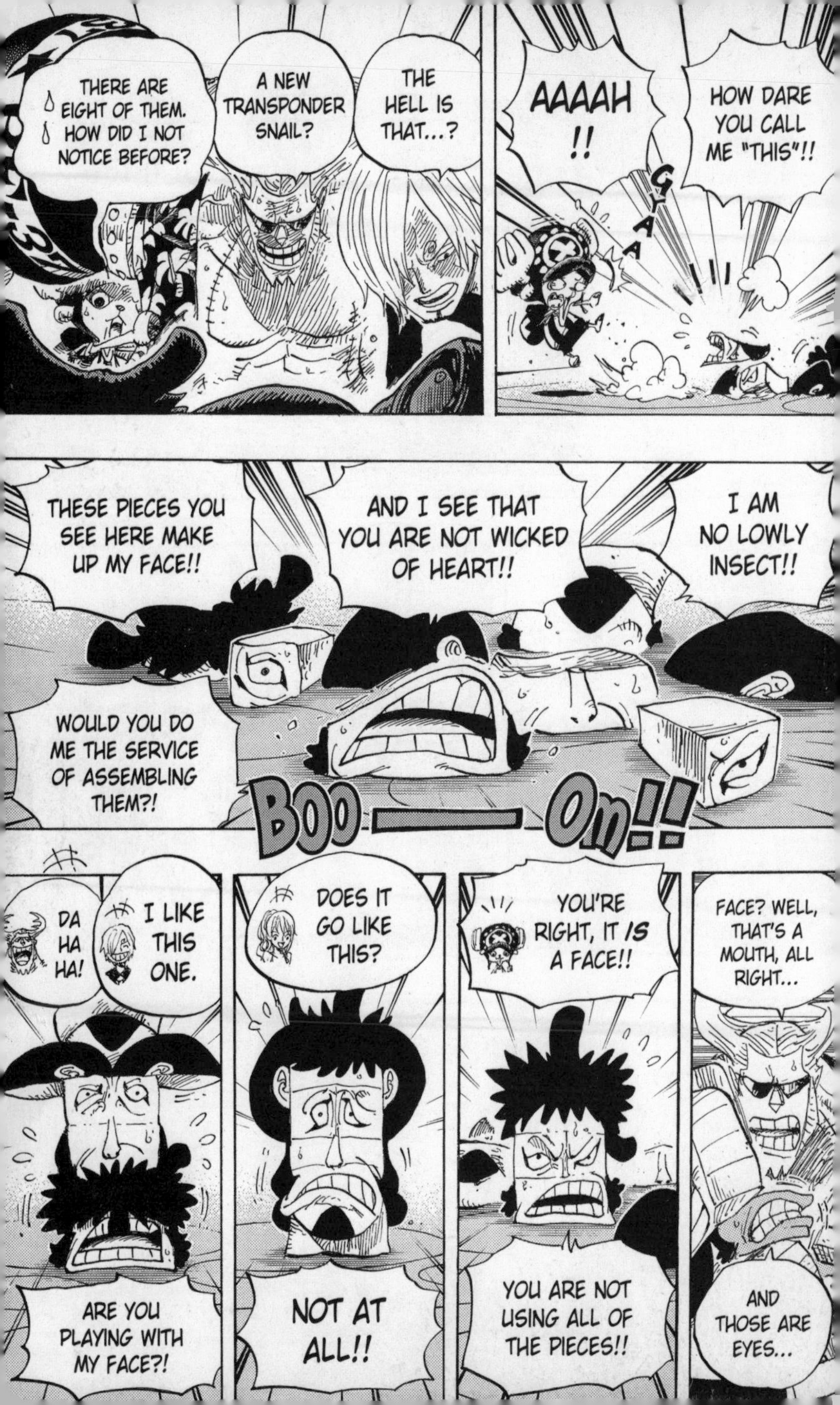
HOW DARE YOU CALL ME "THIS"!!
AAAAH !!
GYAAA
THE HELL IS THAT...?
A NEW TRANSPONDER SNAIL?
THERE ARE EIGHT OF THEM. HOW DID I NOT NOTICE BEFORE?
I AM NO LOWLY INSECT!!
AND I SEE THAT YOU ARE NOT WICKED OF HEART!!
THESE PIECES YOU SEE HERE MAKE UP MY FACE!!
WOULD YOU DO ME THE SERVICE OF ASSEMBLING THEM?!
BOO——OM!!
FACE? WELL, THAT'S A MOUTH, ALL RIGHT...
AND THOSE ARE EYES...
YOU'RE RIGHT, IT *IS* A FACE!!
YOU ARE NOT USING ALL OF THE PIECES!!
DOES IT GO LIKE THIS?
NOT AT ALL!!
I LIKE THIS ONE.
DA HA HA!
ARE YOU PLAYING WITH MY FACE?!

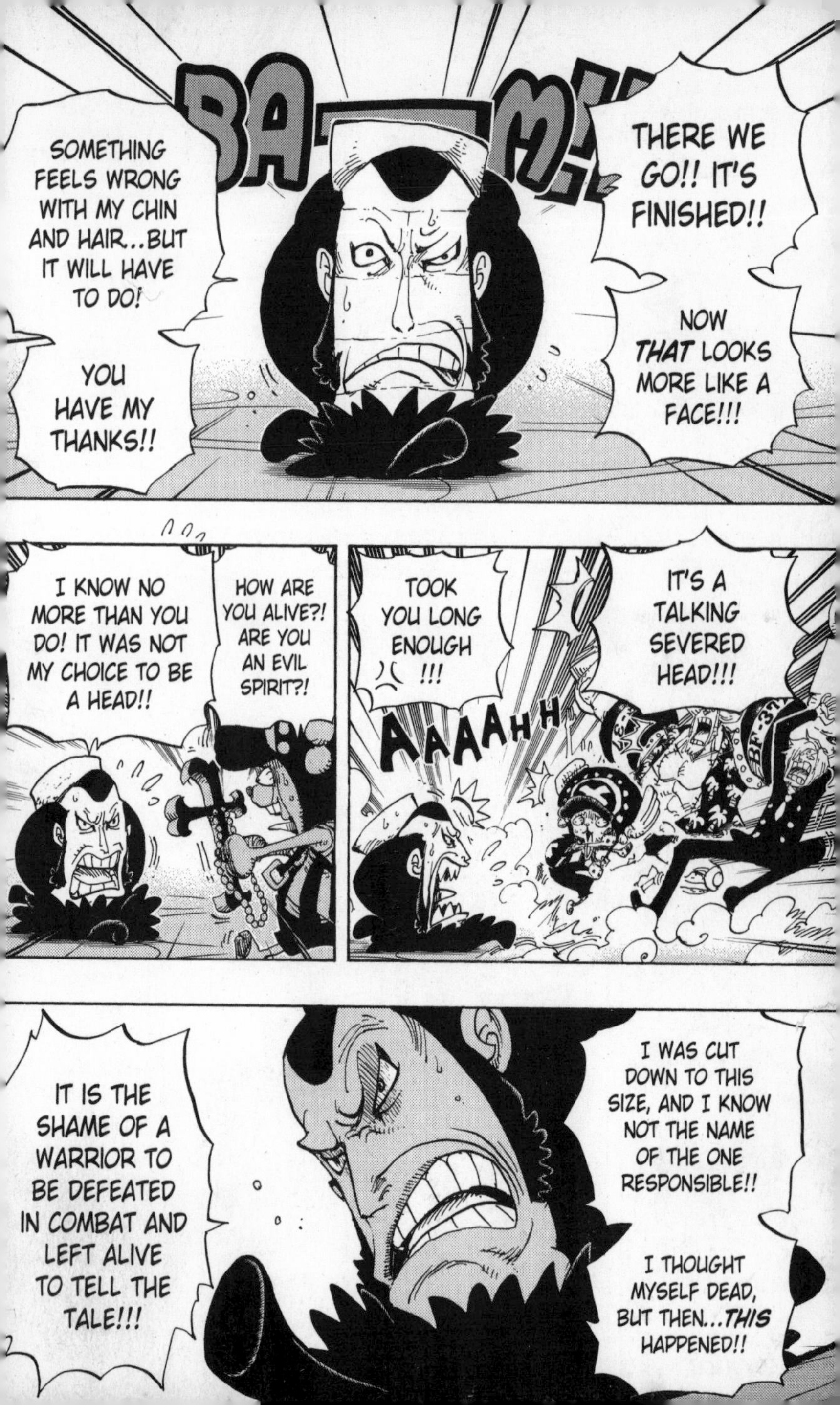

THERE WE GO!! IT'S FINISHED!!
NOW THAT LOOKS MORE LIKE A FACE!!!
BAM!
SOMETHING FEELS WRONG WITH MY CHIN AND HAIR...BUT IT WILL HAVE TO DO!
YOU HAVE MY THANKS!!
IT'S A TALKING SEVERED HEAD!!!
TOOK YOU LONG ENOUGH!!!
AAAAHH
HOW ARE YOU ALIVE?! ARE YOU AN EVIL SPIRIT?!
I KNOW NO MORE THAN YOU DO! IT WAS NOT MY CHOICE TO BE A HEAD!!
I WAS CUT DOWN TO THIS SIZE, AND I KNOW NOT THE NAME OF THE ONE RESPONSIBLE!!
I THOUGHT MYSELF DEAD, BUT THEN...THIS HAPPENED!!
IT IS THE SHAME OF A WARRIOR TO BE DEFEATED IN COMBAT AND LEFT ALIVE TO TELL THE TALE!!!

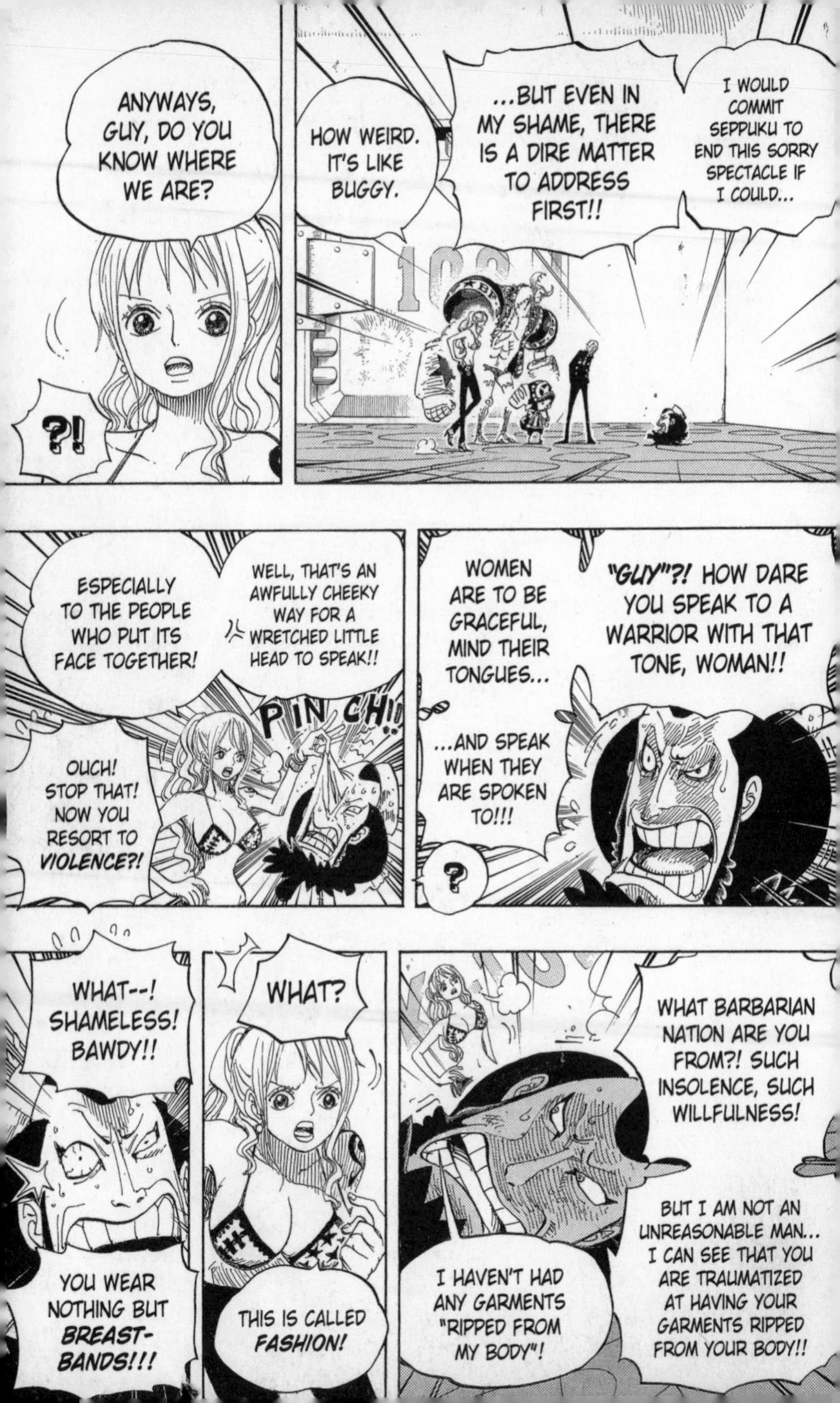
I WOULD COMMIT SEPPUKU TO END THIS SORRY SPECTACLE IF I COULD...
...BUT EVEN IN MY SHAME, THERE IS A DIRE MATTER TO ADDRESS FIRST!!
HOW WEIRD. IT'S LIKE BUGGY.
ANYWAYS, GUY, DO YOU KNOW WHERE WE ARE?
?!
"GUY"?! HOW DARE YOU SPEAK TO A WARRIOR WITH THAT TONE, WOMAN!!
WOMEN ARE TO BE GRACEFUL, MIND THEIR TONGUES...
...AND SPEAK WHEN THEY ARE SPOKEN TO!!!
?
WELL, THAT'S AN AWFULLY CHEEKY WAY FOR A WRETCHED LITTLE HEAD TO SPEAK!!
ESPECIALLY TO THE PEOPLE WHO PUT ITS FACE TOGETHER!
PINCH!!
OUCH! STOP THAT! NOW YOU RESORT TO VIOLENCE?!
WHAT BARBARIAN NATION ARE YOU FROM?! SUCH INSOLENCE, SUCH WILLFULNESS!
BUT I AM NOT AN UNREASONABLE MAN... I CAN SEE THAT YOU ARE TRAUMATIZED AT HAVING YOUR GARMENTS RIPPED FROM YOUR BODY!!
I HAVEN'T HAD ANY GARMENTS "RIPPED FROM MY BODY"!
WHAT?
THIS IS CALLED FASHION!
WHAT--! SHAMELESS! BAWDY!!
YOU WEAR NOTHING BUT BREAST-BANDS!!!

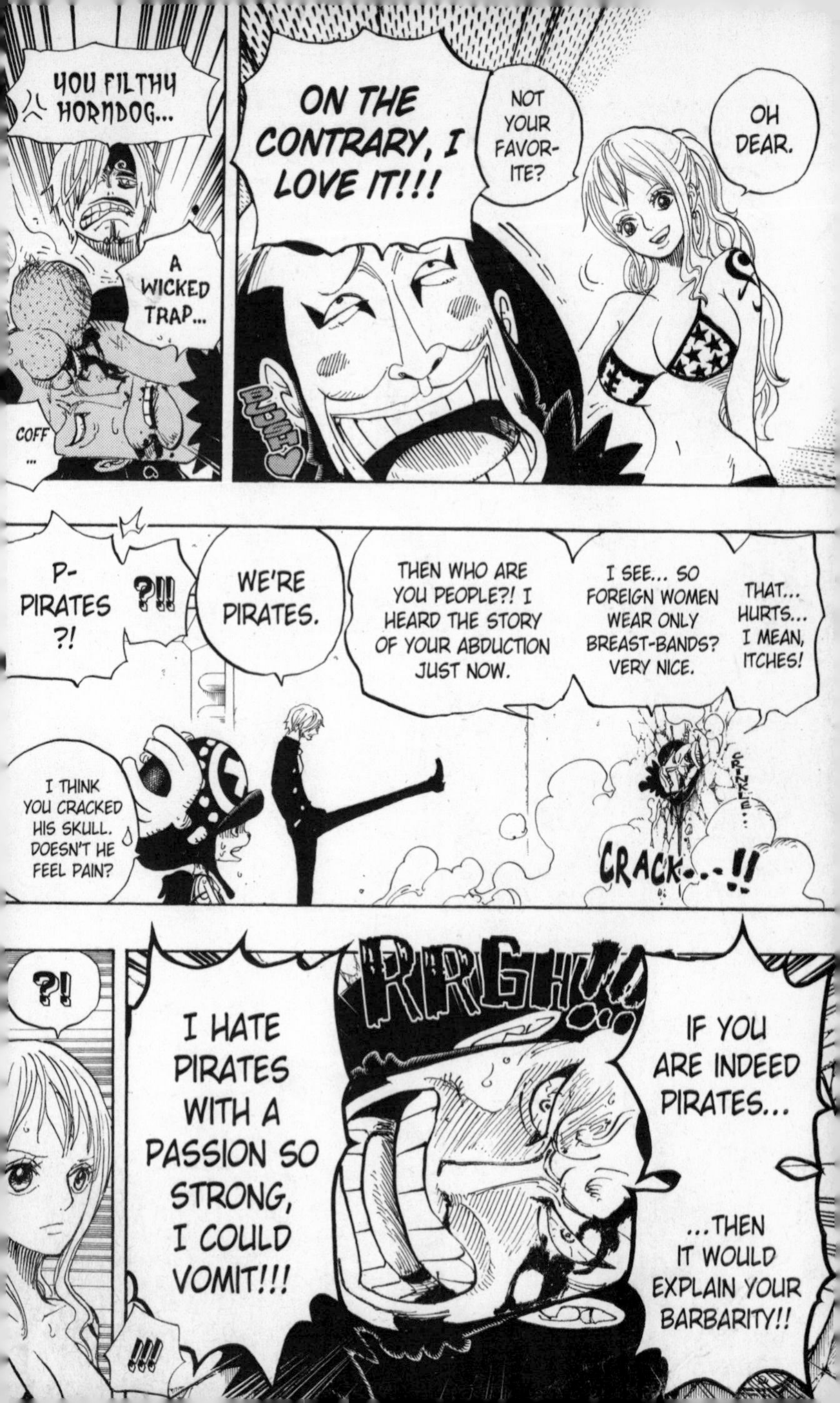
OH DEAR.
NOT YOUR FAVOR-ITE?
ON THE CONTRARY, I LOVE IT!!!
BLUSH
YOU FILTHY HORNDOG...
A WICKED TRAP...
COFF ...
THAT... HURTS... I MEAN, ITCHES!
I SEE... SO FOREIGN WOMEN WEAR ONLY BREAST-BANDS? VERY NICE.
THEN WHO ARE YOU PEOPLE?! I HEARD THE STORY OF YOUR ABDUCTION JUST NOW.
WE'RE PIRATES.
?!!
P-PIRATES?!
CRINKLE...
CRACK...!!
I THINK YOU CRACKED HIS SKULL. DOESN'T HE FEEL PAIN?
RRGH!!
IF YOU ARE INDEED PIRATES...
...THEN IT WOULD EXPLAIN YOUR BARBARITY!!
I HATE PIRATES WITH A PASSION SO STRONG, I COULD VOMIT!!!
?!
!!!

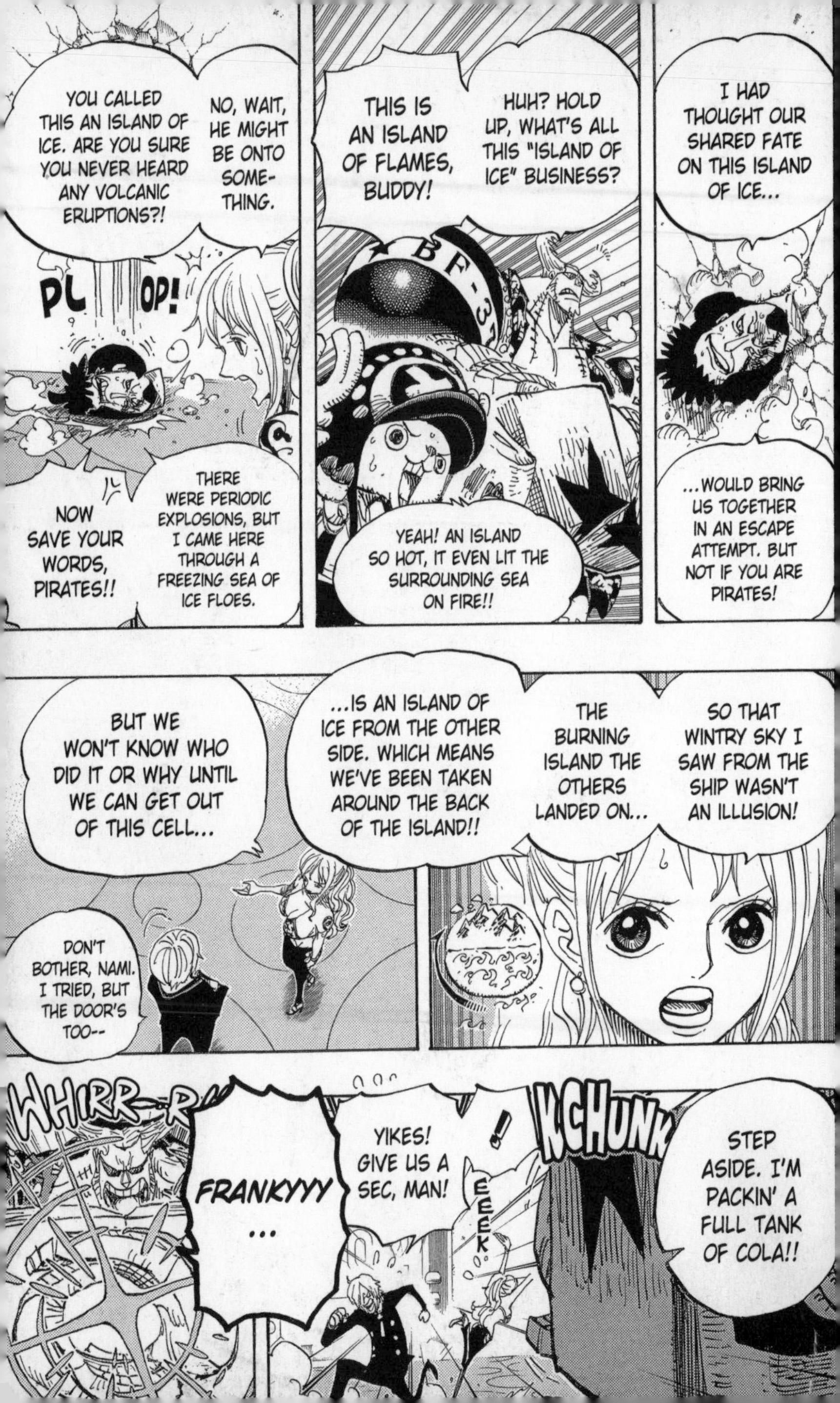
I HAD THOUGHT OUR SHARED FATE ON THIS ISLAND OF ICE...
...WOULD BRING US TOGETHER IN AN ESCAPE ATTEMPT. BUT NOT IF YOU ARE PIRATES!
HUH? HOLD UP, WHAT'S ALL THIS "ISLAND OF ICE" BUSINESS?
THIS IS AN ISLAND OF FLAMES, BUDDY!
YEAH! AN ISLAND SO HOT, IT EVEN LIT THE SURROUNDING SEA ON FIRE!!
NO, WAIT, HE MIGHT BE ONTO SOME-THING.
YOU CALLED THIS AN ISLAND OF ICE. ARE YOU SURE YOU NEVER HEARD ANY VOLCANIC ERUPTIONS?!
PL OP!
THERE WERE PERIODIC EXPLOSIONS, BUT I CAME HERE THROUGH A FREEZING SEA OF ICE FLOES.
NOW SAVE YOUR WORDS, PIRATES!!
SO THAT WINTRY SKY I SAW FROM THE SHIP WASN'T AN ILLUSION!
THE BURNING ISLAND THE OTHERS LANDED ON...
...IS AN ISLAND OF ICE FROM THE OTHER SIDE. WHICH MEANS WE'VE BEEN TAKEN AROUND THE BACK OF THE ISLAND!!
BUT WE WON'T KNOW WHO DID IT OR WHY UNTIL WE CAN GET OUT OF THIS CELL...
DON'T BOTHER, NAMI. I TRIED, BUT THE DOOR'S TOO--
STEP ASIDE. I'M PACKIN' A FULL TANK OF COLA!!
KCHUNK
EEEK
YIKES! GIVE US A SEC, MAN!
FRANKYYY ...
WHIRR-R

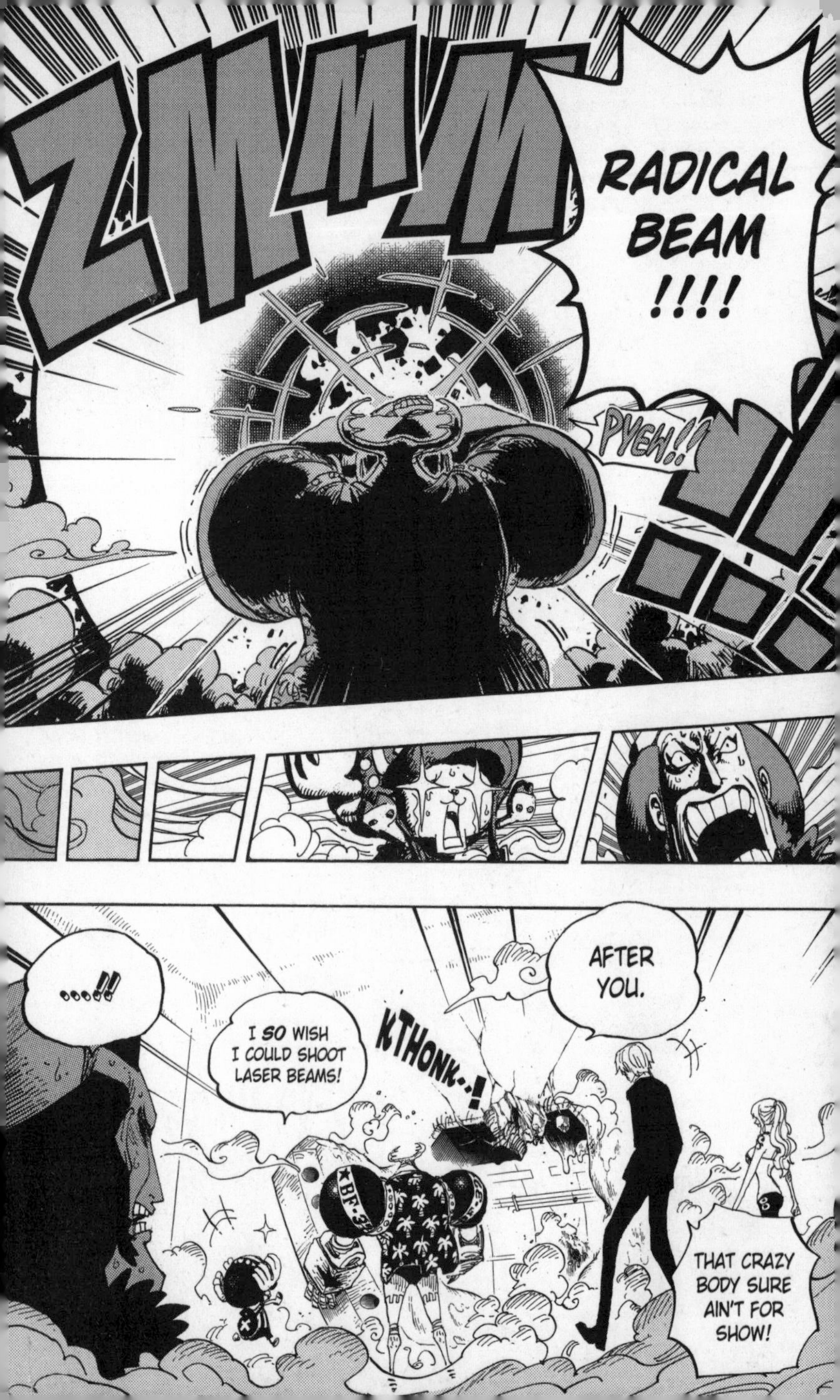
RADICAL BEAM !!!!
ZMMM
PYEW!!
THAT CRAZY BODY SURE AIN'T FOR SHOW!
AFTER YOU.
KTHONK..!
I SO WISH I COULD SHOOT LASER BEAMS!
....!!

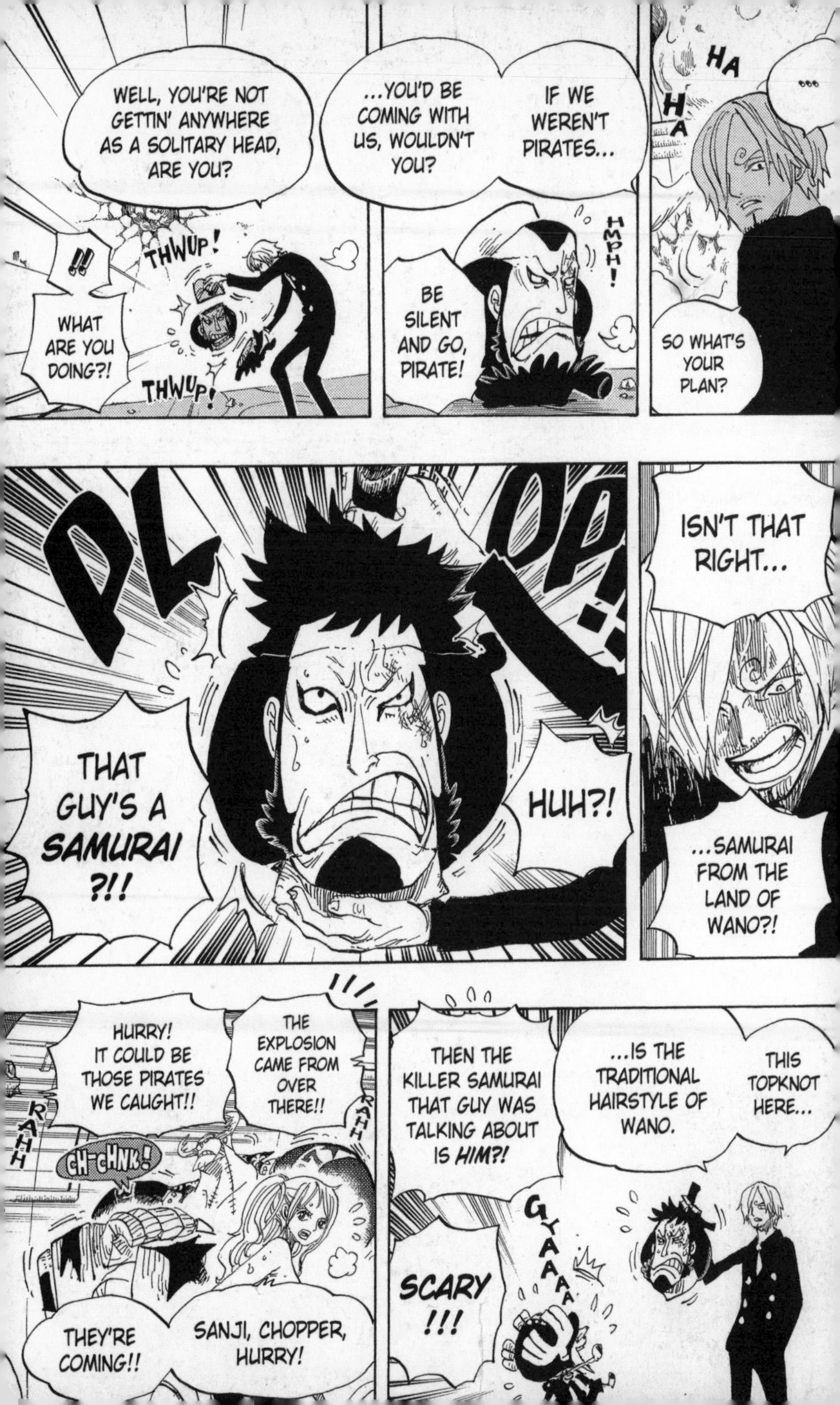
HA
HA
...
SO WHAT'S YOUR PLAN?
IF WE WEREN'T PIRATES...
...YOU'D BE COMING WITH US, WOULDN'T YOU?
HMPH!
BE SILENT AND GO, PIRATE!
WELL, YOU'RE NOT GETTIN' ANYWHERE AS A SOLITARY HEAD, ARE YOU?
THWUP!
!!
WHAT ARE YOU DOING?!
THWUP!
ISN'T THAT RIGHT...
...SAMURAI FROM THE LAND OF WANO?!
PLOP!!
HUH?!
THAT GUY'S A SAMURAI ?!!
THIS TOPKNOT HERE...
...IS THE TRADITIONAL HAIRSTYLE OF WANO.
THEN THE KILLER SAMURAI THAT GUY WAS TALKING ABOUT IS HIM?!
GYAAAA
SCARY !!!
THE EXPLOSION CAME FROM OVER THERE!!
RAHH
HURRY! IT COULD BE THOSE PIRATES WE CAUGHT!!
RAHH
CH-CHNK!
SANJI, CHOPPER, HURRY!
THEY'RE COMING!!

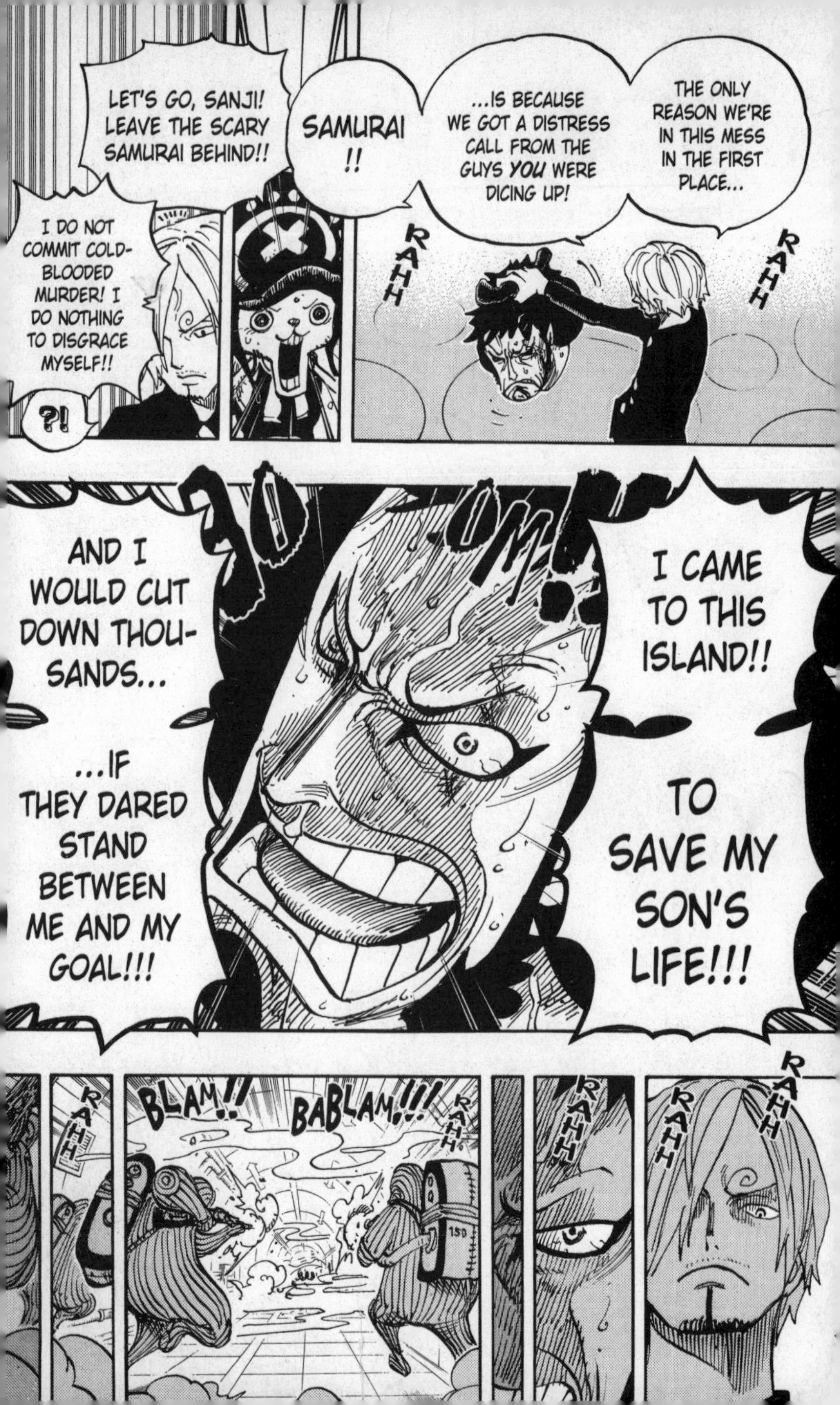
RAHH
THE ONLY REASON WE'RE IN THIS MESS IN THE FIRST PLACE...
...IS BECAUSE WE GOT A DISTRESS CALL FROM THE GUYS YOU WERE DICING UP!
SAMURAI!!
RAHH
LET'S GO, SANJI! LEAVE THE SCARY SAMURAI BEHIND!!
I DO NOT COMMIT COLD-BLOODED MURDER! I DO NOTHING TO DISGRACE MYSELF!!
?!
I CAME TO THIS ISLAND!!
TO SAVE MY SON'S LIFE!!!
AND I WOULD CUT DOWN THOUSANDS...
...IF THEY DARED STAND BETWEEN ME AND MY GOAL!!!
RAHH
RAHH
RAHH
RAHH
BABLAM!!!
BLAM!!
RAHH

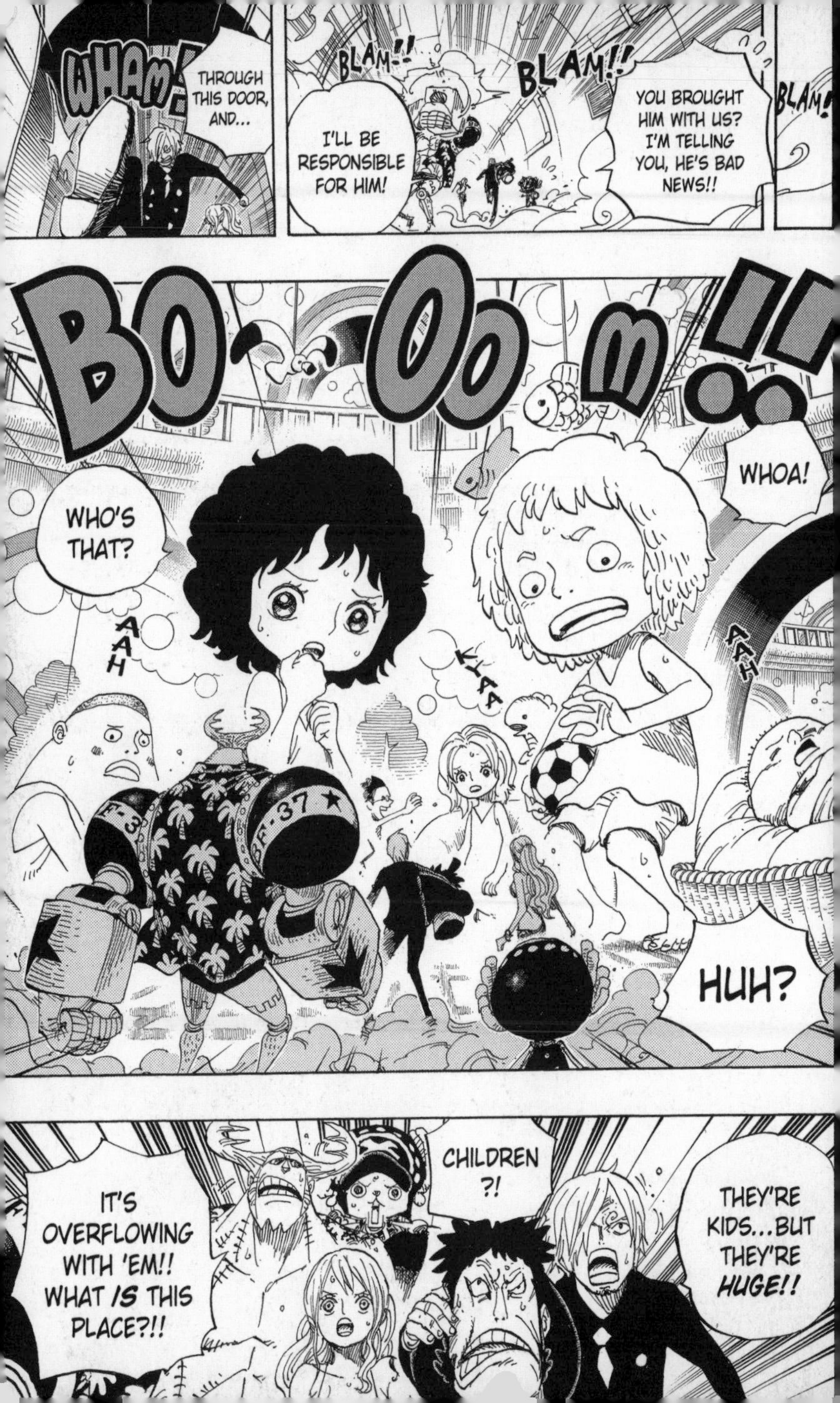
BLAM!
YOU BROUGHT HIM WITH US? I'M TELLING YOU, HE'S BAD NEWS!!
BLAM!!
BLAM!!
I'LL BE RESPONSIBLE FOR HIM!
WHAM!
THROUGH THIS DOOR, AND...
BO-OOM!!
WHOA!
WHO'S THAT?
AAH
KYAA
AAH
HUH?
THEY'RE KIDS...BUT THEY'RE *HUGE!!*
CHILDREN?!
IT'S OVERFLOWING WITH 'EM!! WHAT *IS* THIS PLACE?!!

SBS Question Corner

質問コーナー
エス
ビー
エス
(Hippo Iron, Saitama)

Q: Mr. Oda! I've always dreamed of starting off this section. Let me take it away this time! ♡

Start the BBQ!!! --Muko

A: Whoa, whoa, watch out, the meat's burning! Ahh, nothing like a crisp, refreshing beer in the great outdoors! Good food, good friends...
Wait a minute, this is a barbeque!!!
The only letter that matches is the B! Okay guys, I know this is a rocky start, but if we all try harder to get off on the right foot...

Q: Take this, Odacchi!

Franken General Watch-Your-Step!

--Yosuke

FRU
FRU

A: Hey, watch out!!
We're trying to have an SBS BBQ over here!

Q: There's something that's been eating away at me for years. And that is…when will Sanji's wanted poster be an actual photo?! I'm a Sanji fan! I can't help but feel sorry for him. Anyhow, being such a big fan, I drew a caricature of Sanji that you can use for his next poster. ♡ You're welcome! ♡

--Nanao Style

I'd rather die than kick a woman!

A: What the heck is that?!! That's awful! Just look at Sanji's face! His current eyebrow doesn't go like ⑨ it goes like @ right?! You have to redraw that tail right away, or I'll never use it!

Q: Usopp Rubber Band!

--Baseball-Loving Konosuke

A: Ow! Hey, did you hit me with something?! That move's just supposed to be a bluff! Yeow! It got stuck in my buttcrack!!

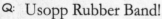

Chapter 658:
THE BISCUITS ROOM

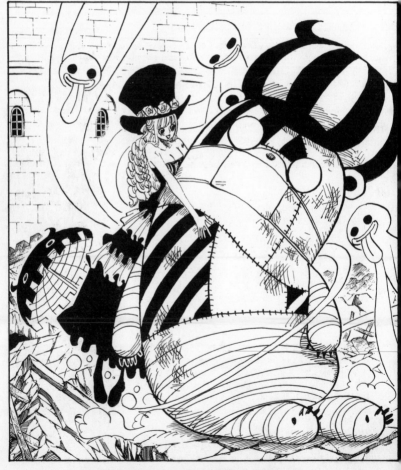

DECKS OF THE WORLD, VOL. 40:
"WANDERING THRILLER BARK—I FOUND KUMACY"

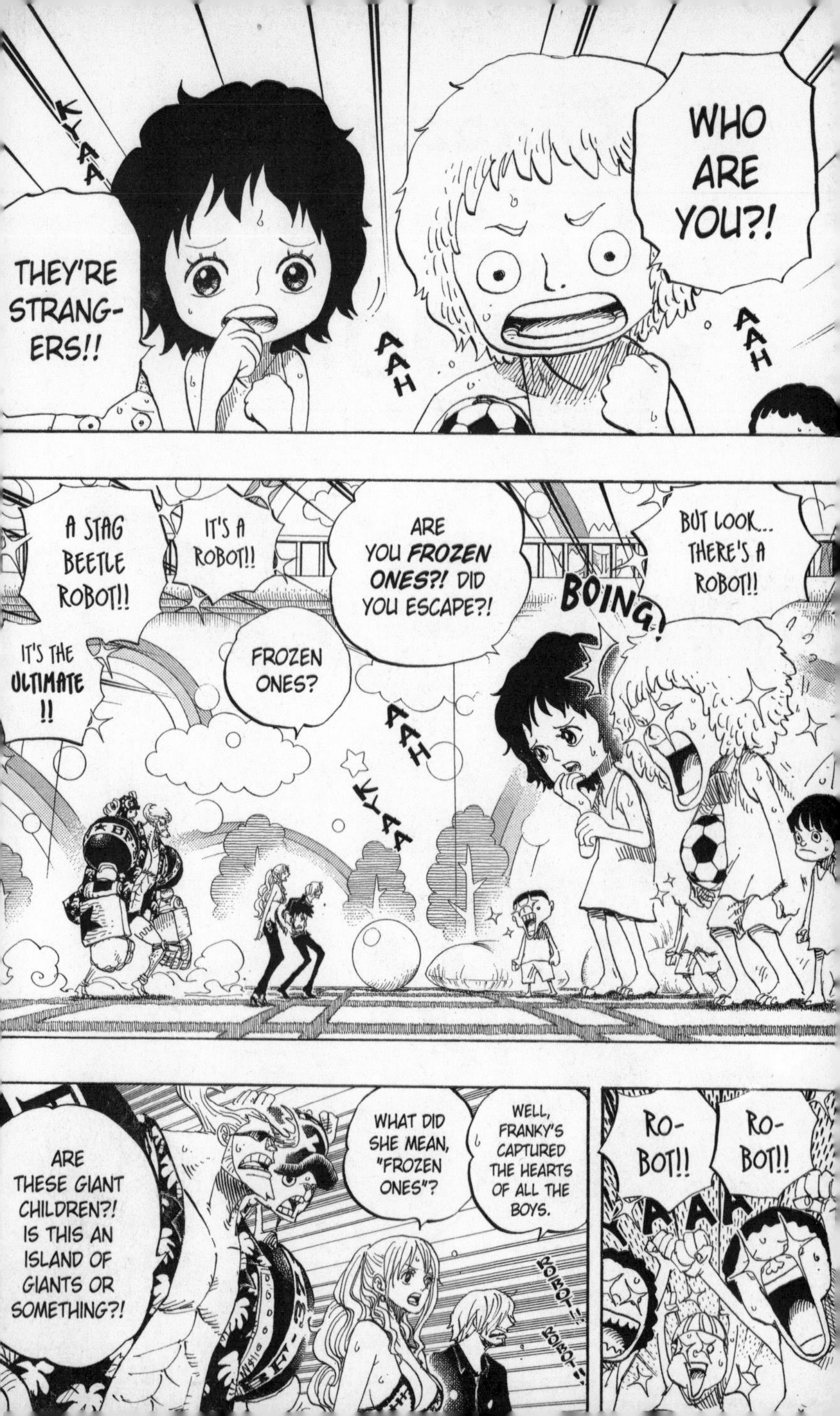
WHO ARE YOU?!
AAH
AAH
THEY'RE STRANGERS!!
KYAA
BUT LOOK... THERE'S A ROBOT!!
BOING
ARE YOU FROZEN ONES?! DID YOU ESCAPE?!
FROZEN ONES?
AAH
KYAA
IT'S A ROBOT!!
A STAG BEETLE ROBOT!!
IT'S THE ULTIMATE!!
RO-BOT!!
RO-BOT!!
AAA
WELL, FRANKY'S CAPTURED THE HEARTS OF ALL THE BOYS.
WHAT DID SHE MEAN, "FROZEN ONES"?
ROBOT!! ROBOT!!
ARE THESE GIANT CHILDREN?! IS THIS AN ISLAND OF GIANTS OR SOMETHING?!

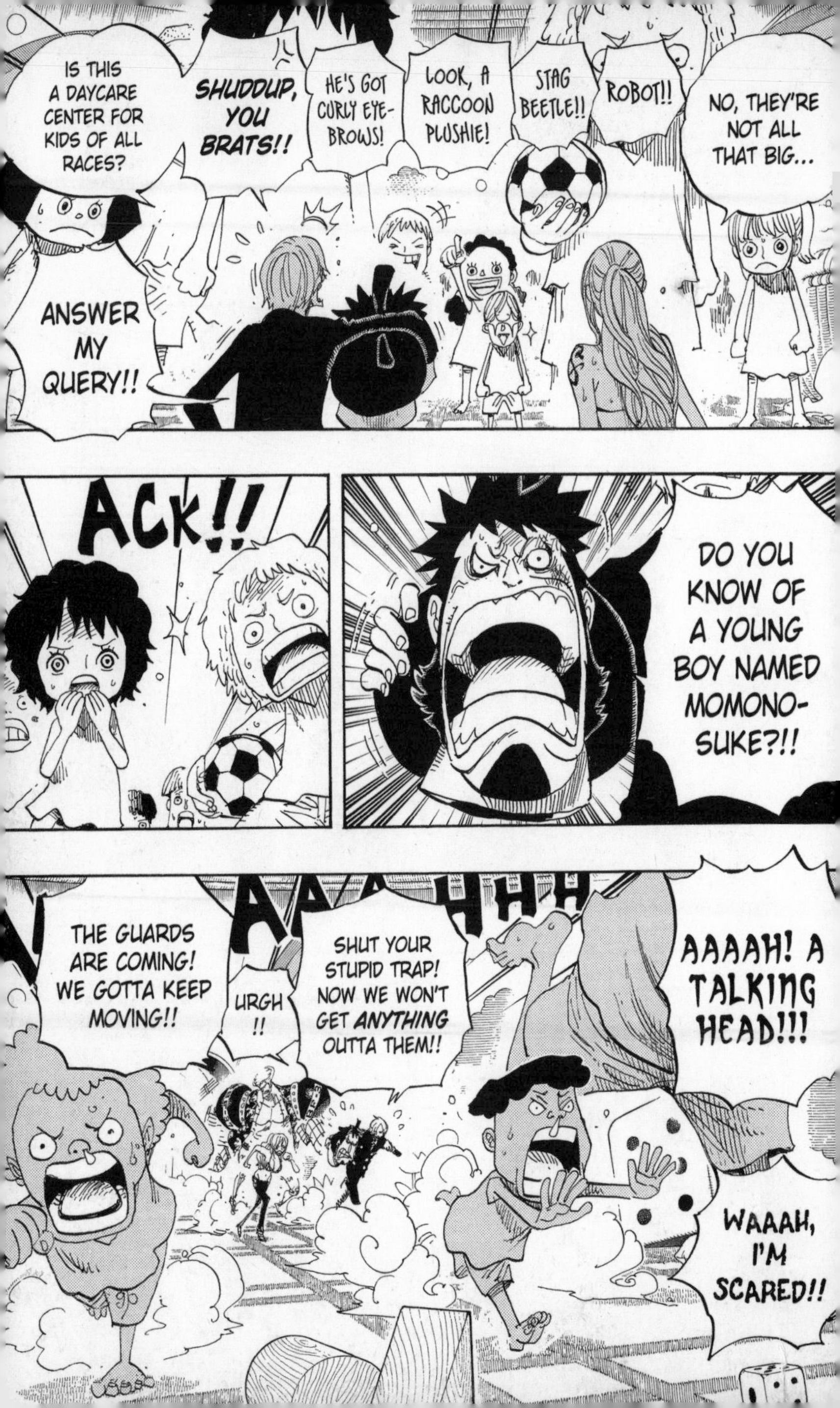
NO, THEY'RE NOT ALL THAT BIG...
ROBOT!!
STAG BEETLE!!
LOOK, A RACCOON PLUSHIE!
HE'S GOT CURLY EYE-BROWS!
SHUDDUP, YOU BRATS!!
IS THIS A DAYCARE CENTER FOR KIDS OF ALL RACES?
ANSWER MY QUERY!!
DO YOU KNOW OF A YOUNG BOY NAMED MOMONO-SUKE?!!
ACK!!
AAAAH! A TALKING HEAD!!!
WAAAH, I'M SCARED!!
SHUT YOUR STUPID TRAP! NOW WE WON'T GET ANYTHING OUTTA THEM!!
URGH !!
THE GUARDS ARE COMING! WE GOTTA KEEP MOVING!!

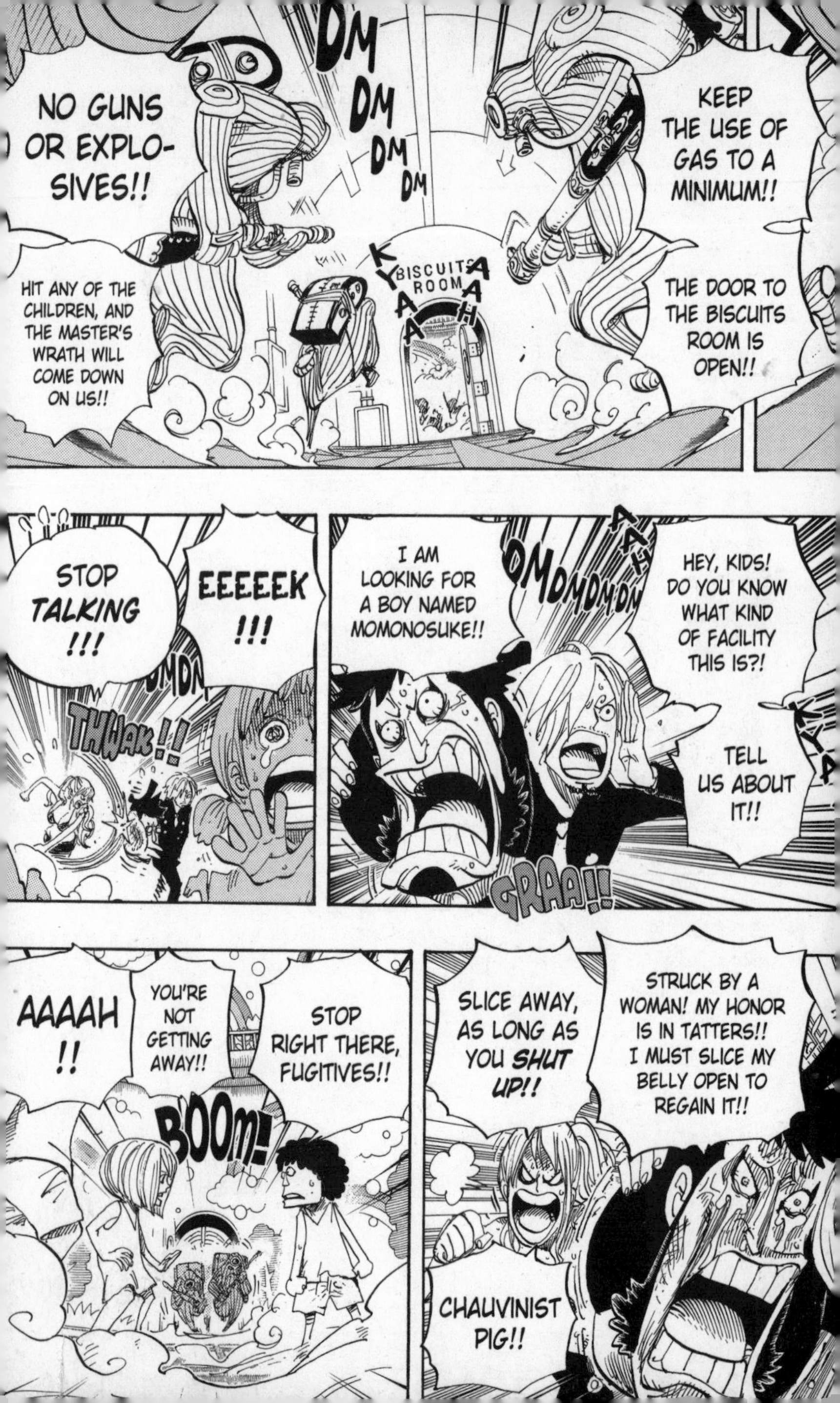
KEEP THE USE OF GAS TO A MINIMUM!!
DM DM DM DM
NO GUNS OR EXPLO-SIVES!!
THE DOOR TO THE BISCUITS ROOM IS OPEN!!
KYAAAAH
BISCUITS ROOM
HIT ANY OF THE CHILDREN, AND THE MASTER'S WRATH WILL COME DOWN ON US!!
HEY, KIDS! DO YOU KNOW WHAT KIND OF FACILITY THIS IS?!
DMDMDMDM
I AM LOOKING FOR A BOY NAMED MOMONOSUKE!!
TELL US ABOUT IT!!
GRAA!!
EEEEEK!!!
STOP TALKING!!!
THWAK!!
STRUCK BY A WOMAN! MY HONOR IS IN TATTERS!! I MUST SLICE MY BELLY OPEN TO REGAIN IT!!
SLICE AWAY, AS LONG AS YOU SHUT UP!!
CHAUVINIST PIG!!
STOP RIGHT THERE, FUGITIVES!!
YOU'RE NOT GETTING AWAY!!
AAAAH!!
BOOM!

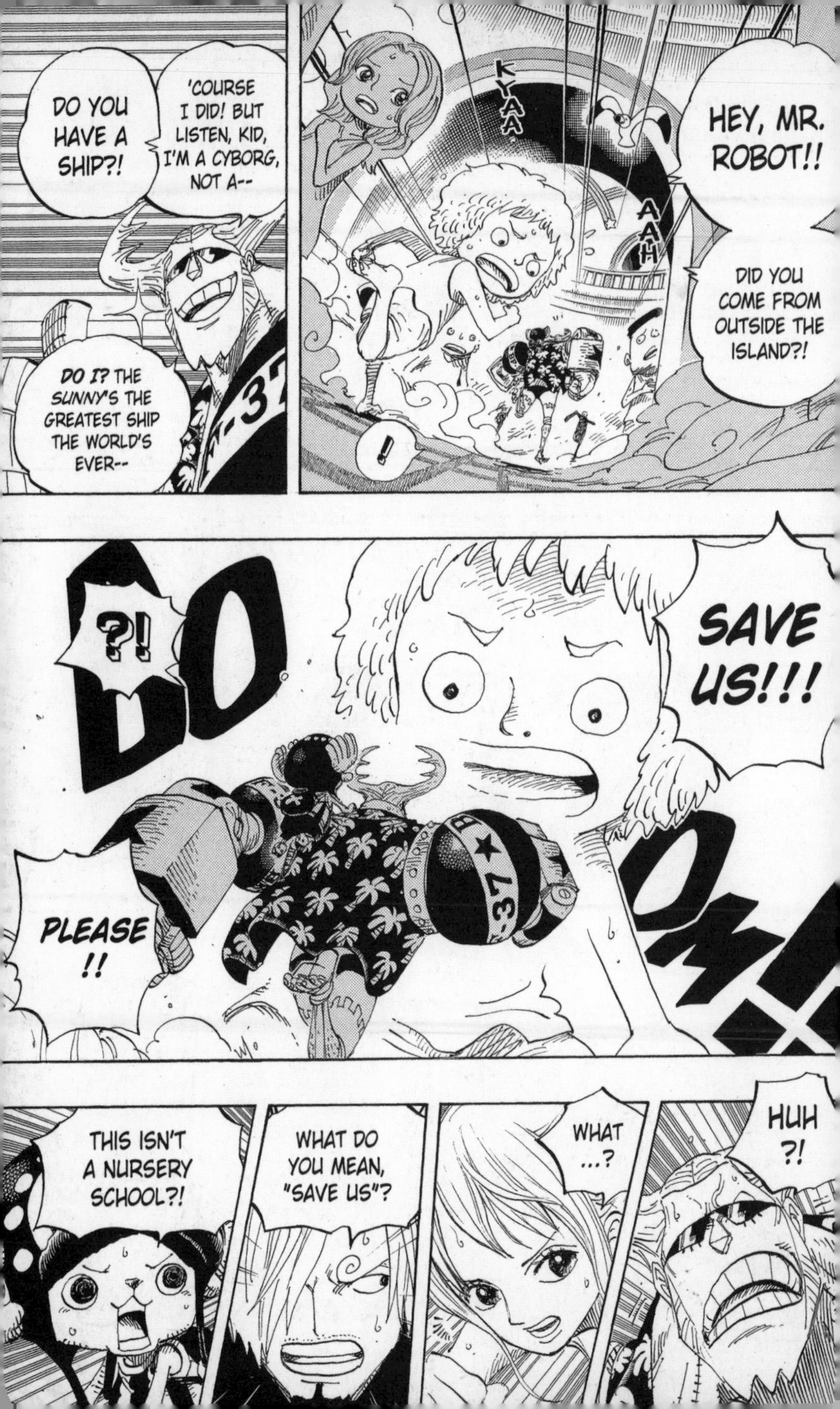
HEY, MR. ROBOT!!
DID YOU COME FROM OUTSIDE THE ISLAND?!
KYAA
AAAH
!
'COURSE I DID! BUT LISTEN, KID, I'M A CYBORG, NOT A--
DO YOU HAVE A SHIP?!
DO I? THE SUNNY'S THE GREATEST SHIP THE WORLD'S EVER--
SAVE US!!!
DOOM!!
?!
PLEASE !!
HUH ?!
WHAT ...?
WHAT DO YOU MEAN, "SAVE US"?
THIS ISN'T A NURSERY SCHOOL?!

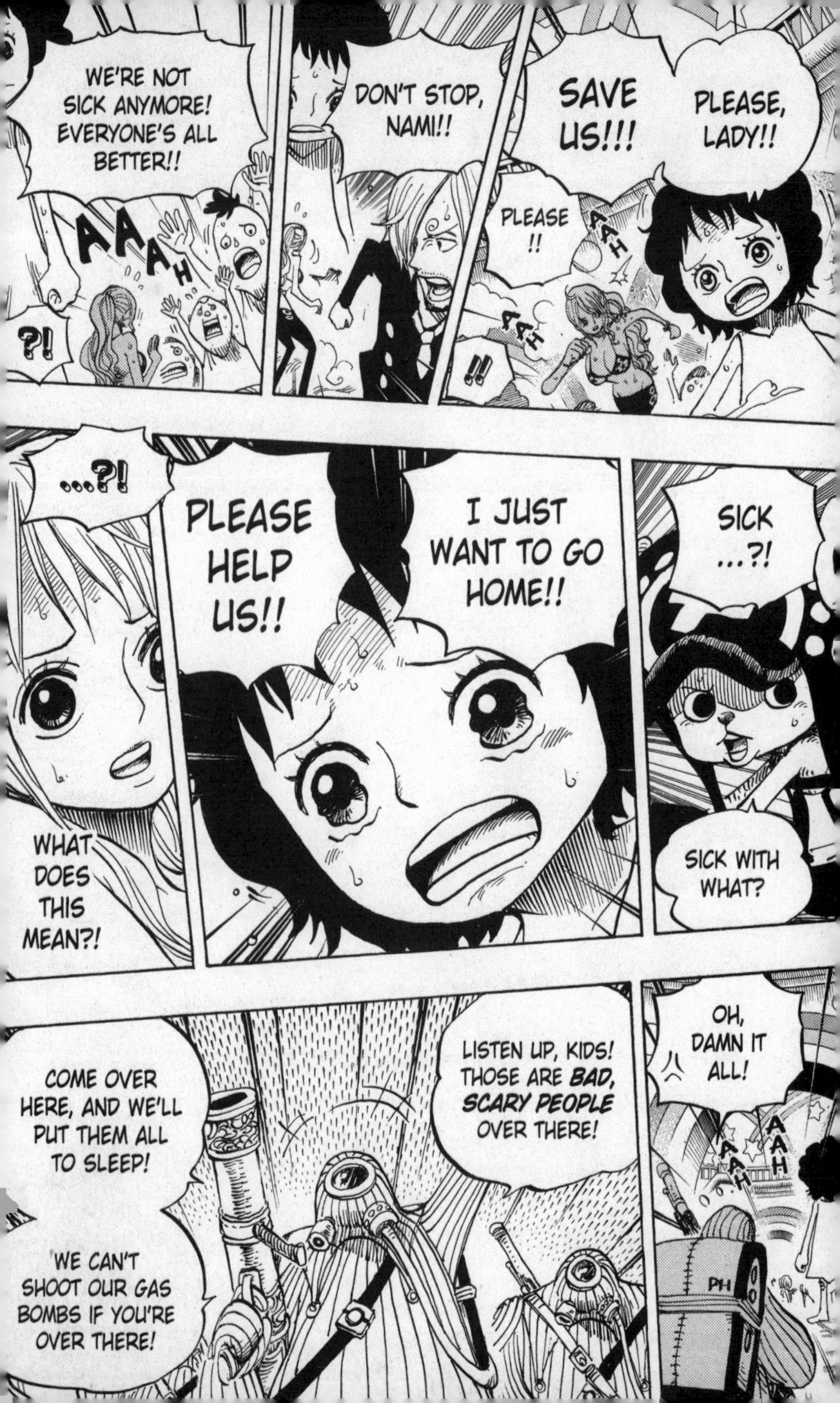
PLEASE, LADY!!
SAVE US!!!
PLEASE !!
AAH
AAH
!!
DON'T STOP, NAMI!!
WE'RE NOT SICK ANYMORE! EVERYONE'S ALL BETTER!!
AAAAH
?!
SICK ...?!
SICK WITH WHAT?
I JUST WANT TO GO HOME!!
PLEASE HELP US!!
...?!
WHAT DOES THIS MEAN?!
OH, DAMN IT ALL!
AAH
AAH
PH
LISTEN UP, KIDS! THOSE ARE *BAD, SCARY PEOPLE* OVER THERE!
COME OVER HERE, AND WE'LL PUT THEM ALL TO SLEEP!
WE CAN'T SHOOT OUR GAS BOMBS IF YOU'RE OVER THERE!

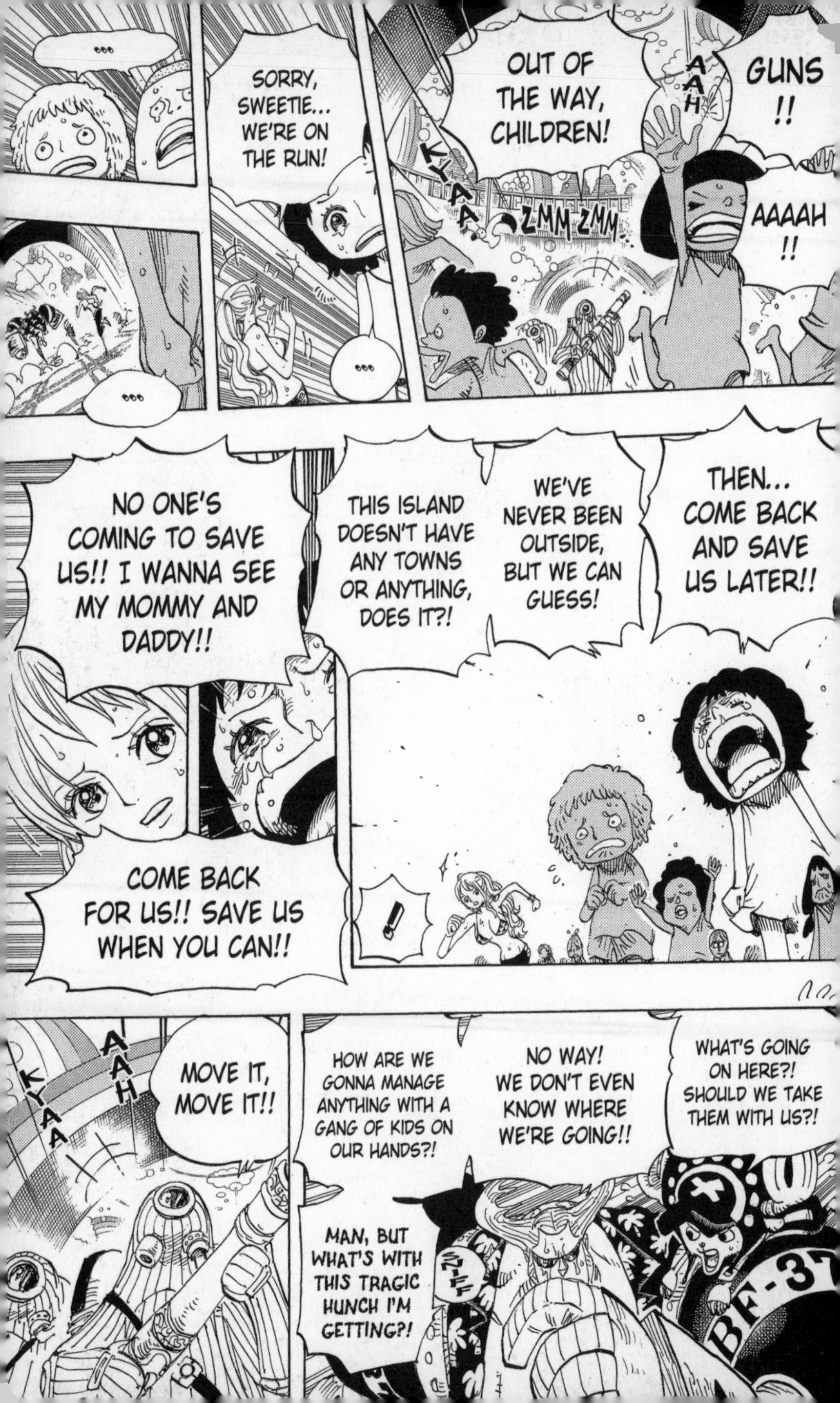
GUNS !!
AAH
OUT OF THE WAY, CHILDREN!
AAAAH !!
KYAAA
ZMM ZMM
SORRY, SWEETIE... WE'RE ON THE RUN!
...
...
...
THEN... COME BACK AND SAVE US LATER!!
WE'VE NEVER BEEN OUTSIDE, BUT WE CAN GUESS!
THIS ISLAND DOESN'T HAVE ANY TOWNS OR ANYTHING, DOES IT?!
NO ONE'S COMING TO SAVE US!! I WANNA SEE MY MOMMY AND DADDY!!
!
COME BACK FOR US!! SAVE US WHEN YOU CAN!!
WHAT'S GOING ON HERE?! SHOULD WE TAKE THEM WITH US?!
NO WAY! WE DON'T EVEN KNOW WHERE WE'RE GOING!!
HOW ARE WE GONNA MANAGE ANYTHING WITH A GANG OF KIDS ON OUR HANDS?!
BF-37
SNIFF
MAN, BUT WHAT'S WITH THIS TRAGIC HUNCH I'M GETTING?!
MOVE IT, MOVE IT!!
AAH
KYAAA

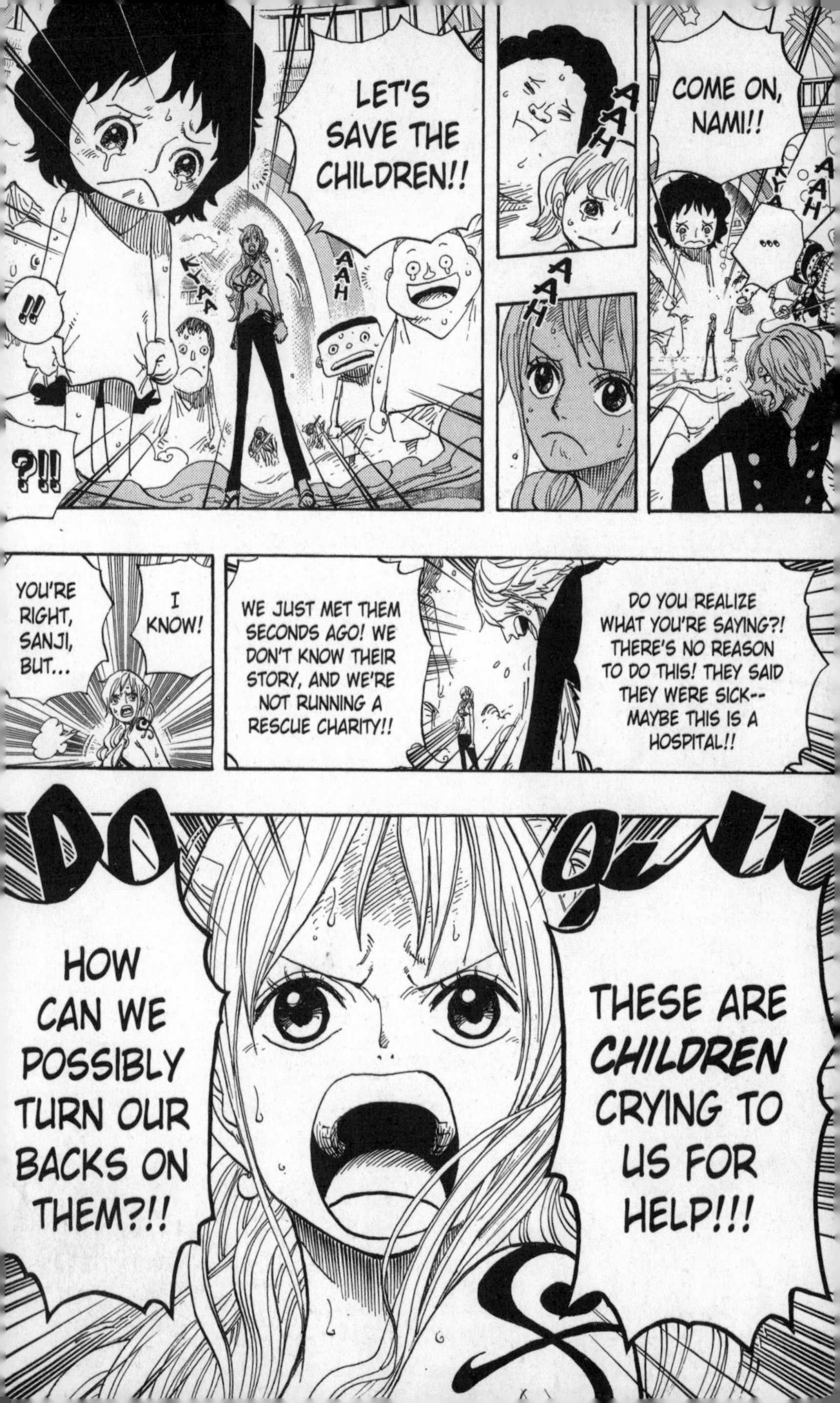
COME ON, NAMI!!
KYAA
AAH
...
AAH
AAH
LET'S SAVE THE CHILDREN!!
AAH
KYAA
!!
?!!
DO YOU REALIZE WHAT YOU'RE SAYING?! THERE'S NO REASON TO DO THIS! THEY SAID THEY WERE SICK-- MAYBE THIS IS A HOSPITAL!!
WE JUST MET THEM SECONDS AGO! WE DON'T KNOW THEIR STORY, AND WE'RE NOT RUNNING A RESCUE CHARITY!!
I KNOW!
YOU'RE RIGHT, SANJI, BUT...
DO
THESE ARE CHILDREN CRYING TO US FOR HELP!!!
HOW CAN WE POSSIBLY TURN OUR BACKS ON THEM?!!

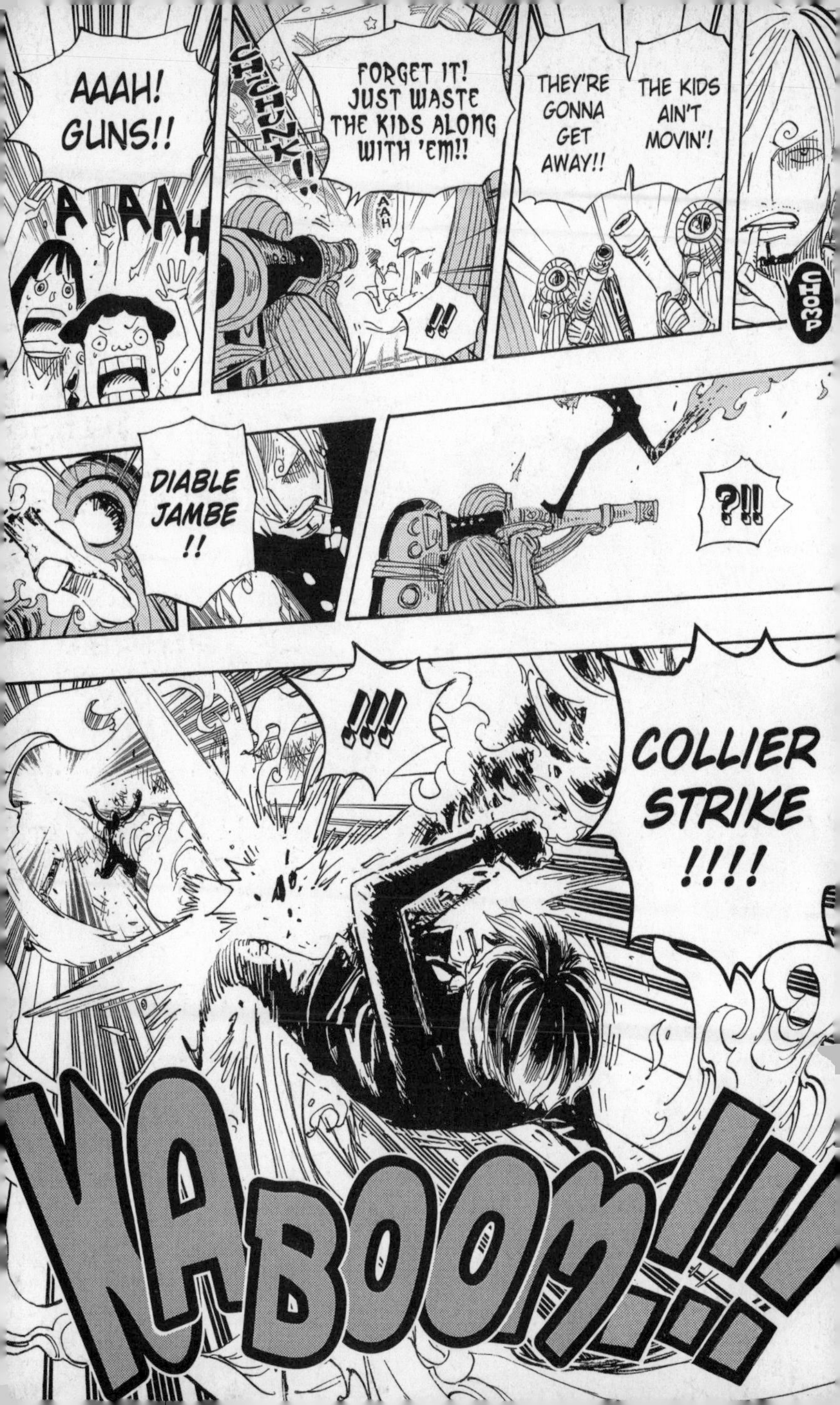
CHOMP
THE KIDS AIN'T MOVIN'!
THEY'RE GONNA GET AWAY!!
FORGET IT! JUST WASTE THE KIDS ALONG WITH 'EM!!
CHCHUNK!!
AAH
!!
AAAH! GUNS!!
AAAH
?!!
DIABLE JAMBE !!
COLLIER STRIKE !!!!
!!!
KABOOM!!!

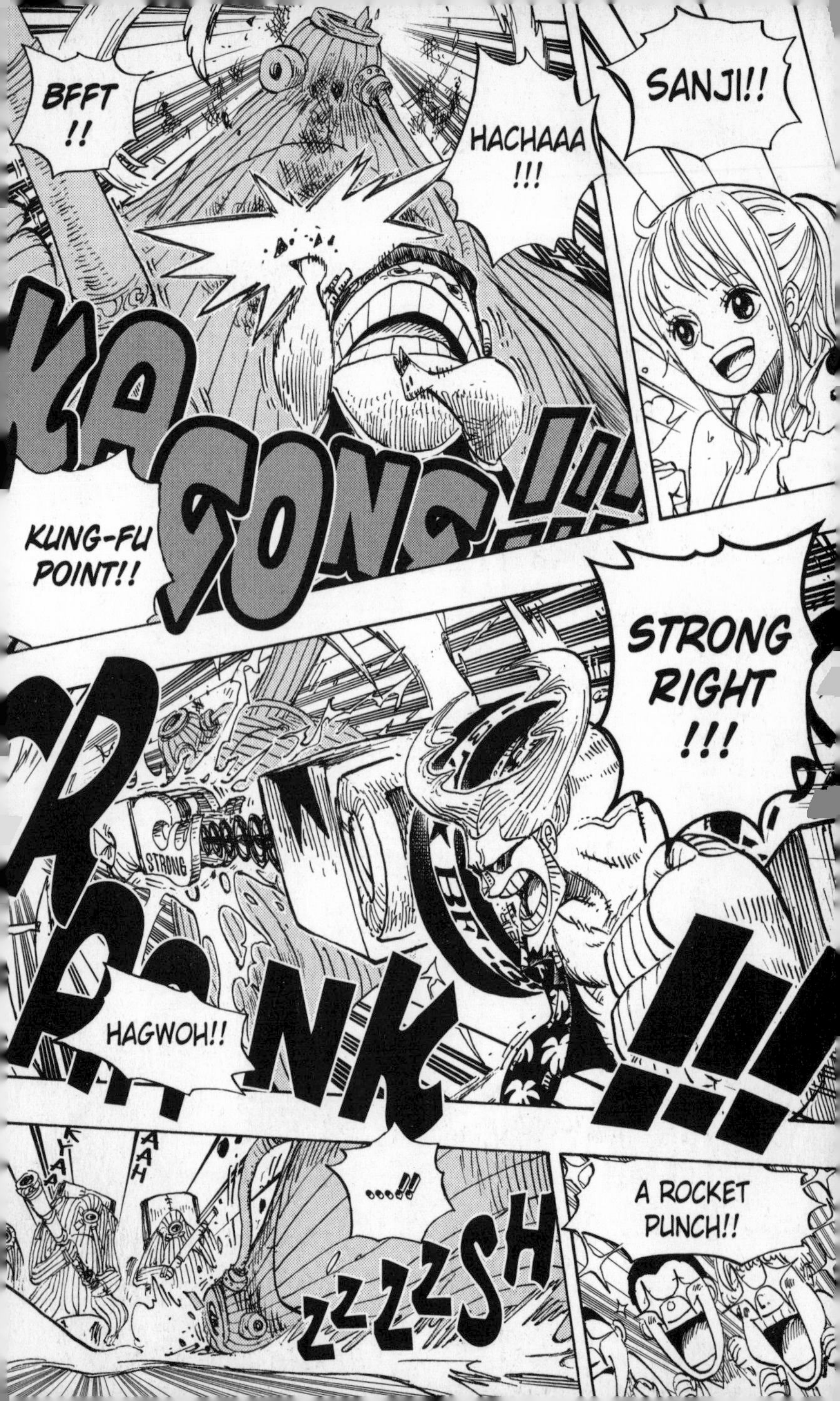
SANJI!!
HACHAAA!!!
BFFT!!
KA GONG!!
KUNG-FU POINT!!
STRONG RIGHT!!!
STRONG
HAGWOH!!
A ROCKET PUNCH!!
...!!
ZZZZZSH
AAH
KYAA

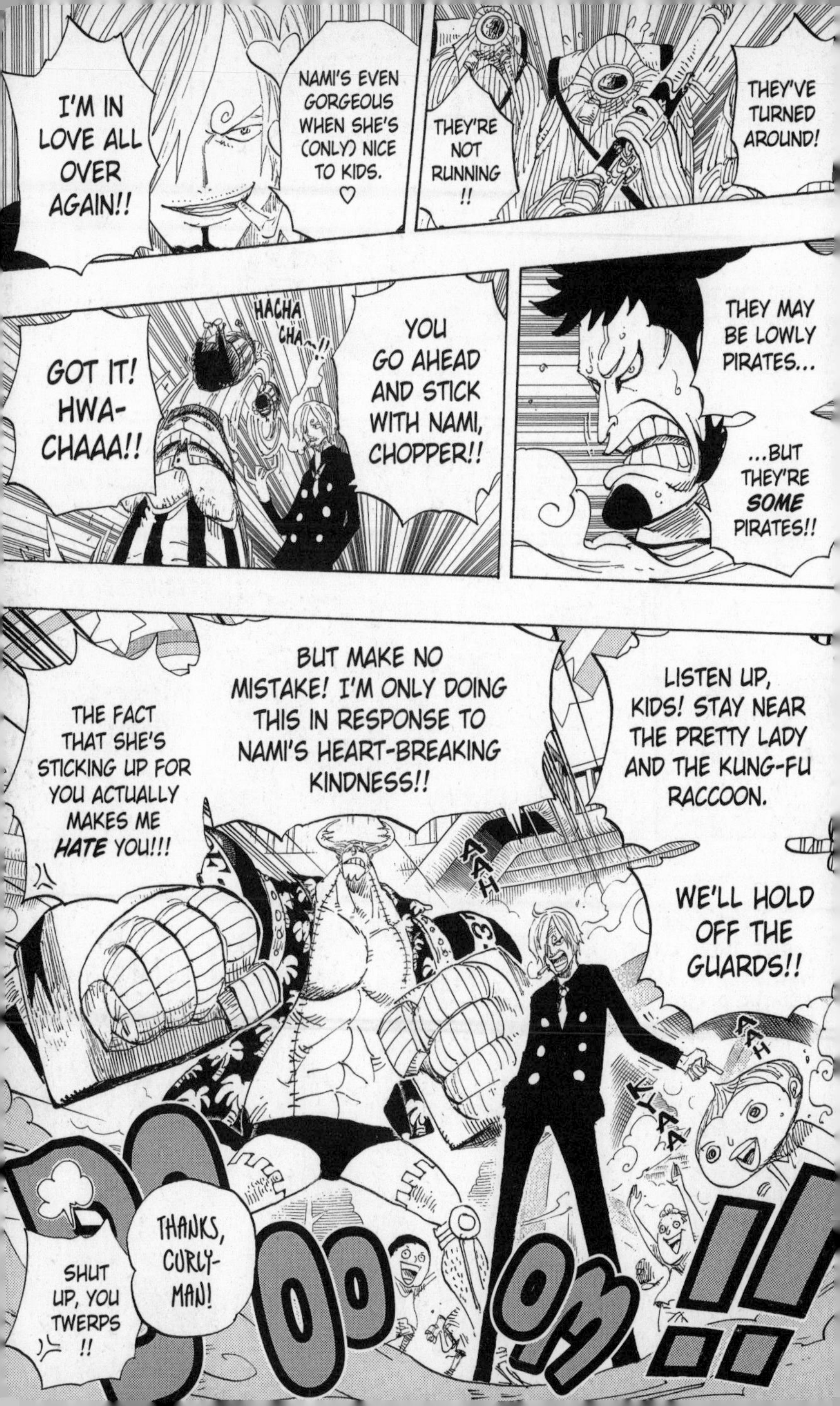
THEY'VE TURNED AROUND!
THEY'RE NOT RUNNING!!
NAMI'S EVEN GORGEOUS WHEN SHE'S (ONLY) NICE TO KIDS. ♥
I'M IN LOVE ALL OVER AGAIN!!
THEY MAY BE LOWLY PIRATES...
...BUT THEY'RE SOME PIRATES!!
YOU GO AHEAD AND STICK WITH NAMI, CHOPPER!!
HACHA CHA...!!
GOT IT! HWA-CHAAA!!
LISTEN UP, KIDS! STAY NEAR THE PRETTY LADY AND THE KUNG-FU RACCOON.
WE'LL HOLD OFF THE GUARDS!!
AAH
AAH
KYAA
BUT MAKE NO MISTAKE! I'M ONLY DOING THIS IN RESPONSE TO NAMI'S HEART-BREAKING KINDNESS!!
THE FACT THAT SHE'S STICKING UP FOR YOU ACTUALLY MAKES ME *HATE* YOU!!!
THANKS, CURLY-MAN!
SHUT UP, YOU TWERPS!!
OOOM!!

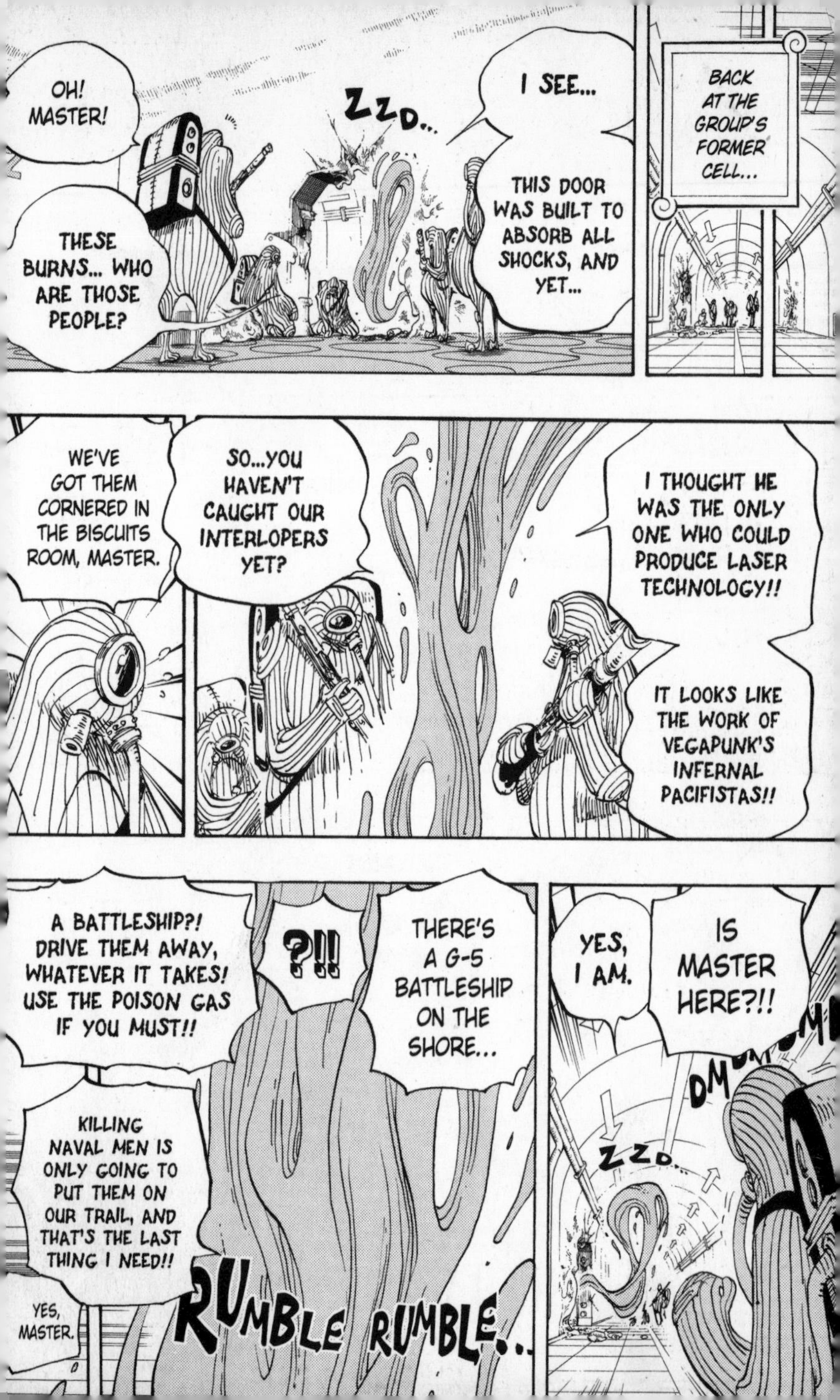
BACK AT THE GROUP'S FORMER CELL...
I SEE...
THIS DOOR WAS BUILT TO ABSORB ALL SHOCKS, AND YET...
ZZD...
OH! MASTER!
THESE BURNS... WHO ARE THOSE PEOPLE?
I THOUGHT HE WAS THE ONLY ONE WHO COULD PRODUCE LASER TECHNOLOGY!!
IT LOOKS LIKE THE WORK OF VEGAPUNK'S INFERNAL PACIFISTAS!!
SO...YOU HAVEN'T CAUGHT OUR INTERLOPERS YET?
WE'VE GOT THEM CORNERED IN THE BISCUITS ROOM, MASTER.
IS MASTER HERE?!!
YES, I AM.
ZZD...
THERE'S A G-5 BATTLESHIP ON THE SHORE...
?!!
A BATTLESHIP?! DRIVE THEM AWAY, WHATEVER IT TAKES! USE THE POISON GAS IF YOU MUST!!
KILLING NAVAL MEN IS ONLY GOING TO PUT THEM ON OUR TRAIL, AND THAT'S THE LAST THING I NEED!!
YES, MASTER.
RUMBLE RUMBLE...

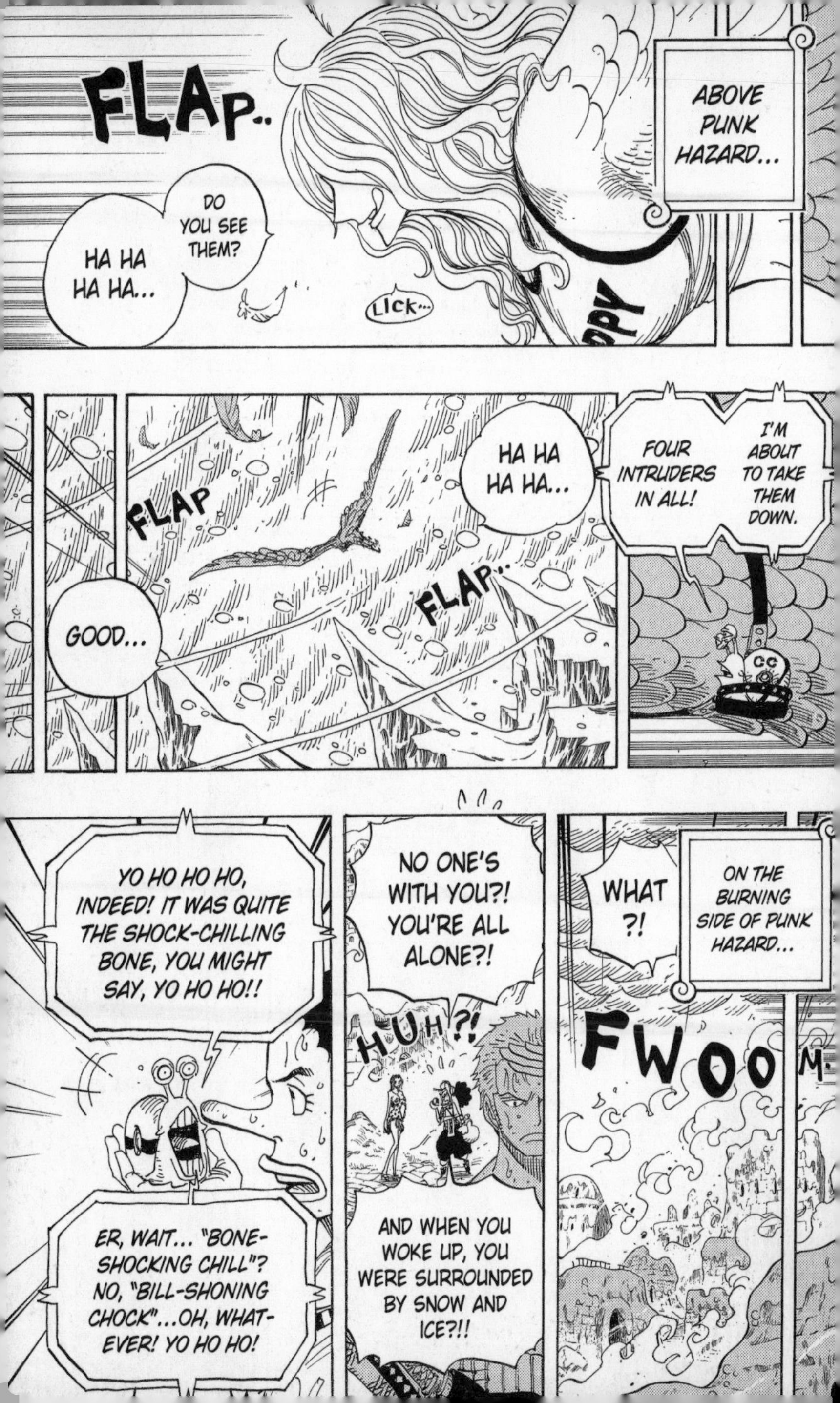

ABOVE PUNK HAZARD...
FLAP..
DO YOU SEE THEM?
HA HA HA HA...
LICK...
FOUR INTRUDERS IN ALL!
I'M ABOUT TO TAKE THEM DOWN.
HA HA HA HA...
FLAP
FLAP..
GOOD...
ON THE BURNING SIDE OF PUNK HAZARD...
WHAT?!
FWOOM.
NO ONE'S WITH YOU?! YOU'RE ALL ALONE?!
HUH?!
AND WHEN YOU WOKE UP, YOU WERE SURROUNDED BY SNOW AND ICE?!!
YO HO HO HO, INDEED! IT WAS QUITE THE SHOCK-CHILLING BONE, YOU MIGHT SAY, YO HO HO!!
ER, WAIT... "BONE-SHOCKING CHILL"? NO, "BILL-SHONING CHOCK"...OH, WHAT-EVER! YO HO HO!

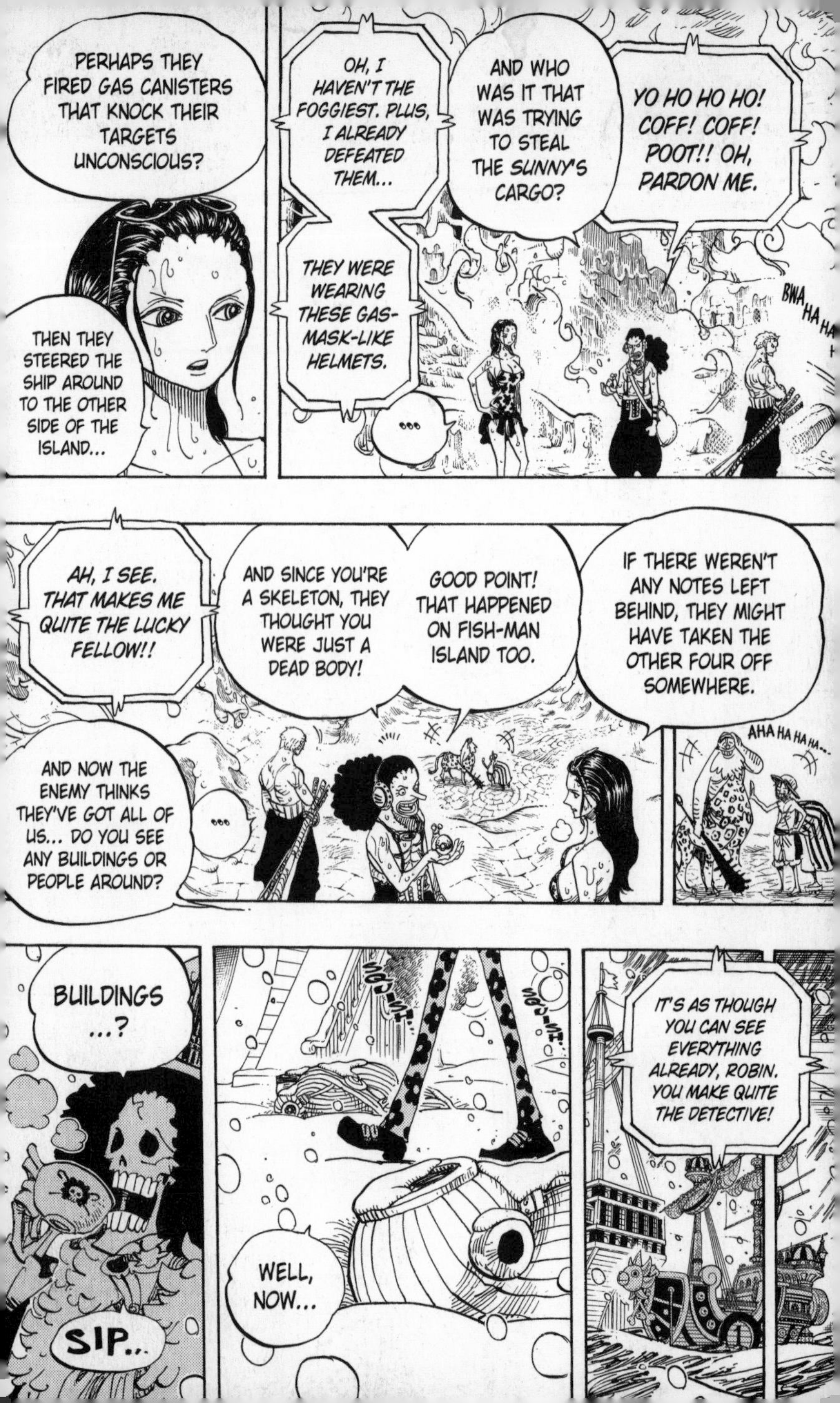
YO HO HO HO! COFF! COFF! POOT!! OH, PARDON ME.
AND WHO WAS IT THAT WAS TRYING TO STEAL THE SUNNY'S CARGO?
BWA HA HA
OH, I HAVEN'T THE FOGGIEST. PLUS, I ALREADY DEFEATED THEM...
THEY WERE WEARING THESE GAS-MASK-LIKE HELMETS.
...
PERHAPS THEY FIRED GAS CANISTERS THAT KNOCK THEIR TARGETS UNCONSCIOUS?
THEN THEY STEERED THE SHIP AROUND TO THE OTHER SIDE OF THE ISLAND...
AHA HA HA HA...
IF THERE WEREN'T ANY NOTES LEFT BEHIND, THEY MIGHT HAVE TAKEN THE OTHER FOUR OFF SOMEWHERE.
GOOD POINT! THAT HAPPENED ON FISH-MAN ISLAND TOO.
AND SINCE YOU'RE A SKELETON, THEY THOUGHT YOU WERE JUST A DEAD BODY!
AH, I SEE. THAT MAKES ME QUITE THE LUCKY FELLOW!!
AND NOW THE ENEMY THINKS THEY'VE GOT ALL OF US... DO YOU SEE ANY BUILDINGS OR PEOPLE AROUND?
...
IT'S AS THOUGH YOU CAN SEE EVERYTHING ALREADY, ROBIN. YOU MAKE QUITE THE DETECTIVE!
WELL, NOW...
BUILDINGS ...?
SIP...

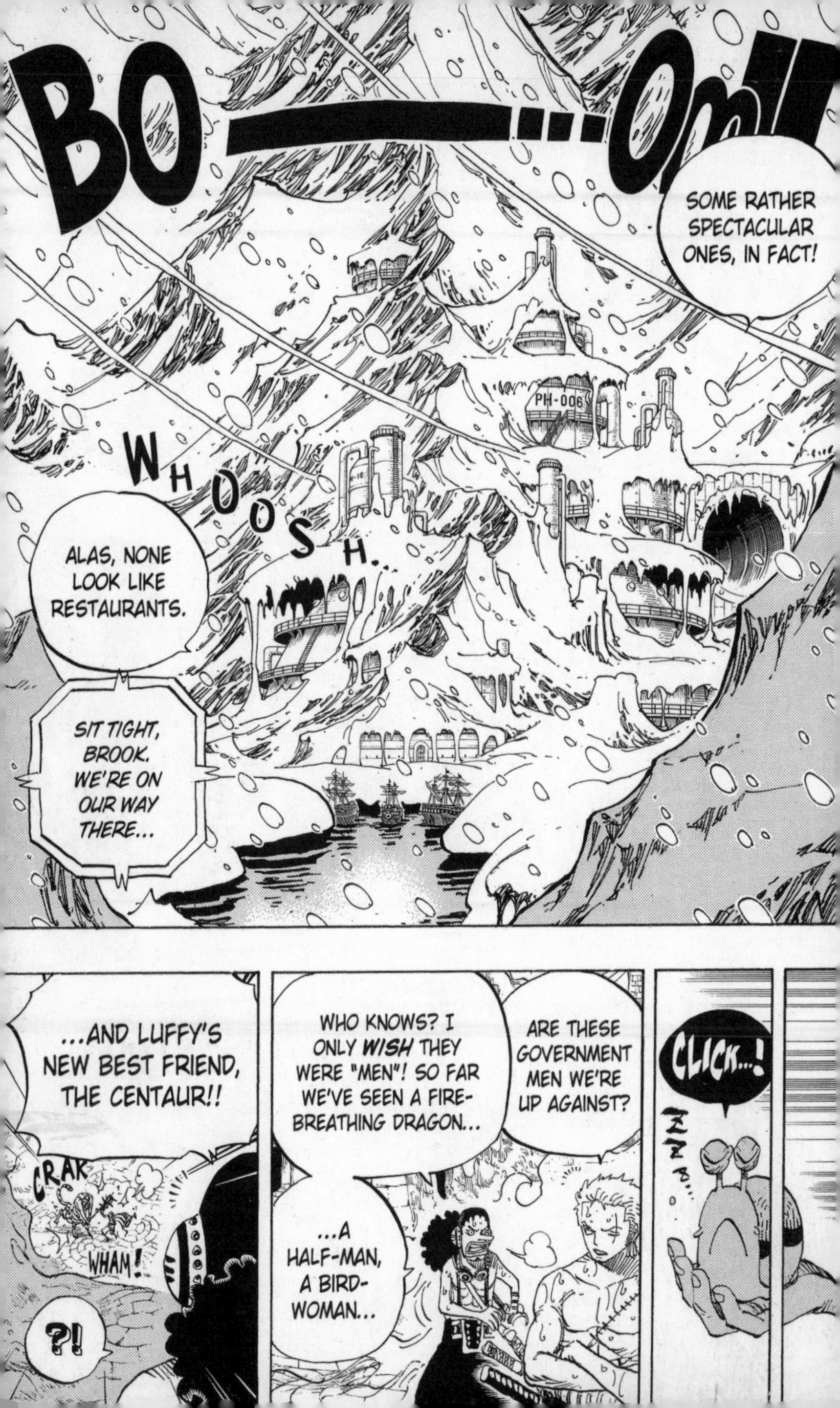
BO———...Om!!
SOME RATHER SPECTACULAR ONES, IN FACT!
WHOOSH...
ALAS, NONE LOOK LIKE RESTAURANTS.
SIT TIGHT, BROOK. WE'RE ON OUR WAY THERE...
CLICK...!
ARE THESE GOVERNMENT MEN WE'RE UP AGAINST?
WHO KNOWS? I ONLY *WISH* THEY WERE "MEN"! SO FAR WE'VE SEEN A FIRE-BREATHING DRAGON...
...A HALF-MAN, A BIRD-WOMAN...
...AND LUFFY'S NEW BEST FRIEND, THE CENTAUR!!
CRAK
WHAM!
?!

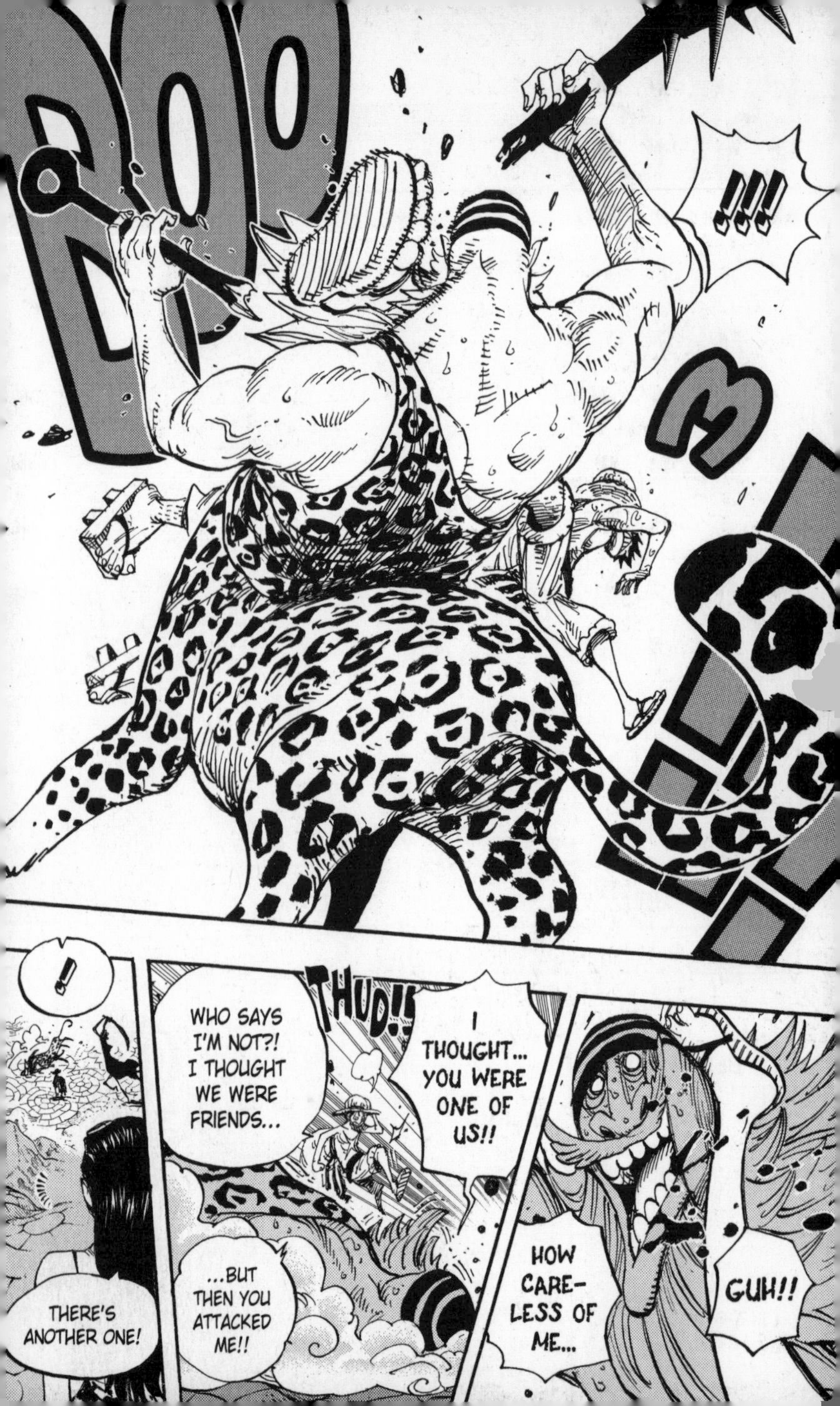
!!!
GUH!!
HOW CARE-LESS OF ME...
I THOUGHT... YOU WERE ONE OF US!!
WHO SAYS I'M NOT?! I THOUGHT WE WERE FRIENDS...
THUD!!
...BUT THEN YOU ATTACKED ME!!
!
THERE'S ANOTHER ONE!

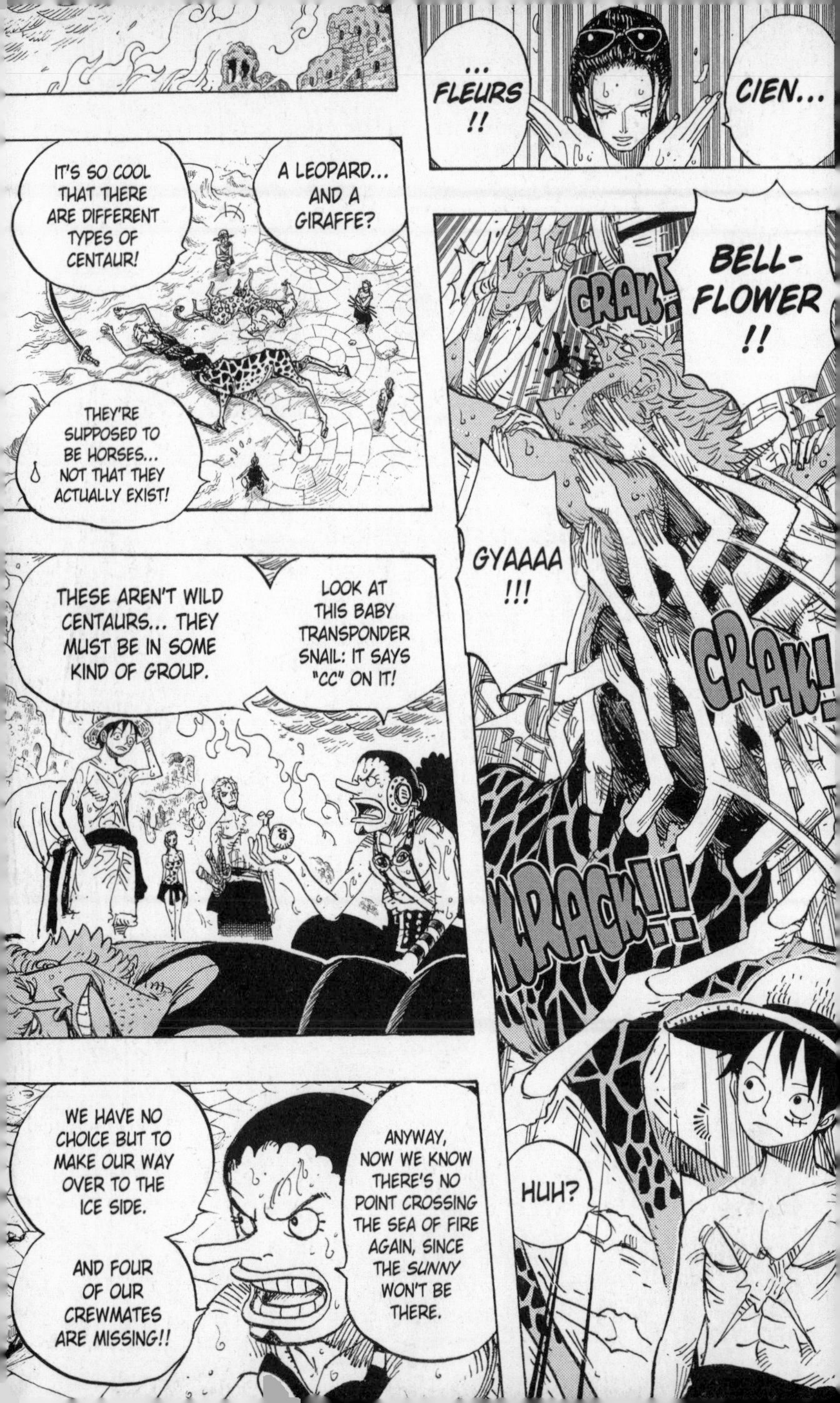
CIEN...
... FLEURS !!
BELL-FLOWER !!
CRAK!
GYAAAA !!!
CRAK!
KRACK!!
HUH?
A LEOPARD... AND A GIRAFFE?
IT'S SO COOL THAT THERE ARE DIFFERENT TYPES OF CENTAUR!
THEY'RE SUPPOSED TO BE HORSES... NOT THAT THEY ACTUALLY EXIST!
LOOK AT THIS BABY TRANSPONDER SNAIL: IT SAYS "CC" ON IT!
THESE AREN'T WILD CENTAURS... THEY MUST BE IN SOME KIND OF GROUP.
ANYWAY, NOW WE KNOW THERE'S NO POINT CROSSING THE SEA OF FIRE AGAIN, SINCE THE *SUNNY* WON'T BE THERE.
WE HAVE NO CHOICE BUT TO MAKE OUR WAY OVER TO THE ICE SIDE.
AND FOUR OF OUR CREWMATES ARE MISSING!!

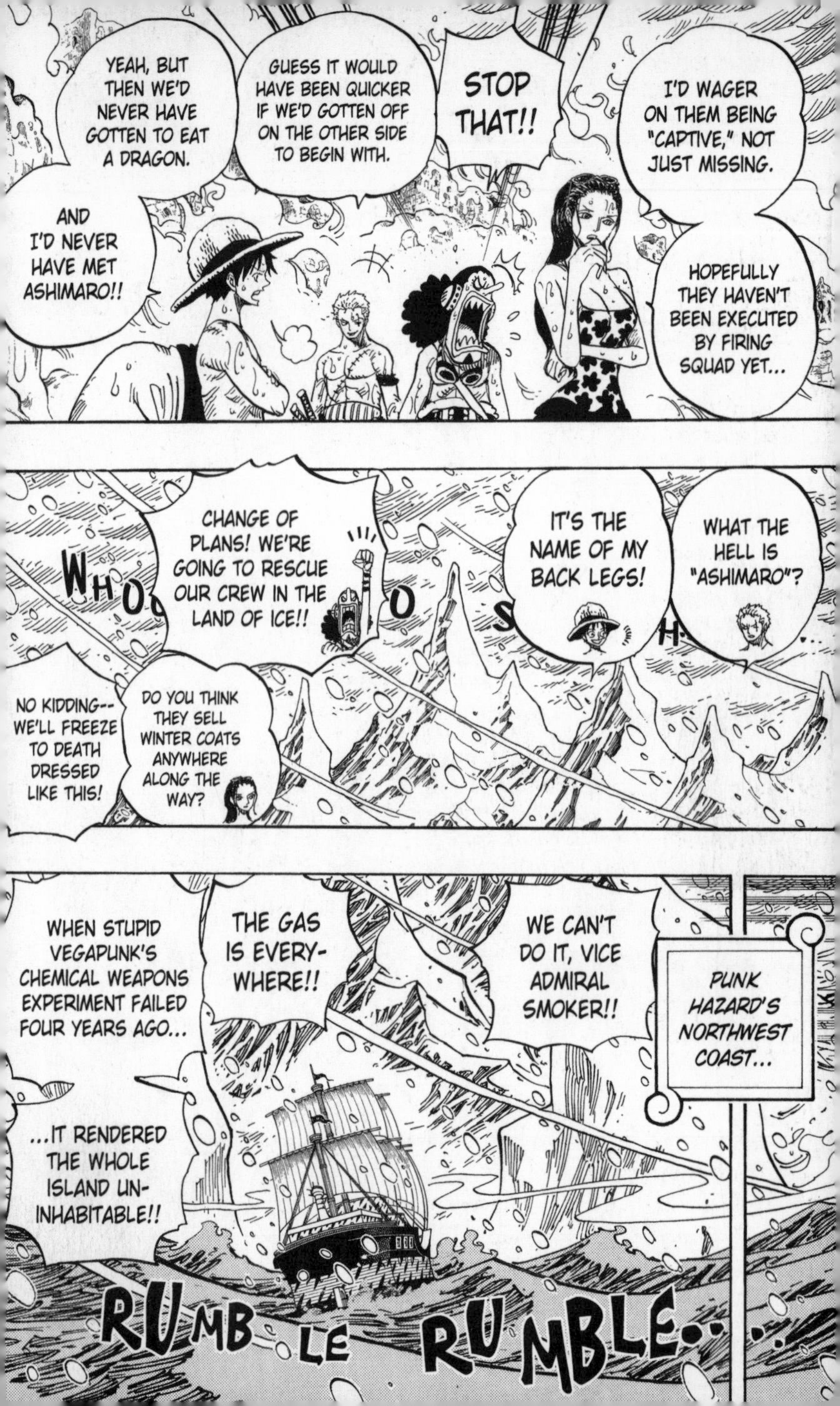
I'D WAGER ON THEM BEING "CAPTIVE," NOT JUST MISSING.
HOPEFULLY THEY HAVEN'T BEEN EXECUTED BY FIRING SQUAD YET...
STOP THAT!!
GUESS IT WOULD HAVE BEEN QUICKER IF WE'D GOTTEN OFF ON THE OTHER SIDE TO BEGIN WITH.
YEAH, BUT THEN WE'D NEVER HAVE GOTTEN TO EAT A DRAGON.
AND I'D NEVER HAVE MET ASHIMARO!!
WHAT THE HELL IS "ASHIMARO"?
IT'S THE NAME OF MY BACK LEGS!
CHANGE OF PLANS! WE'RE GOING TO RESCUE OUR CREW IN THE LAND OF ICE!!
WHOOSH...
DO YOU THINK THEY SELL WINTER COATS ANYWHERE ALONG THE WAY?
NO KIDDING-- WE'LL FREEZE TO DEATH DRESSED LIKE THIS!
PUNK HAZARD'S NORTHWEST COAST...
WE CAN'T DO IT, VICE ADMIRAL SMOKER!!
THE GAS IS EVERY-WHERE!!
WHEN STUPID VEGAPUNK'S CHEMICAL WEAPONS EXPERIMENT FAILED FOUR YEARS AGO...
...IT RENDERED THE WHOLE ISLAND UN-INHABITABLE!!
RUMBLE RUMBLE...

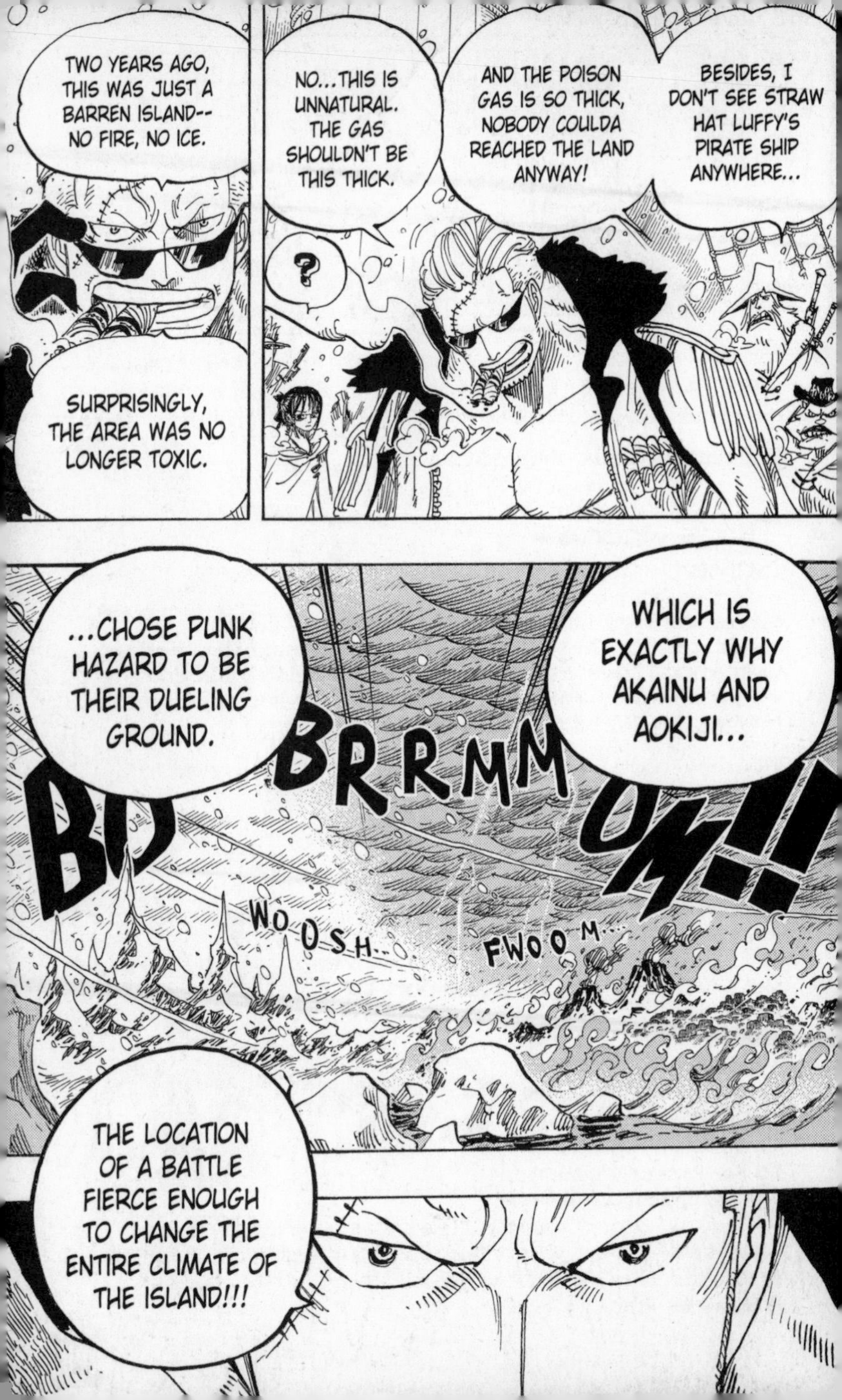

BESIDES, I DON'T SEE STRAW HAT LUFFY'S PIRATE SHIP ANYWHERE...
AND THE POISON GAS IS SO THICK, NOBODY COULDA REACHED THE LAND ANYWAY!
NO...THIS IS UNNATURAL. THE GAS SHOULDN'T BE THIS THICK.
?
TWO YEARS AGO, THIS WAS JUST A BARREN ISLAND-- NO FIRE, NO ICE.
SURPRISINGLY, THE AREA WAS NO LONGER TOXIC.
WHICH IS EXACTLY WHY AKAINU AND AOKIJI...
...CHOSE PUNK HAZARD TO BE THEIR DUELING GROUND.
BO BRRMM OW!!
FWOOM...
WOOSH...
THE LOCATION OF A BATTLE FIERCE ENOUGH TO CHANGE THE ENTIRE CLIMATE OF THE ISLAND!!!

SBS Question Corner

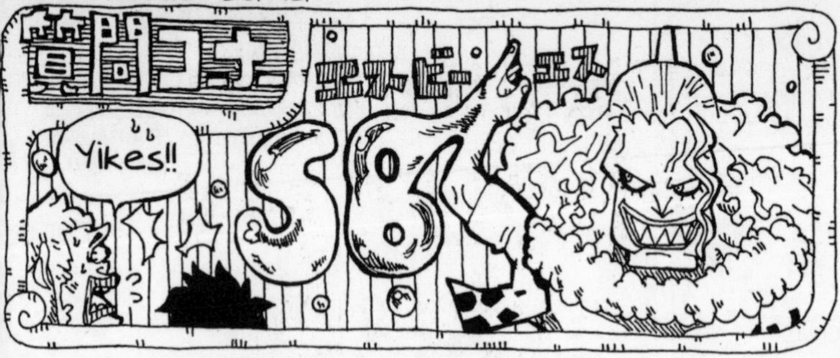
Yikes!!

(Haru, Nagano)

Q: Hello, hello, Odacchi!! When I was staring at a pretty lady handing out packs of tissue near the train station, Jimbei was thinking of his plan to make Luffy a hero in Volume 64! So what was the name of his plan, anyway?

--God of Manga

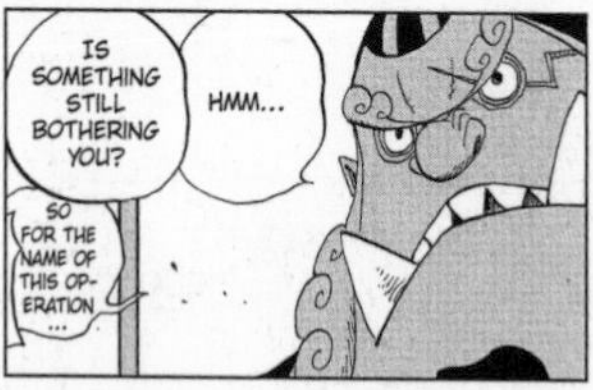
HMM...
IS SOMETHING STILL BOTHERING YOU?
SO FOR THE NAME OF THIS OPERATION...

A: That's wrong. Something was wrong with the first half of your sentence! Well, here were the candidates for Jimbei's plan: Operation Straw Hat Heroes, Operation I Love Humans, and Operation Who Cares About History Anyway. Hmm...did it really need a name, anyway? Maybe it's best he never came up with one.

Q: Odacchi! Odacchi! On page 152 of Volume 65, there's a very sweet little mermaid wearing a hood, right? C-c-c-could that be… ♡♡ Madam Sharley? ♡♡

--I'll Be A Pirate!

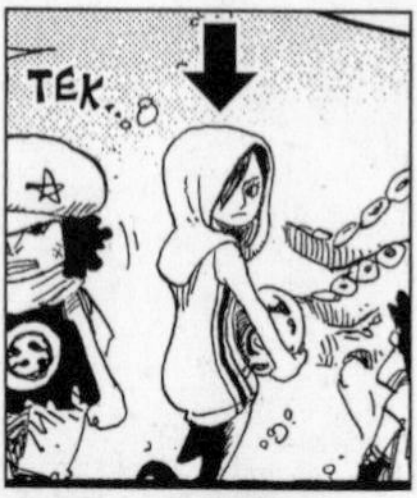
TEK...

A: That's right. They call her Madam Sharley, but she's only 29. Her brother Arlong is 41 and Hody is 30, which means she's part of Hody's generation. When Arlong was young, he was abandoned in the Fish-man District by his father, so he never really knew his dad. But when he was 15, a man claiming to be his father returned with a daughter he had with a different woman. That was Sharley. By the way, it's said that when she was four years old, Sharley predicted the "Age of Voyaging" that began the following year.

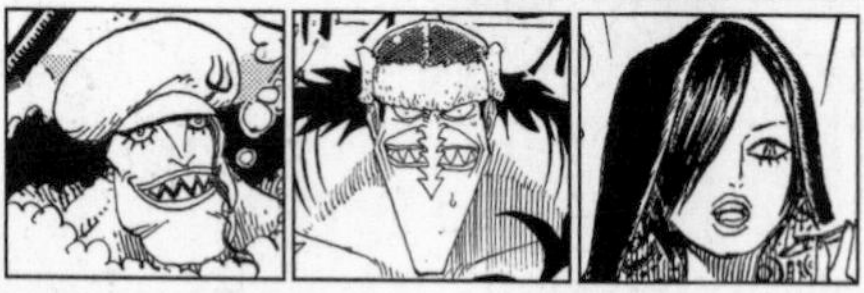

Chapter 659: ABOUT MY TORSO

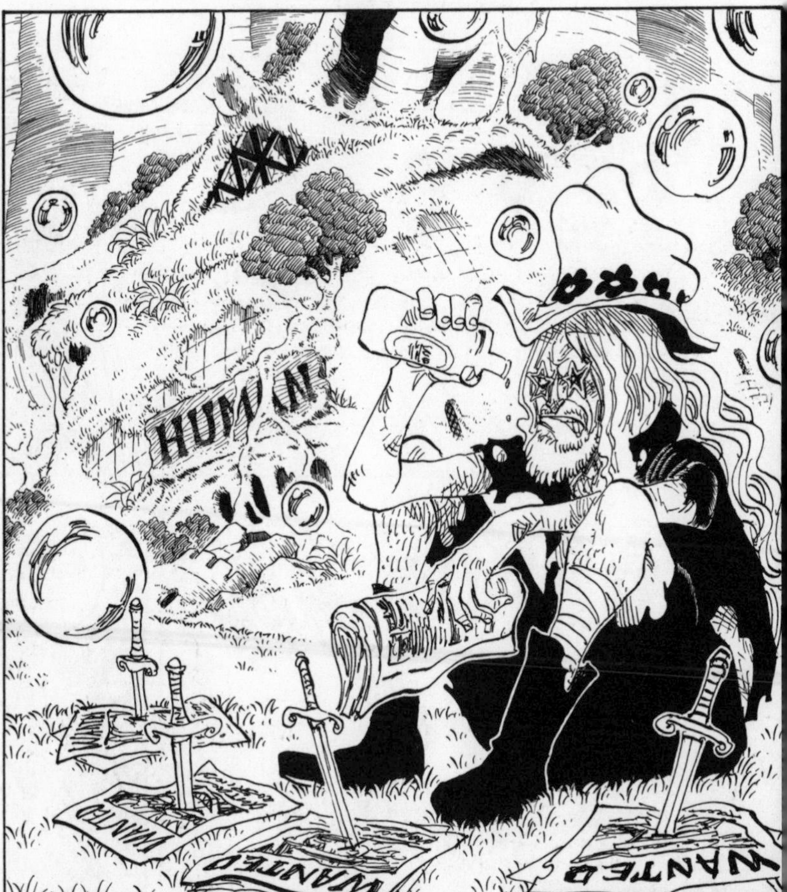
WANTED
WANTED
WANTED
WANTED

DECKS OF THE WORLD, VOL. 41: "SABAODY ARCHIPELAGO—
DISCO THE SLAVER, DOWN ON HIS LUCK"

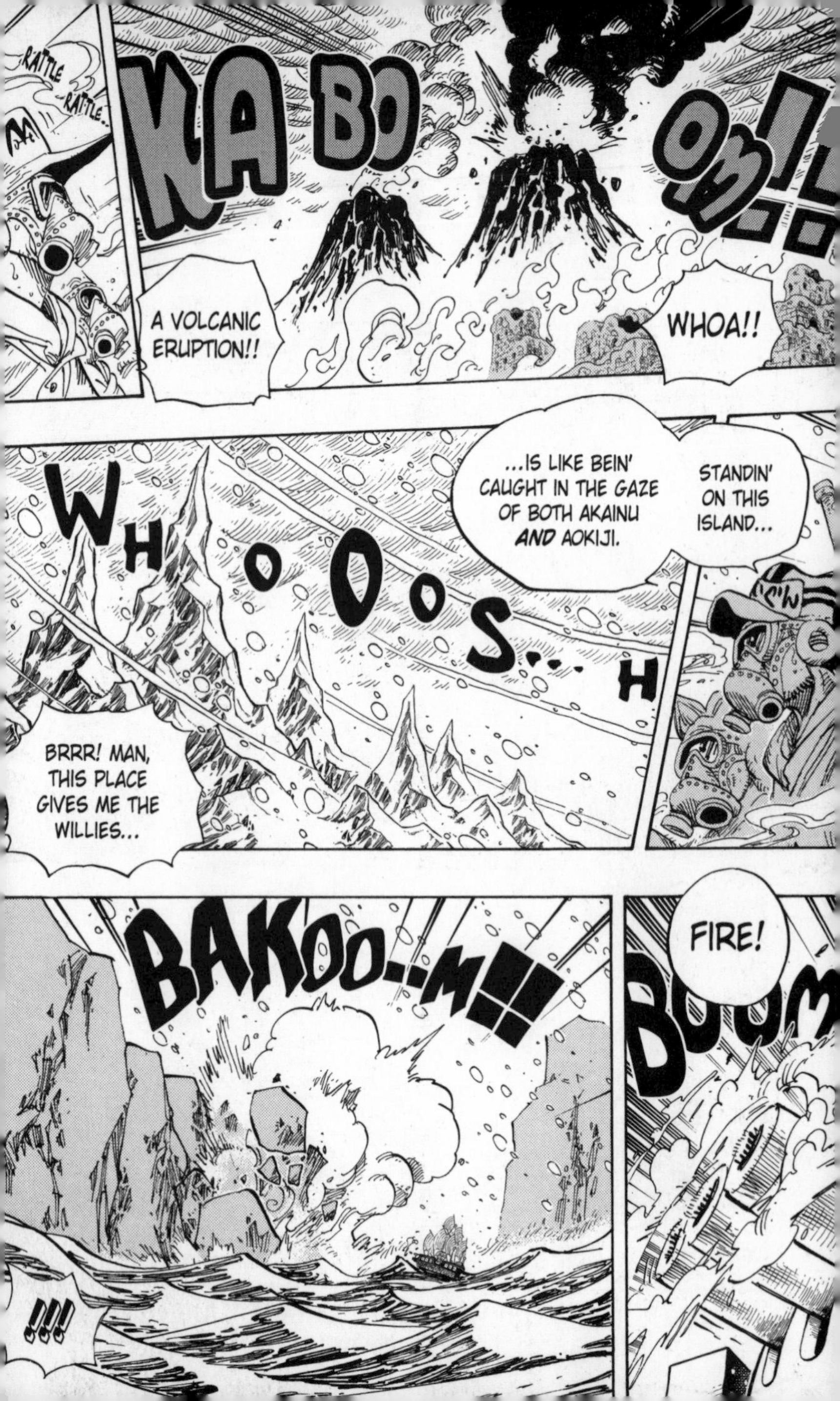
KABOOM!!
WHOA!!
A VOLCANIC ERUPTION!!
RATTLE RATTLE...
STANDIN' ON THIS ISLAND...
...IS LIKE BEIN' CAUGHT IN THE GAZE OF BOTH AKAINU AND AOKIJI.
WHOOOOSH...H
BRRR! MAN, THIS PLACE GIVES ME THE WILLIES...
FIRE!
BOOM
BAKOO--M!!
!!!

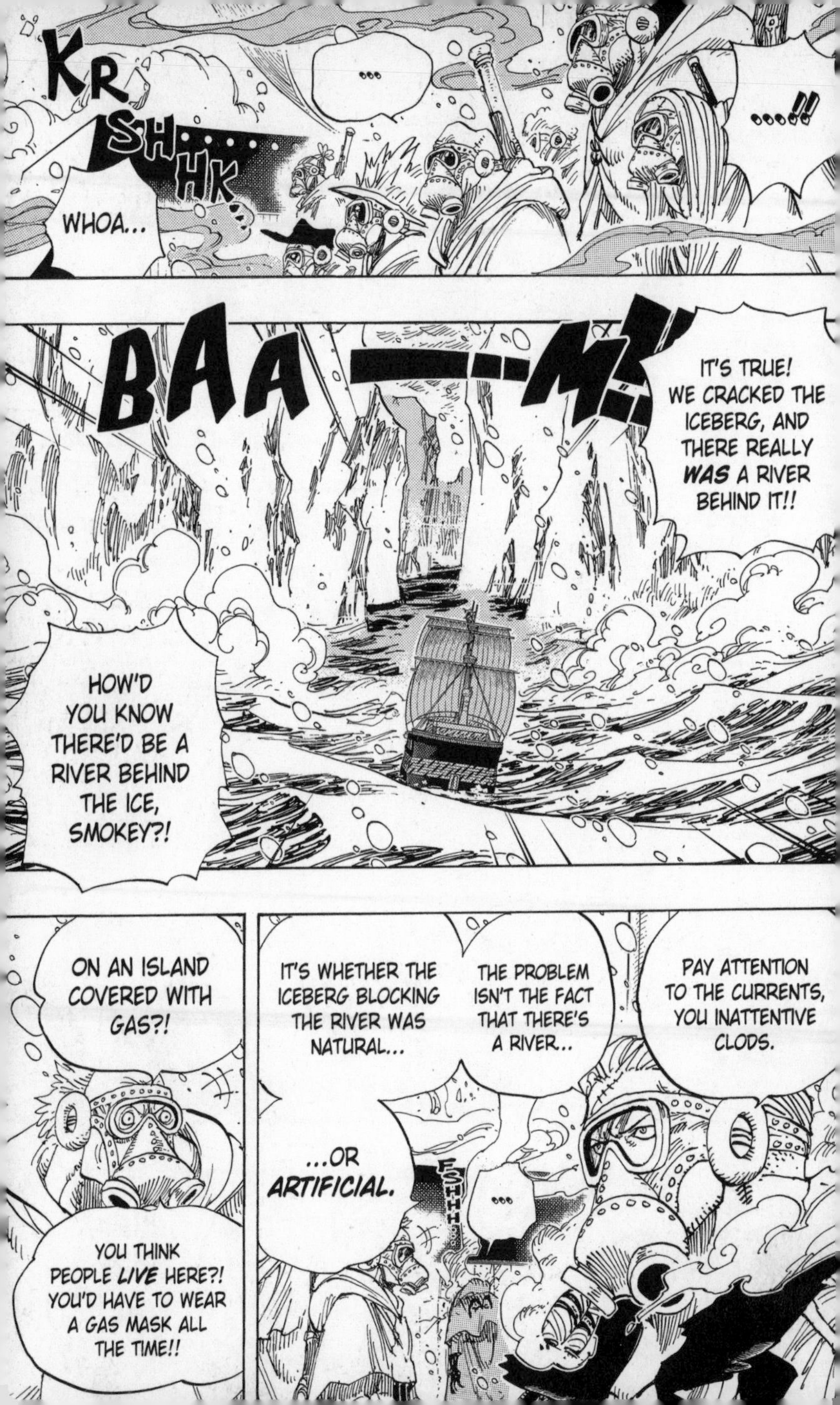
...!!
...
KR SHHK
WHOA...
BAA—M!!
IT'S TRUE! WE CRACKED THE ICEBERG, AND THERE REALLY *WAS* A RIVER BEHIND IT!!
HOW'D YOU KNOW THERE'D BE A RIVER BEHIND THE ICE, SMOKEY?!
PAY ATTENTION TO THE CURRENTS, YOU INATTENTIVE CLODS.
THE PROBLEM ISN'T THE FACT THAT THERE'S A RIVER...
IT'S WHETHER THE ICEBERG BLOCKING THE RIVER WAS NATURAL...
...OR *ARTIFICIAL.*
FSHHH
...
ON AN ISLAND COVERED WITH GAS?!
YOU THINK PEOPLE *LIVE* HERE?! YOU'D HAVE TO WEAR A GAS MASK ALL THE TIME!!

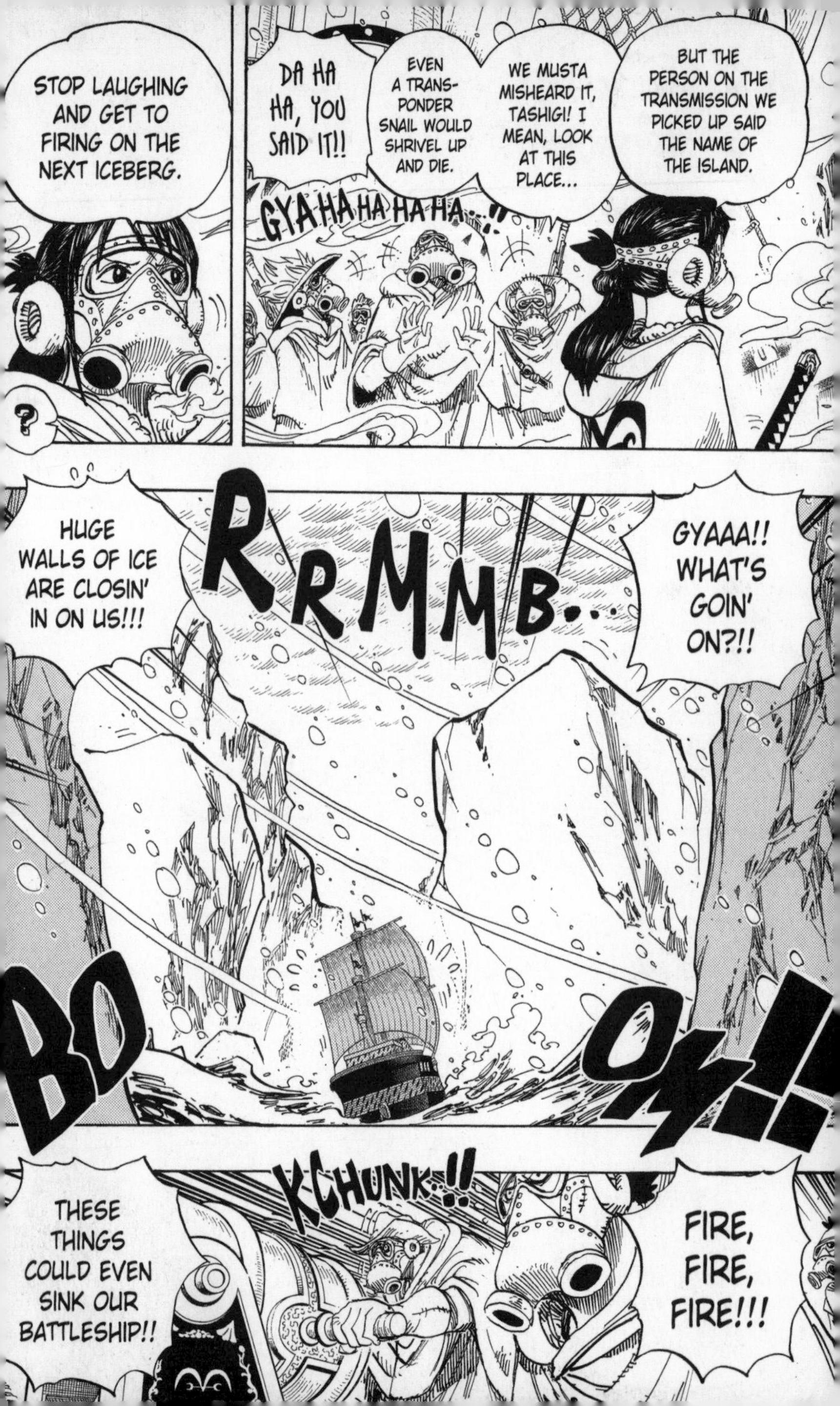
BUT THE PERSON ON THE TRANSMISSION WE PICKED UP SAID THE NAME OF THE ISLAND.
WE MUSTA MISHEARD IT, TASHIGI! I MEAN, LOOK AT THIS PLACE...
EVEN A TRANS-PONDER SNAIL WOULD SHRIVEL UP AND DIE.
DA HA HA, YOU SAID IT!!
GYAHA HA HA HA...!!
STOP LAUGHING AND GET TO FIRING ON THE NEXT ICEBERG.
?
GYAAA!! WHAT'S GOIN' ON?!!
RRMMB...
HUGE WALLS OF ICE ARE CLOSIN' IN ON US!!!
BOOM!!
FIRE, FIRE, FIRE!!!
KCHUNK!!
THESE THINGS COULD EVEN SINK OUR BATTLESHIP!!

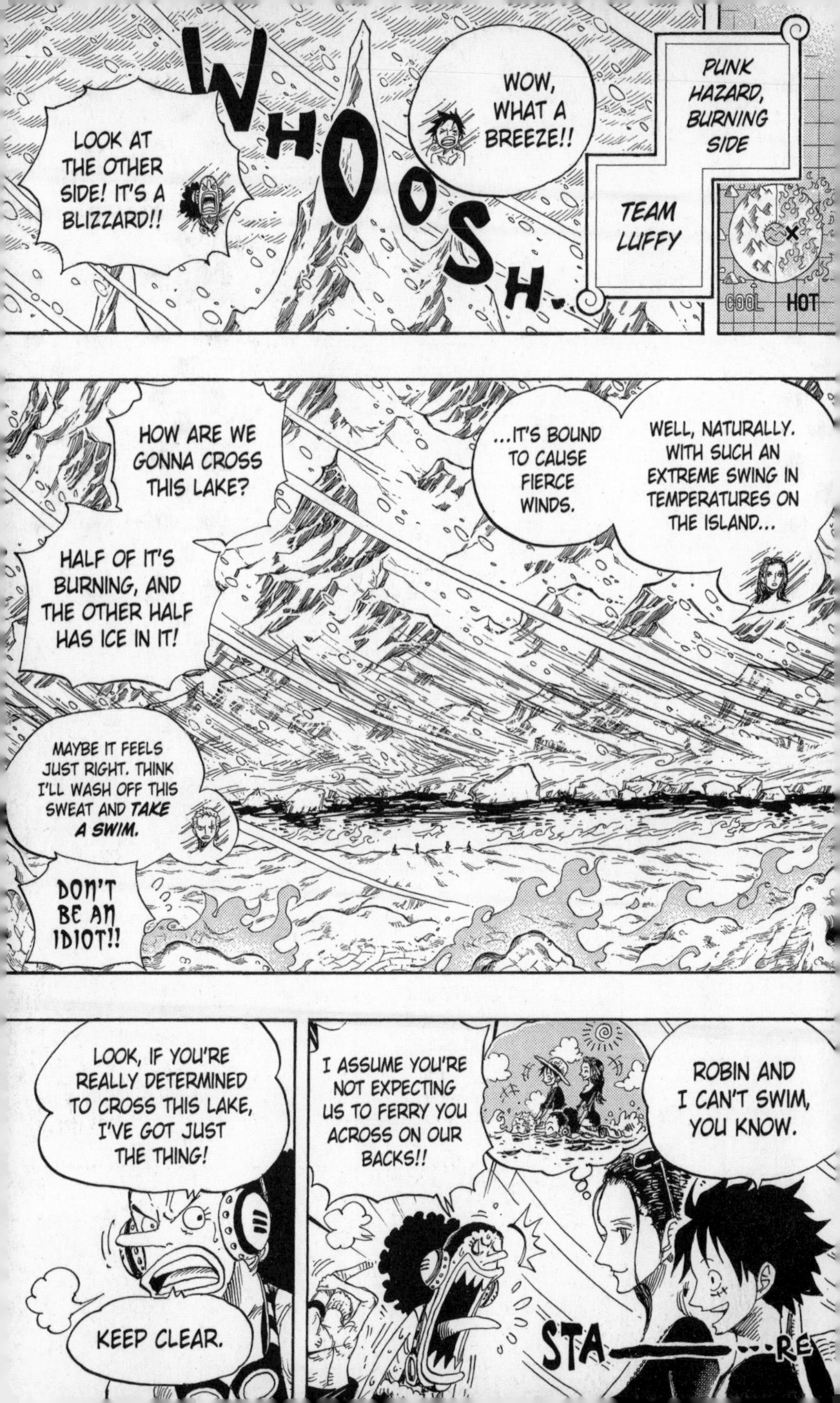
PUNK HAZARD, BURNING SIDE
TEAM LUFFY
COOL
HOT
WOW, WHAT A BREEZE!!
WHOOSH
LOOK AT THE OTHER SIDE! IT'S A BLIZZARD!!
WELL, NATURALLY. WITH SUCH AN EXTREME SWING IN TEMPERATURES ON THE ISLAND...
...IT'S BOUND TO CAUSE FIERCE WINDS.
HOW ARE WE GONNA CROSS THIS LAKE?
HALF OF IT'S BURNING, AND THE OTHER HALF HAS ICE IN IT!
MAYBE IT FEELS JUST RIGHT. THINK I'LL WASH OFF THIS SWEAT AND TAKE A SWIM.
DON'T BE AN IDIOT!!
ROBIN AND I CAN'T SWIM, YOU KNOW.
I ASSUME YOU'RE NOT EXPECTING US TO FERRY YOU ACROSS ON OUR BACKS!!
STA...RE
LOOK, IF YOU'RE REALLY DETERMINED TO CROSS THIS LAKE, I'VE GOT JUST THE THING!
KEEP CLEAR.

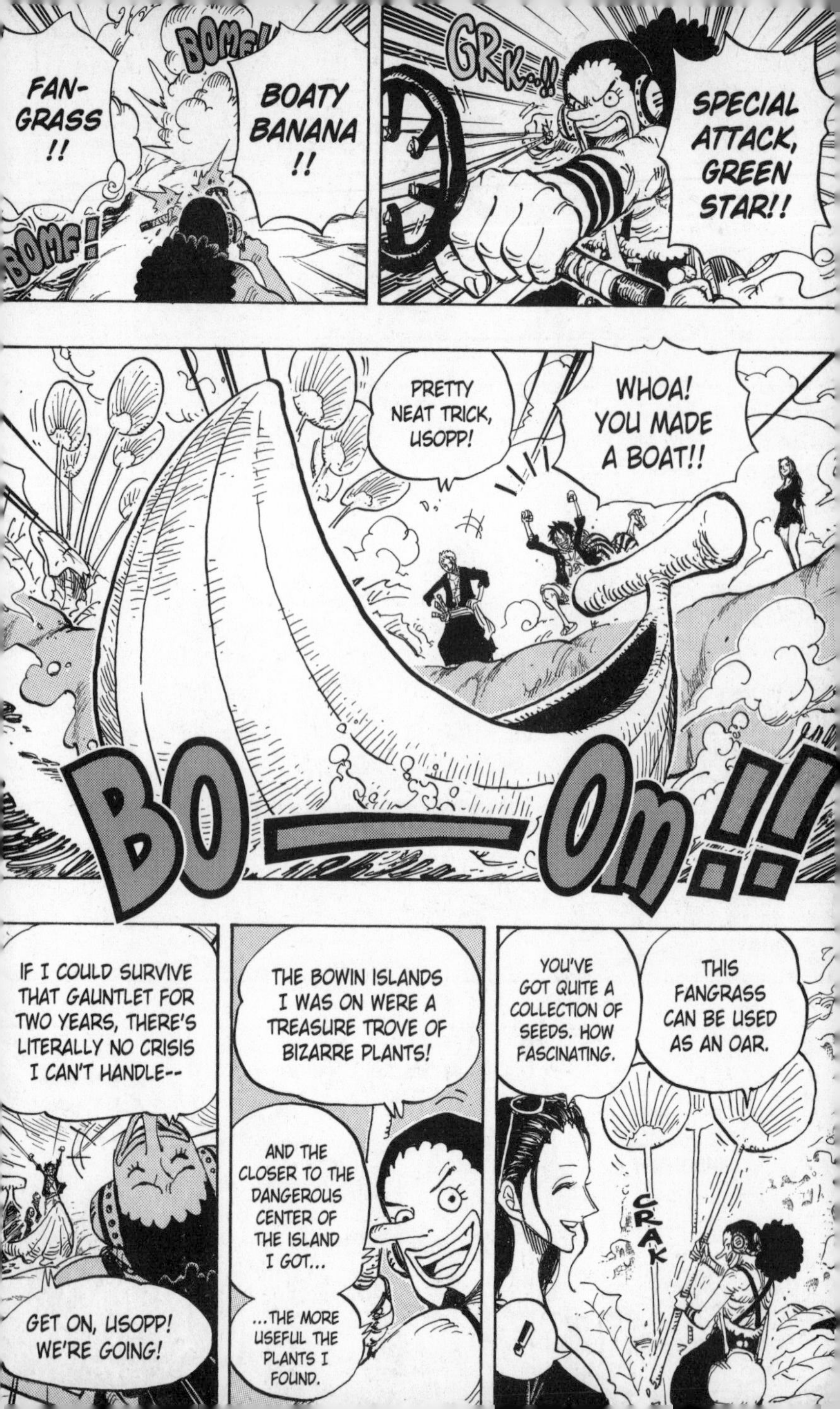
GRK..!!
SPECIAL ATTACK, GREEN STAR!!
BOMF!
BOATY BANANA!!
FAN-GRASS!!
BOMF!
WHOA! YOU MADE A BOAT!!
PRETTY NEAT TRICK, USOPP!
BO—OM!!
THIS FANGRASS CAN BE USED AS AN OAR.
YOU'VE GOT QUITE A COLLECTION OF SEEDS. HOW FASCINATING.
CRAK
!
THE BOWIN ISLANDS I WAS ON WERE A TREASURE TROVE OF BIZARRE PLANTS!
AND THE CLOSER TO THE DANGEROUS CENTER OF THE ISLAND I GOT...
...THE MORE USEFUL THE PLANTS I FOUND.
IF I COULD SURVIVE THAT GAUNTLET FOR TWO YEARS, THERE'S LITERALLY NO CRISIS I CAN'T HANDLE--
GET ON, USOPP! WE'RE GOING!

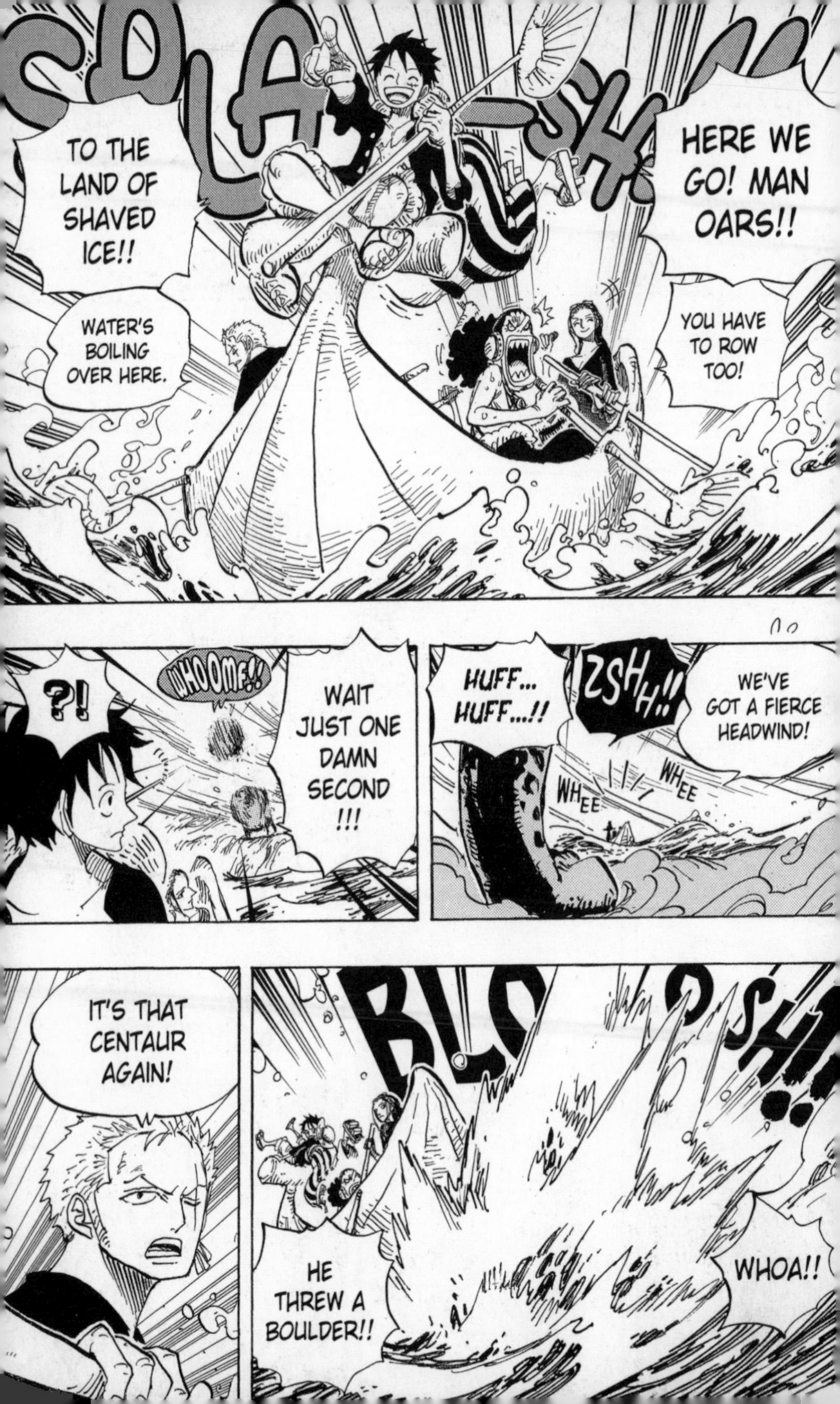
SPLA-SH
HERE WE GO! MAN OARS!!
TO THE LAND OF SHAVED ICE!!
YOU HAVE TO ROW TOO!
WATER'S BOILING OVER HERE.
WE'VE GOT A FIERCE HEADWIND!
ZSHH!!
HUFF... HUFF...!!
WHEE
WHEE
WAIT JUST ONE DAMN SECOND!!!
WHOOMF!!
?!
BLO
SH!!
WHOA!!
HE THREW A BOULDER!!
IT'S THAT CENTAUR AGAIN!

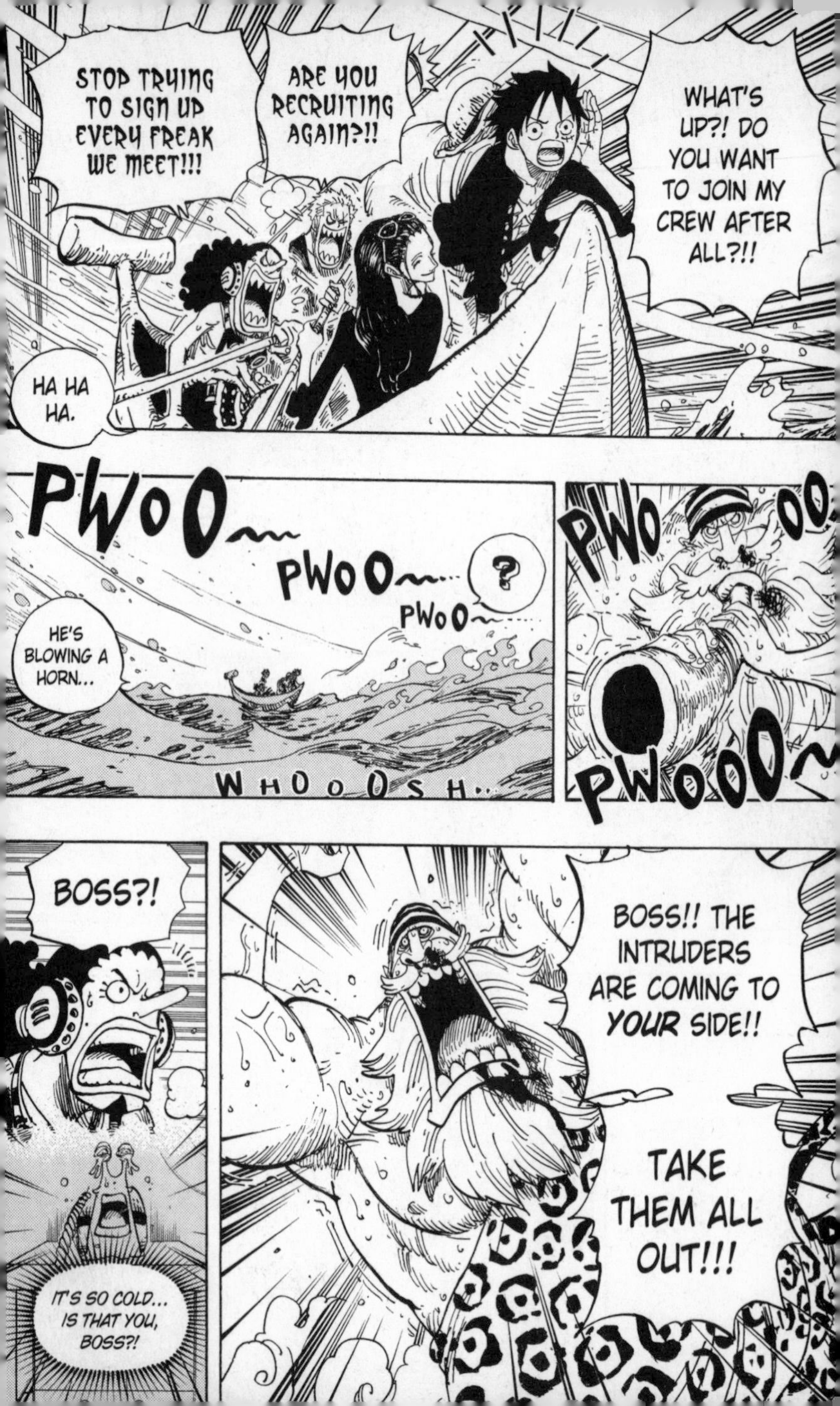
WHAT'S UP?! DO YOU WANT TO JOIN MY CREW AFTER ALL?!!
ARE YOU RECRUITING AGAIN?!!
STOP TRYING TO SIGN UP EVERY FREAK WE MEET!!!
HA HA HA.
PWOOO
PWOOOO~
PWOO~
PWOO~...
?
PWOO~...
HE'S BLOWING A HORN...
WHOOOOSH...
BOSS!! THE INTRUDERS ARE COMING TO *YOUR* SIDE!!
TAKE THEM ALL OUT!!!
BOSS?!
IT'S SO COLD... IS THAT YOU, BOSS?!

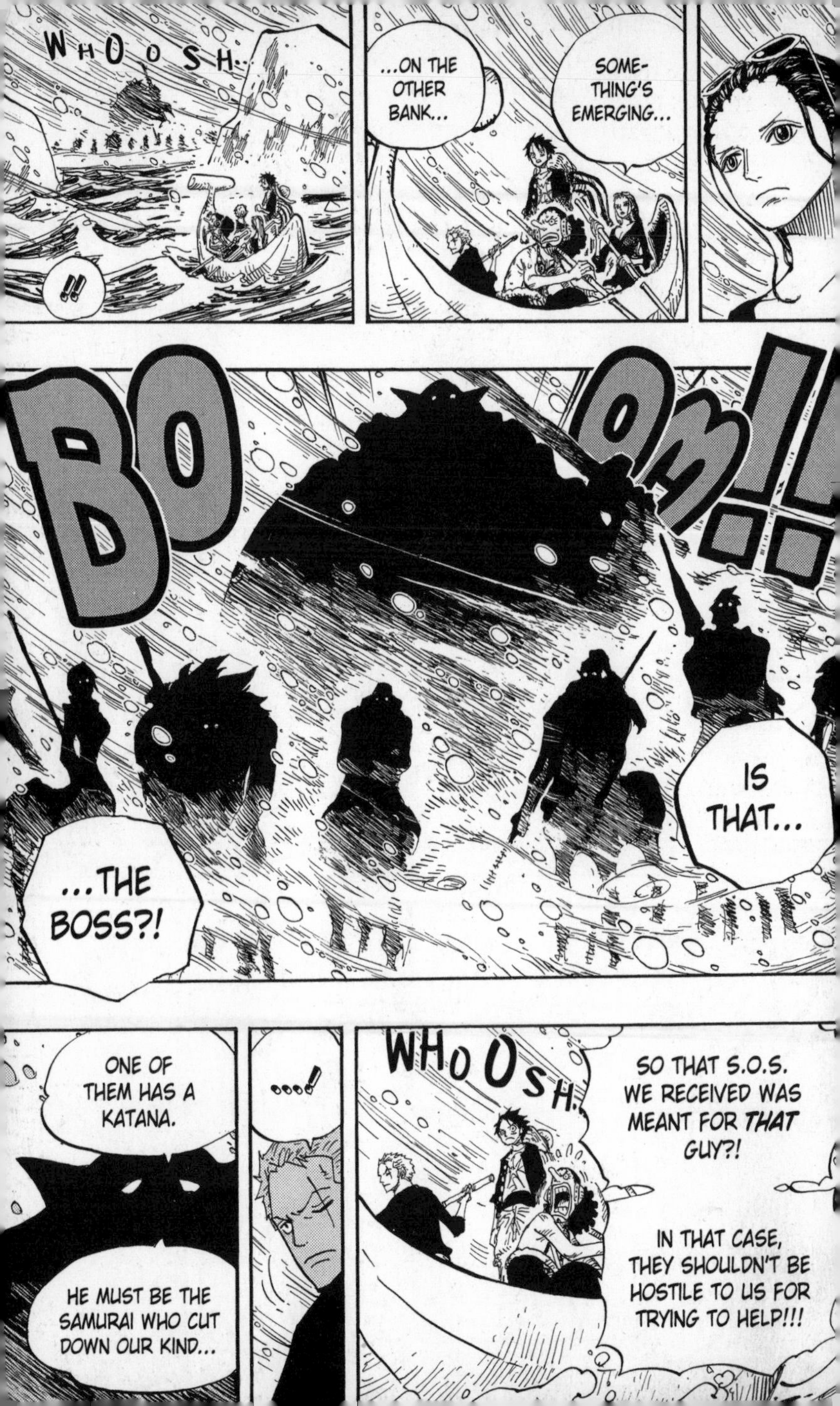
SOME-THING'S EMERGING...
...ON THE OTHER BANK...
WHOOSH
!!
BOOM!!
IS THAT...
...THE BOSS?!
SO THAT S.O.S. WE RECEIVED WAS MEANT FOR *THAT* GUY?!
WHOOSH
IN THAT CASE, THEY SHOULDN'T BE HOSTILE TO US FOR TRYING TO HELP!!!
...!
ONE OF THEM HAS A KATANA.
HE MUST BE THE SAMURAI WHO CUT DOWN OUR KIND...

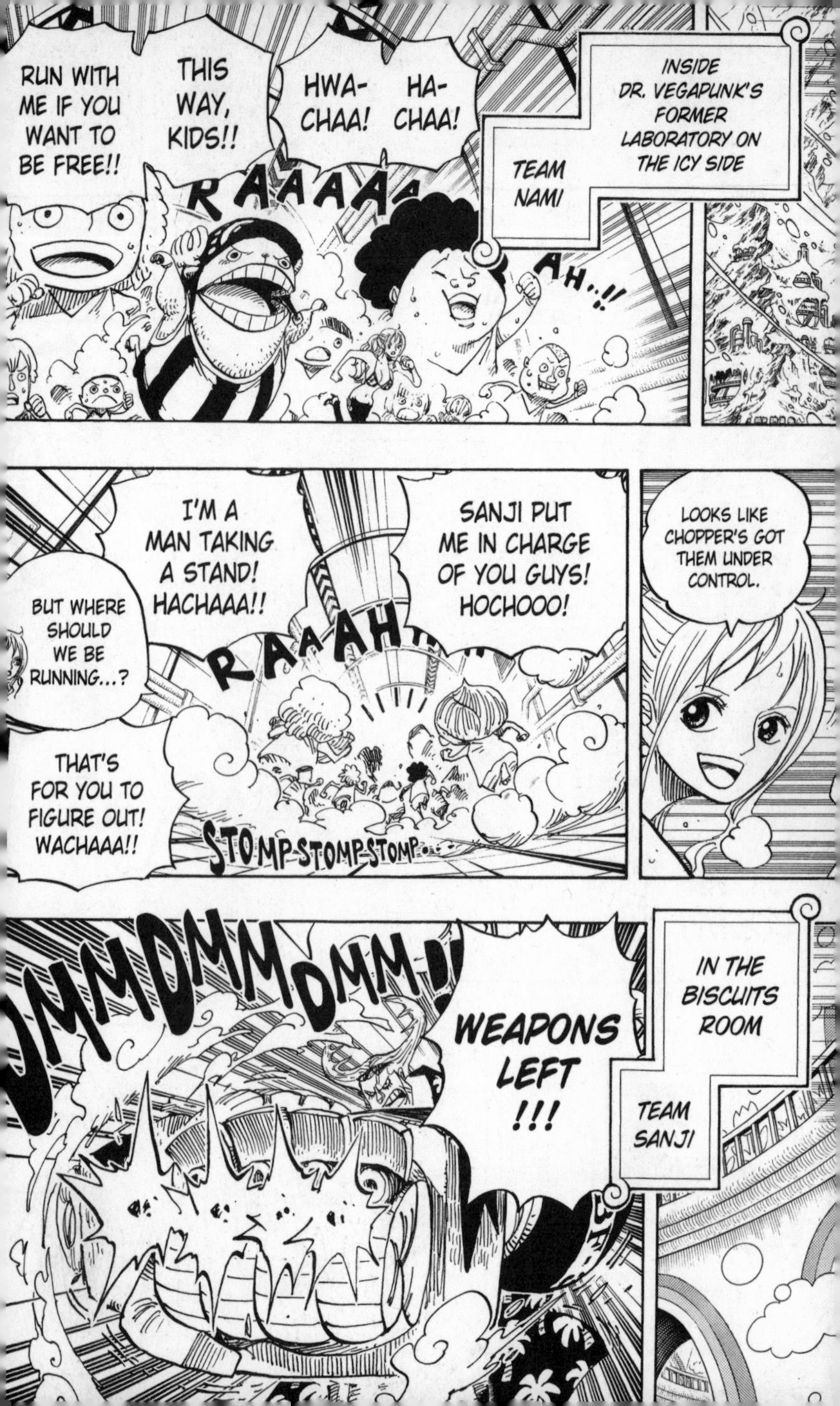

INSIDE DR. VEGAPUNK'S FORMER LABORATORY ON THE ICY SIDE
TEAM NAMI
HA- CHAA!
HWA- CHAA!
THIS WAY, KIDS!!
RUN WITH ME IF YOU WANT TO BE FREE!!
RAAAAA
AH..!!
LOOKS LIKE CHOPPER'S GOT THEM UNDER CONTROL.
SANJI PUT ME IN CHARGE OF YOU GUYS! HOCHOOO!
I'M A MAN TAKING A STAND! HACHAAA!!
BUT WHERE SHOULD WE BE RUNNING...?
RAAAH
THAT'S FOR YOU TO FIGURE OUT! WACHAAA!!
STOMP-STOMP-STOMP
IN THE BISCUITS ROOM
TEAM SANJI
WEAPONS LEFT!!!
MMDMMMDMM!!

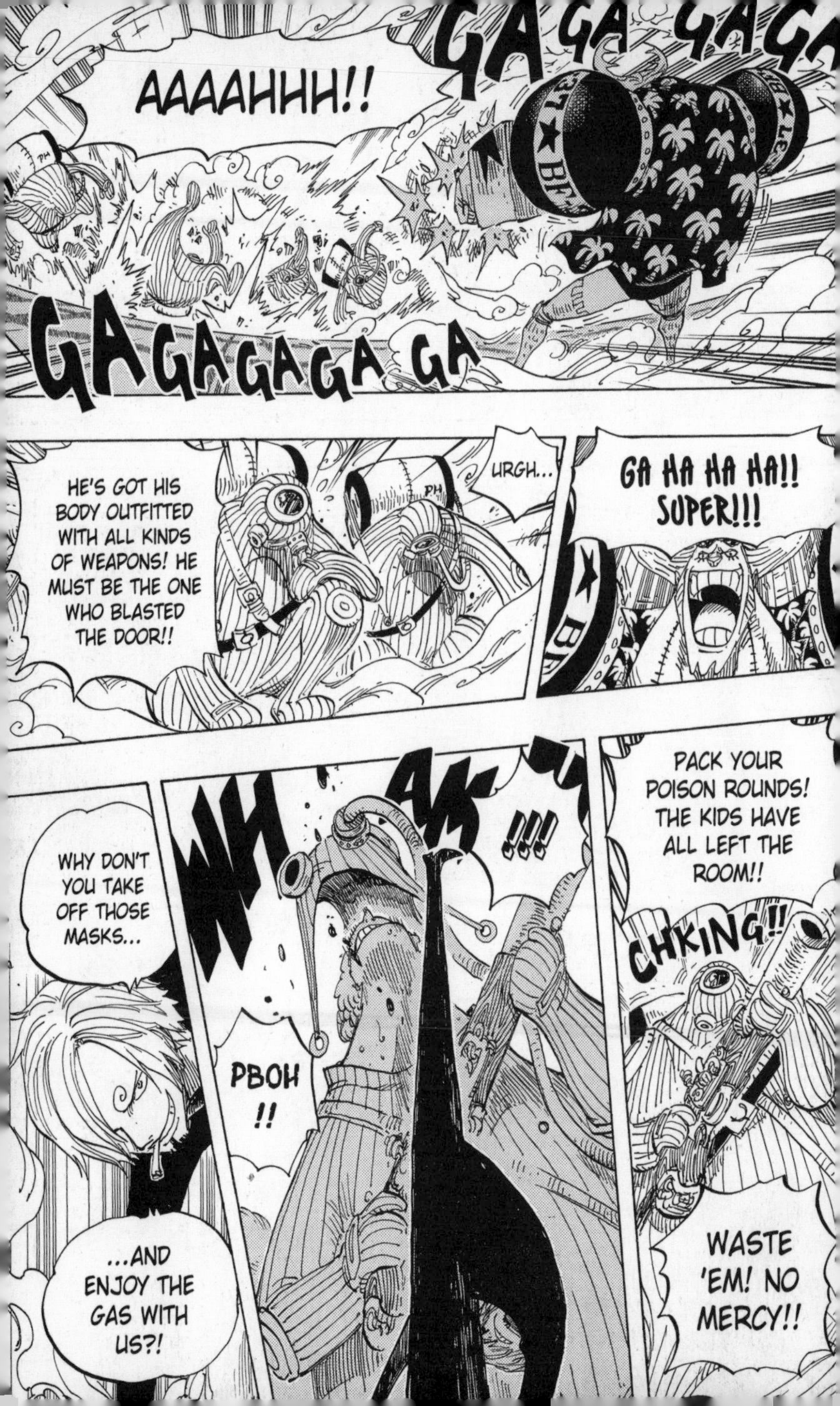
GA GA GA GA
AAAAHHH!!
GAGAGAGA GA
GA HA HA HA!! SUPER!!!
URGH...
HE'S GOT HIS BODY OUTFITTED WITH ALL KINDS OF WEAPONS! HE MUST BE THE ONE WHO BLASTED THE DOOR!!
PACK YOUR POISON ROUNDS! THE KIDS HAVE ALL LEFT THE ROOM!!
CHKING!!
WASTE 'EM! NO MERCY!!
WHAK!!!
PBOH!!
WHY DON'T YOU TAKE OFF THOSE MASKS...
...AND ENJOY THE GAS WITH US?!

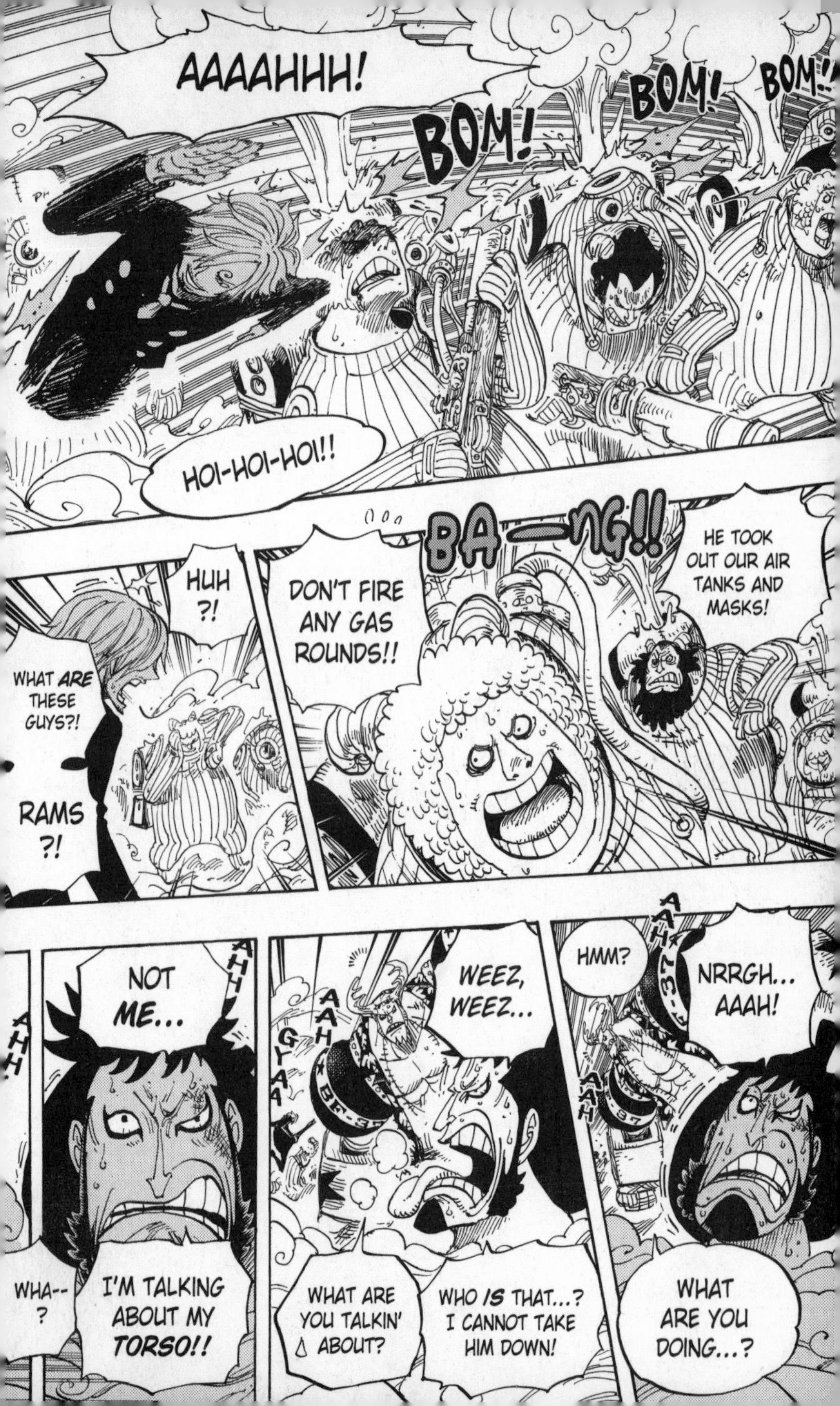
BOM!!
BOM!
AAAAHHH!
BOM!
HOI-HOI-HOI!!
HE TOOK OUT OUR AIR TANKS AND MASKS!
BA—NG!!
DON'T FIRE ANY GAS ROUNDS!!
HUH ?!
WHAT *ARE* THESE GUYS?!
RAMS ?!
NRRGH... AAAH!
AAH
HMM?
AAH
WHAT ARE YOU DOING...?
WEEZ, WEEZ...
AAH
GYAA
WHO *IS* THAT...? I CANNOT TAKE HIM DOWN!
WHAT ARE YOU TALKIN' ABOUT?
NOT *ME*...
AHH
I'M TALKING ABOUT MY *TORSO!!*
AHH
WHA-- ?

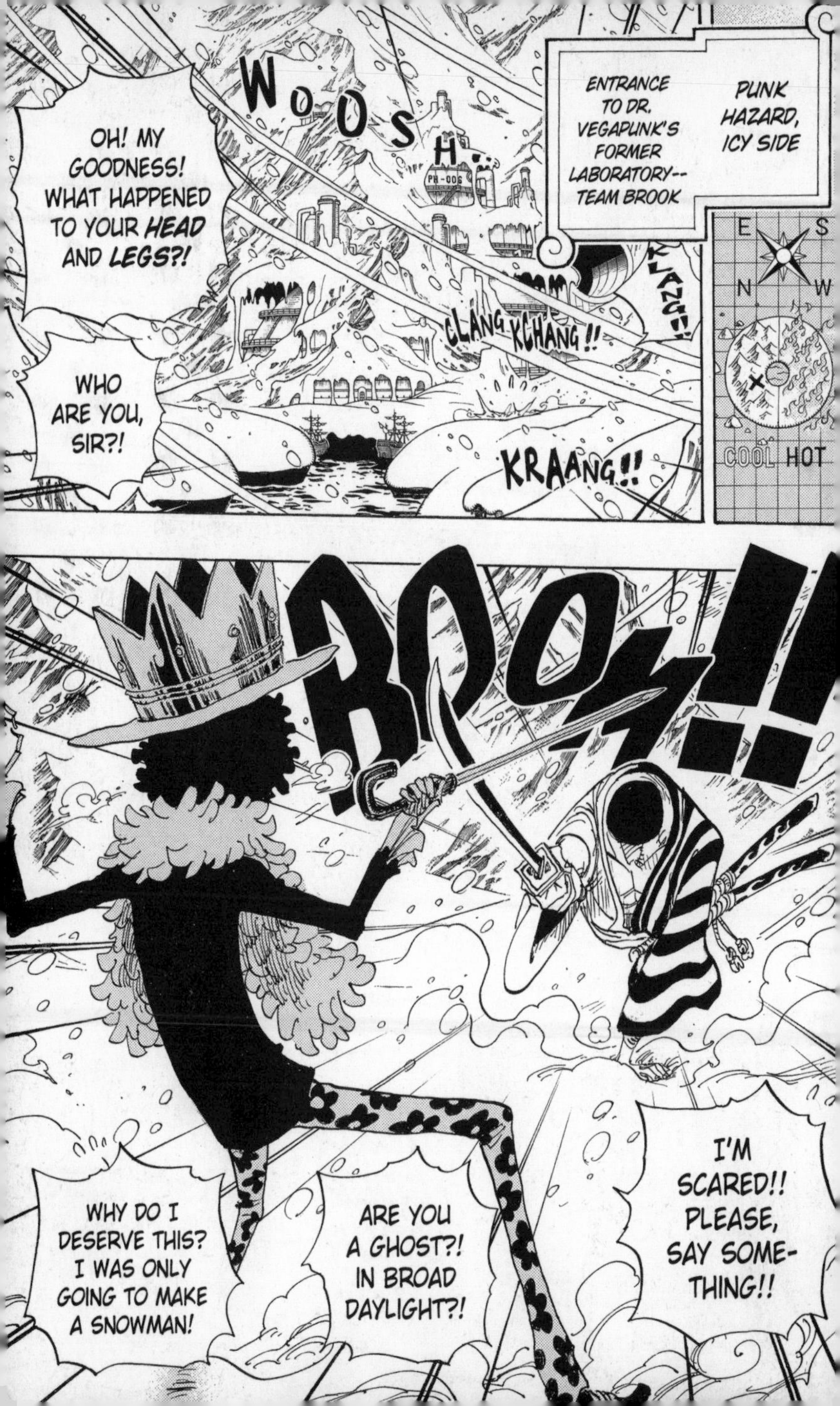
PUNK HAZARD, ICY SIDE
ENTRANCE TO DR. VEGAPUNK'S FORMER LABORATORY-- TEAM BROOK
E
S
N
W
COOL
HOT
KLANG!!
WOOSH
PH-006
CLANG KCHANG!!
KRAANG!!
OH! MY GOODNESS! WHAT HAPPENED TO YOUR HEAD AND LEGS?!
WHO ARE YOU, SIR?!
I'M SCARED!! PLEASE, SAY SOME-THING!!
ARE YOU A GHOST?! IN BROAD DAYLIGHT?!
WHY DO I DESERVE THIS? I WAS ONLY GOING TO MAKE A SNOWMAN!

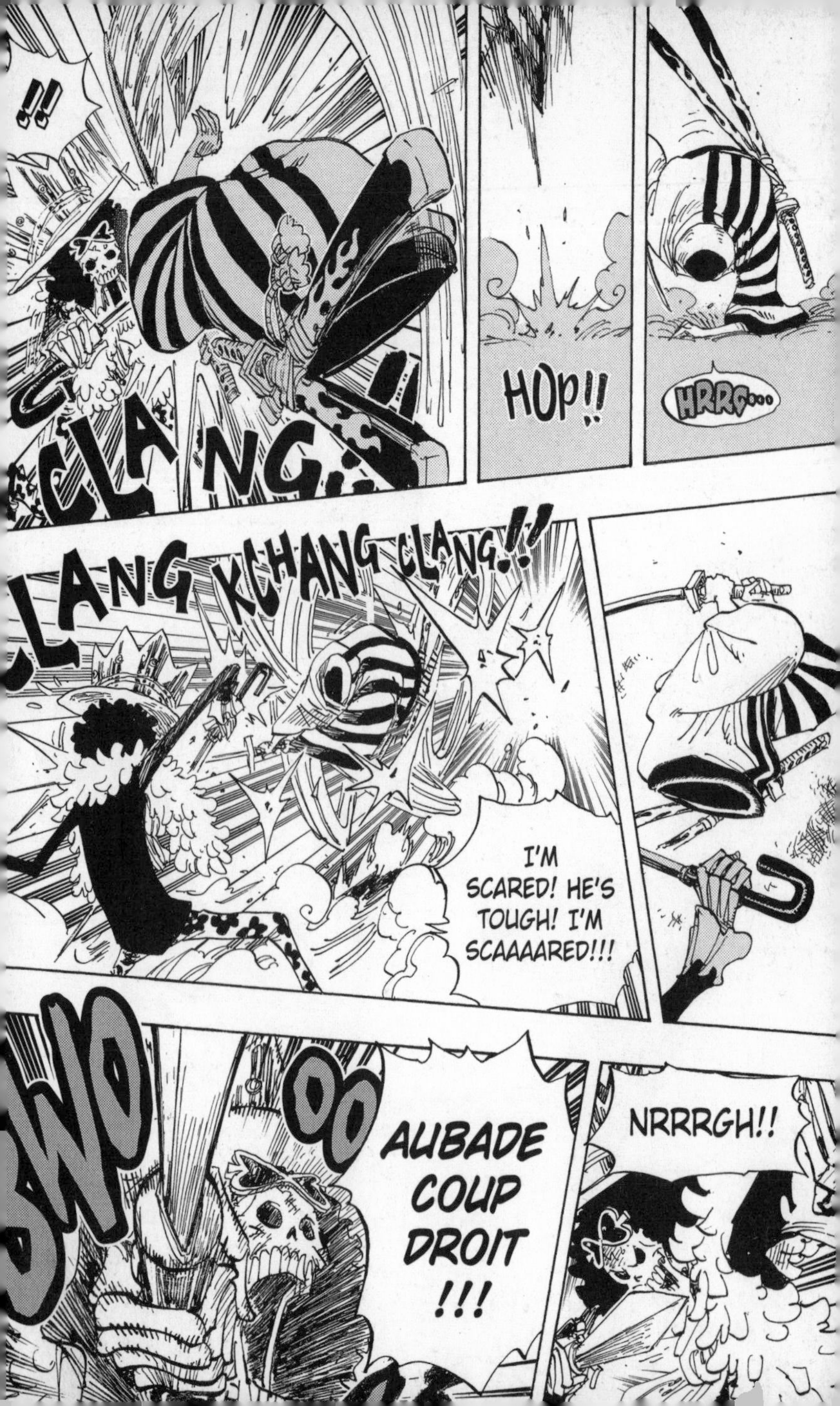
HRRG...
HOP!!
!!
CLANG
CLANG KCHANG CLANG!!
I'M SCARED! HE'S TOUGH! I'M SCAAAARED!!!
NRRRGH!!
SWOOO
AUBADE COUP DROIT !!!

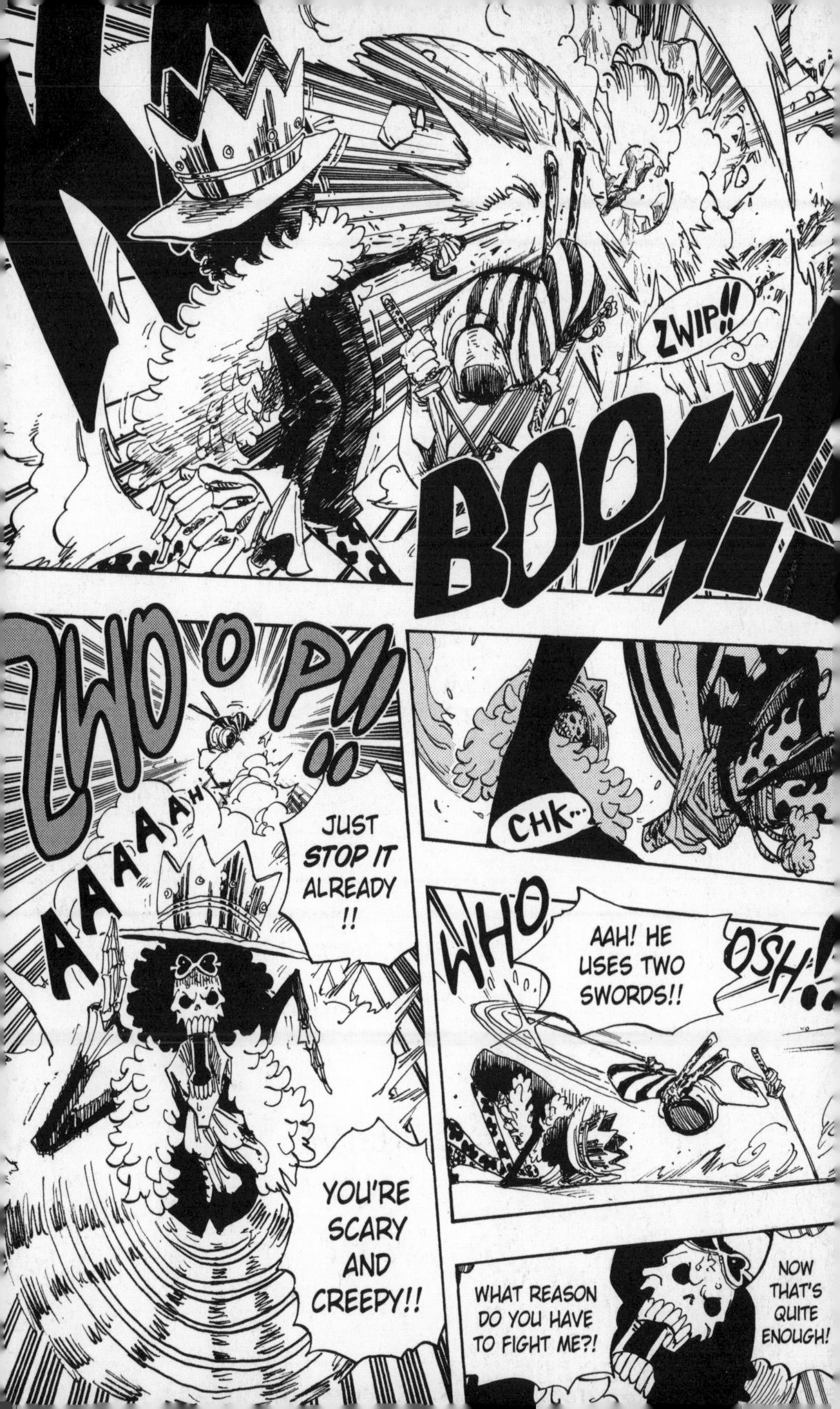
ZWIP!!
BOOM!!
CHK...
WHOOSH!!
AAH! HE USES TWO SWORDS!!
NOW THAT'S QUITE ENOUGH!
WHAT REASON DO YOU HAVE TO FIGHT ME?!
ZWOOP!!
AAAAAAH
JUST STOP IT ALREADY!!
YOU'RE SCARY AND CREEPY!!

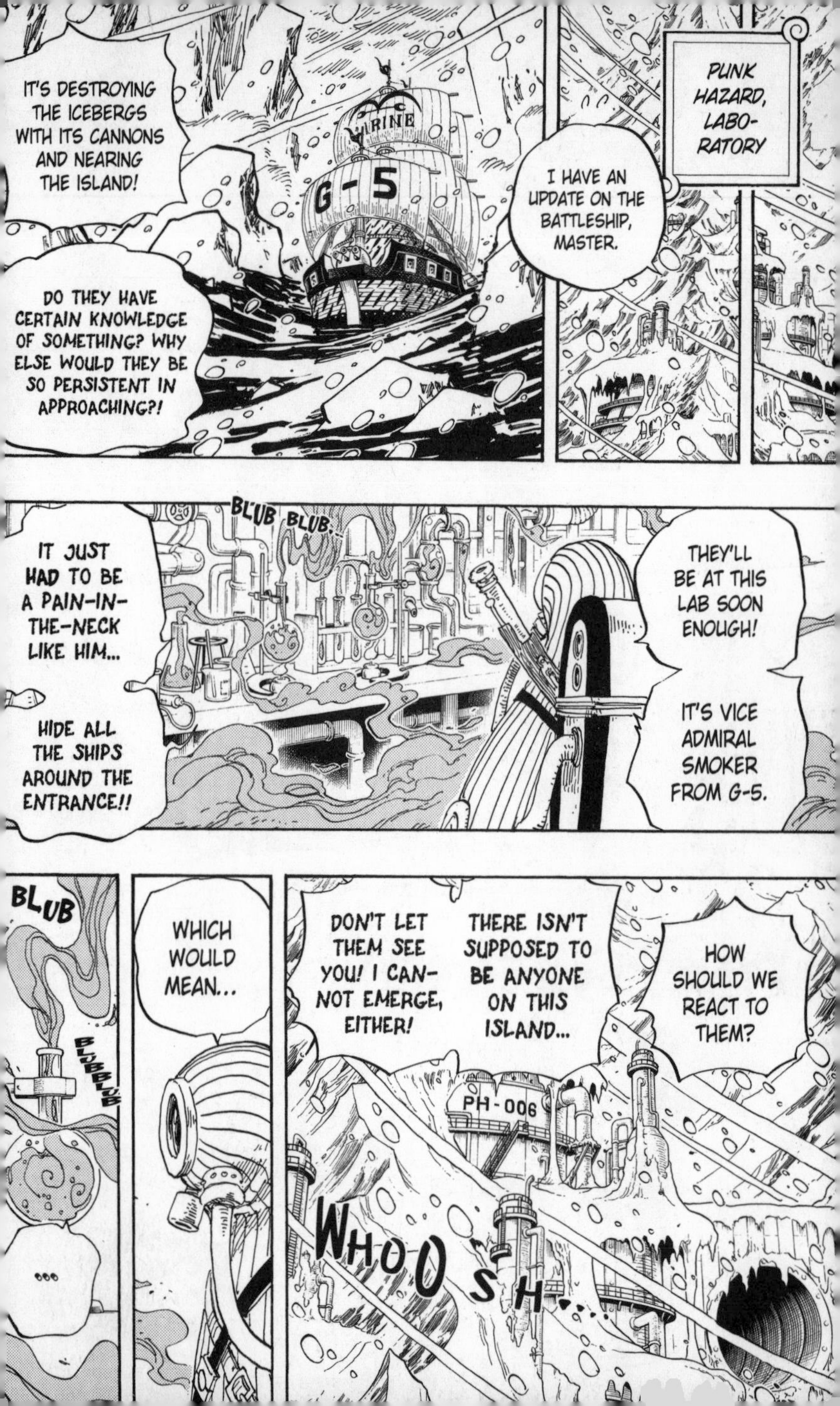
PUNK HAZARD, LABORATORY
I HAVE AN UPDATE ON THE BATTLESHIP, MASTER.
MARINE
G-5
IT'S DESTROYING THE ICEBERGS WITH ITS CANNONS AND NEARING THE ISLAND!
DO THEY HAVE CERTAIN KNOWLEDGE OF SOMETHING? WHY ELSE WOULD THEY BE SO PERSISTENT IN APPROACHING?!
THEY'LL BE AT THIS LAB SOON ENOUGH!
IT'S VICE ADMIRAL SMOKER FROM G-5.
BLUB BLUB...
IT JUST HAD TO BE A PAIN-IN-THE-NECK LIKE HIM...
HIDE ALL THE SHIPS AROUND THE ENTRANCE!!
HOW SHOULD WE REACT TO THEM?
THERE ISN'T SUPPOSED TO BE ANYONE ON THIS ISLAND...
DON'T LET THEM SEE YOU! I CANNOT EMERGE, EITHER!
PH-006
WHOOSH...
WHICH WOULD MEAN...
BLUB
BLUBBLUB
...

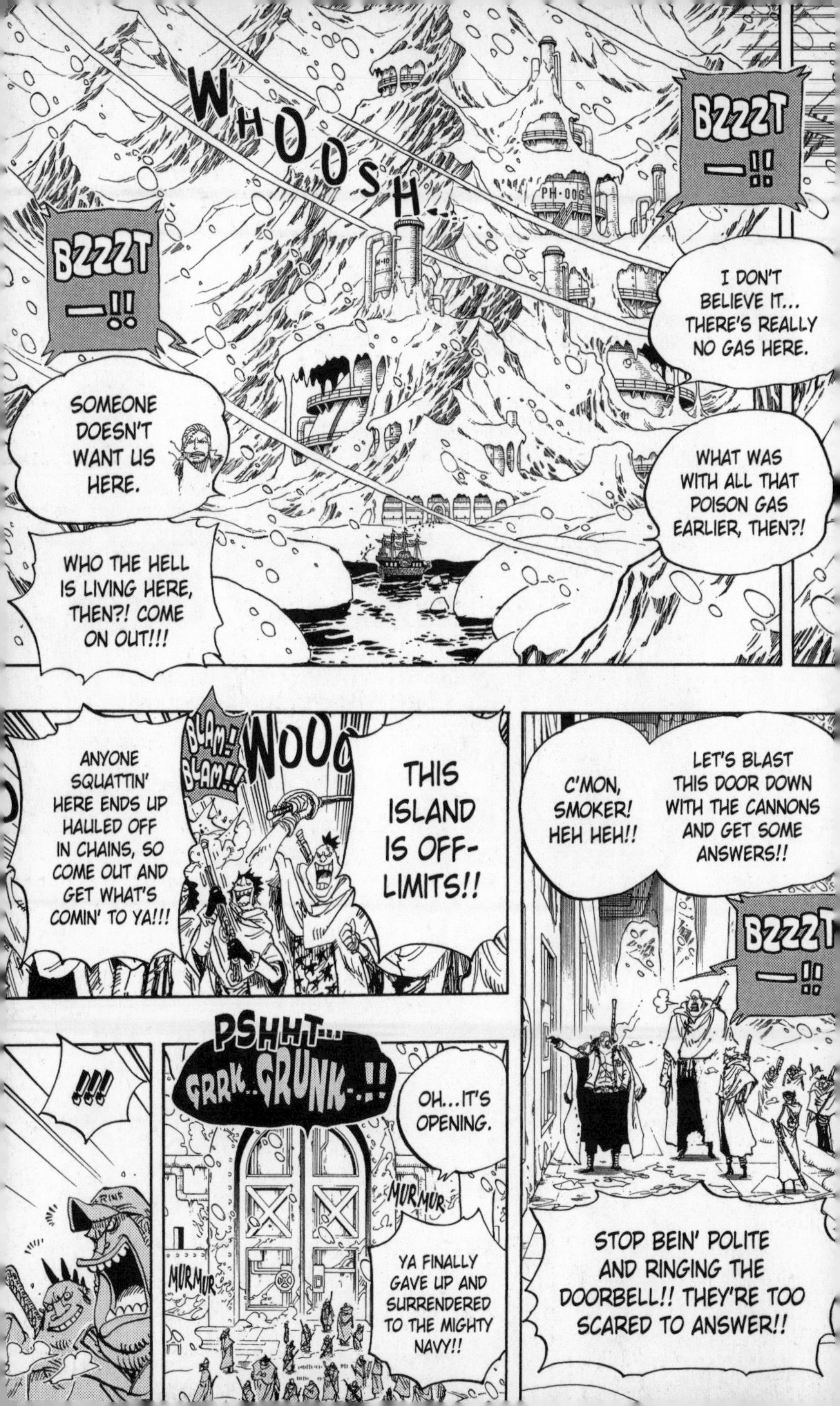
BZZZT—!!
I DON'T BELIEVE IT... THERE'S REALLY NO GAS HERE.
WHAT WAS WITH ALL THAT POISON GAS EARLIER, THEN?!
WHOOSH
BZZZT—!!
SOMEONE DOESN'T WANT US HERE.
WHO THE HELL IS LIVING HERE, THEN?! COME ON OUT!!!
LET'S BLAST THIS DOOR DOWN WITH THE CANNONS AND GET SOME ANSWERS!!
C'MON, SMOKER! HEH HEH!!
BZZZT—!!
STOP BEIN' POLITE AND RINGING THE DOORBELL!! THEY'RE TOO SCARED TO ANSWER!!
THIS ISLAND IS OFF-LIMITS!!
WOOO
BLAM! BLAM!!
ANYONE SQUATTIN' HERE ENDS UP HAULED OFF IN CHAINS, SO COME OUT AND GET WHAT'S COMIN' TO YA!!!
PSHHT... GRRK..GRUNK..!!
OH...IT'S OPENING.
MURMUR
YA FINALLY GAVE UP AND SURRENDERED TO THE MIGHTY NAVY!!
MURMUR
!!!

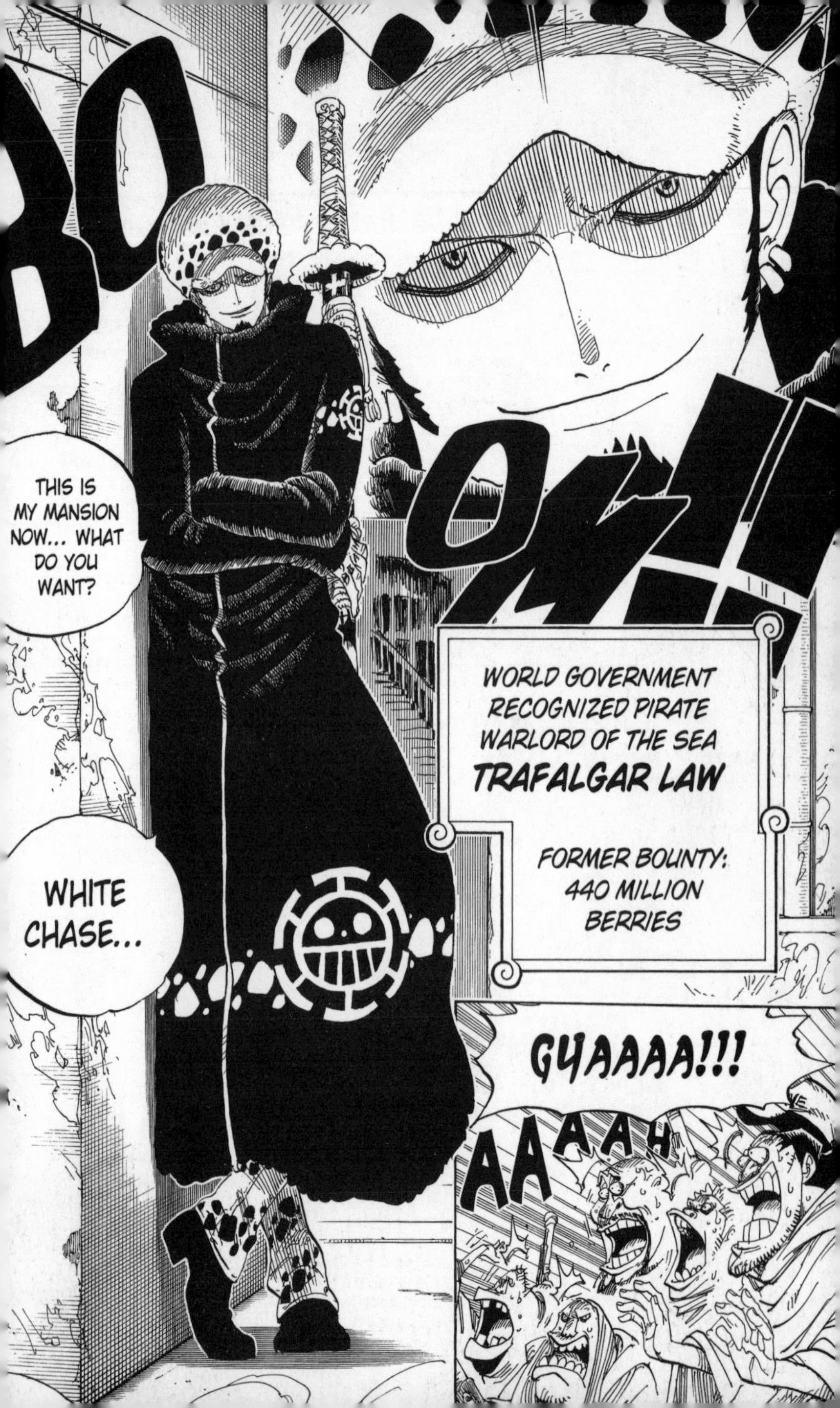
BOOM!!
WORLD GOVERNMENT RECOGNIZED PIRATE WARLORD OF THE SEA
TRAFALGAR LAW
FORMER BOUNTY: 440 MILLION BERRIES
GYAAAA!!!
AAAAH
THIS IS MY MANSION NOW... WHAT DO YOU WANT?
WHITE CHASE...

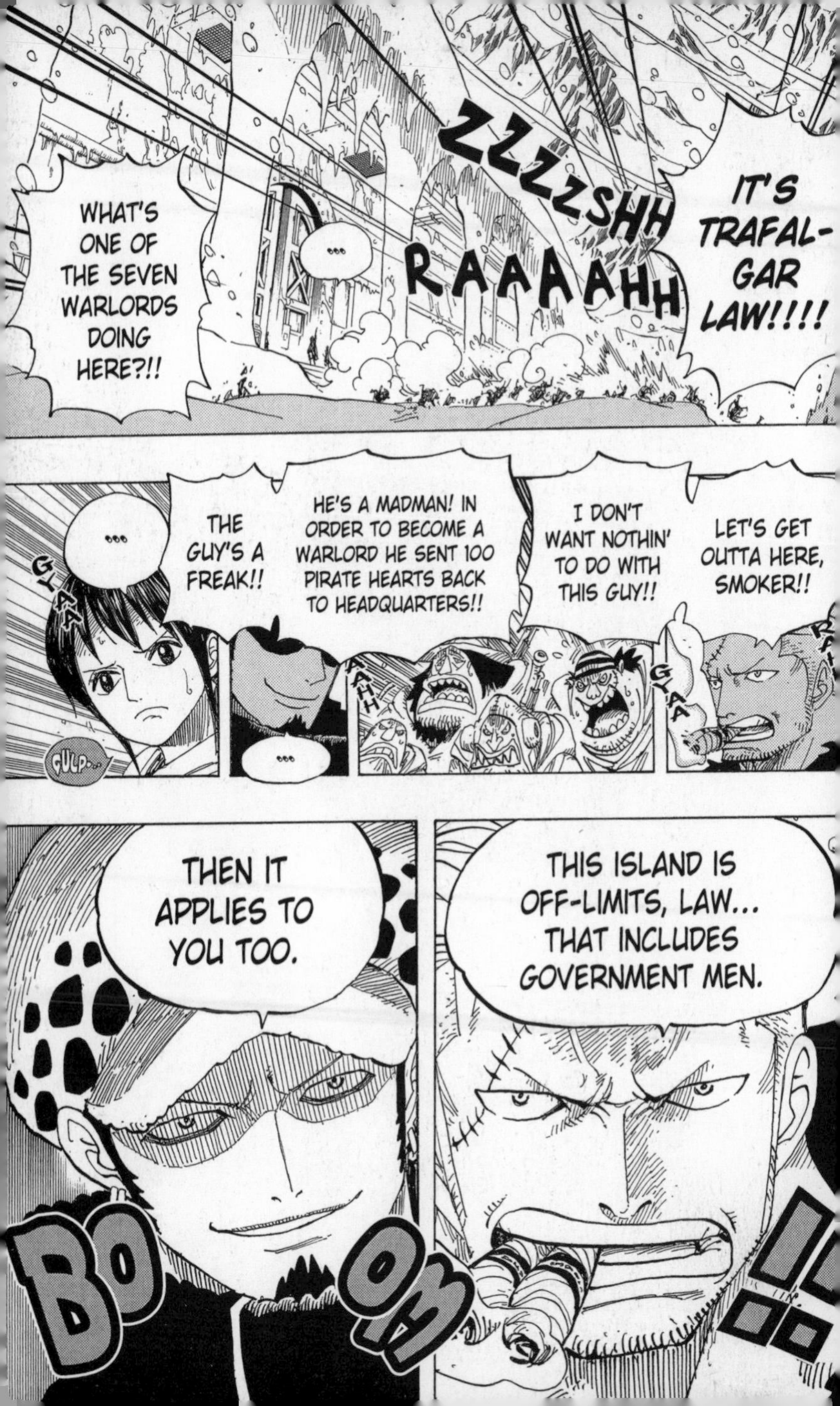

IT'S TRAFAL-GAR LAW!!!!
ZZZZSHH
RAAAAHH
...
WHAT'S ONE OF THE SEVEN WARLORDS DOING HERE?!!
LET'S GET OUTTA HERE, SMOKER!!
GYAA
I DON'T WANT NOTHIN' TO DO WITH THIS GUY!!
AAHH
HE'S A MADMAN! IN ORDER TO BECOME A WARLORD HE SENT 100 PIRATE HEARTS BACK TO HEADQUARTERS!!
...
THE GUY'S A FREAK!!
...
GYAA
GULP...
THIS ISLAND IS OFF-LIMITS, LAW... THAT INCLUDES GOVERNMENT MEN.
!!
THEN IT APPLIES TO YOU TOO.
BOOM

WARLORD OF THE SEA

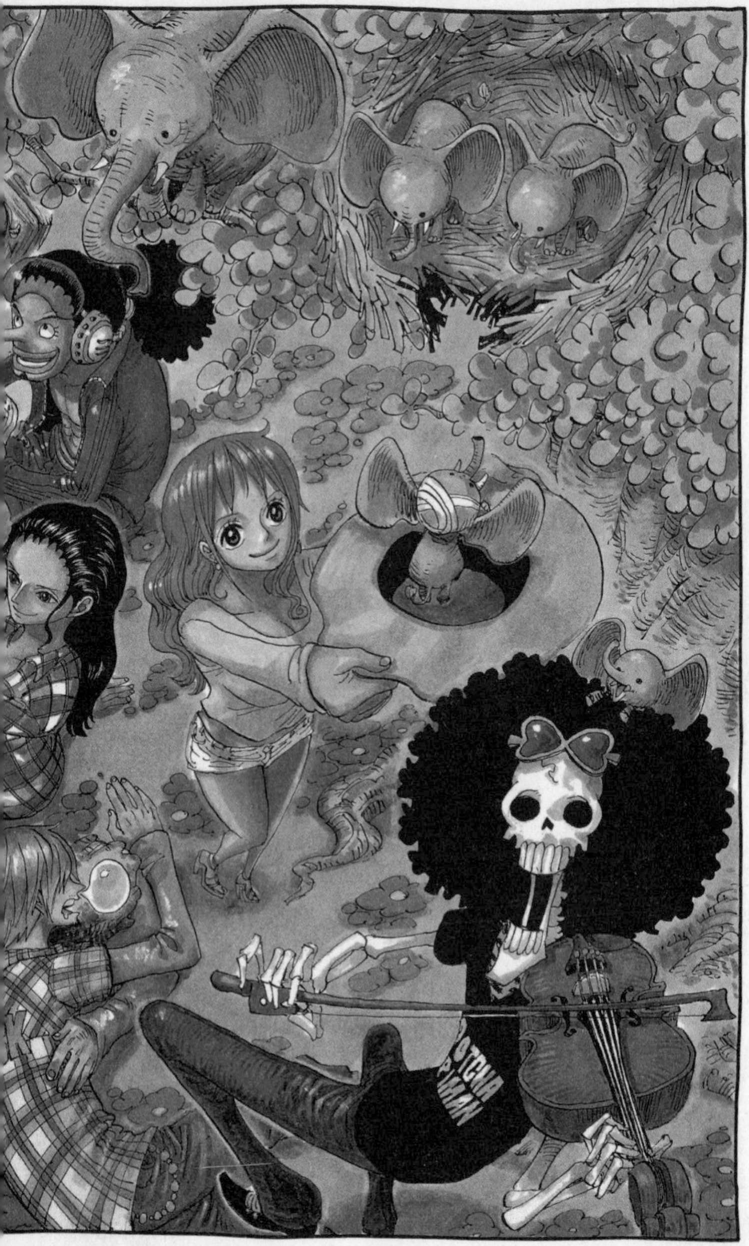

Chapter 660: TRAFALGAR LAW,

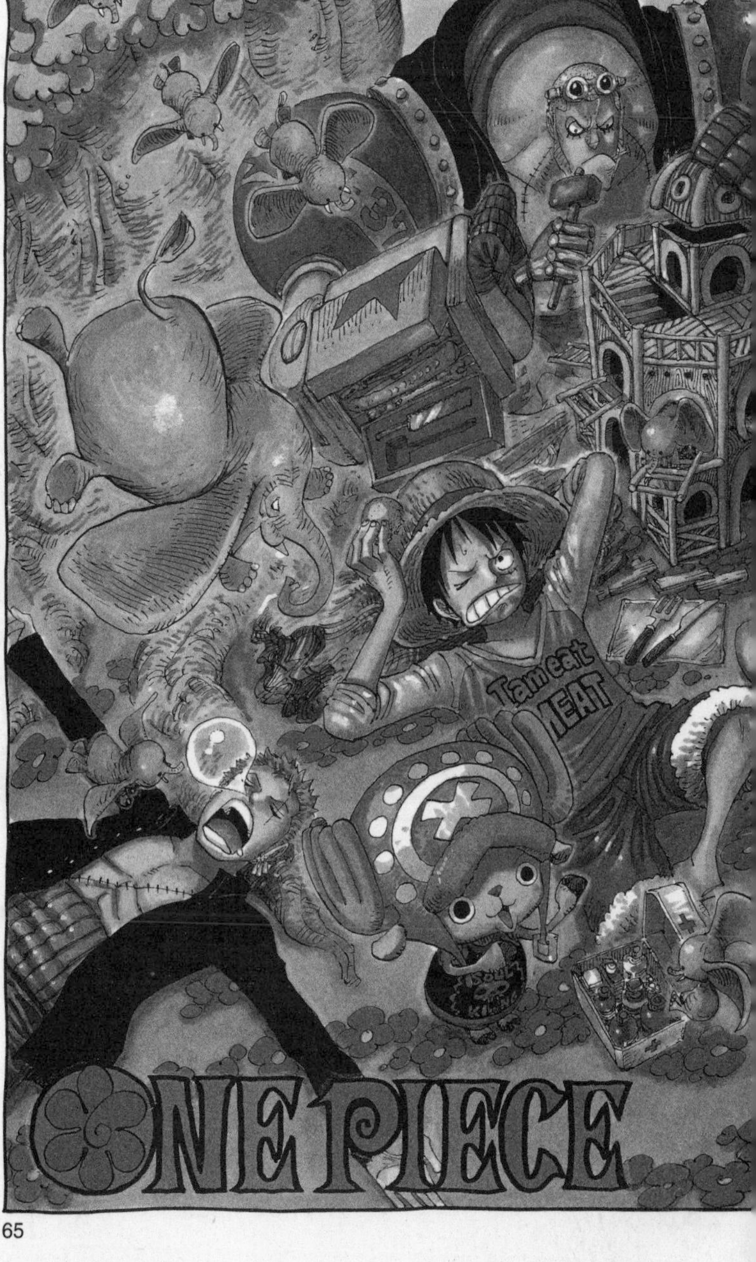

Tam eat
MEAT
ONE PIECE

vol.67
ONE PIECE

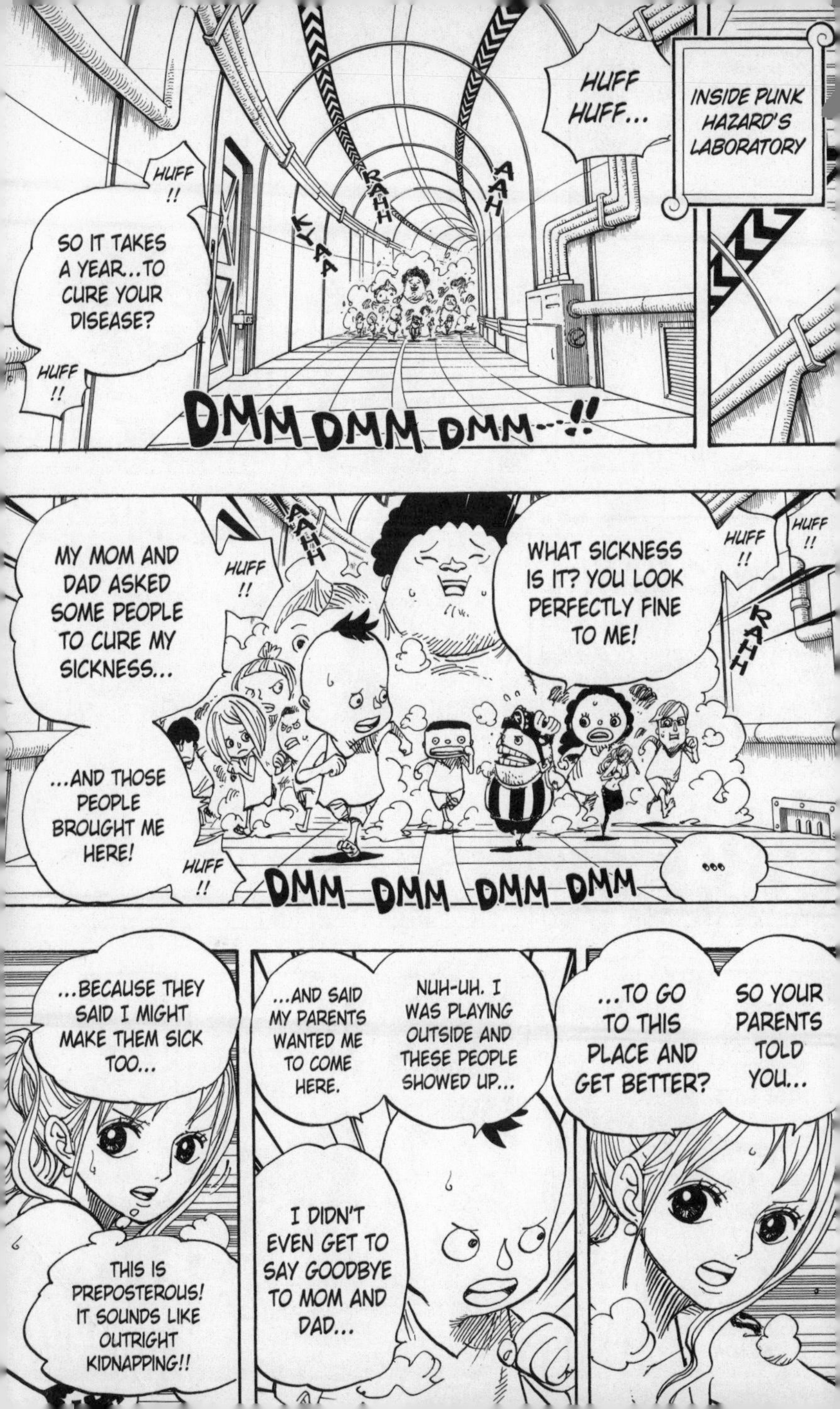
INSIDE PUNK HAZARD'S LABORATORY
HUFF HUFF...
AAH
RAHH
KYAA
HUFF !!
SO IT TAKES A YEAR...TO CURE YOUR DISEASE?
HUFF !!
DMM DMM DMM...!!
HUFF !!
HUFF !!
RAHH
WHAT SICKNESS IS IT? YOU LOOK PERFECTLY FINE TO ME!
AAHH
HUFF !!
MY MOM AND DAD ASKED SOME PEOPLE TO CURE MY SICKNESS...
...AND THOSE PEOPLE BROUGHT ME HERE!
...
HUFF !!
DMM DMM DMM DMM
SO YOUR PARENTS TOLD YOU...
...TO GO TO THIS PLACE AND GET BETTER?
NUH-UH. I WAS PLAYING OUTSIDE AND THESE PEOPLE SHOWED UP...
...AND SAID MY PARENTS WANTED ME TO COME HERE.
I DIDN'T EVEN GET TO SAY GOODBYE TO MOM AND DAD...
...BECAUSE THEY SAID I MIGHT MAKE THEM SICK TOO...
THIS IS PREPOSTEROUS! IT SOUNDS LIKE OUTRIGHT KIDNAPPING!!

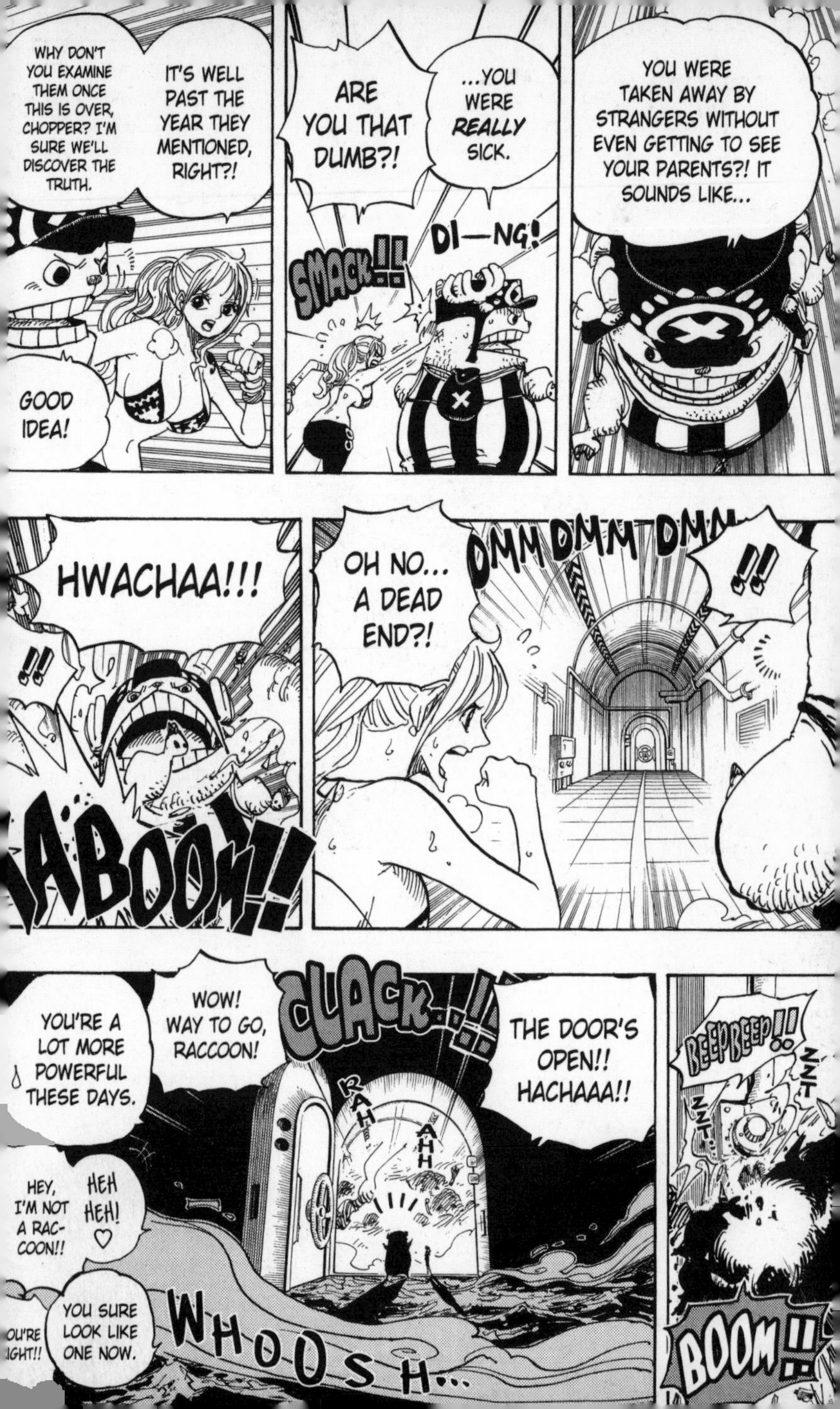
YOU WERE TAKEN AWAY BY STRANGERS WITHOUT EVEN GETTING TO SEE YOUR PARENTS?! IT SOUNDS LIKE...
...YOU WERE REALLY SICK.
ARE YOU THAT DUMB?!
DI—NG!
SMACK!!
IT'S WELL PAST THE YEAR THEY MENTIONED, RIGHT?!
WHY DON'T YOU EXAMINE THEM ONCE THIS IS OVER, CHOPPER? I'M SURE WE'LL DISCOVER THE TRUTH.
GOOD IDEA!
!!
DMM DMM DMM
OH NO... A DEAD END?!
HWACHAA!!!
!!
ABOOM!!
BEEP BEEP!!
ZZT
ZZT
BOOM!!
THE DOOR'S OPEN!! HACHAAA!!
CLACK!!
WOW! WAY TO GO, RACCOON!
YOU'RE A LOT MORE POWERFUL THESE DAYS.
RAH
AHH
HEH HEH! ♡
HEY, I'M NOT A RAC-COON!!
YOU SURE LOOK LIKE ONE NOW.
OU'RE IGHT!!
WHOOSH...

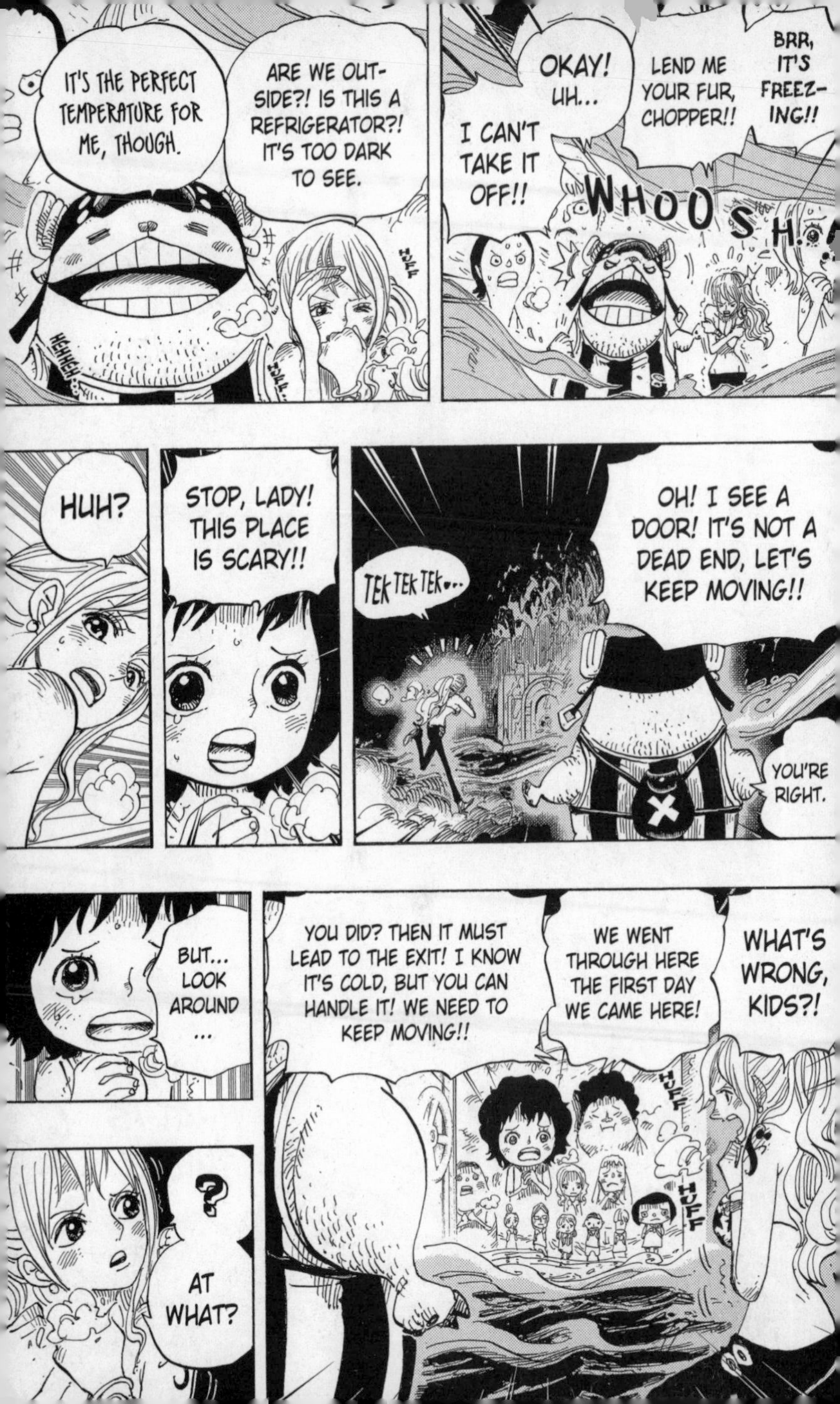
BRR, IT'S FREEZ-ING!!
LEND ME YOUR FUR, CHOPPER!!
OKAY! UH...
I CAN'T TAKE IT OFF!!
WHOOSH
ARE WE OUT-SIDE?! IS THIS A REFRIGERATOR?! IT'S TOO DARK TO SEE.
IT'S THE PERFECT TEMPERATURE FOR ME, THOUGH.
HUFF
HUFF
HEH HEH
OH! I SEE A DOOR! IT'S NOT A DEAD END, LET'S KEEP MOVING!!
TEK TEK TEK...
YOU'RE RIGHT.
STOP, LADY! THIS PLACE IS SCARY!!
HUH?
WHAT'S WRONG, KIDS?!
WE WENT THROUGH HERE THE FIRST DAY WE CAME HERE!
YOU DID? THEN IT MUST LEAD TO THE EXIT! I KNOW IT'S COLD, BUT YOU CAN HANDLE IT! WE NEED TO KEEP MOVING!!
HUFF
HUFF
BUT... LOOK AROUND ...
?
AT WHAT?

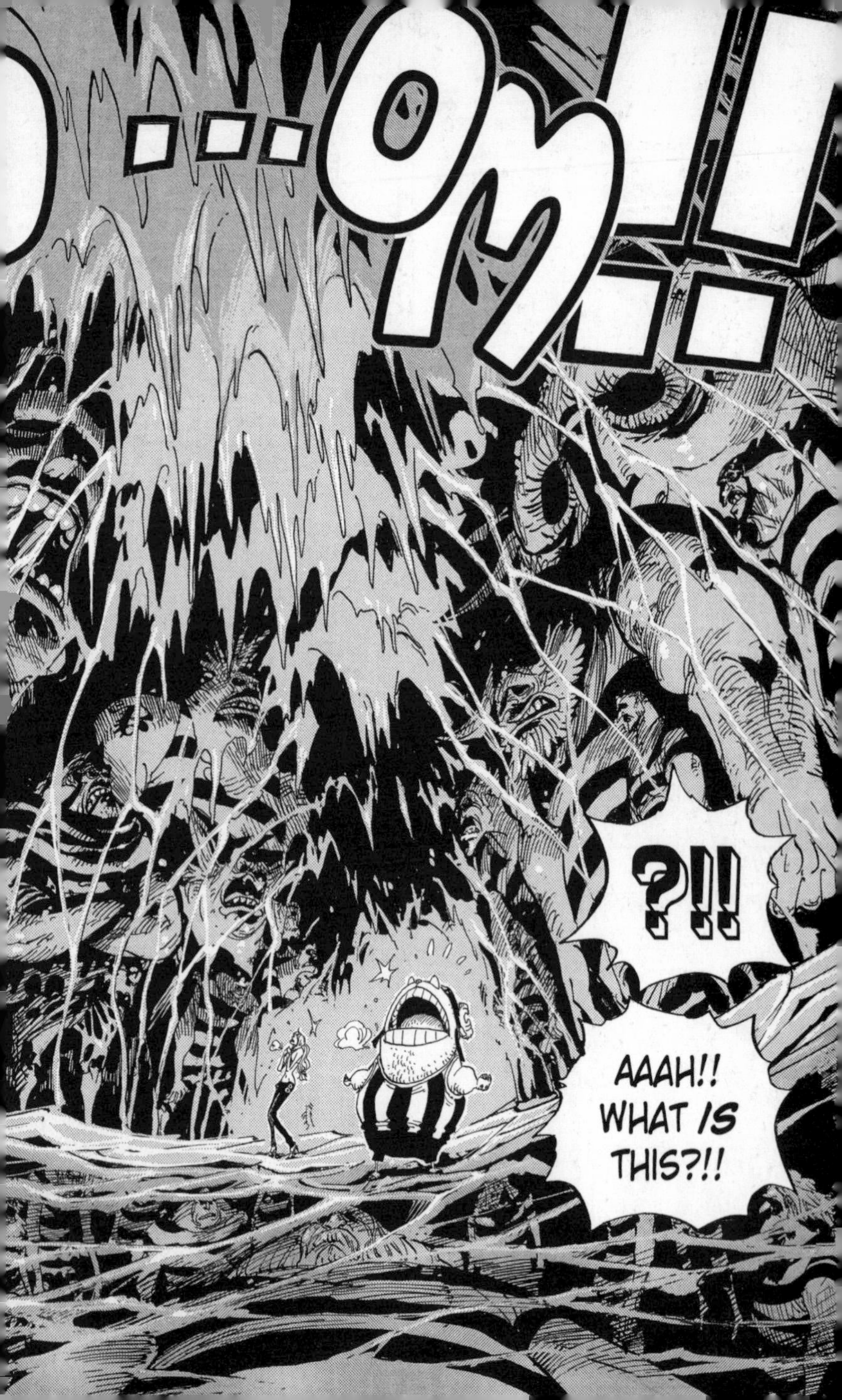
?!!
AAAH!! WHAT *IS* THIS?!!

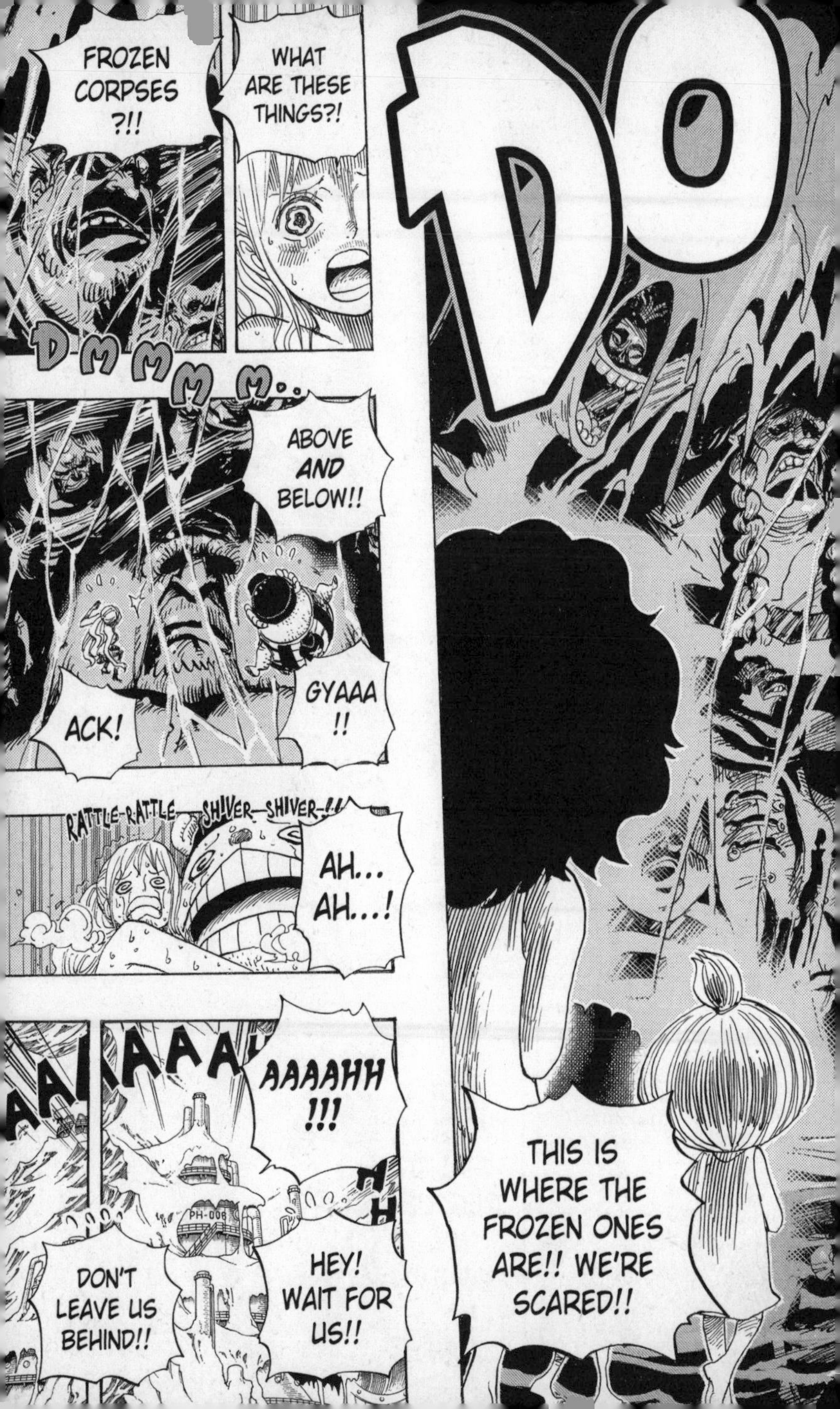
DO
THIS IS WHERE THE FROZEN ONES ARE!! WE'RE SCARED!!
WHAT ARE THESE THINGS?!
FROZEN CORPSES ?!!
D-MMMM M...
ABOVE AND BELOW!!
GYAAA !!
ACK!
RATTLE-RATTLE SHIVER-SHIVER-!!
AH... AH...!
AAAAHH !!!
PH-006
HEY! WAIT FOR US!!
DON'T LEAVE US BEHIND!!

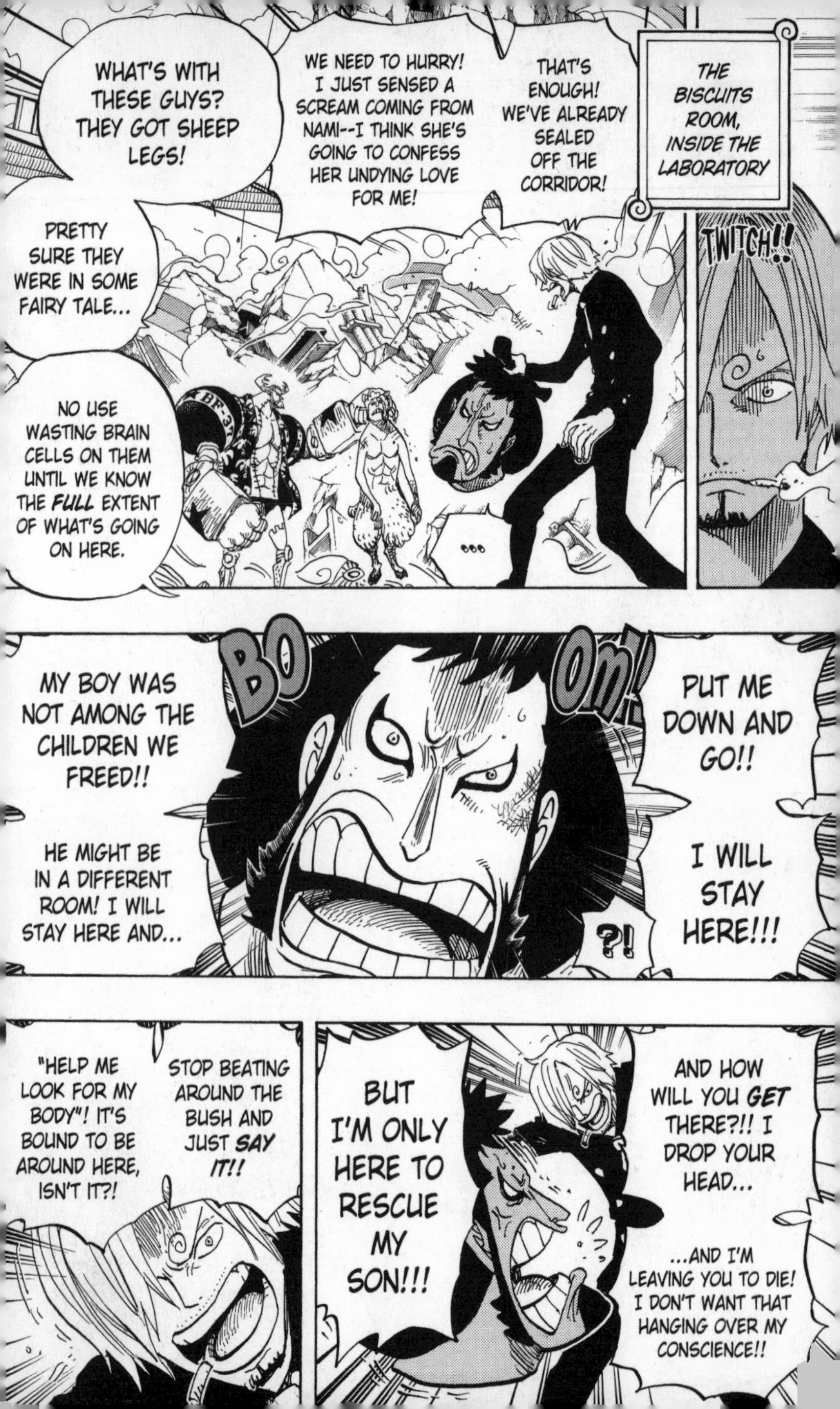
THE BISCUITS ROOM, INSIDE THE LABORATORY
TWITCH!!
THAT'S ENOUGH! WE'VE ALREADY SEALED OFF THE CORRIDOR!
WE NEED TO HURRY! I JUST SENSED A SCREAM COMING FROM NAMI--I THINK SHE'S GOING TO CONFESS HER UNDYING LOVE FOR ME!
WHAT'S WITH THESE GUYS? THEY GOT SHEEP LEGS!
PRETTY SURE THEY WERE IN SOME FAIRY TALE...
...
NO USE WASTING BRAIN CELLS ON THEM UNTIL WE KNOW THE FULL EXTENT OF WHAT'S GOING ON HERE.
BOOM!!
PUT ME DOWN AND GO!!
I WILL STAY HERE!!!
?!
MY BOY WAS NOT AMONG THE CHILDREN WE FREED!!
HE MIGHT BE IN A DIFFERENT ROOM! I WILL STAY HERE AND...
AND HOW WILL YOU GET THERE?!! I DROP YOUR HEAD...
BUT I'M ONLY HERE TO RESCUE MY SON!!!
...AND I'M LEAVING YOU TO DIE! I DON'T WANT THAT HANGING OVER MY CONSCIENCE!!
STOP BEATING AROUND THE BUSH AND JUST SAY IT!!
"HELP ME LOOK FOR MY BODY"! IT'S BOUND TO BE AROUND HERE, ISN'T IT?!

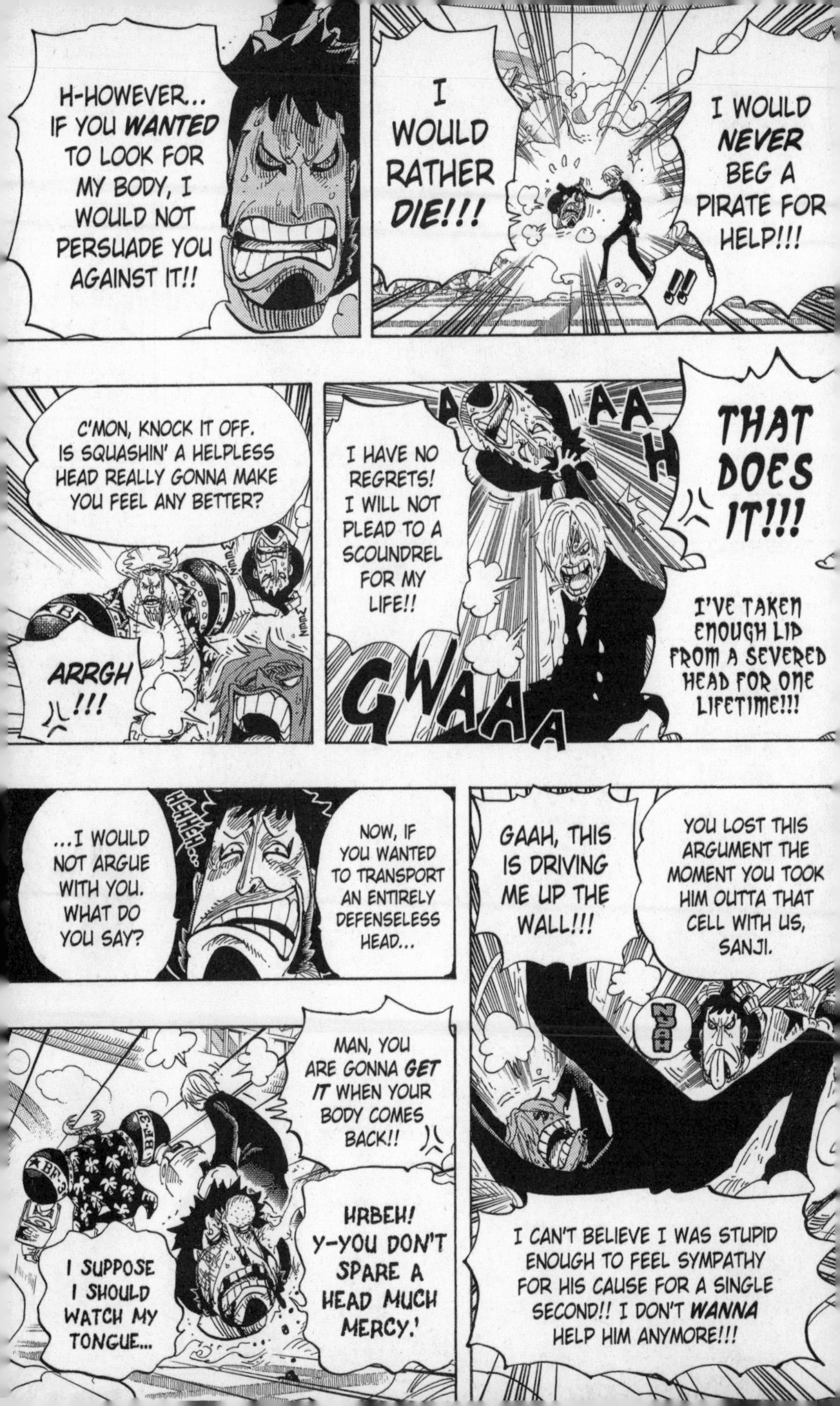
I WOULD NEVER BEG A PIRATE FOR HELP!!!
I WOULD RATHER DIE!!!
!!
H-HOWEVER... IF YOU WANTED TO LOOK FOR MY BODY, I WOULD NOT PERSUADE YOU AGAINST IT!!
THAT DOES IT!!!
AAAH
I'VE TAKEN ENOUGH LIP FROM A SEVERED HEAD FOR ONE LIFETIME!!!
I HAVE NO REGRETS! I WILL NOT PLEAD TO A SCOUNDREL FOR MY LIFE!!
GWAAAA
C'MON, KNOCK IT OFF. IS SQUASHIN' A HELPLESS HEAD REALLY GONNA MAKE YOU FEEL ANY BETTER?
ARRGH!!!
YOU LOST THIS ARGUMENT THE MOMENT YOU TOOK HIM OUTTA THAT CELL WITH US, SANJI.
GAAH, THIS IS DRIVING ME UP THE WALL!!!
NYAH
I CAN'T BELIEVE I WAS STUPID ENOUGH TO FEEL SYMPATHY FOR HIS CAUSE FOR A SINGLE SECOND!! I DON'T WANNA HELP HIM ANYMORE!!!
NOW, IF YOU WANTED TO TRANSPORT AN ENTIRELY DEFENSELESS HEAD...
HEHHEH
...I WOULD NOT ARGUE WITH YOU. WHAT DO YOU SAY?
MAN, YOU ARE GONNA GET IT WHEN YOUR BODY COMES BACK!!
HRBEH! Y-YOU DON'T SPARE A HEAD MUCH MERCY.'
I SUPPOSE I SHOULD WATCH MY TONGUE...

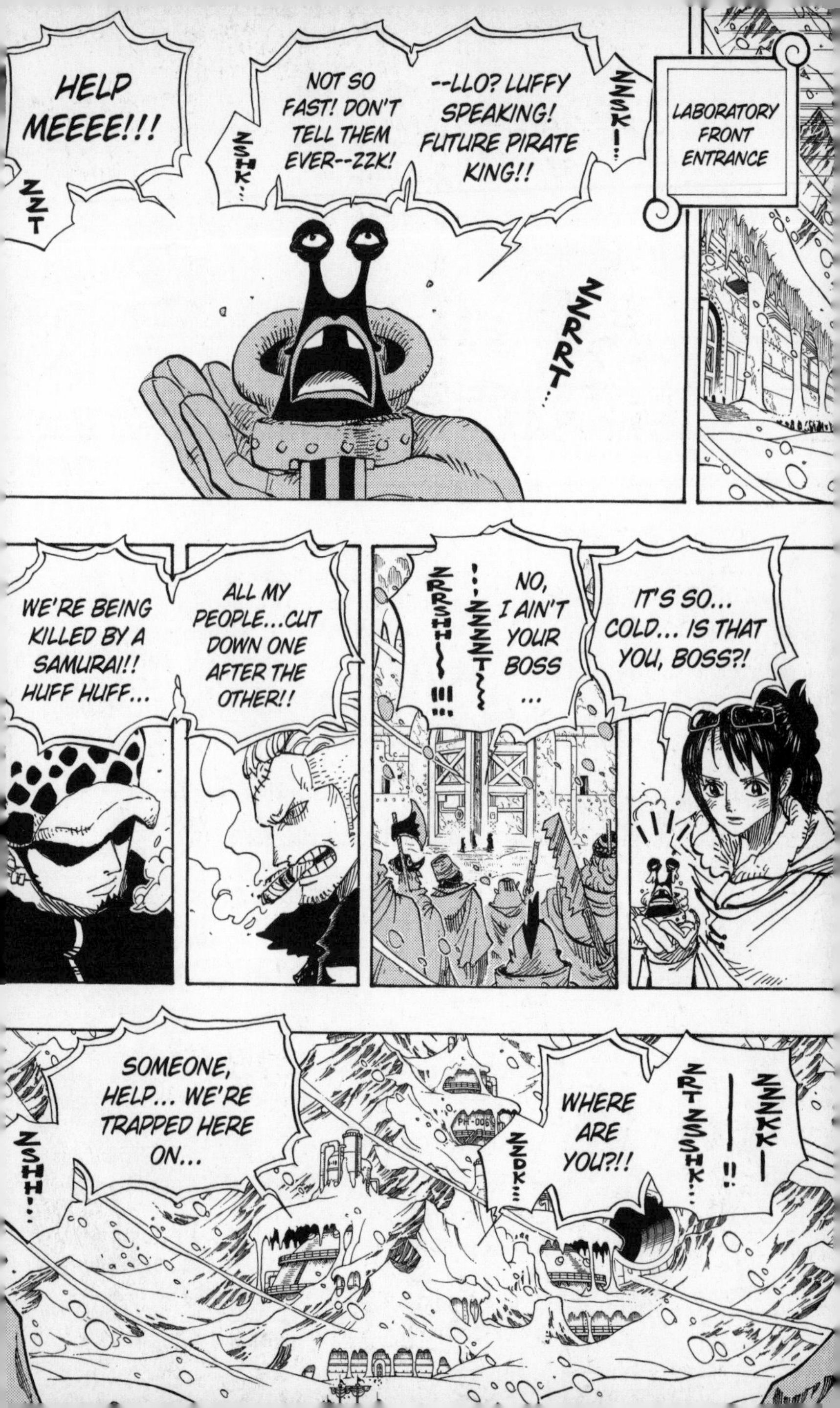
LABORATORY FRONT ENTRANCE
ZZSK!..
--LLO? LUFFY SPEAKING! FUTURE PIRATE KING!!
NOT SO FAST! DON'T TELL THEM EVER--ZZK!
ZSHK...
HELP MEEEE!!!
ZZT
ZZRRT...
IT'S SO... COLD... IS THAT YOU, BOSS?!
NO, I AIN'T YOUR BOSS ...
ZZZZT~~
ZRRSHH~~!!!
ALL MY PEOPLE...CUT DOWN ONE AFTER THE OTHER!!
WE'RE BEING KILLED BY A SAMURAI!! HUFF HUFF...
ZZZKK——!!
ZRT ZSSHK...
WHERE ARE YOU?!!
ZZDK!!..
PH-006
SOMEONE, HELP... WE'RE TRAPPED HERE ON...
ZSHH!..

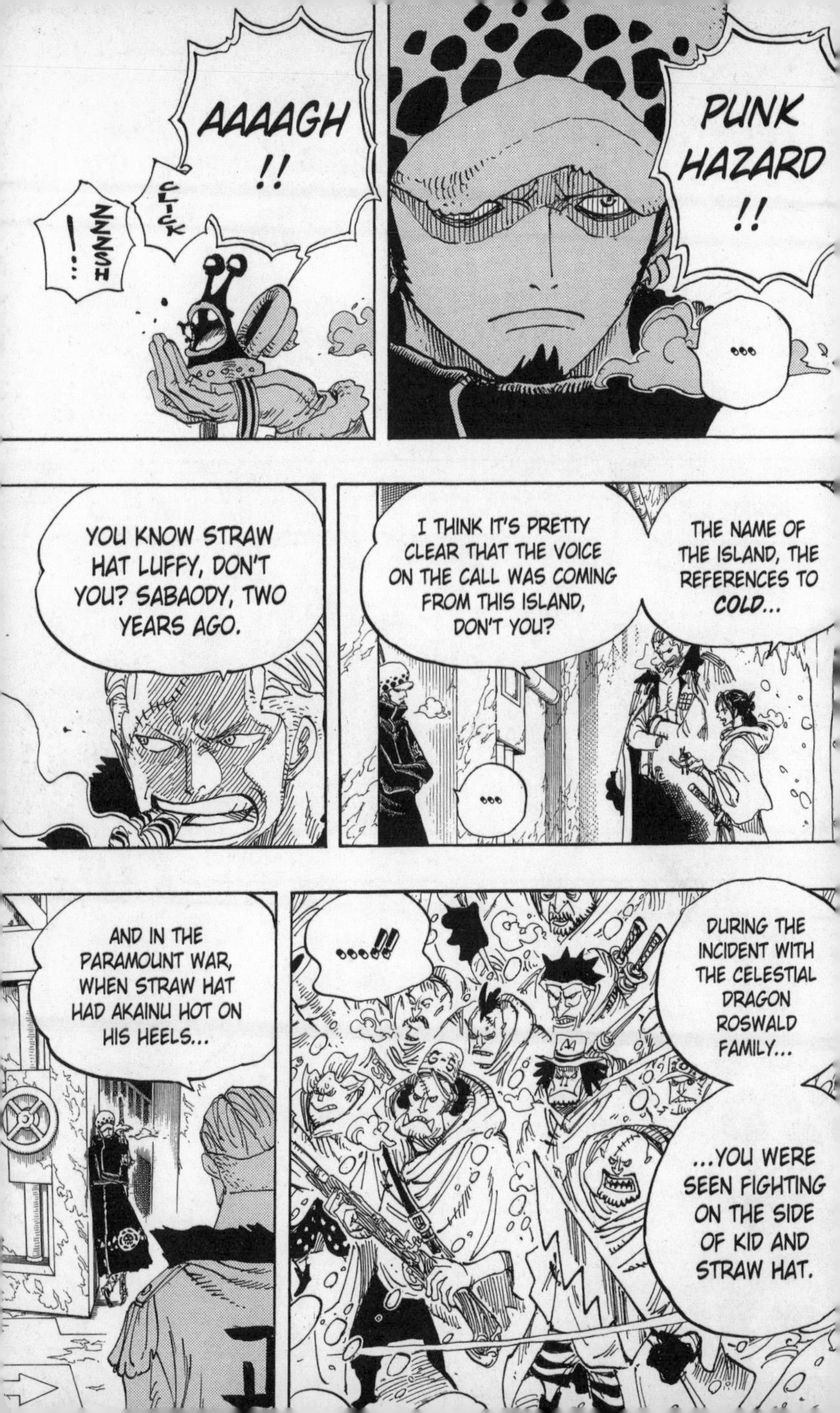
PUNK HAZARD !!
...
AAAAGH !!
CLICK
ZZZZSH !...
THE NAME OF THE ISLAND, THE REFERENCES TO *COLD*...
I THINK IT'S PRETTY CLEAR THAT THE VOICE ON THE CALL WAS COMING FROM THIS ISLAND, DON'T YOU?
...
YOU KNOW STRAW HAT LUFFY, DON'T YOU? SABAODY, TWO YEARS AGO.
DURING THE INCIDENT WITH THE CELESTIAL DRAGON ROSWALD FAMILY...
....!!
...YOU WERE SEEN FIGHTING ON THE SIDE OF KID AND STRAW HAT.
AND IN THE PARAMOUNT WAR, WHEN STRAW HAT HAD AKAINU HOT ON HIS HEELS...

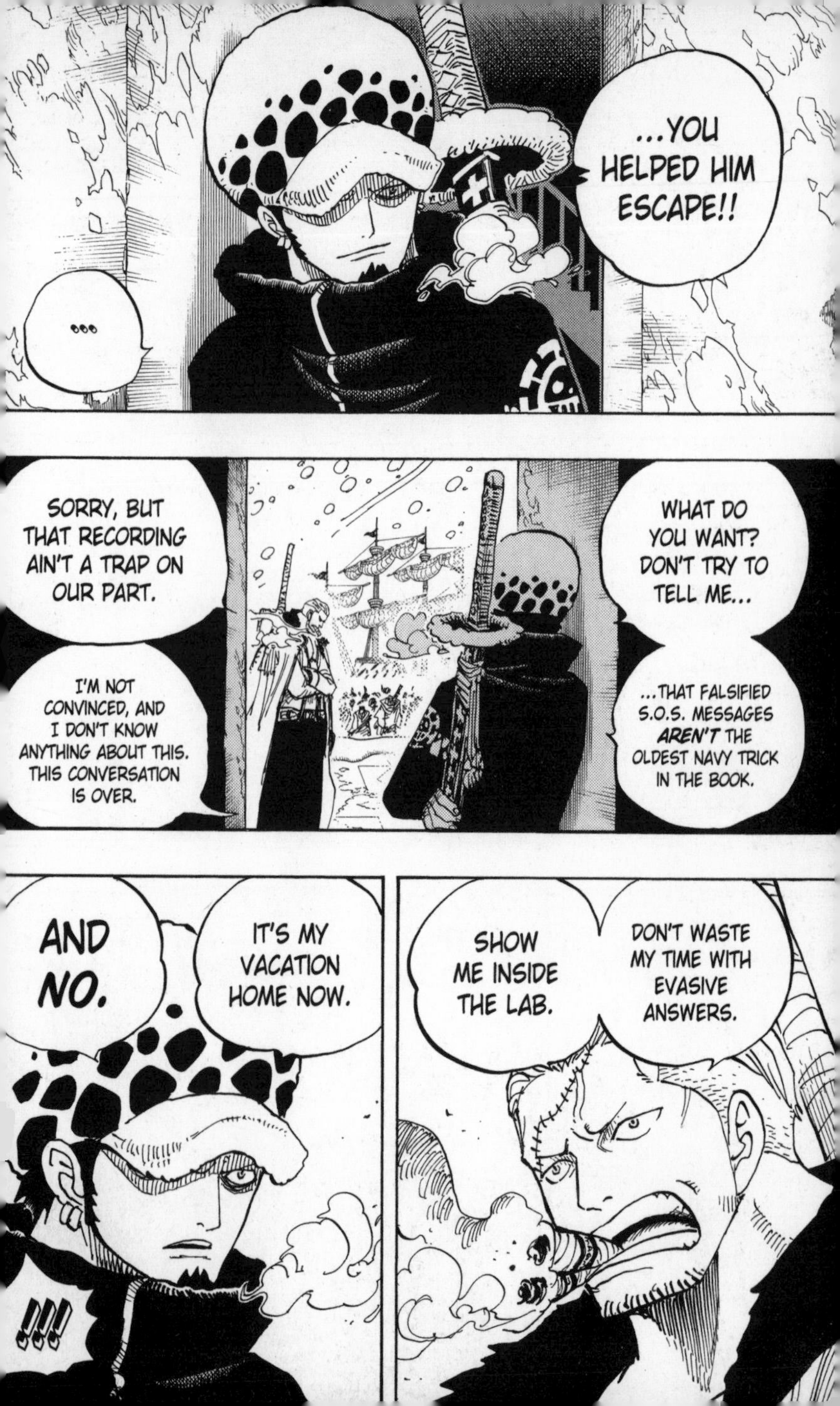
...YOU HELPED HIM ESCAPE!!
...
WHAT DO YOU WANT? DON'T TRY TO TELL ME...
...THAT FALSIFIED S.O.S. MESSAGES *AREN'T* THE OLDEST NAVY TRICK IN THE BOOK.
SORRY, BUT THAT RECORDING AIN'T A TRAP ON OUR PART.
I'M NOT CONVINCED, AND I DON'T KNOW ANYTHING ABOUT THIS. THIS CONVERSATION IS OVER.
DON'T WASTE MY TIME WITH EVASIVE ANSWERS.
SHOW ME INSIDE THE LAB.
IT'S MY VACATION HOME NOW.
AND NO.
!!!

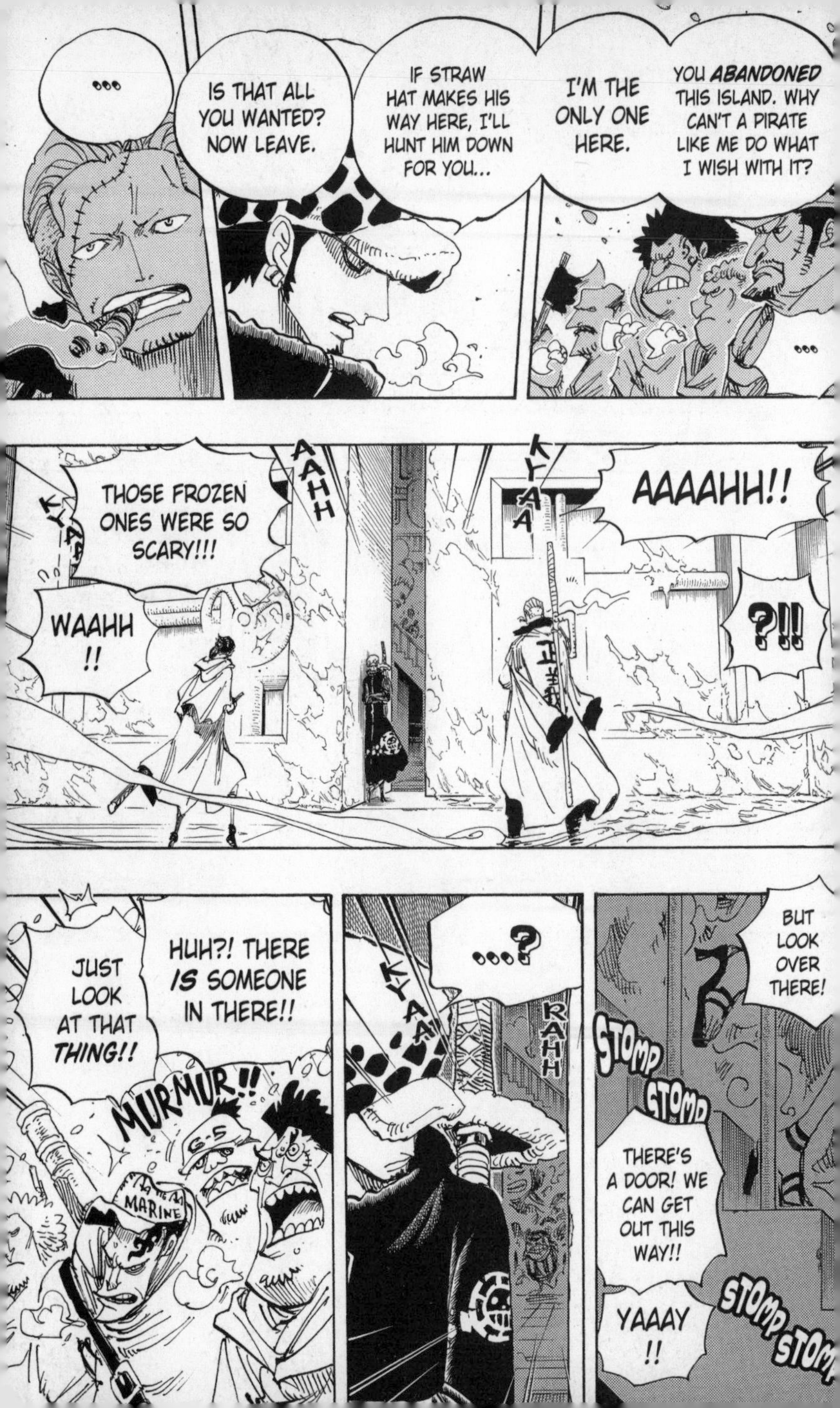
YOU ABANDONED THIS ISLAND. WHY CAN'T A PIRATE LIKE ME DO WHAT I WISH WITH IT?
I'M THE ONLY ONE HERE.
...
IF STRAW HAT MAKES HIS WAY HERE, I'LL HUNT HIM DOWN FOR YOU...
IS THAT ALL YOU WANTED? NOW LEAVE.
...
AAAAHH!!
KYAA
?!!
AAHH
THOSE FROZEN ONES WERE SO SCARY!!!
KYAA
WAAHH !!
BUT LOOK OVER THERE!
STOMP
STOMP
THERE'S A DOOR! WE CAN GET OUT THIS WAY!!
STOMP STOM
YAAAY !!
...?
KYAA
RAHH
HUH?! THERE IS SOMEONE IN THERE!!
JUST LOOK AT THAT THING!!
MURMUR!!
G-5
MARINE

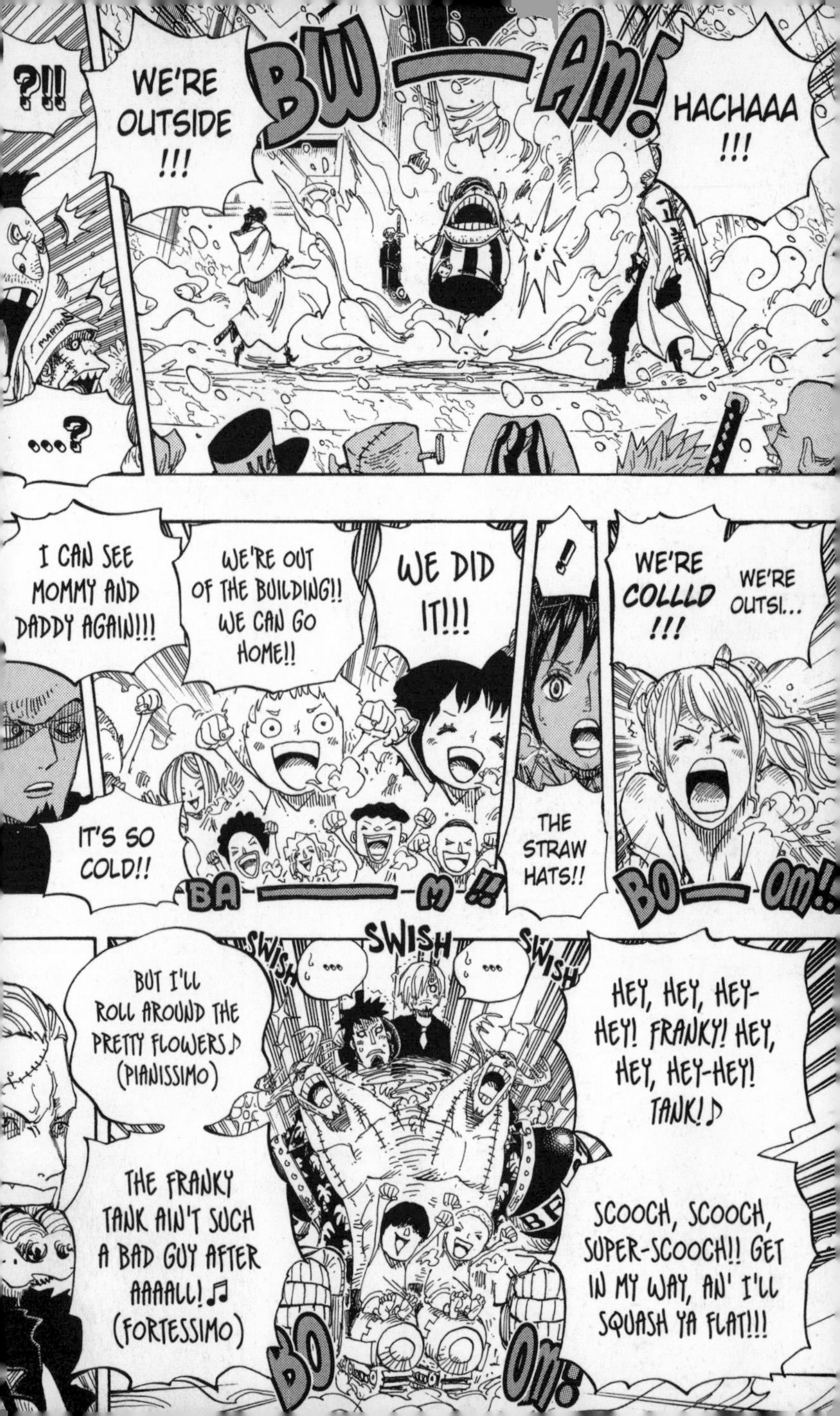
HACHAAA!!!
BW—AM!
WE'RE OUTSIDE!!!
?!!
...?
WE'RE OUTSI...
WE'RE COLLLD!!!
BO—OM!!
!
THE STRAW HATS!!
WE DID IT!!!
WE'RE OUT OF THE BUILDING!! WE CAN GO HOME!!
I CAN SEE MOMMY AND DADDY AGAIN!!!
IT'S SO COLD!!
BA—M!!
SWISH
SWISH
SWISH
...
...
HEY, HEY, HEY-HEY! FRANKY! HEY, HEY, HEY-HEY! TANK!♪
SCOOCH, SCOOCH, SUPER-SCOOCH!! GET IN MY WAY, AN' I'LL SQUASH YA FLAT!!!
BUT I'LL ROLL AROUND THE PRETTY FLOWERS♪ (PIANISSIMO)
THE FRANKY TANK AIN'T SUCH A BAD GUY AFTER AAAALL!♫ (FORTESSIMO)
BO—OM!

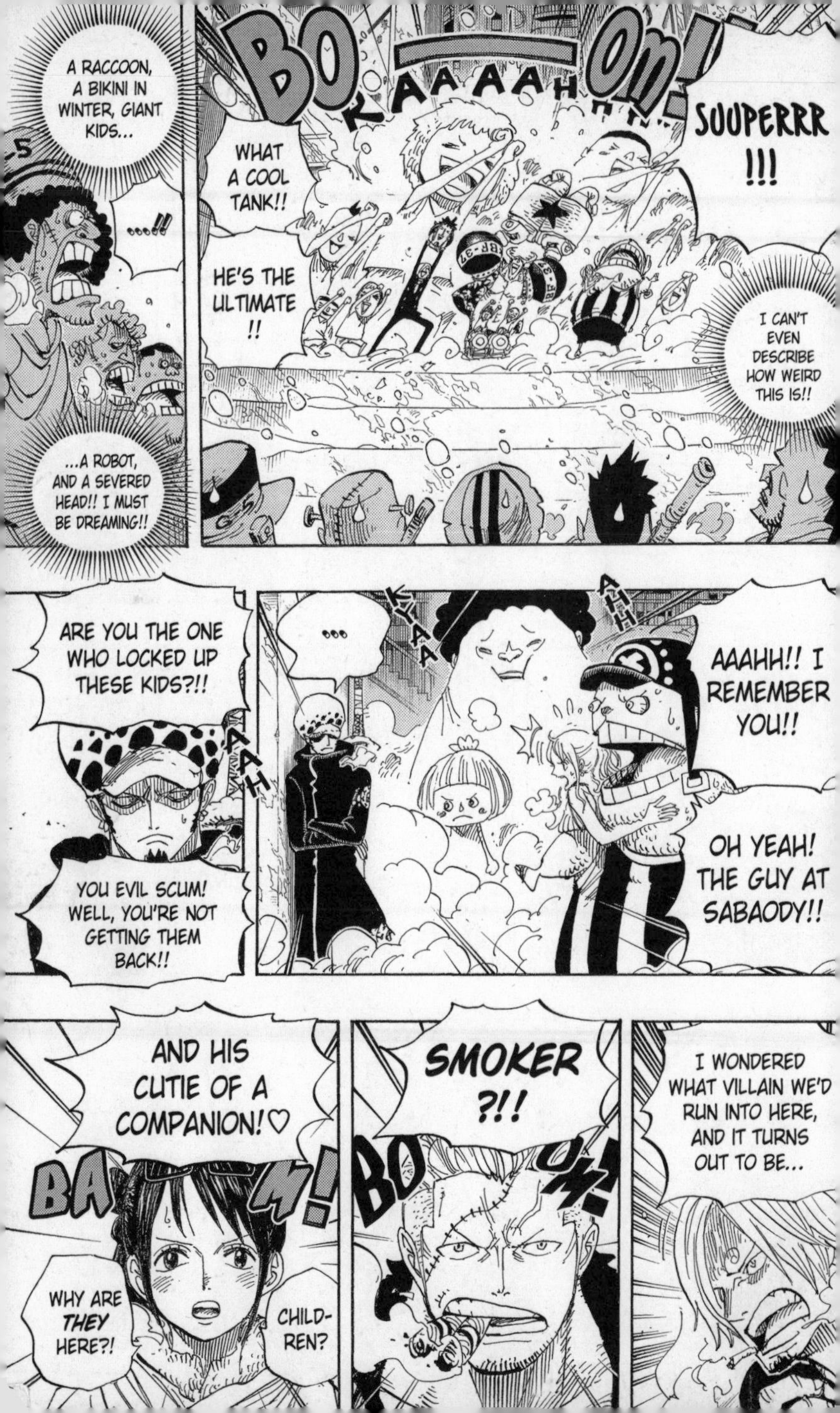
SUUPERRR!!!
BO—OM!
KAAAAAHH
WHAT A COOL TANK!!
I CAN'T EVEN DESCRIBE HOW WEIRD THIS IS!!
HE'S THE ULTIMATE!!
A RACCOON, A BIKINI IN WINTER, GIANT KIDS...
....!!
...A ROBOT, AND A SEVERED HEAD!! I MUST BE DREAMING!!
AAAHH!! I REMEMBER YOU!!
AHH
KYAA
...
OH YEAH! THE GUY AT SABAODY!!
ARE YOU THE ONE WHO LOCKED UP THESE KIDS?!!
AAH
YOU EVIL SCUM! WELL, YOU'RE NOT GETTING THEM BACK!!
I WONDERED WHAT VILLAIN WE'D RUN INTO HERE, AND IT TURNS OUT TO BE...
SMOKER?!!
BO OM!
CHILD-REN?
AND HIS CUTIE OF A COMPANION!♡
BA M!
WHY ARE *THEY* HERE?!

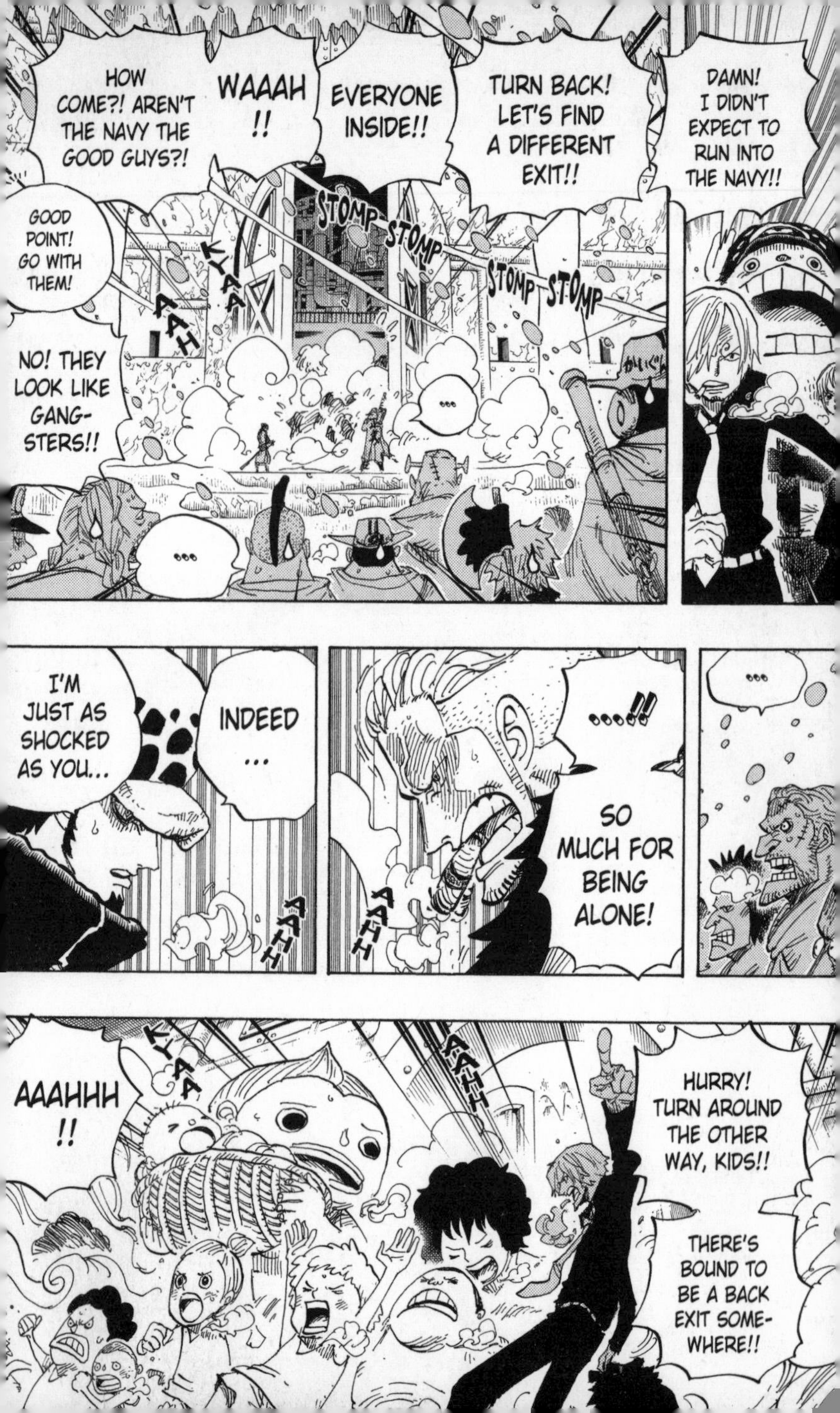
DAMN! I DIDN'T EXPECT TO RUN INTO THE NAVY!!
TURN BACK! LET'S FIND A DIFFERENT EXIT!!
EVERYONE INSIDE!!
WAAAH !!
HOW COME?! AREN'T THE NAVY THE GOOD GUYS?!
STOMP STOMP
STOMP STOMP
KYAA
GOOD POINT! GO WITH THEM!
AAH
...
NO! THEY LOOK LIKE GANG-STERS!!
...
...
....!!
SO MUCH FOR BEING ALONE!
AAHH
INDEED ...
I'M JUST AS SHOCKED AS YOU...
AAHH
HURRY! TURN AROUND THE OTHER WAY, KIDS!!
THERE'S BOUND TO BE A BACK EXIT SOME-WHERE!!
AAHH
KYAA
AAAHHH !!

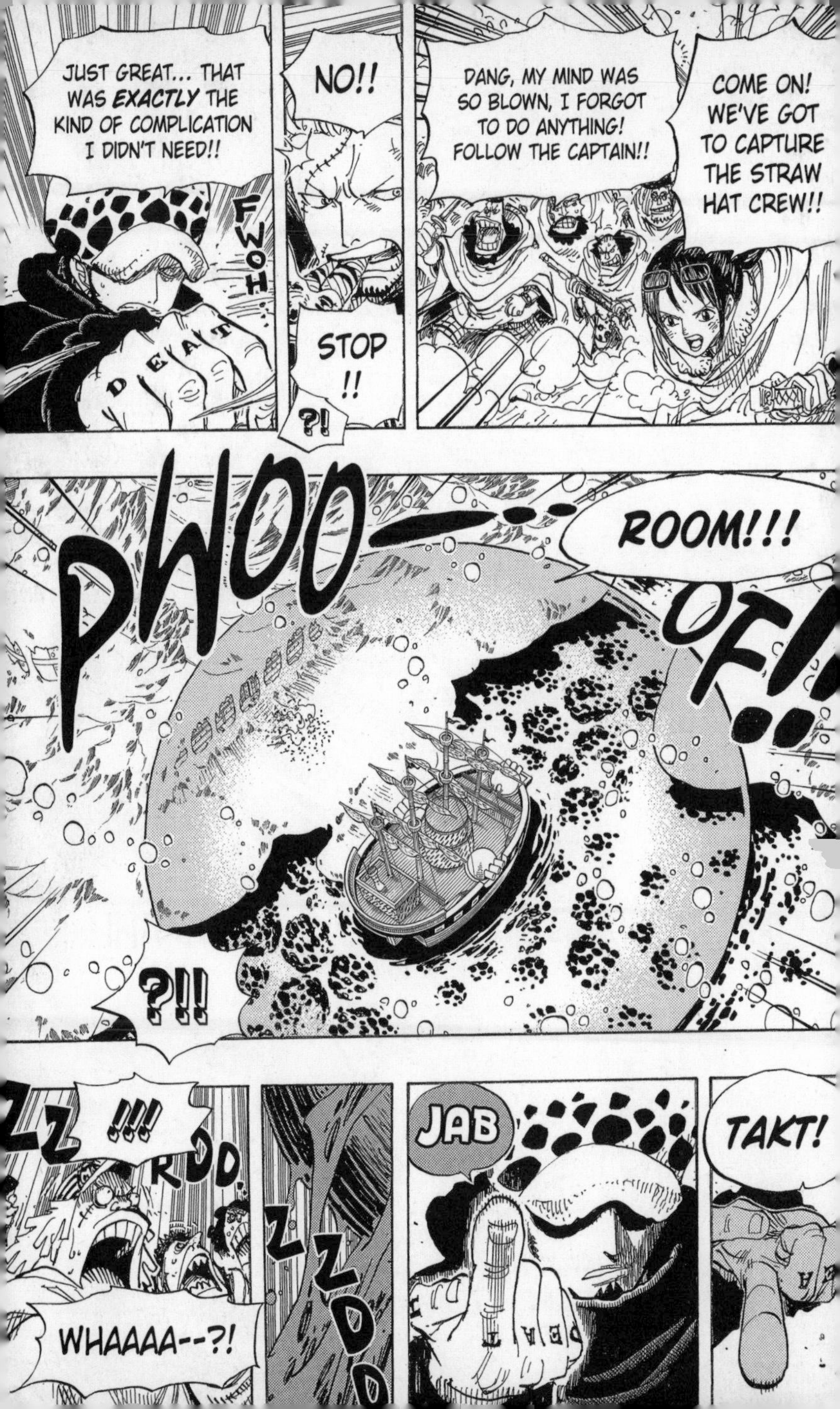
COME ON! WE'VE GOT TO CAPTURE THE STRAW HAT CREW!!
DANG, MY MIND WAS SO BLOWN, I FORGOT TO DO ANYTHING! FOLLOW THE CAPTAIN!!
NO!!
STOP !!
?!
JUST GREAT... THAT WAS *EXACTLY* THE KIND OF COMPLICATION I DIDN'T NEED!!
FWOH
ROOM!!!
PHOOO--OF!!
?!!
TAKT!
JAB
!!!
WHAAAA--?!

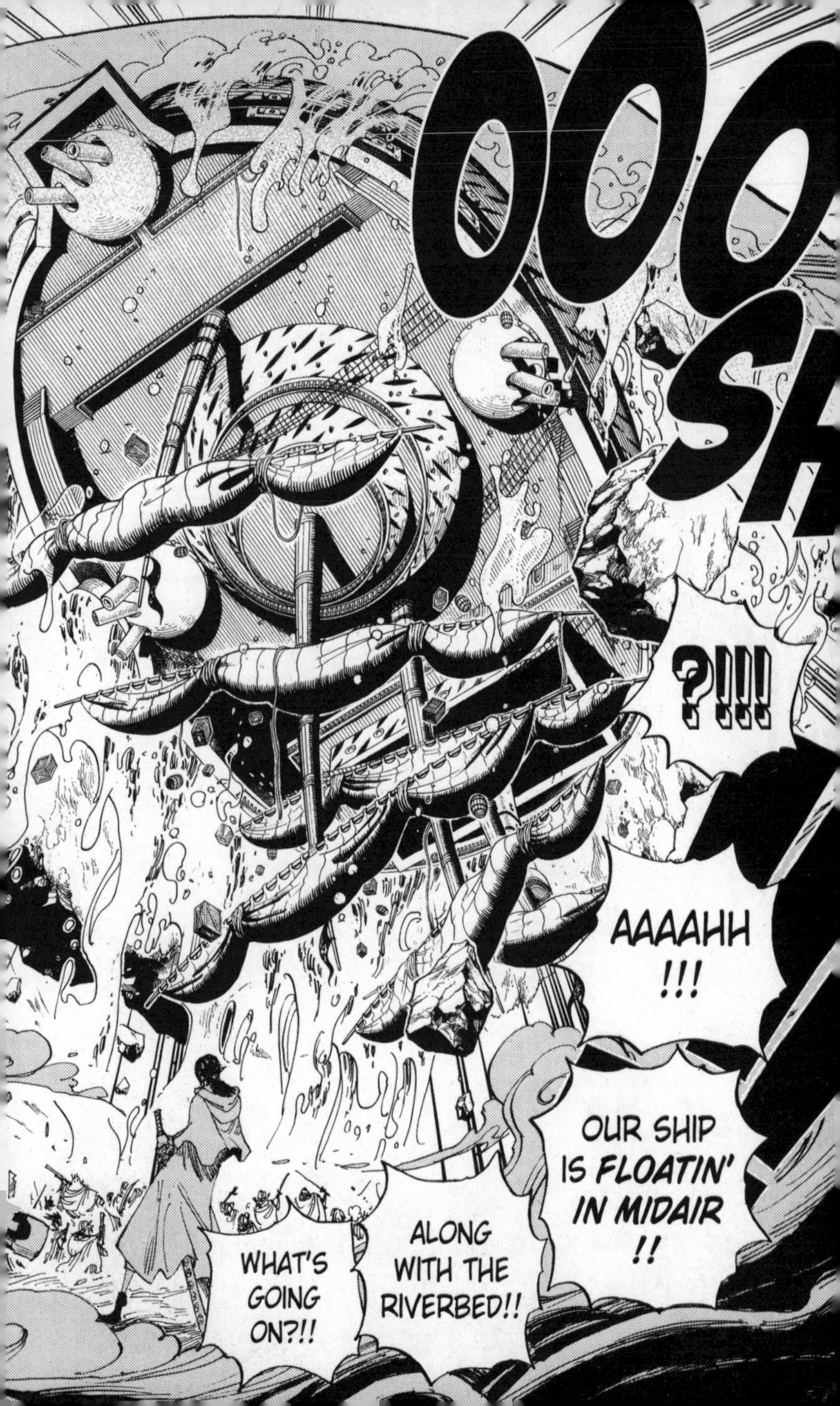
OOOSH
?!!!
AAAAHH !!!
OUR SHIP IS *FLOATIN' IN MIDAIR* !!
ALONG WITH THE RIVERBED!!
WHAT'S GOING ON?!!

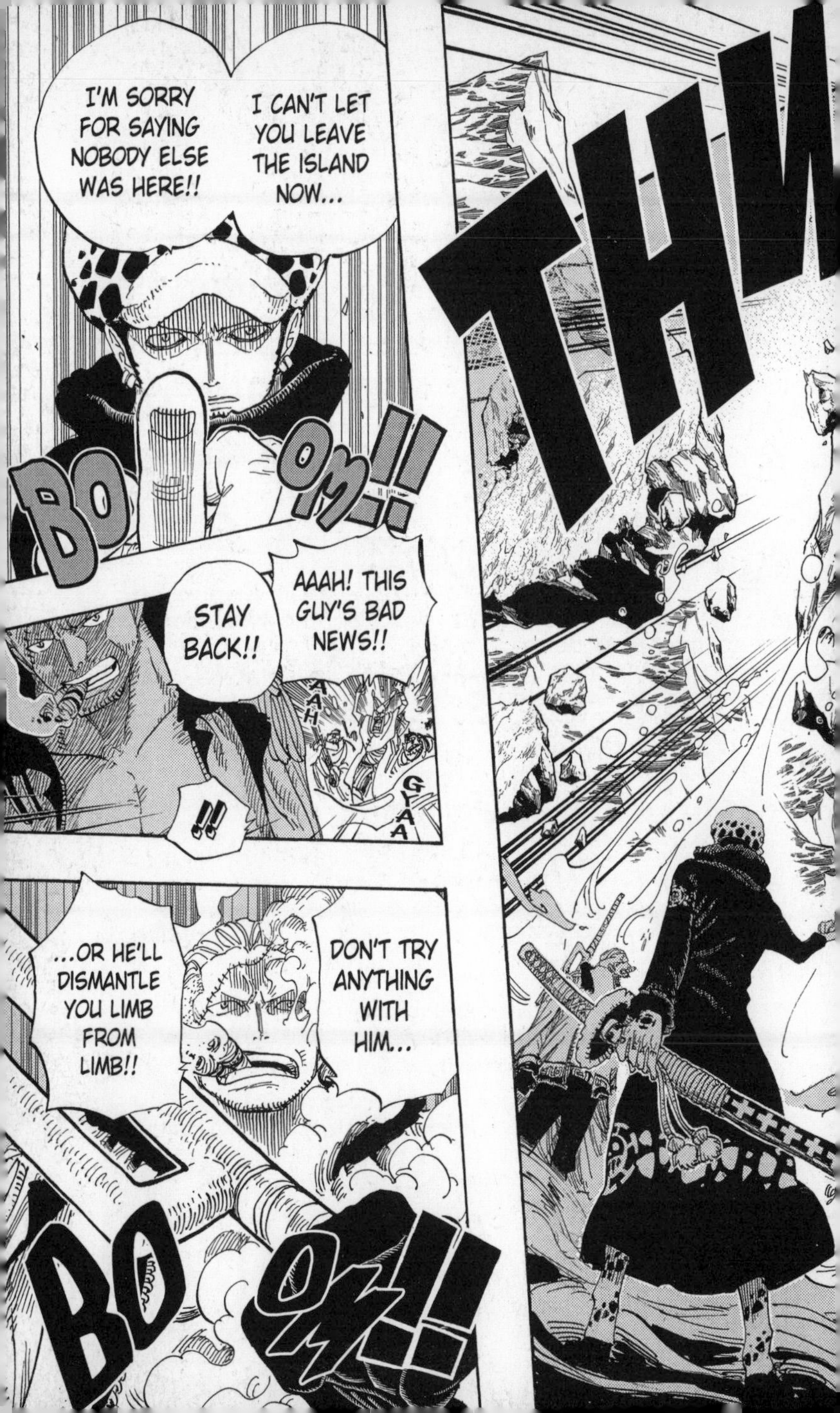
THW
I CAN'T LET YOU LEAVE THE ISLAND NOW...
I'M SORRY FOR SAYING NOBODY ELSE WAS HERE!!
BOOM!!
AAAH! THIS GUY'S BAD NEWS!!
STAY BACK!!
AAAH
GYAAA
!!
DON'T TRY ANYTHING WITH HIM...
...OR HE'LL DISMANTLE YOU LIMB FROM LIMB!!
BOOM!!

SBS Question Corner

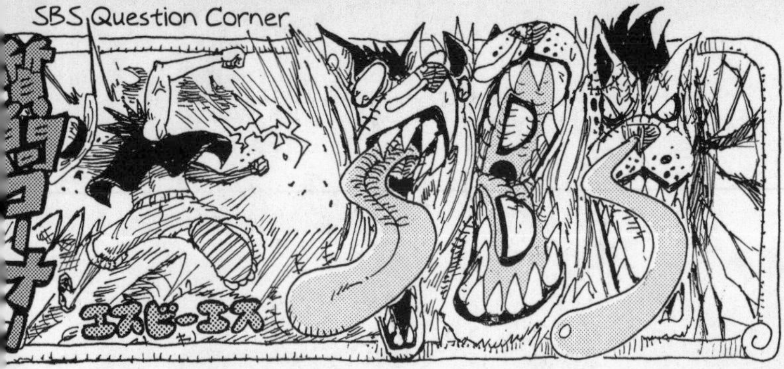
質問コーナー!
エスビーエス

(Ponio, Aichi)

Q: In Volumes 64 and 65, Nami and Robin watch Franky's cyborg moves and stare silently. What's wrong with them? Please explain.

--CPDX

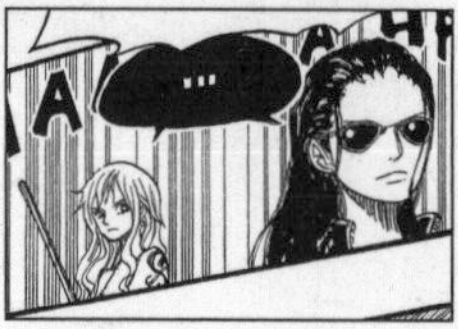

A: Hmm. You're 17, right, CPDX? Let me give you a little life lesson. See, men and women are like totally different species. We might be human, but we don't see eye-to-eye. No matter how well you describe the awesomeness of robots, girls just won't get it. They're into all these weird sparkly things and puffy things and junk like that. And we don't get *that*, do we?! So you see, it's all right if they see that cool stuff and just ignore it. That's how it works!! Hang in there, Franky!!

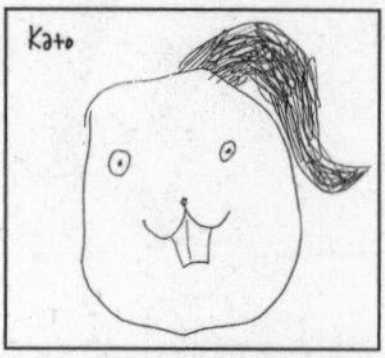
Kato

Q: Why is Law the new Warlord and not Kato?!

--Lah

A: Because, judging by the shape of Kato's nose, he's not even human. His bounty would be like two berries.

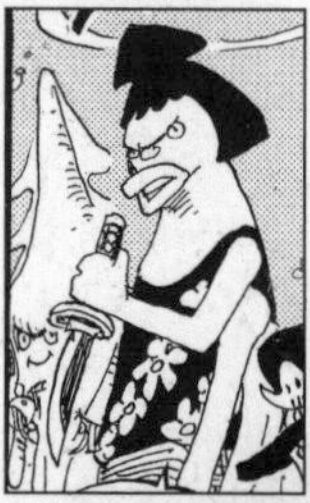

Q: Hello, Mr. Oda! On p.151 of Volume 65, there's a squid next to Ikaros as a child. Could this be Daedalus? I'm right, aren't I?! Aren't I?!!!

--Iwaken, Friend of Chagero

A: Yes, yes, now take it easy! At the time they were both alive and best friends. But then Daedalus had an accident and turned into dried squid, and ever since, Ikaros has been traumatized by the sight of fire. He can't help but be afraid he'll be turned into dried squid himself.

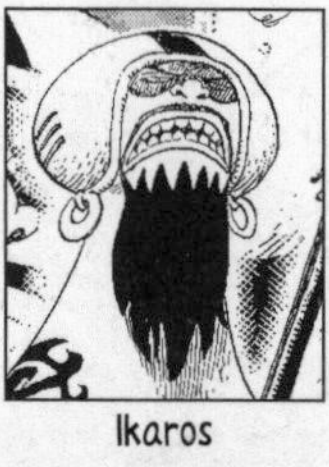

Ikaros

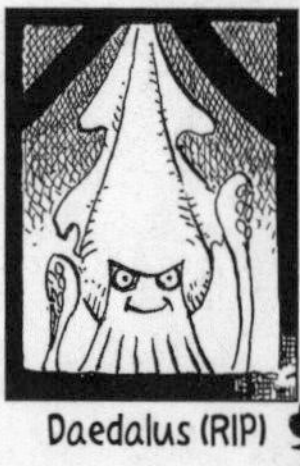

Daedalus (RIP)

Chapter 661:
LAKESIDE BANDITS

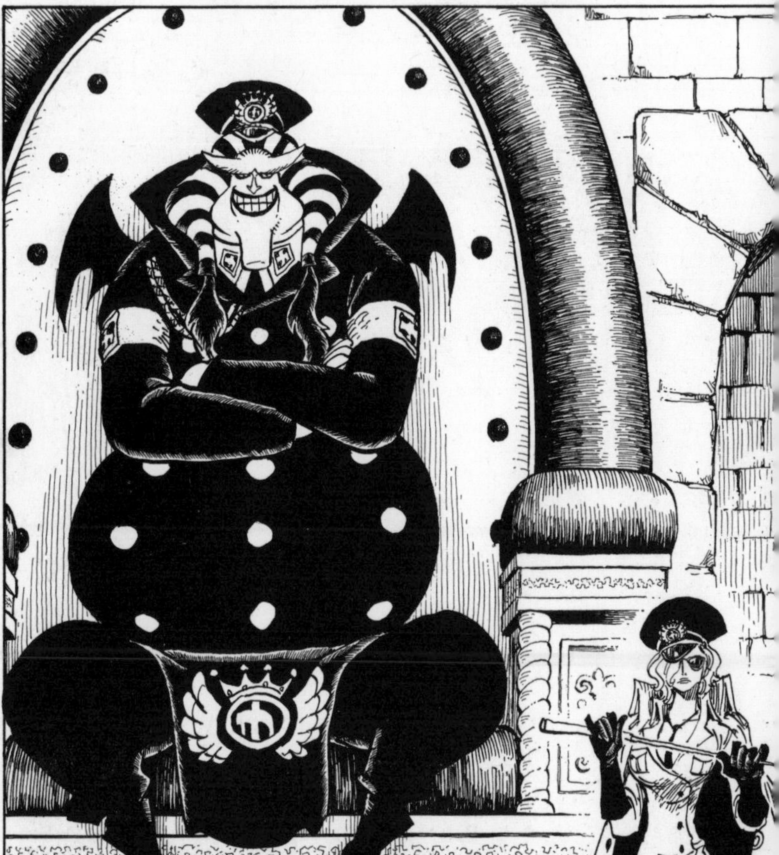

DECKS OF THE WORLD, VOL. 42: "IMPEL DOWN—PRISON WARDEN HANNYABAL & CHIEF JAILER DOMINO"

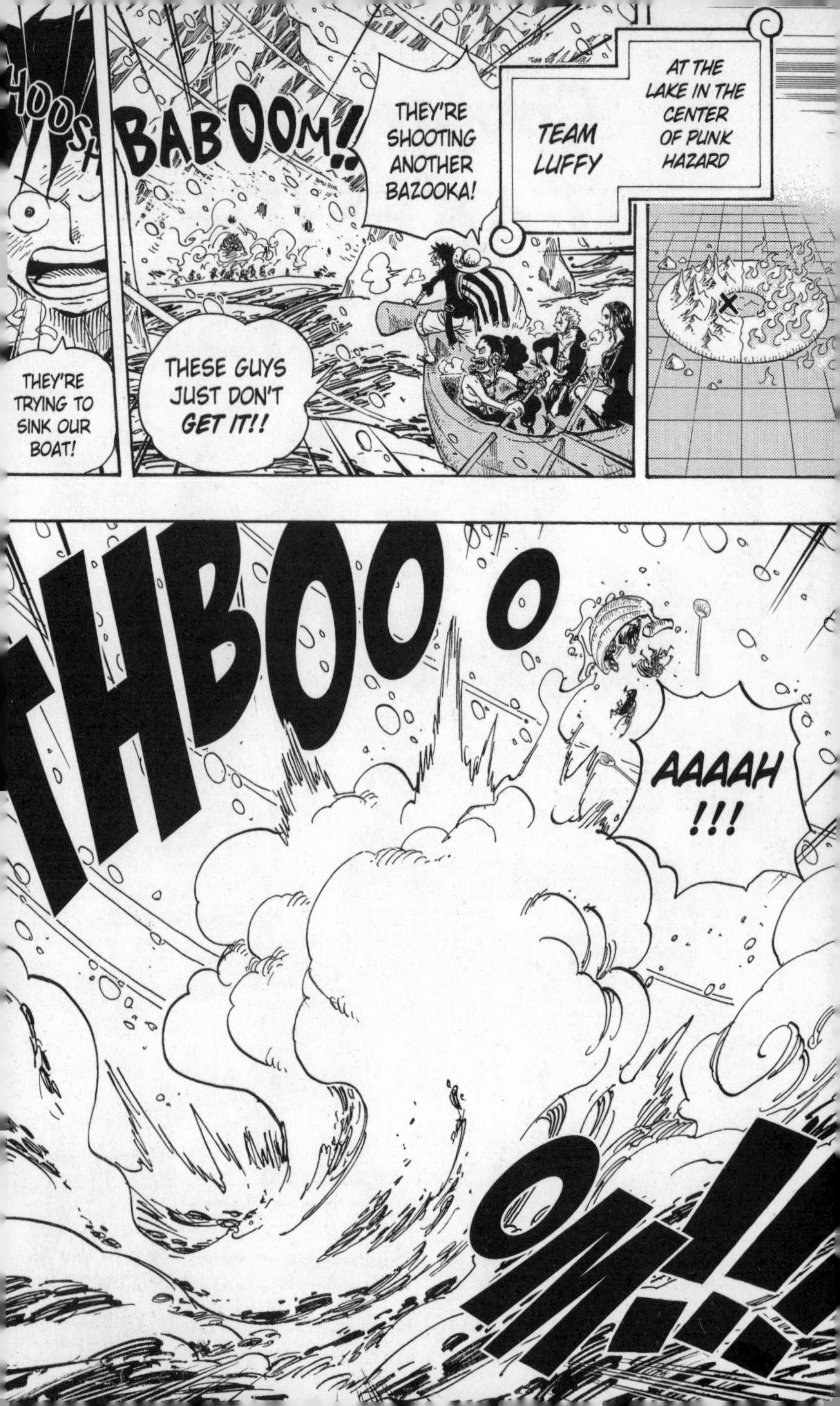

AT THE LAKE IN THE CENTER OF PUNK HAZARD
TEAM LUFFY
THEY'RE SHOOTING ANOTHER BAZOOKA!
BABOOM!!
THESE GUYS JUST DON'T GET IT!!
HOOSH
THEY'RE TRYING TO SINK OUR BOAT!
AAAAH !!!
THBOOO
M!!!

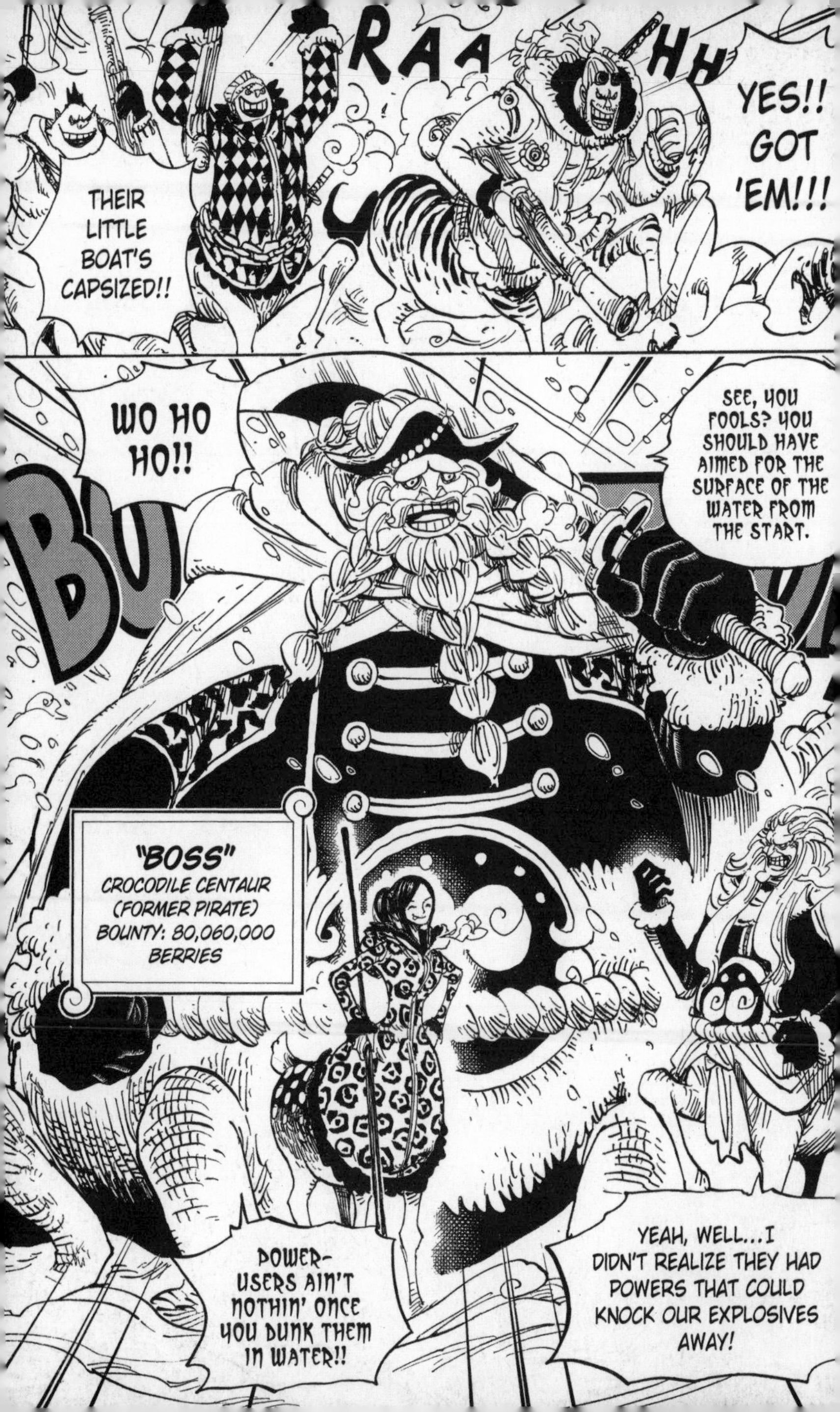
RAA HH
YES!! GOT 'EM!!!
THEIR LITTLE BOAT'S CAPSIZED!!
SEE, YOU FOOLS? YOU SHOULD HAVE AIMED FOR THE SURFACE OF THE WATER FROM THE START.
WO HO HO!!
"BOSS" CROCODILE CENTAUR (FORMER PIRATE) BOUNTY: 80,060,000 BERRIES
YEAH, WELL...I DIDN'T REALIZE THEY HAD POWERS THAT COULD KNOCK OUR EXPLOSIVES AWAY!
POWER-USERS AIN'T NOTHIN' ONCE YOU DUNK THEM IN WATER!!

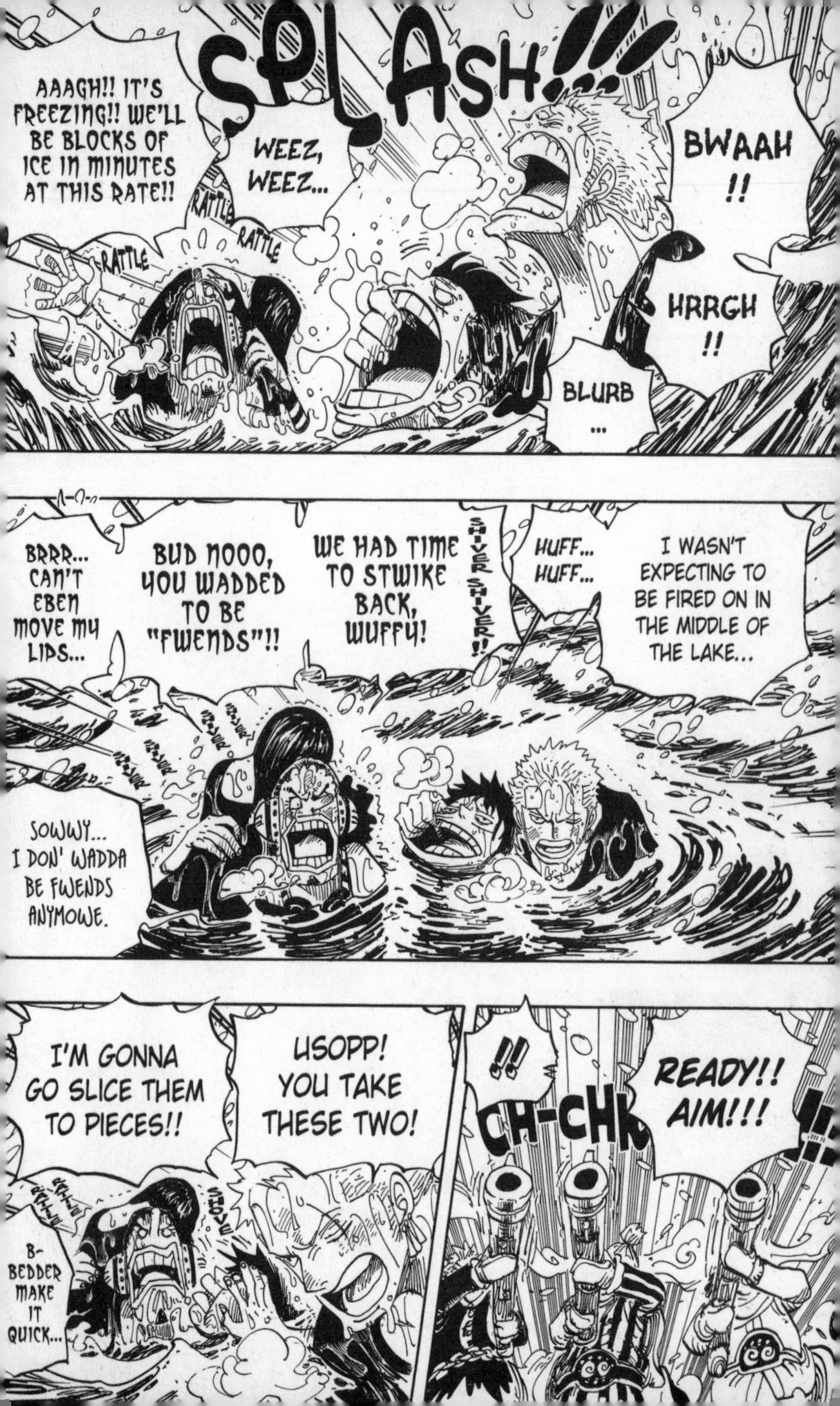
SPLASH!!!
BWAAH !!
WEEZ, WEEZ...
AAAGH!! IT'S FREEZING!! WE'LL BE BLOCKS OF ICE IN MINUTES AT THIS RATE!!
RATTLE RATTLE
RATTLE
HRRGH !!
BLURB ...
I WASN'T EXPECTING TO BE FIRED ON IN THE MIDDLE OF THE LAKE...
HUFF... HUFF...
SHIVER SHIVER!!
WE HAD TIME TO STWIKE BACK, WUFFY!
BUD NOOO, YOU WADDED TO BE "FWENDS"!!
BRRR... CAN'T EBEN MOVE MY LIPS...
SOWWY... I DON' WADDA BE FWENDS ANYMOWE.
READY!! AIM!!!
!!
CH-CHK
!!
USOPP! YOU TAKE THESE TWO!
I'M GONNA GO SLICE THEM TO PIECES!!
SHOVE
RATTLE RATTLE
B-BEDDER MAKE IT QUICK...

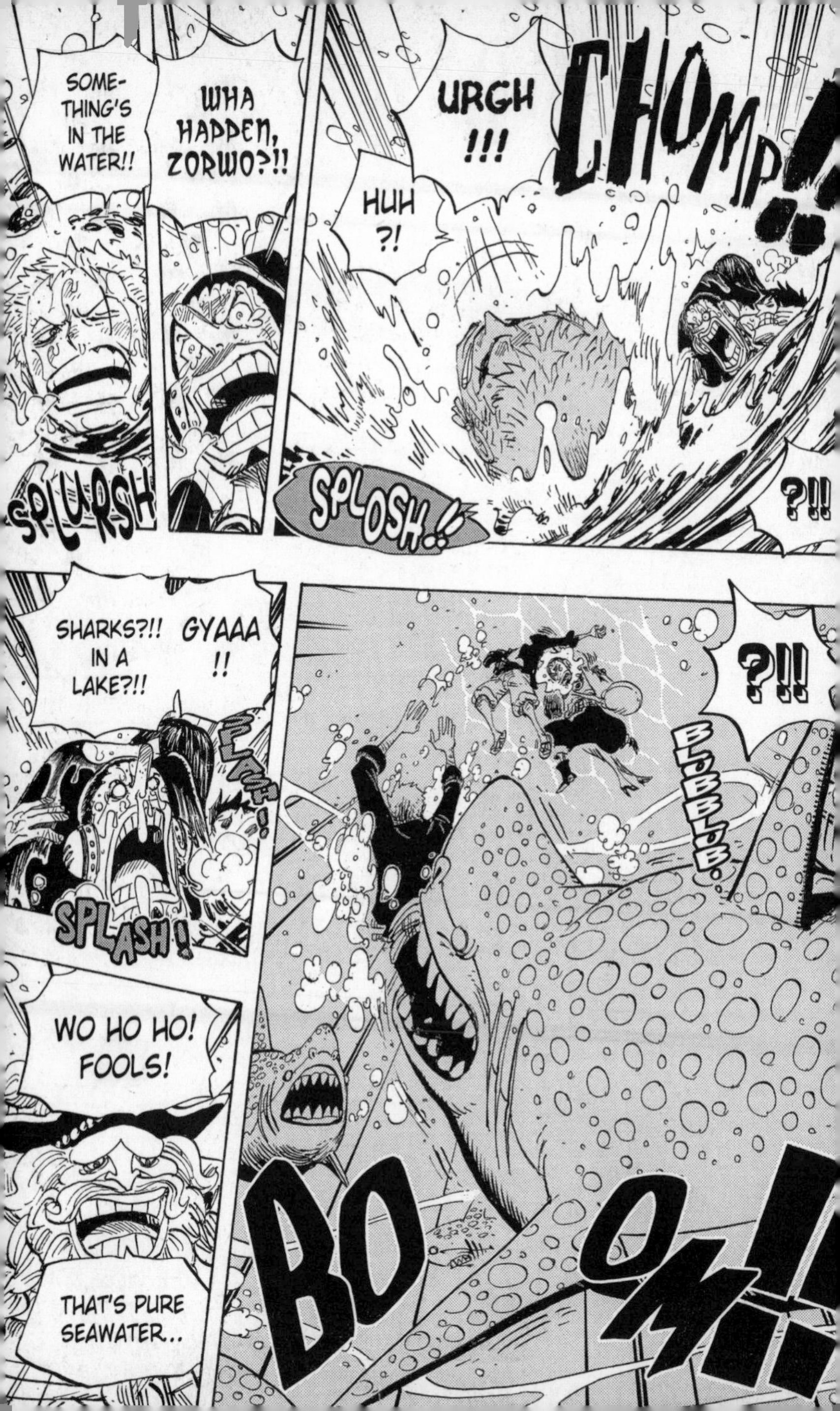
CHOMP!!
URGH!!!
HUH?!
?!!
SPLOSH!!
WHA HAPPEN, ZORWO?!!
SOME-THING'S IN THE WATER!!
SPLURSH
?!!
BLBBLB
BOOM!!
GYAAA!!
SHARKS?!! IN A LAKE?!!
FLASH!
SPLASH!
WO HO HO! FOOLS!
THAT'S PURE SEAWATER...

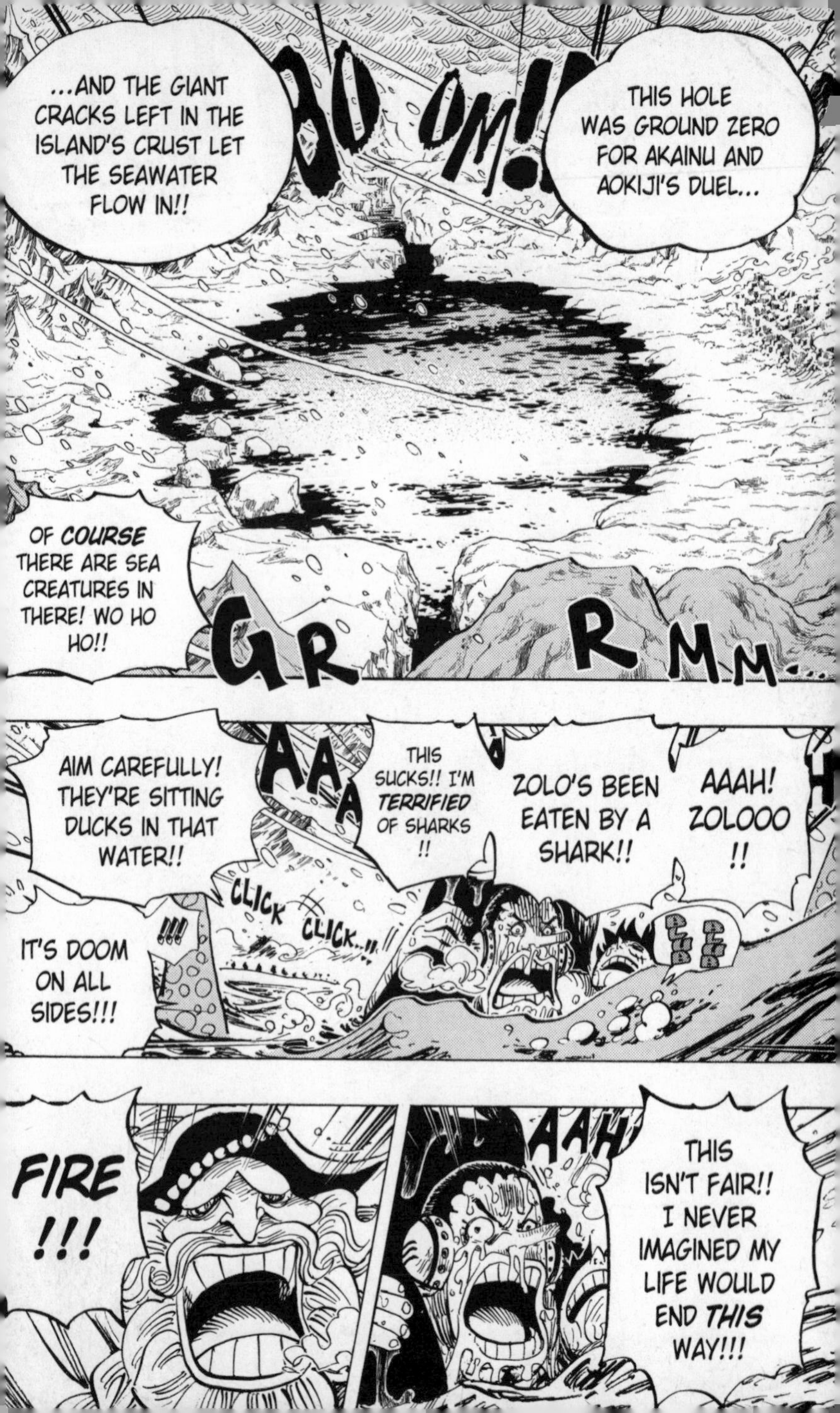
THIS HOLE WAS GROUND ZERO FOR AKAINU AND AOKIJI'S DUEL...
BOOM!!
...AND THE GIANT CRACKS LEFT IN THE ISLAND'S CRUST LET THE SEAWATER FLOW IN!!
OF COURSE THERE ARE SEA CREATURES IN THERE! WO HO HO!!
GRRMM...
AAAH! ZOLOOO!!
ZOLO'S BEEN EATEN BY A SHARK!!
THIS SUCKS!! I'M TERRIFIED OF SHARKS!!
AAA
AIM CAREFULLY! THEY'RE SITTING DUCKS IN THAT WATER!!
CLICK
CLICK..!!
!!!
IT'S DOOM ON ALL SIDES!!!
AAH
THIS ISN'T FAIR!! I NEVER IMAGINED MY LIFE WOULD END THIS WAY!!!
FIRE!!!

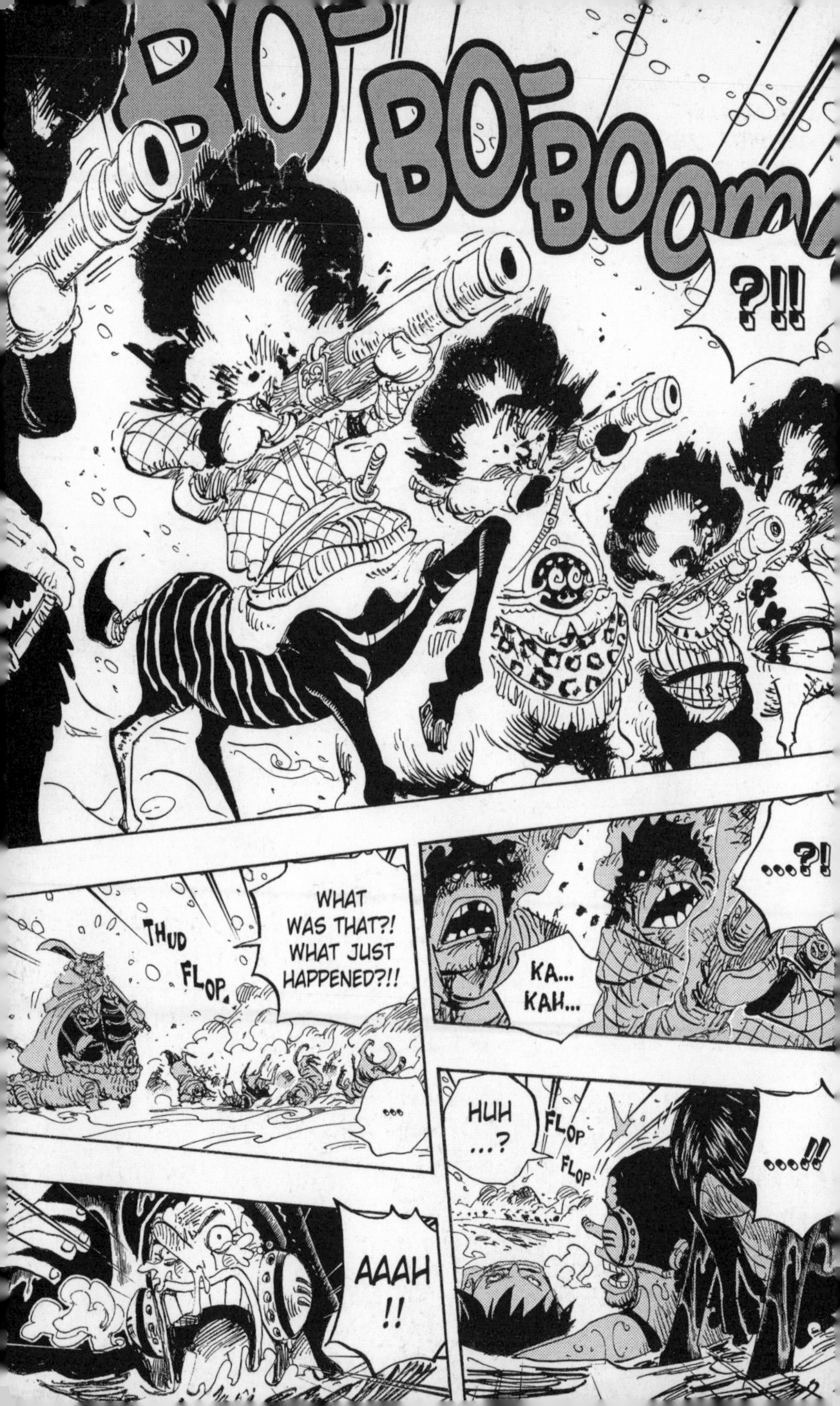
BO-BO-BOOM
?!!
...?!
KA... KAH...
WHAT WAS THAT?! WHAT JUST HAPPENED?!!
THUD
FLOP
...
...!!
HUH ...?
FLOP
FLOP
AAAH !!

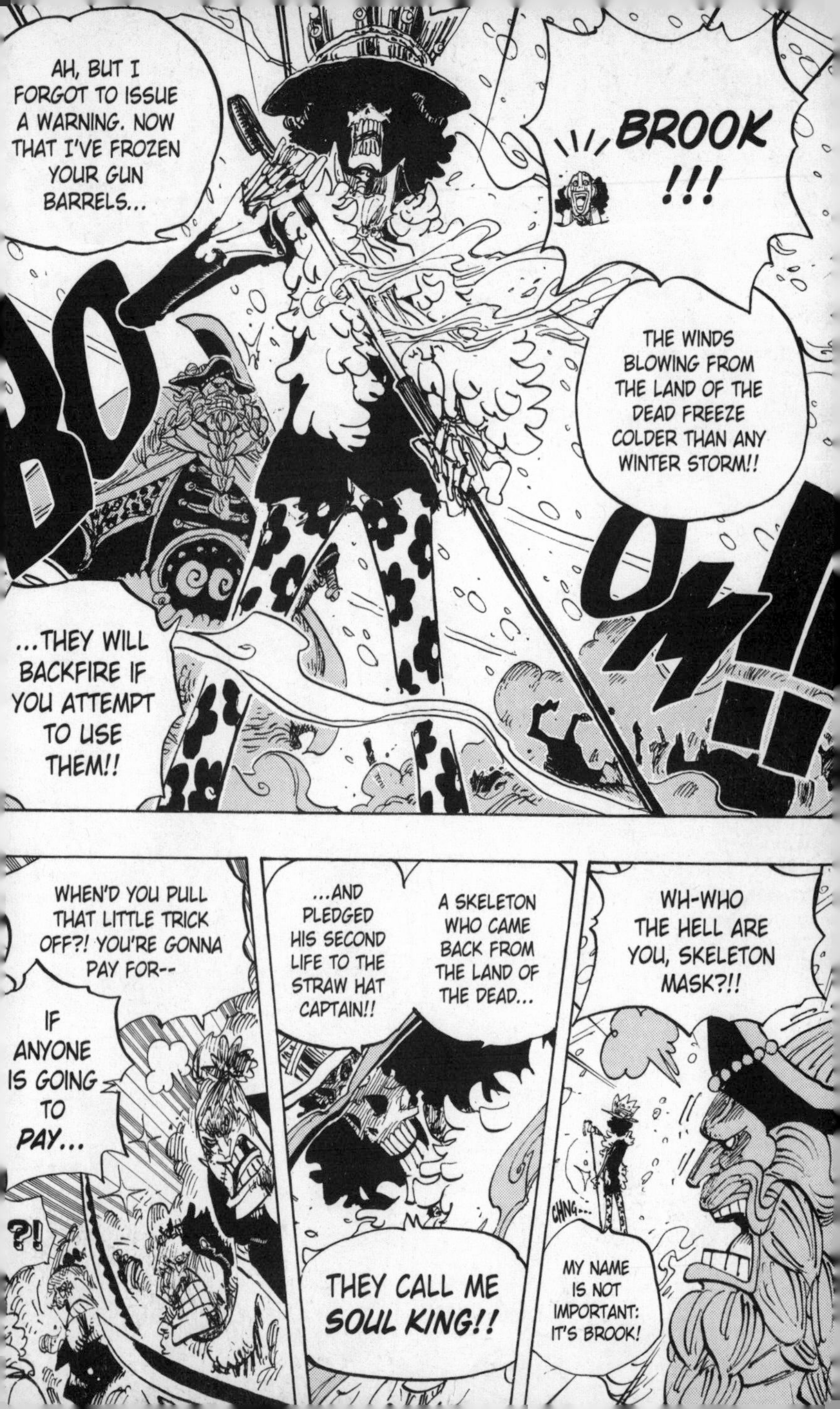
BROOK!!!
AH, BUT I FORGOT TO ISSUE A WARNING. NOW THAT I'VE FROZEN YOUR GUN BARRELS...
THE WINDS BLOWING FROM THE LAND OF THE DEAD FREEZE COLDER THAN ANY WINTER STORM!!
BO
OM!!
...THEY WILL BACKFIRE IF YOU ATTEMPT TO USE THEM!!
WH-WHO THE HELL ARE YOU, SKELETON MASK?!!
CHNG...
MY NAME IS NOT IMPORTANT: IT'S BROOK!
A SKELETON WHO CAME BACK FROM THE LAND OF THE DEAD...
...AND PLEDGED HIS SECOND LIFE TO THE STRAW HAT CAPTAIN!!
THEY CALL ME SOUL KING!!
WHEN'D YOU PULL THAT LITTLE TRICK OFF?! YOU'RE GONNA PAY FOR--
IF ANYONE IS GOING TO PAY...
?!

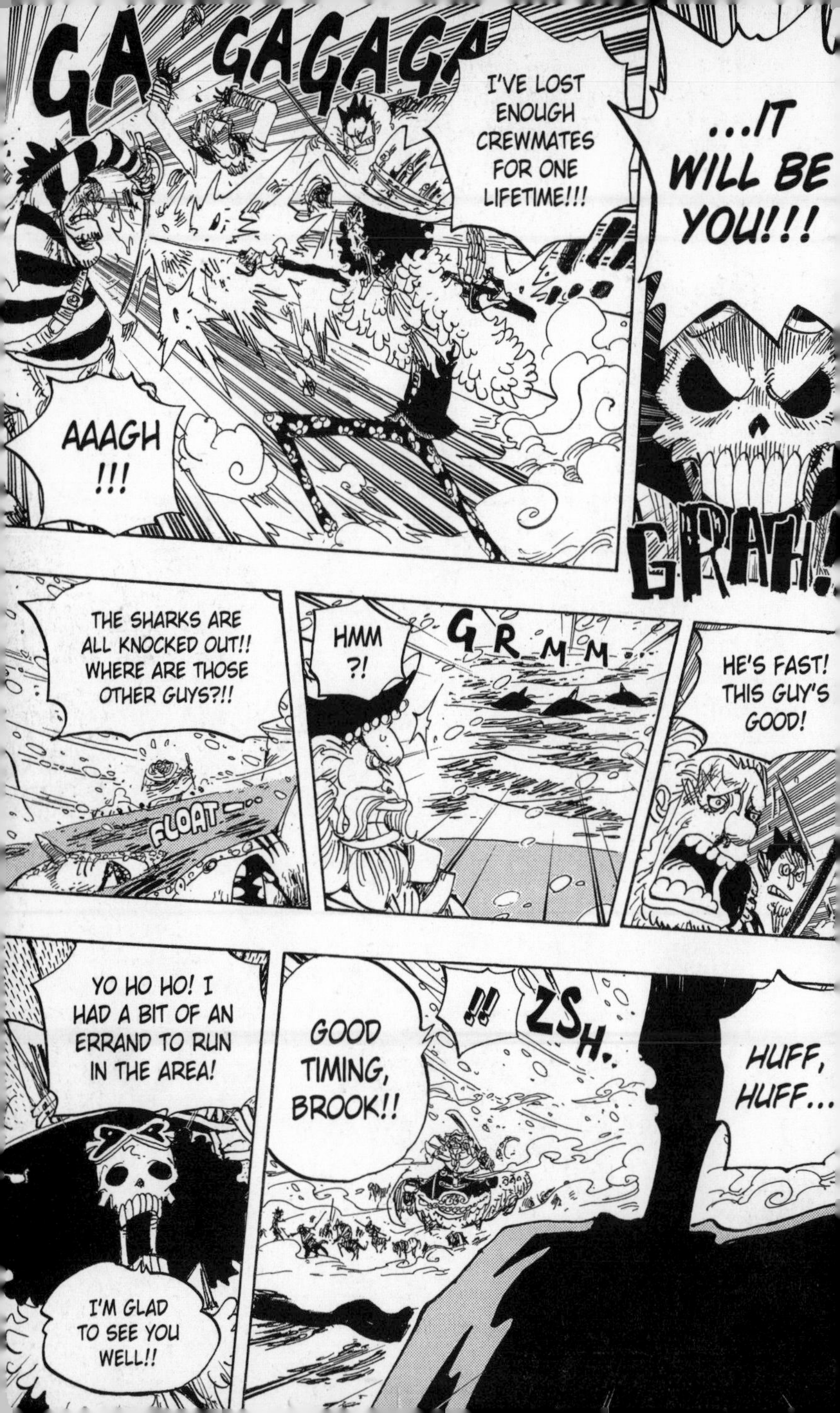
...IT WILL BE YOU!!!
GRAH!!
GA GAGAGA
I'VE LOST ENOUGH CREWMATES FOR ONE LIFETIME!!!
AAAGH !!!
HE'S FAST! THIS GUY'S GOOD!
HMM ?!
GRMMM
THE SHARKS ARE ALL KNOCKED OUT!! WHERE ARE THOSE OTHER GUYS?!!
FLOAT
HUFF, HUFF...
!!
ZSH
GOOD TIMING, BROOK!!
YO HO HO! I HAD A BIT OF AN ERRAND TO RUN IN THE AREA!
I'M GLAD TO SEE YOU WELL!!

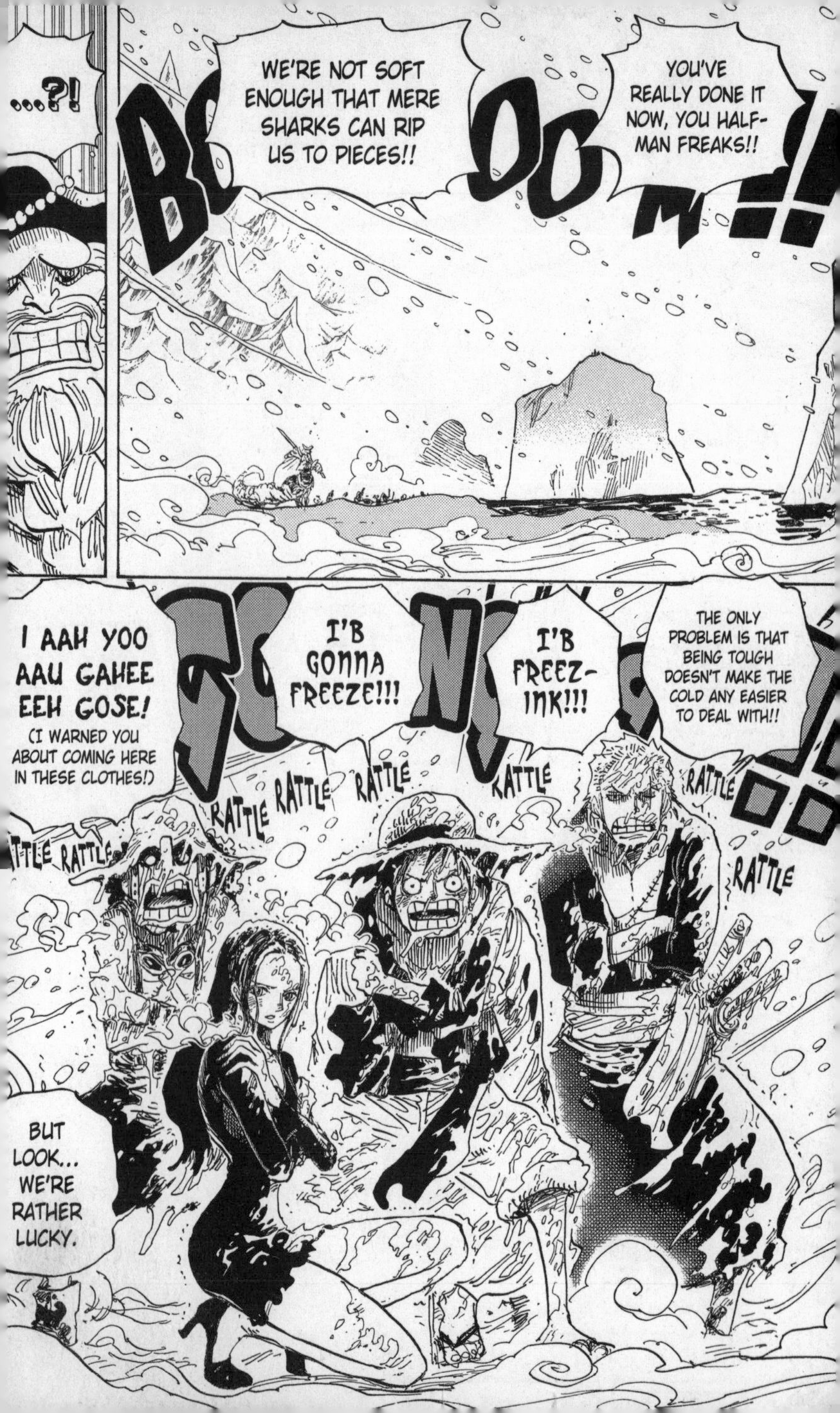
YOU'VE REALLY DONE IT NOW, YOU HALF-MAN FREAKS!!
WE'RE NOT SOFT ENOUGH THAT MERE SHARKS CAN RIP US TO PIECES!!
...?!
THE ONLY PROBLEM IS THAT BEING TOUGH DOESN'T MAKE THE COLD ANY EASIER TO DEAL WITH!!
RATTLE
RATTLE
I'B FREEZ-INK!!!
RATTLE
I'B GONNA FREEZE!!!
RATTLE
RATTLE
RATTLE
I AAH YOO AAU GAHEE EEH GOSE!
(I WARNED YOU ABOUT COMING HERE IN THESE CLOTHES!)
RATTLE
RATTLE
BUT LOOK... WE'RE RATHER LUCKY.

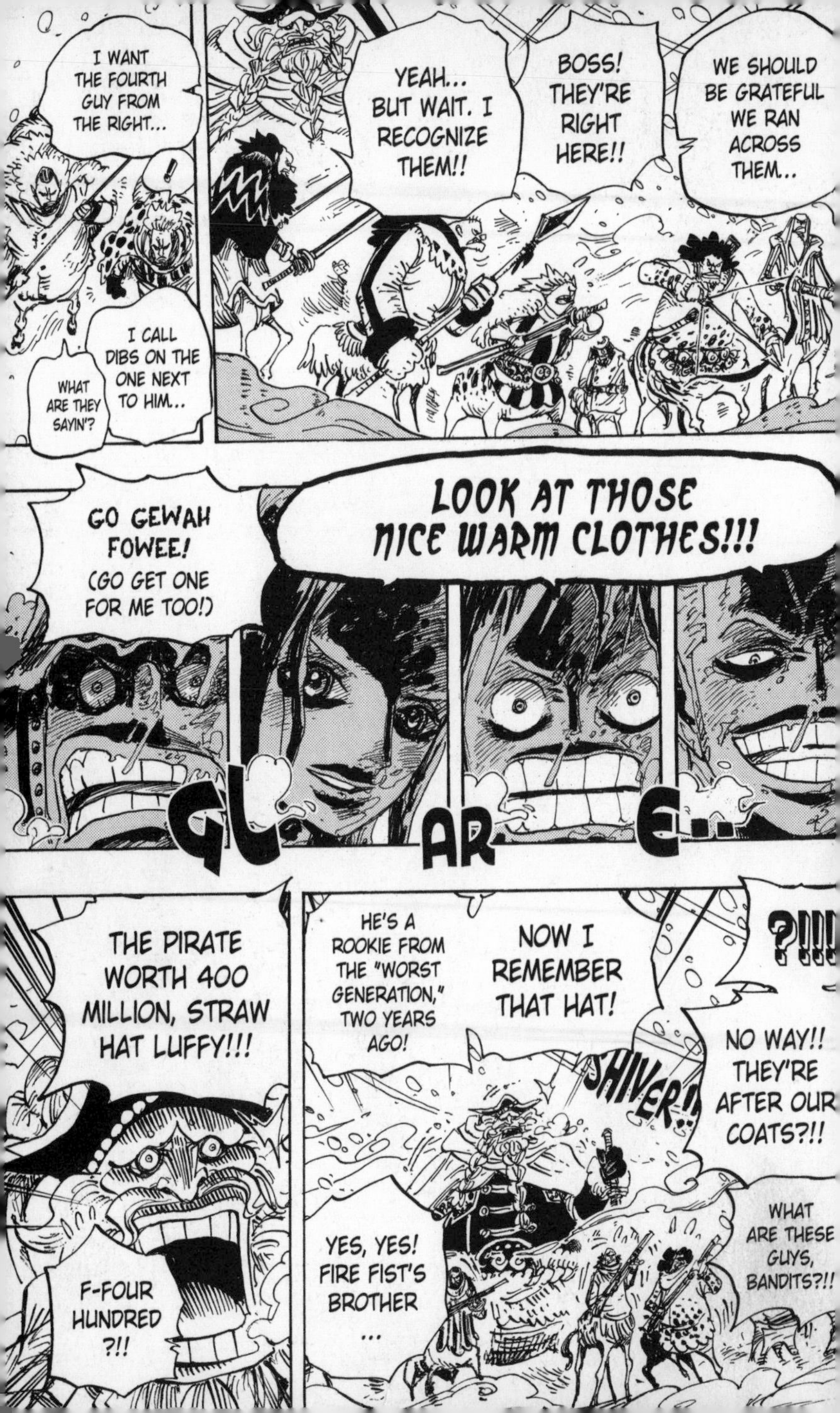
WE SHOULD BE GRATEFUL WE RAN ACROSS THEM...
BOSS! THEY'RE RIGHT HERE!!
YEAH... BUT WAIT. I RECOGNIZE THEM!!
I WANT THE FOURTH GUY FROM THE RIGHT...
!
I CALL DIBS ON THE ONE NEXT TO HIM...
WHAT ARE THEY SAYIN'?
LOOK AT THOSE NICE WARM CLOTHES!!!
GO GEWAH FOWEE! (GO GET ONE FOR ME TOO!)
GLARE...
?!!!
NO WAY!! THEY'RE AFTER OUR COATS?!!
NOW I REMEMBER THAT HAT!
HE'S A ROOKIE FROM THE "WORST GENERATION," TWO YEARS AGO!
SHIVER!!
WHAT ARE THESE GUYS, BANDITS?!!
YES, YES! FIRE FIST'S BROTHER ...
THE PIRATE WORTH 400 MILLION, STRAW HAT LUFFY!!!
F-FOUR HUNDRED ?!!

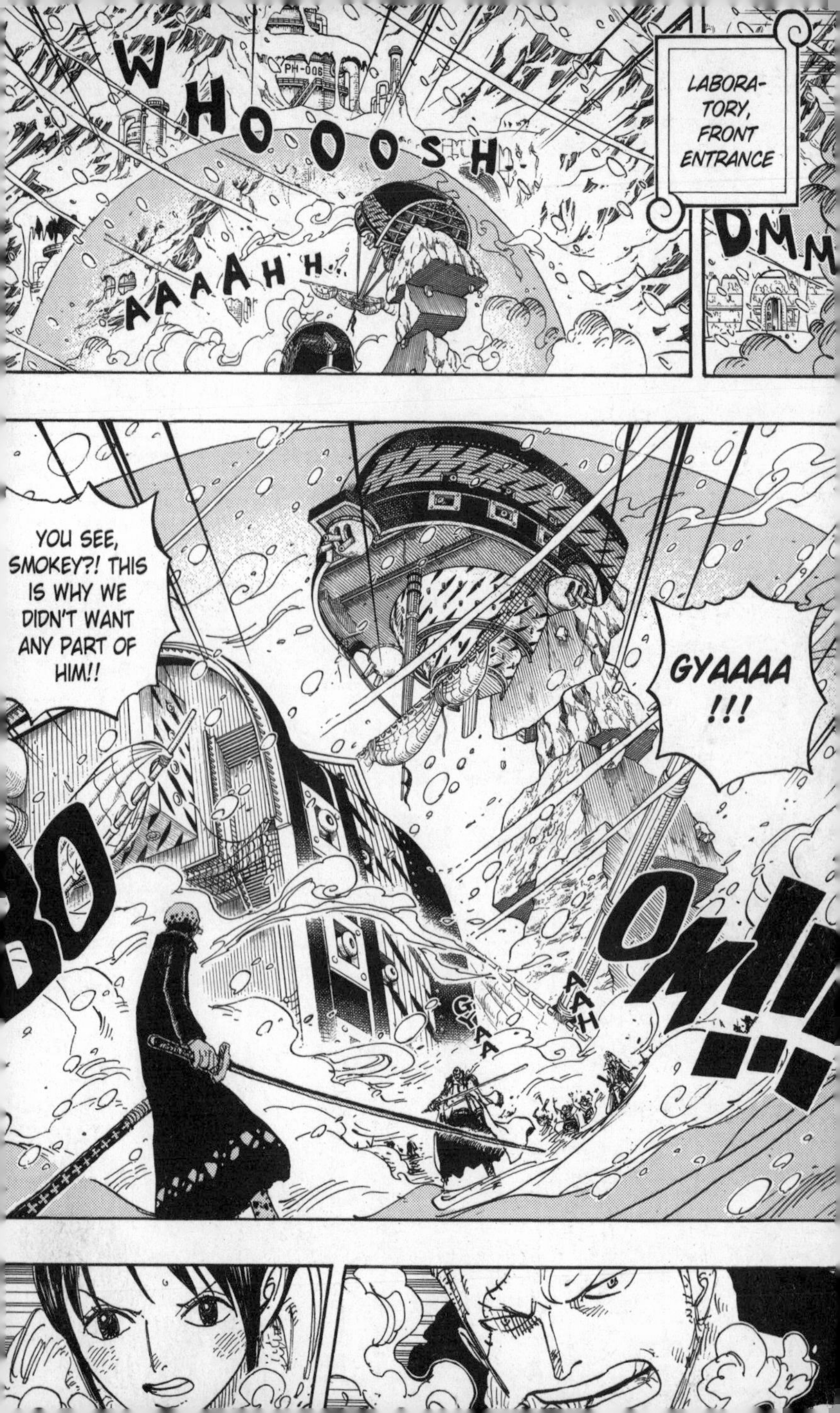

LABORA-TORY, FRONT ENTRANCE
DMM
WHOOOSH
PH-006
AAAAHH
GYAAAA!!!
YOU SEE, SMOKEY?! THIS IS WHY WE DIDN'T WANT ANY PART OF HIM!!
BOOM!!
AAH
GYAA

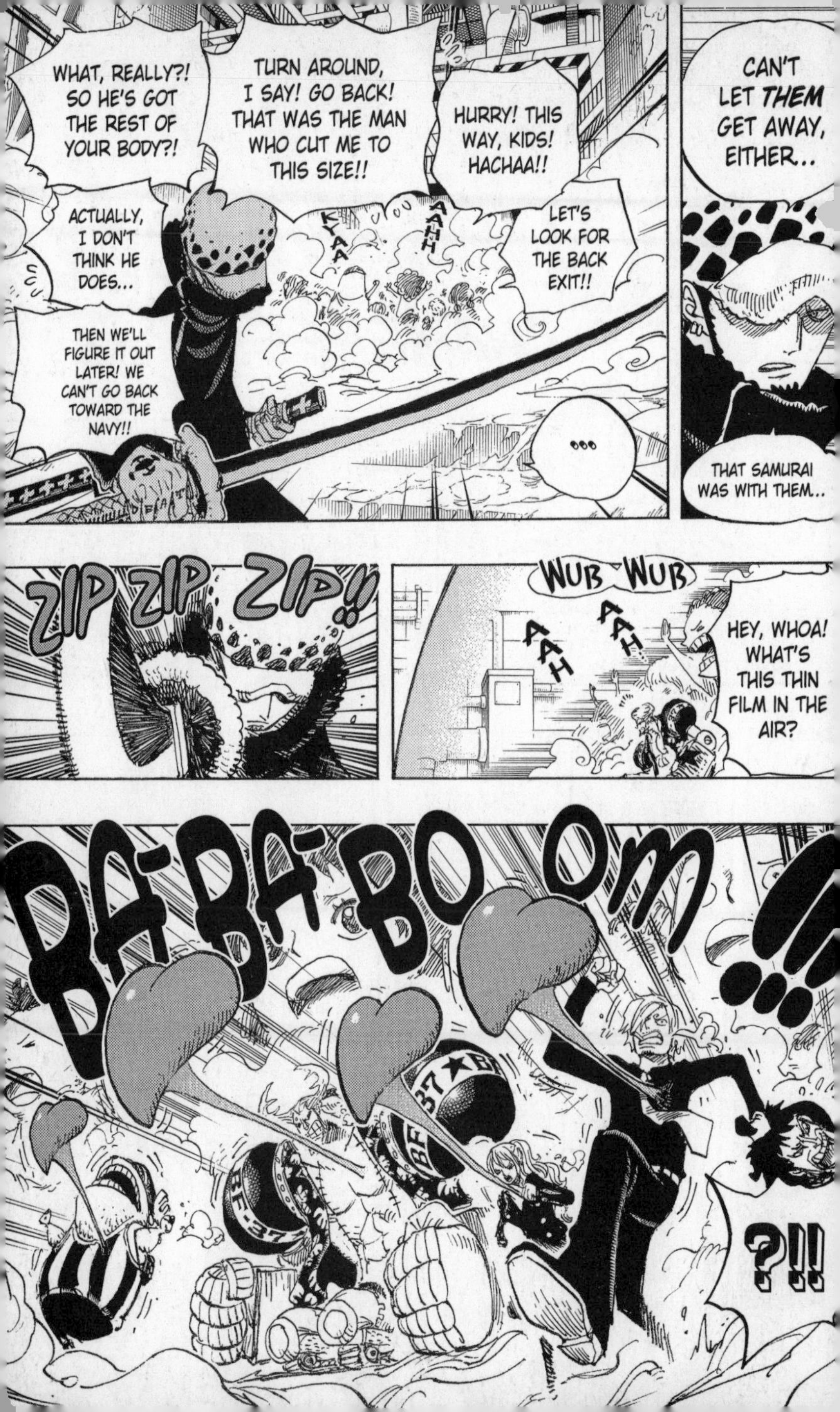
CAN'T LET *THEM* GET AWAY, EITHER...
THAT SAMURAI WAS WITH THEM..
HURRY! THIS WAY, KIDS! HACHAA!!
TURN AROUND, I SAY! GO BACK! THAT WAS THE MAN WHO CUT ME TO THIS SIZE!!
WHAT, REALLY?! SO HE'S GOT THE REST OF YOUR BODY?!
LET'S LOOK FOR THE BACK EXIT!!
AAHH
KYAA
ACTUALLY, I DON'T THINK HE DOES...
THEN WE'LL FIGURE IT OUT LATER! WE CAN'T GO BACK TOWARD THE NAVY!!
...
WUB WUB
HEY, WHOA! WHAT'S THIS THIN FILM IN THE AIR?
AAH
AAH
ZIP ZIP ZIP!!
BA-BA-BOOM...!!!
?!!

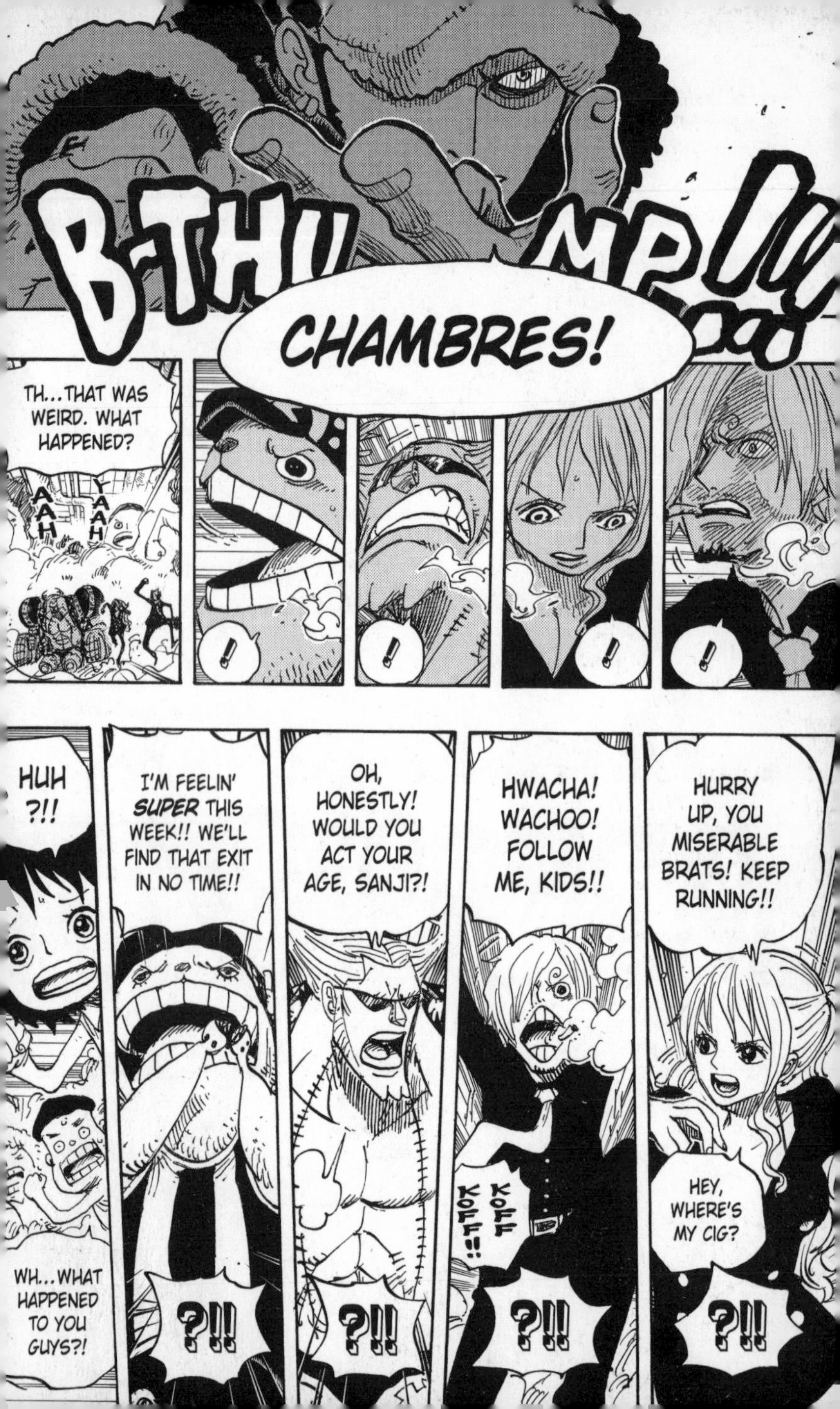
B-THUMP
CHAMBRES!
!
!
!
!
TH...THAT WAS WEIRD. WHAT HAPPENED?
YAAH
AAH
HURRY UP, YOU MISERABLE BRATS! KEEP RUNNING!!
HEY, WHERE'S MY CIG?
?!!
HWACHA! WACHOO! FOLLOW ME, KIDS!!
KOFF KOFF!!
?!!
OH, HONESTLY! WOULD YOU ACT YOUR AGE, SANJI?!
?!!
I'M FEELIN' **SUPER** THIS WEEK!! WE'LL FIND THAT EXIT IN NO TIME!!
?!!
HUH ?!!
WH...WHAT HAPPENED TO YOU GUYS?!

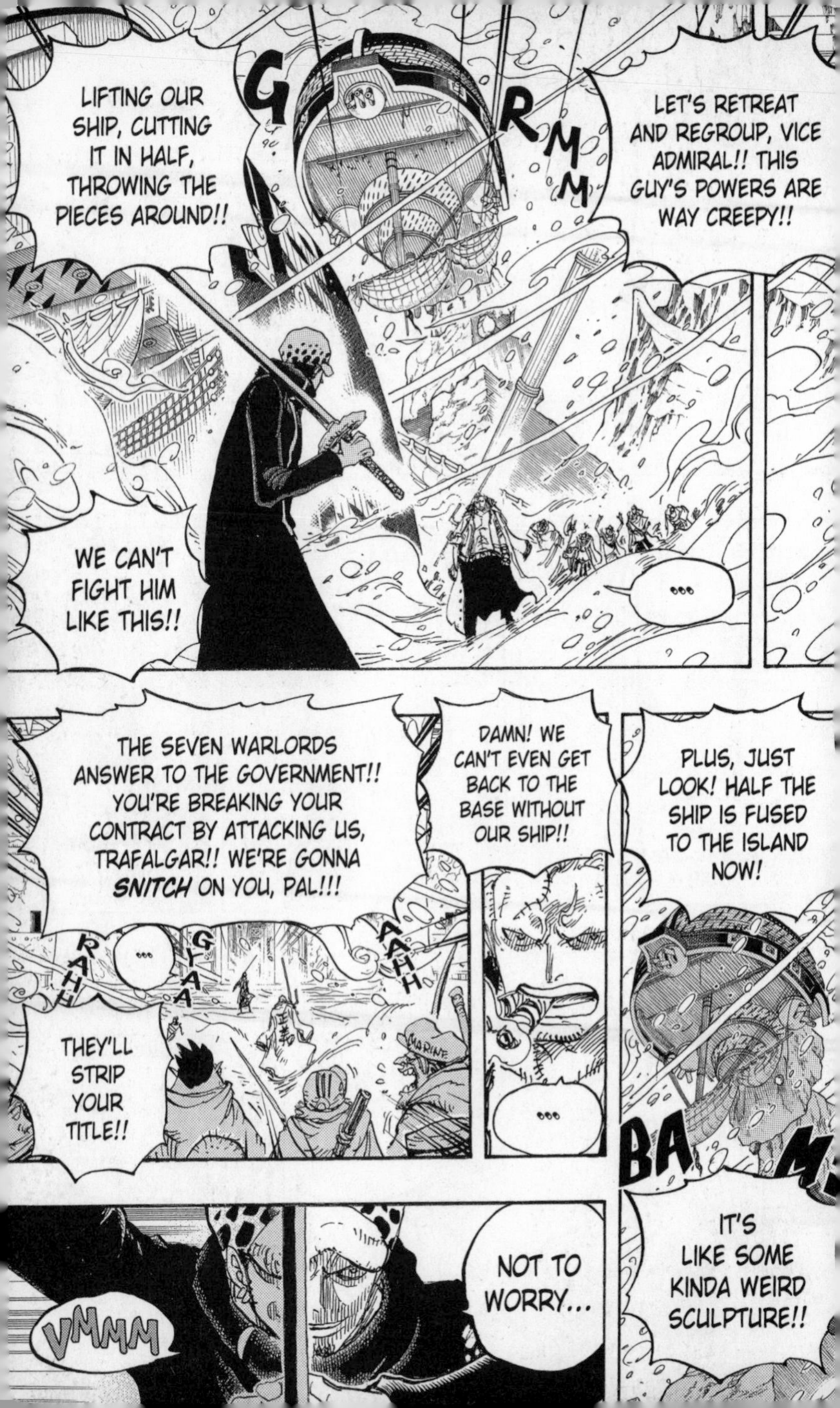
LET'S RETREAT AND REGROUP, VICE ADMIRAL!! THIS GUY'S POWERS ARE WAY CREEPY!!
GRMM
LIFTING OUR SHIP, CUTTING IT IN HALF, THROWING THE PIECES AROUND!!
...
WE CAN'T FIGHT HIM LIKE THIS!!
PLUS, JUST LOOK! HALF THE SHIP IS FUSED TO THE ISLAND NOW!
BAM
IT'S LIKE SOME KINDA WEIRD SCULPTURE!!
DAMN! WE CAN'T EVEN GET BACK TO THE BASE WITHOUT OUR SHIP!!
...
THE SEVEN WARLORDS ANSWER TO THE GOVERNMENT!! YOU'RE BREAKING YOUR CONTRACT BY ATTACKING US, TRAFALGAR!! WE'RE GONNA SNITCH ON YOU, PAL!!!
AAHH
GYAA
...
RAHH
THEY'LL STRIP YOUR TITLE!!
NOT TO WORRY...
VMMM

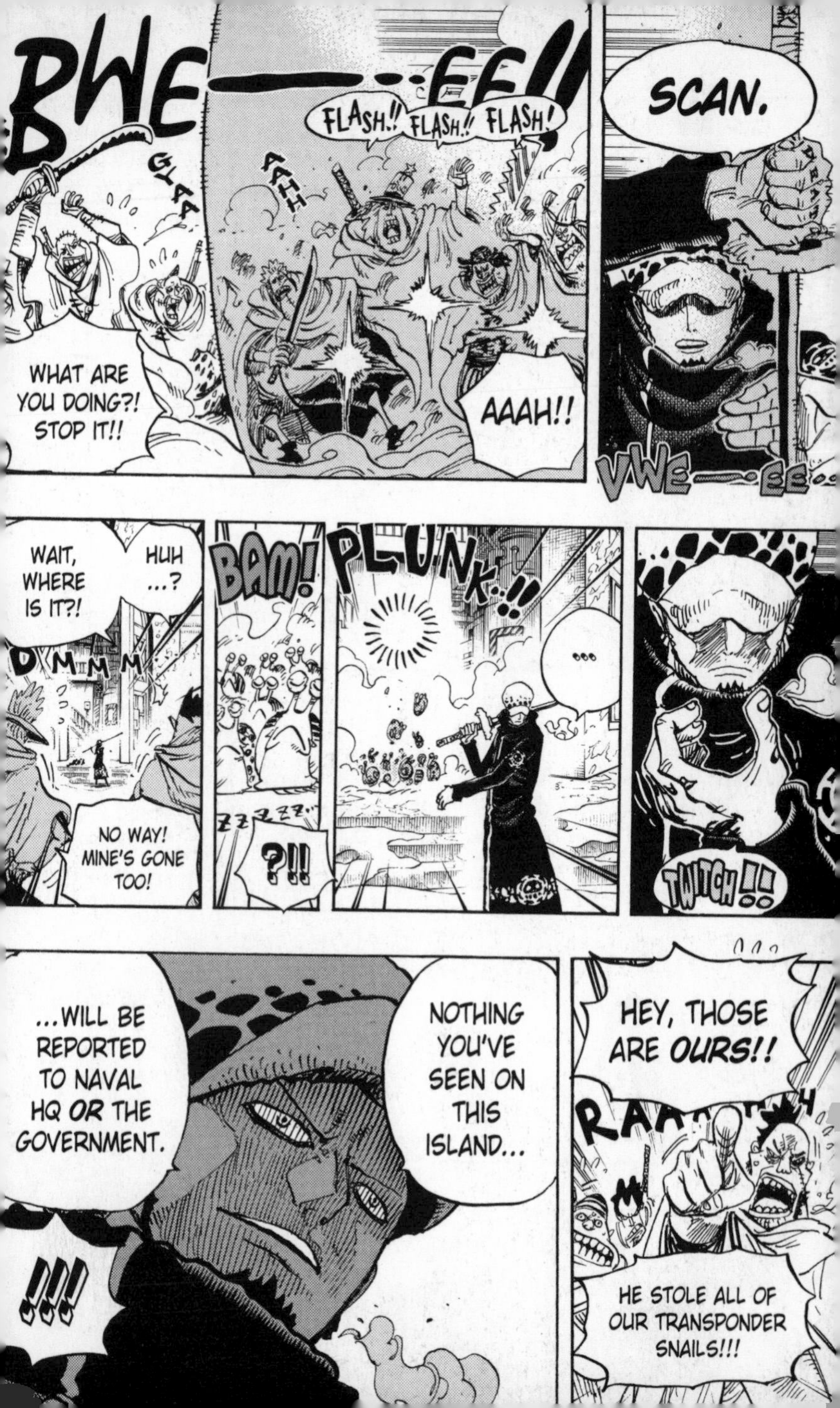
SCAN.
VWE——EE
BWE——EE!!
FLASH!!
FLASH!!
FLASH!
AAHH
AAAH!!
GYAA
WHAT ARE YOU DOING?! STOP IT!!
TWITCH!!
PLUNK!!
...
BAM!
ZZZZZ
?!!
HUH ...?
WAIT, WHERE IS IT?!
DMMM
NO WAY! MINE'S GONE TOO!
HEY, THOSE ARE *OURS*!!
HE STOLE ALL OF OUR TRANSPONDER SNAILS!!!
NOTHING YOU'VE SEEN ON THIS ISLAND...
...WILL BE REPORTED TO NAVAL HQ *OR* THE GOVERNMENT.
!!!

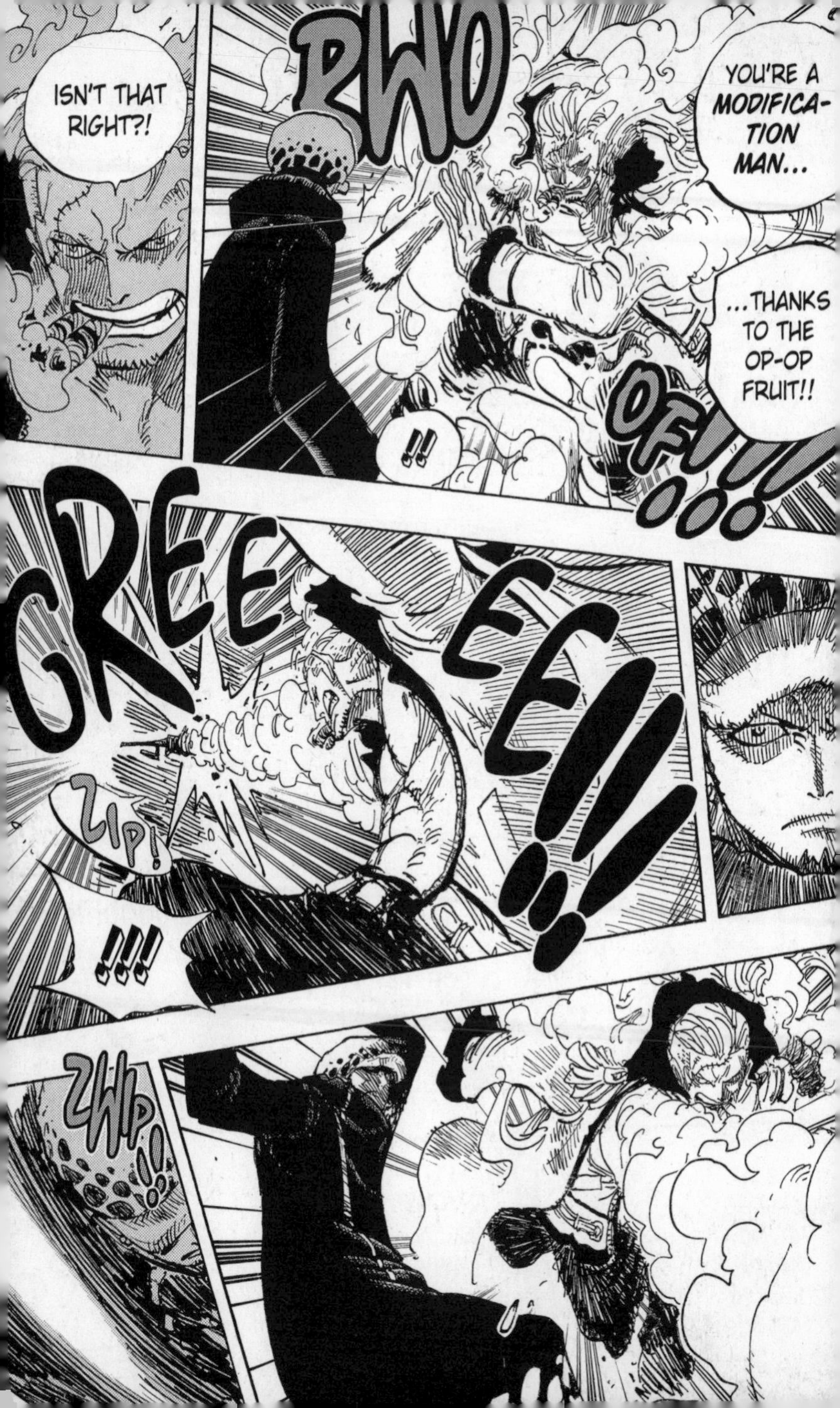

RWO
YOU'RE A MODIFICATION MAN...
...THANKS TO THE OP-OP FRUIT!!
!!
OF!!!
ISN'T THAT RIGHT?!
GREEEE!!!
ZIP!
!!!
ZWIP!!

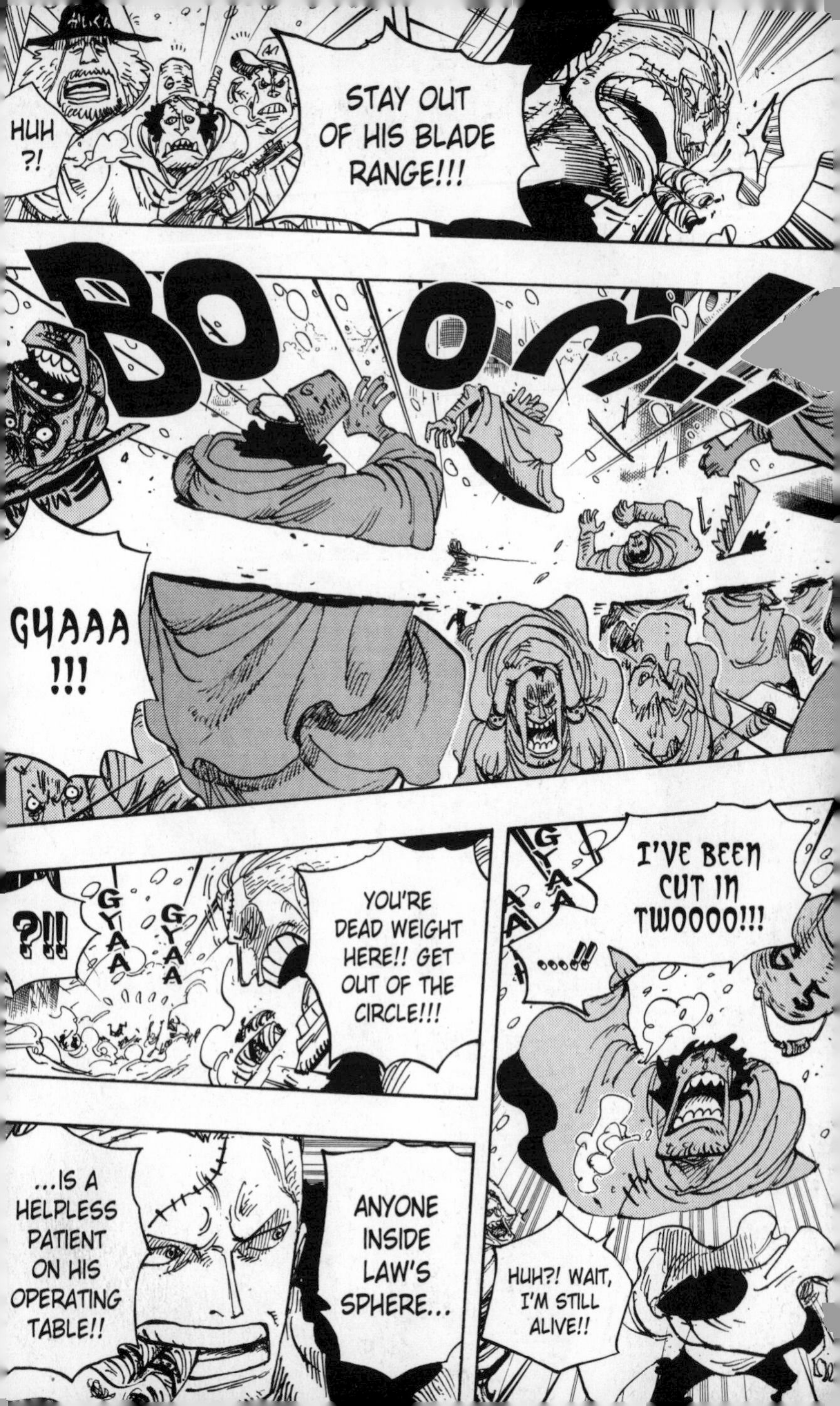
STAY OUT OF HIS BLADE RANGE!!!
HUH ?!
BOOM!!
GYAAA !!!
I'VE BEEN CUT IN TWOOOO!!!
GYAAAA
....!!
HUH?! WAIT, I'M STILL ALIVE!!
YOU'RE DEAD WEIGHT HERE!! GET OUT OF THE CIRCLE!!!
GYAA
GYAA
?!!
ANYONE INSIDE LAW'S SPHERE...
...IS A HELPLESS PATIENT ON HIS OPERATING TABLE!!

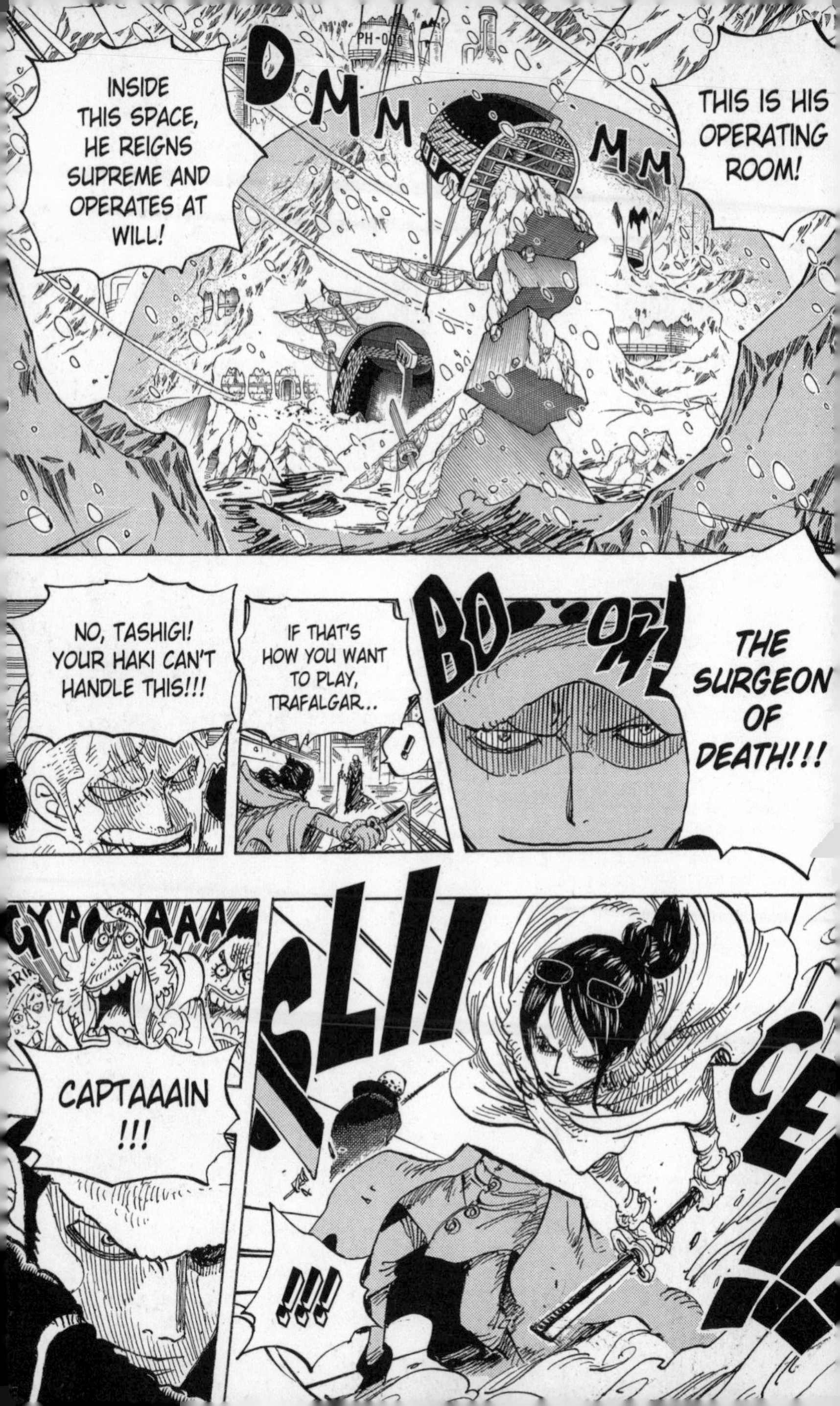
THIS IS HIS OPERATING ROOM!
DMMMM
INSIDE THIS SPACE, HE REIGNS SUPREME AND OPERATES AT WILL!
THE SURGEON OF DEATH!!!
IF THAT'S HOW YOU WANT TO PLAY, TRAFALGAR..
!
NO, TASHIGI! YOUR HAKI CAN'T HANDLE THIS!!!
!!!
CAPTAAAIN !!!

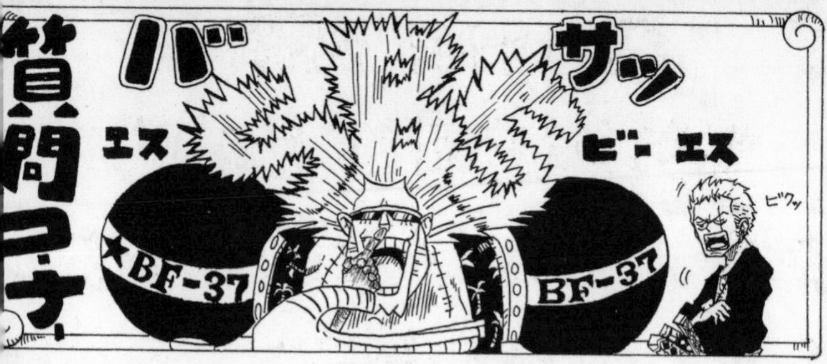
バ
サッ
エス
ビー エス
BF-37
BF-37
ビクッ
(Michi Nakahara, Tottori)

Q: Mr. Oda, have you ever wiped your butt with sandpaper?

--Sara Mama

A: No!!!

Q: Hello, Mr. Oda! ★ In Chapter 655 from Volume 66, the scene where they're eating the deep sea fish lunches, Robin says it's tasty, and Luffy and Usopp are munching away, but Zolo's going "crunch crunch." Did Sanji make good on his threat to slip razor blades into Zolo's lunch?

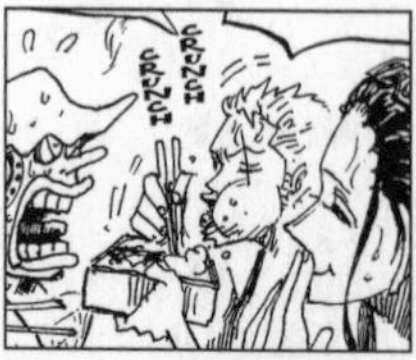
CRUNCH
CRUNCH

--Gillette

A: Mmm! WOW!! Thanks for reading into it! Of course, I wasn't really expecting that anyone would pick up on it, but you can see the beginnings in this scene in Chapter 653(⬇). Normally, you wouldn't draw someone eating their lunch with the sound effects "crunch crunch," but in my mind, Zolo's lunch was full of razor blades and poison, so the effect came out that way. The funny part about their fights are how seriously they take it.

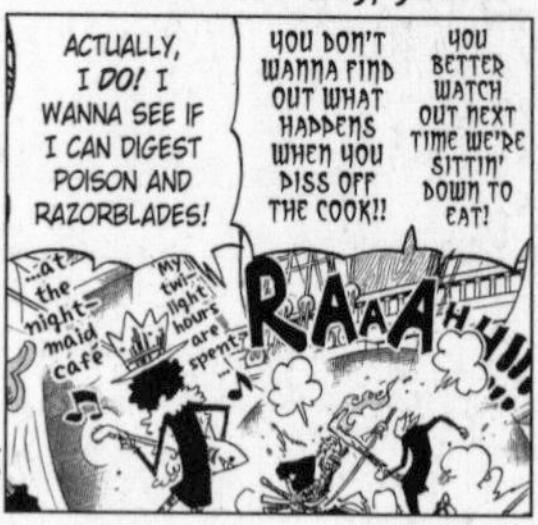
YOU BETTER WATCH OUT NEXT TIME WE'RE SITTIN' DOWN TO EAT!
YOU DON'T WANNA FIND OUT WHAT HAPPENS WHEN YOU PISS OFF THE COOK!!
ACTUALLY, I DO! I WANNA SEE IF I CAN DIGEST POISON AND RAZORBLADES!
RAAAH!!!
My twilight hours are spent...
...at the night-maid cafe

Q: Everyone remembers Wanze from the Water Seven arc. At some point, my little sister starting copying his mannerisms. When she says, "Ra... Ramen Kung Fuuuu?!" and shakes her hands around her face, it's incredibly annoying. She says she has a bad case of "Wanze-itis." How do you cure Wanze-itis, anyway?

--Midori

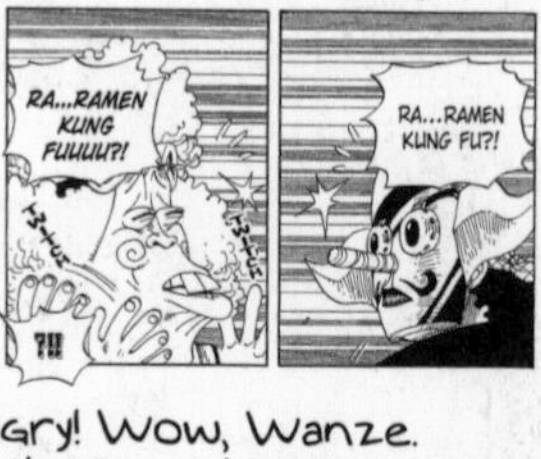
RA...RAMEN KUNG FU?!
RA...RAMEN KUNG FUUUU?!
TWITCH
TWITCH
?!!

A: "Boo hoo hoo (twitch twitch), how do you cure Wanze-itis, boo hoo (twitch twitch)" Ow! Ow, ow!! That hurts! Stop hitting me! Geez, you sure got angry! Wow, Wanze. What a character, huh? Don't cure it, let's all get Wanze-itis together! Wave your hands in front of your cheeks, stick out your lips, make a dumb face, and repeat what the other person says! It's the easiest way ever to get punched in the face!

Chapter 662:
WARLORD LAW VS. VICE ADMIRAL SMOKER

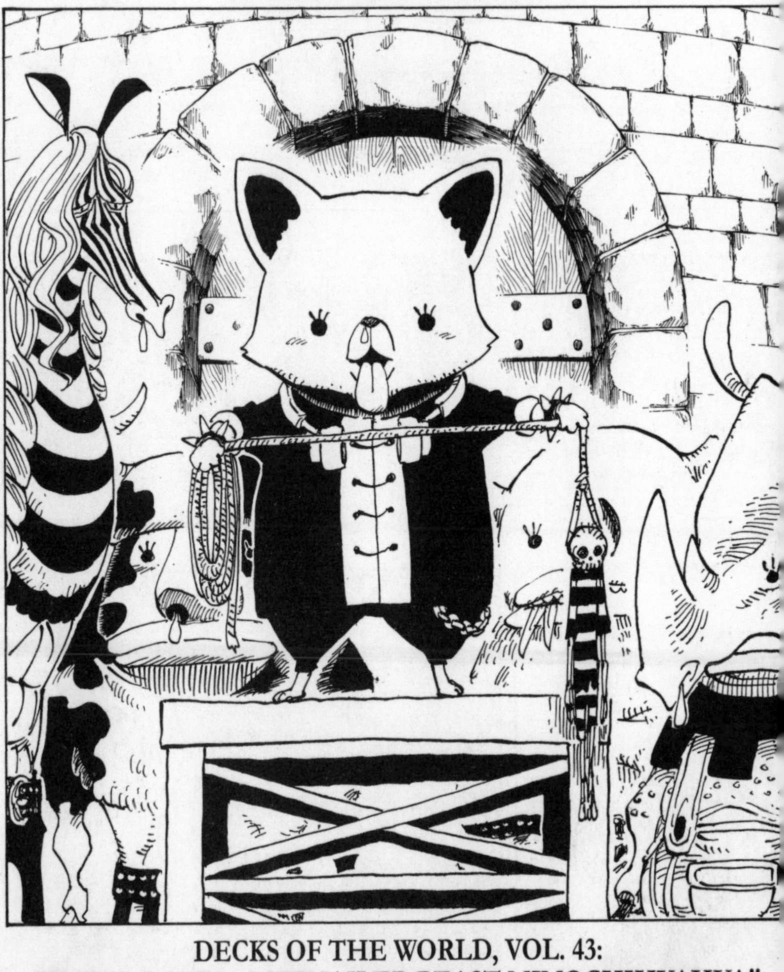

DECKS OF THE WORLD, VOL. 43:
"IMPEL DOWN—NEW JAILER BEAST MINOCHIHUAHUA"

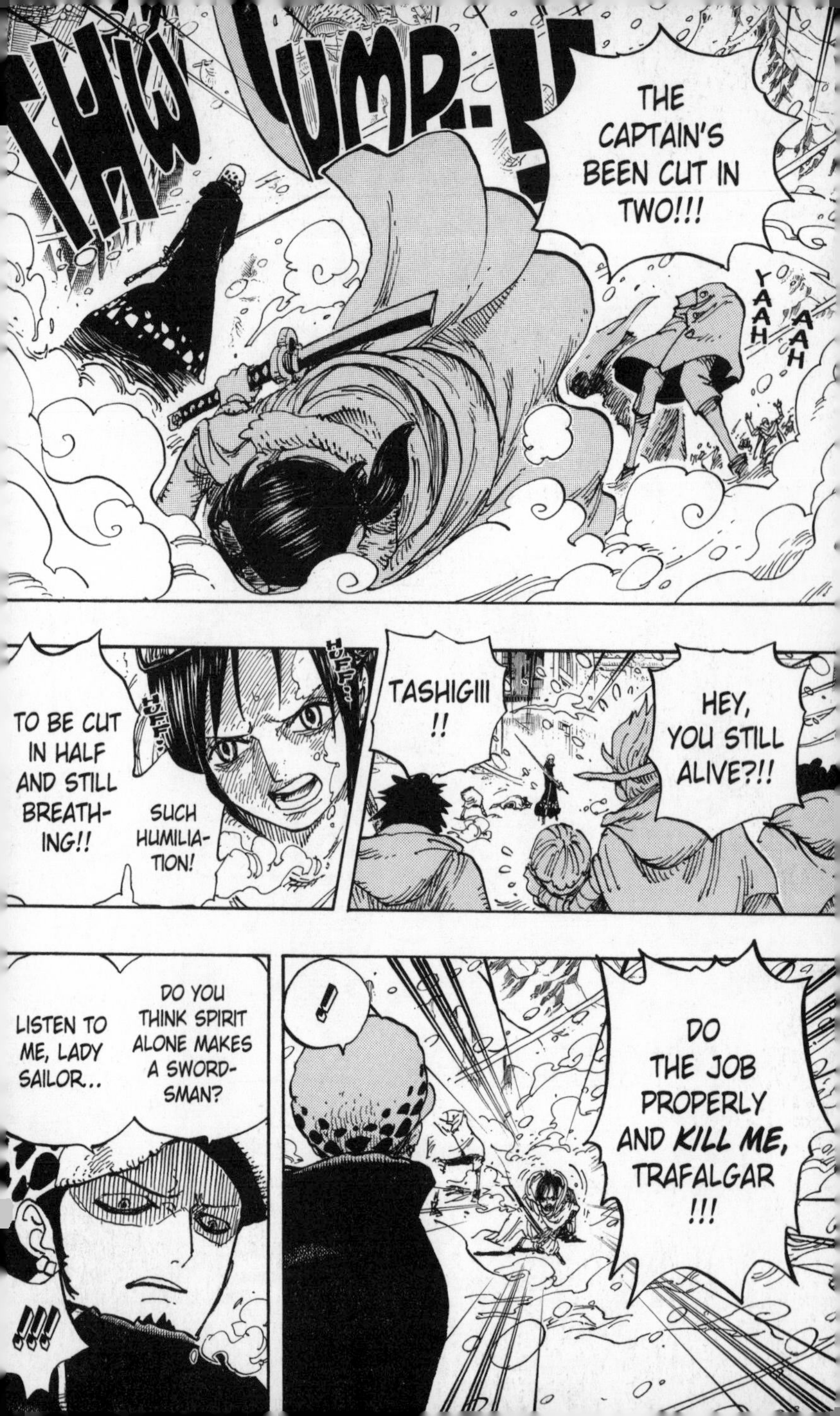
THWUMP..!!
THE CAPTAIN'S BEEN CUT IN TWO!!!
YAAH AAH
HEY, YOU STILL ALIVE?!!
TASHIGIII !!
HUFF...
HUFF...
SUCH HUMILIATION!
TO BE CUT IN HALF AND STILL BREATHING!!
!
DO THE JOB PROPERLY AND KILL ME, TRAFALGAR !!!
DO YOU THINK SPIRIT ALONE MAKES A SWORDSMAN?
LISTEN TO ME, LADY SAILOR...
!!!

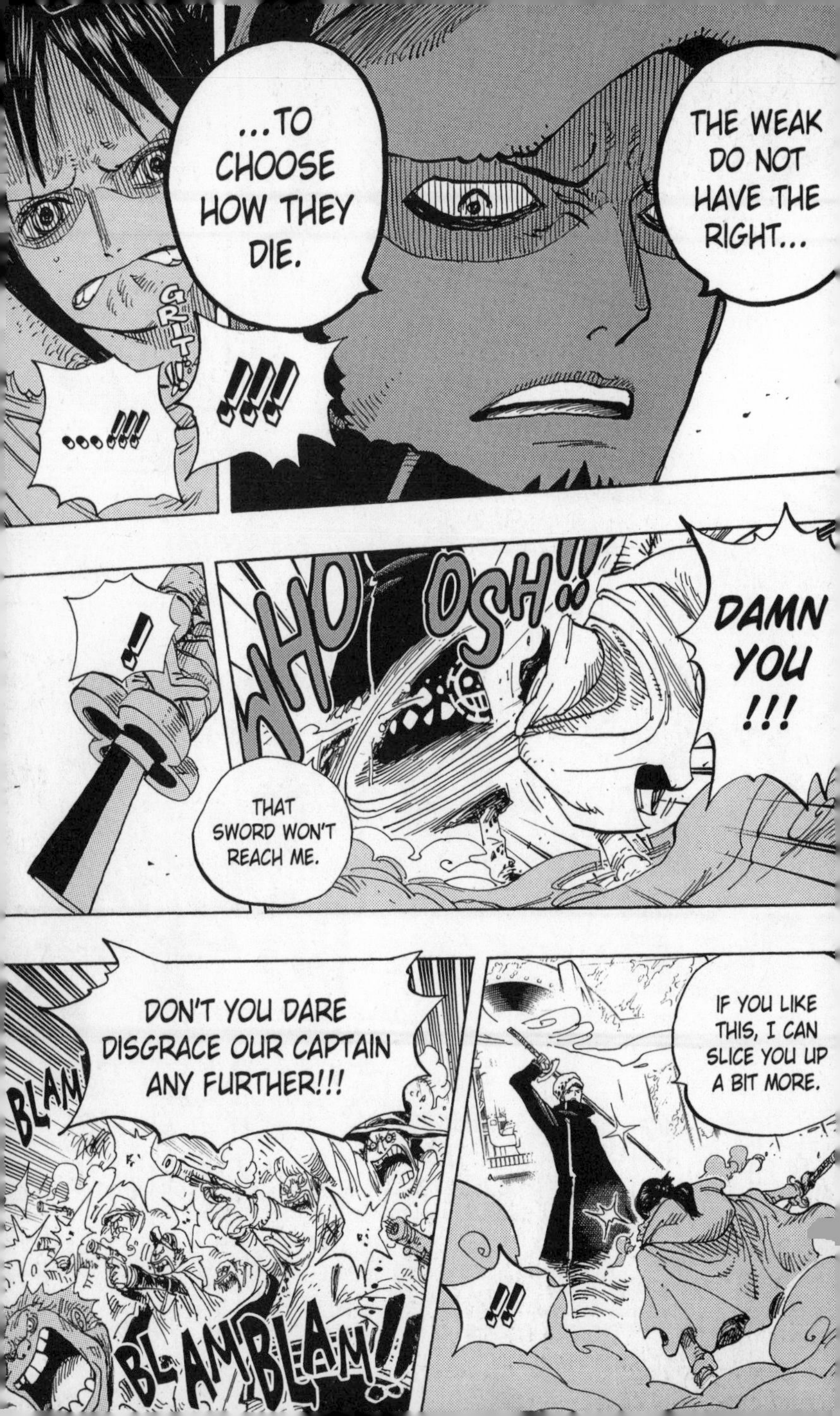
THE WEAK DO NOT HAVE THE RIGHT...
...TO CHOOSE HOW THEY DIE.
GRIT!!
!!!
...!!!
DAMN YOU !!!
WHOOSH!!
THAT SWORD WON'T REACH ME.
!
IF YOU LIKE THIS, I CAN SLICE YOU UP A BIT MORE.
!!
DON'T YOU DARE DISGRACE OUR CAPTAIN ANY FURTHER!!!
BLAM
BLAMBLAM!!

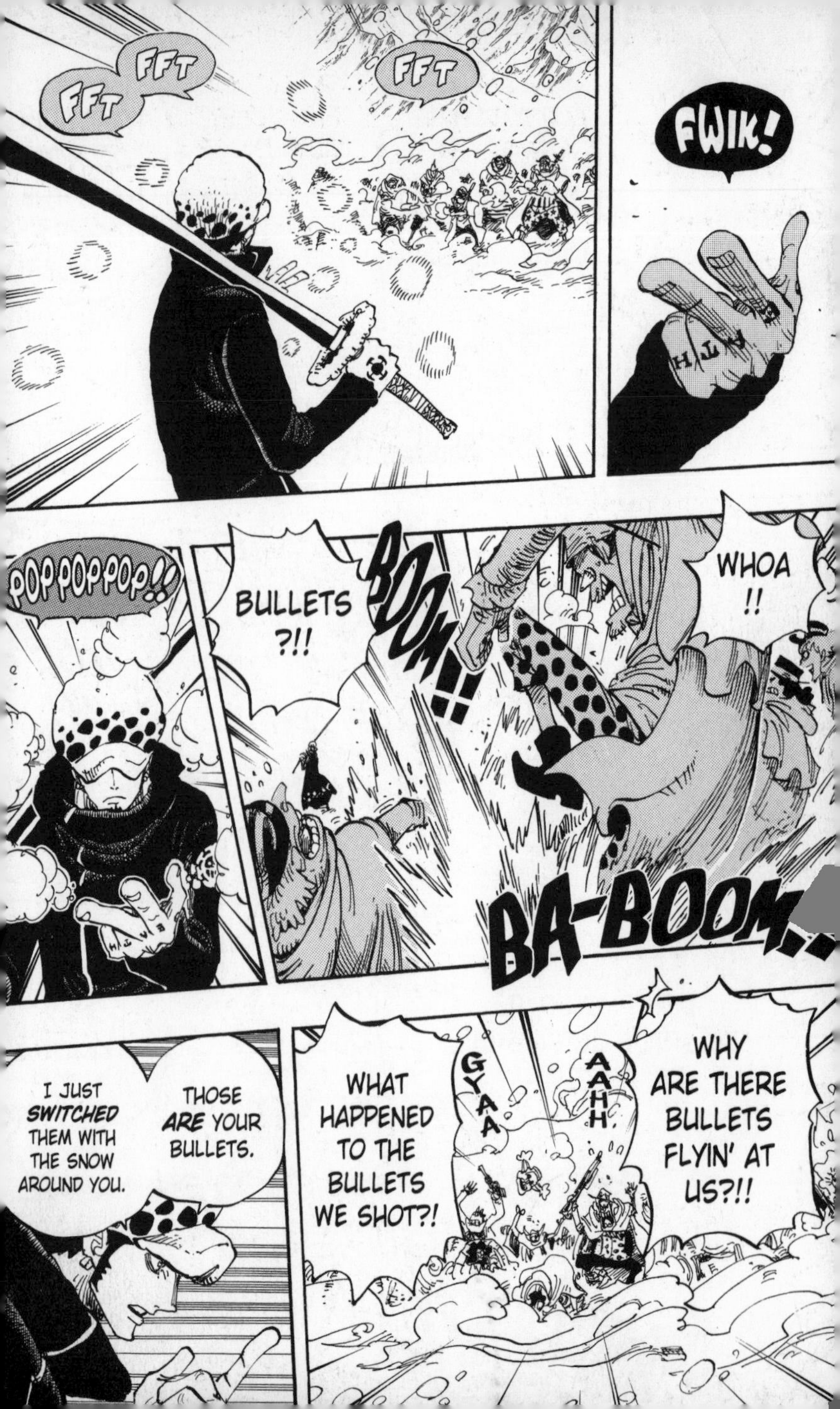
FWIK!
FFT
FFT
FFT
WHOA !!
BA-BOOM!!
BOOM!!
BULLETS ?!!
POPPOPPOP!!
WHY ARE THERE BULLETS FLYIN' AT US?!!
AAHH
GYAA
WHAT HAPPENED TO THE BULLETS WE SHOT?!
THOSE *ARE* YOUR BULLETS.
I JUST *SWITCHED* THEM WITH THE SNOW AROUND YOU.

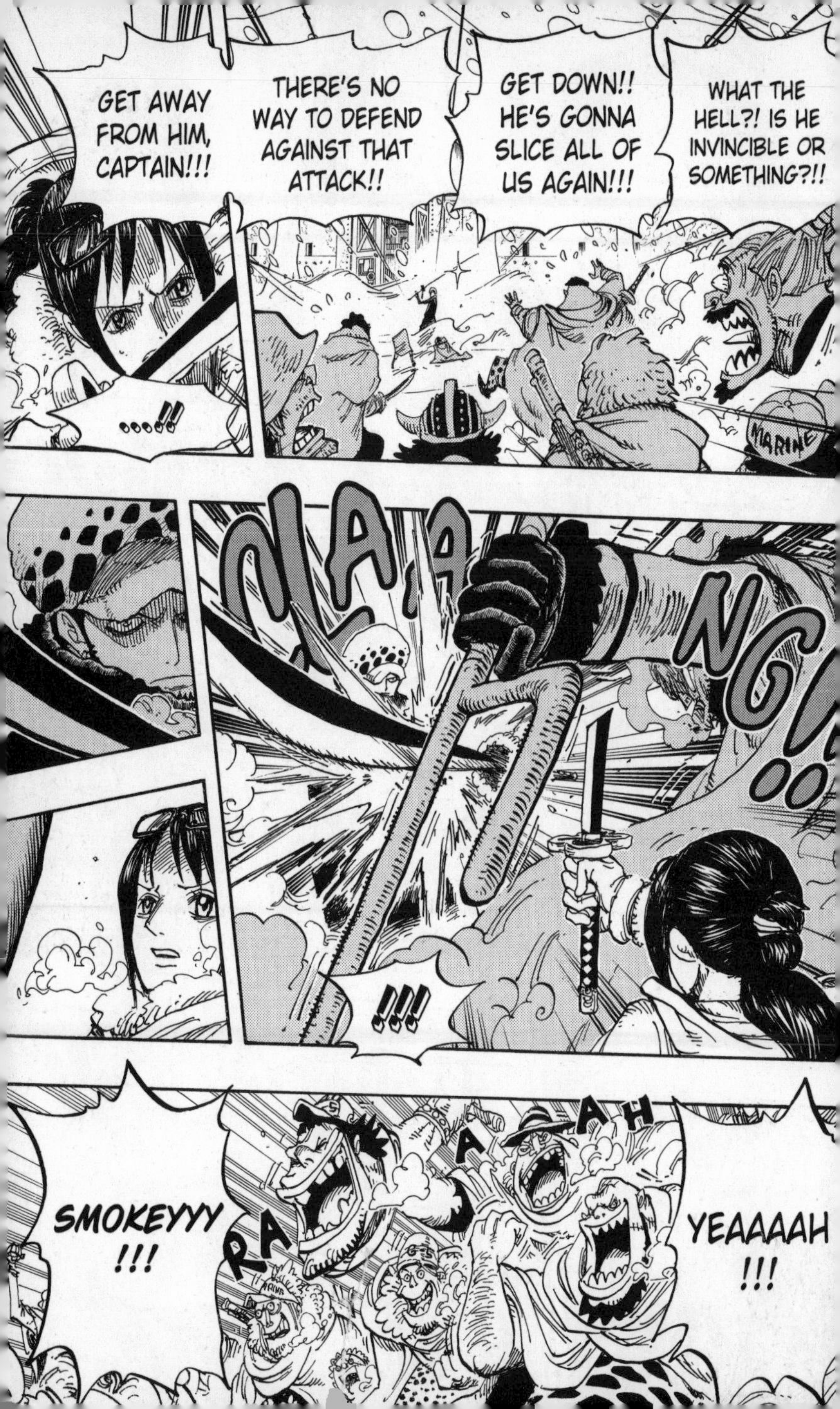
WHAT THE HELL?! IS HE INVINCIBLE OR SOMETHING?!!
GET DOWN!! HE'S GONNA SLICE ALL OF US AGAIN!!!
THERE'S NO WAY TO DEFEND AGAINST THAT ATTACK!!
MARINE
GET AWAY FROM HIM, CAPTAIN!!!
....!!
GAAANG!!
!!!
YEAAAAH!!!
RAAAH
SMOKEYYY!!!

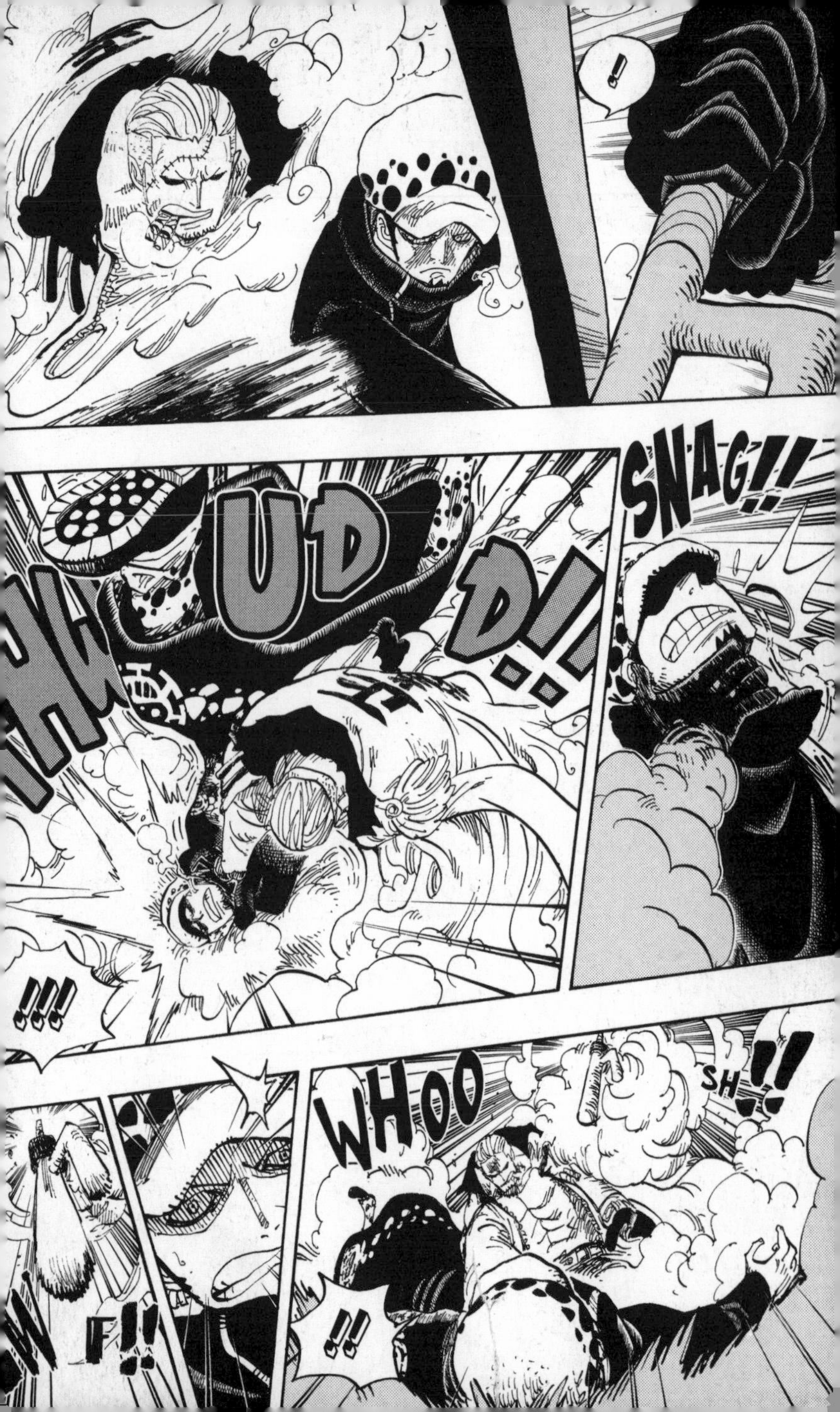
!
SNAG!!
THUDD!!
!!!
WHOOSH!!
!!
WH
F!!

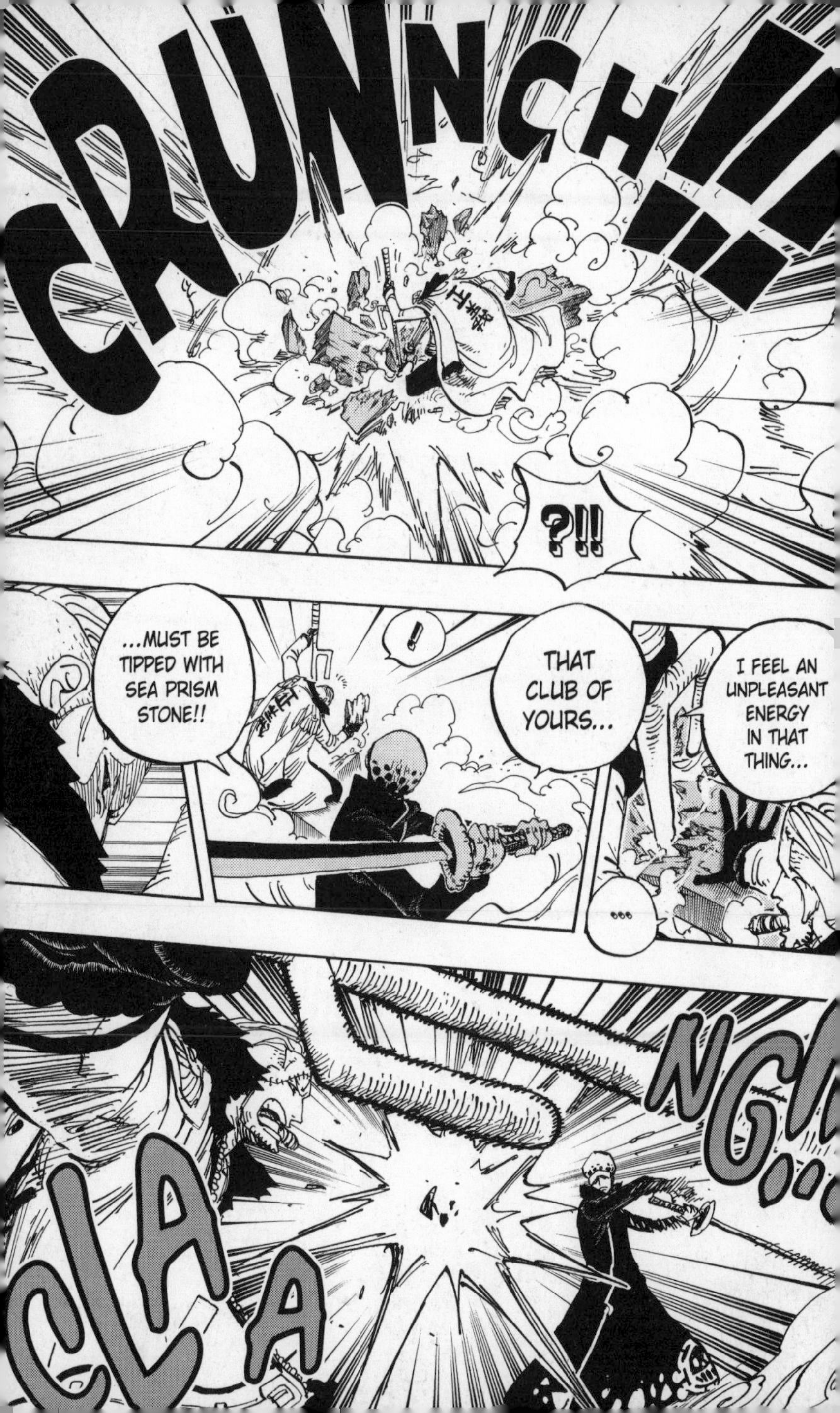
CRUNNCH!!!
?!!
I FEEL AN UNPLEASANT ENERGY IN THAT THING...
...
THAT CLUB OF YOURS...
!
...MUST BE TIPPED WITH SEA PRISM STONE!!
NG...
CLA A

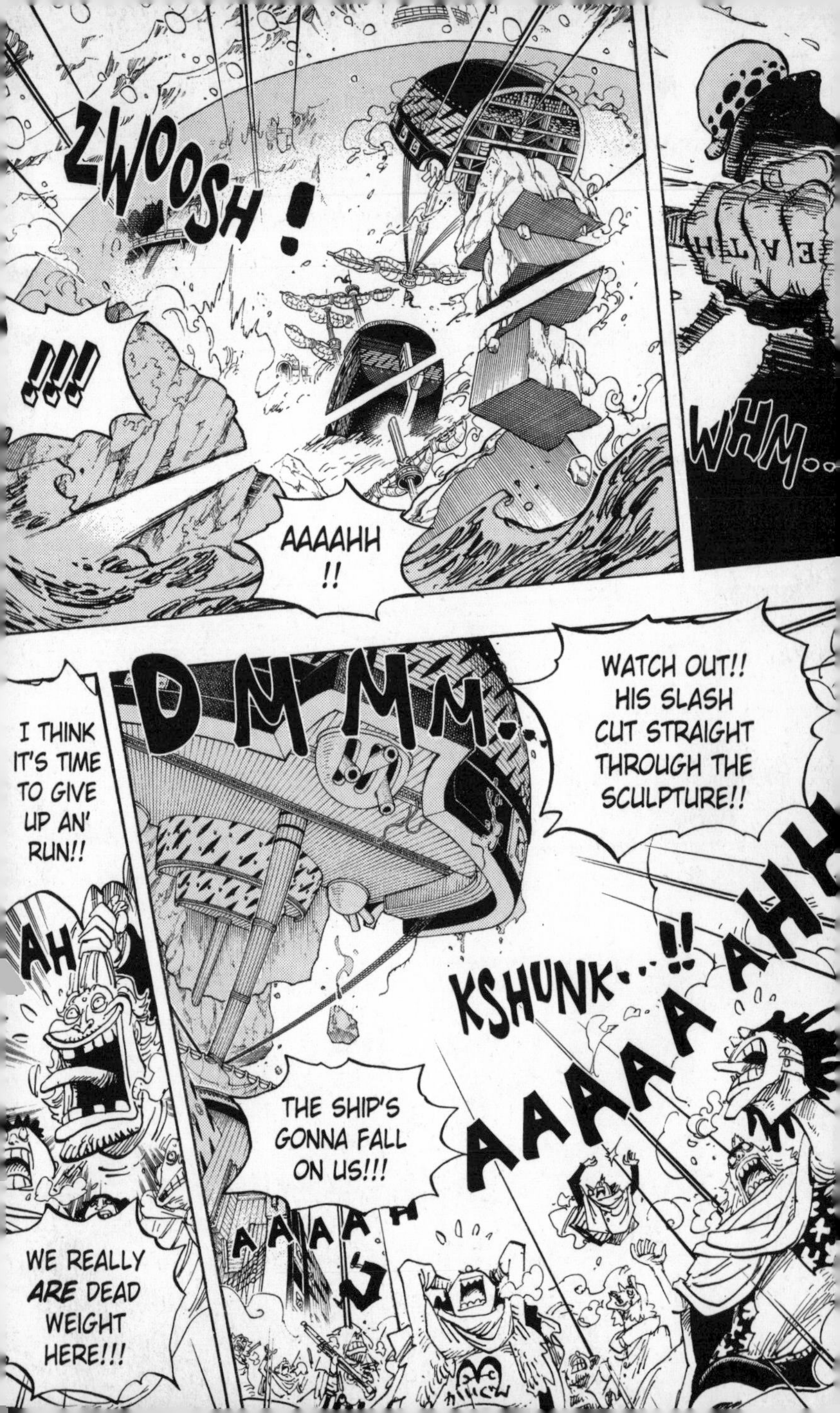
WHM...
ZWOOSH!
!!!
AAAAHH!!
WATCH OUT!! HIS SLASH CUT STRAIGHT THROUGH THE SCULPTURE!!
KSHUNK...!!
AAAAAAHH
THE SHIP'S GONNA FALL ON US!!!
DMMM..
I THINK IT'S TIME TO GIVE UP AN' RUN!!
AH
AAAAH
WE REALLY *ARE* DEAD WEIGHT HERE!!!

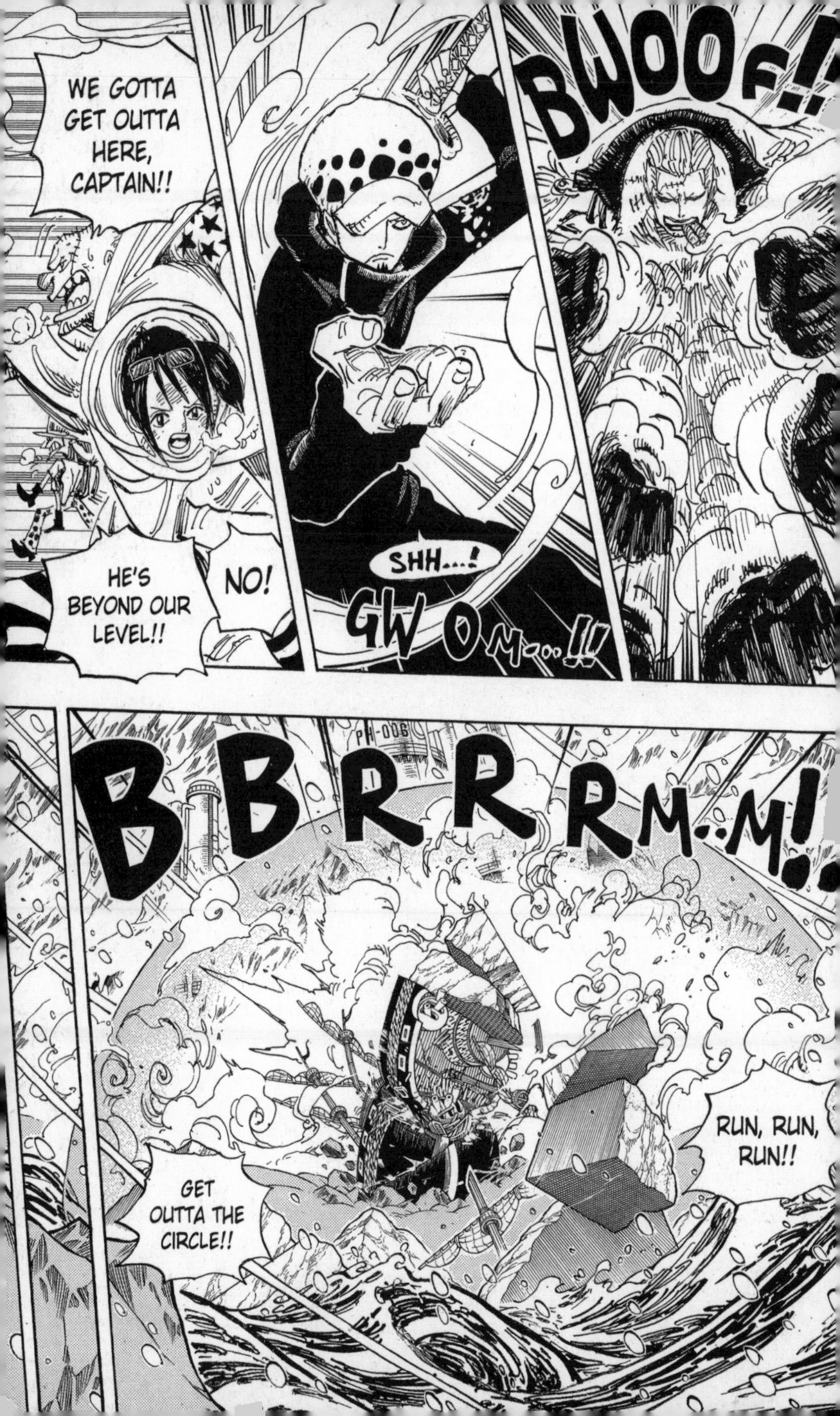
BWOOF!!
SHH...!
GWOM...!!
WE GOTTA GET OUTTA HERE, CAPTAIN!!
NO!
HE'S BEYOND OUR LEVEL!!
PH-006
BBRRRM..M!!
RUN, RUN, RUN!!
GET OUTTA THE CIRCLE!!

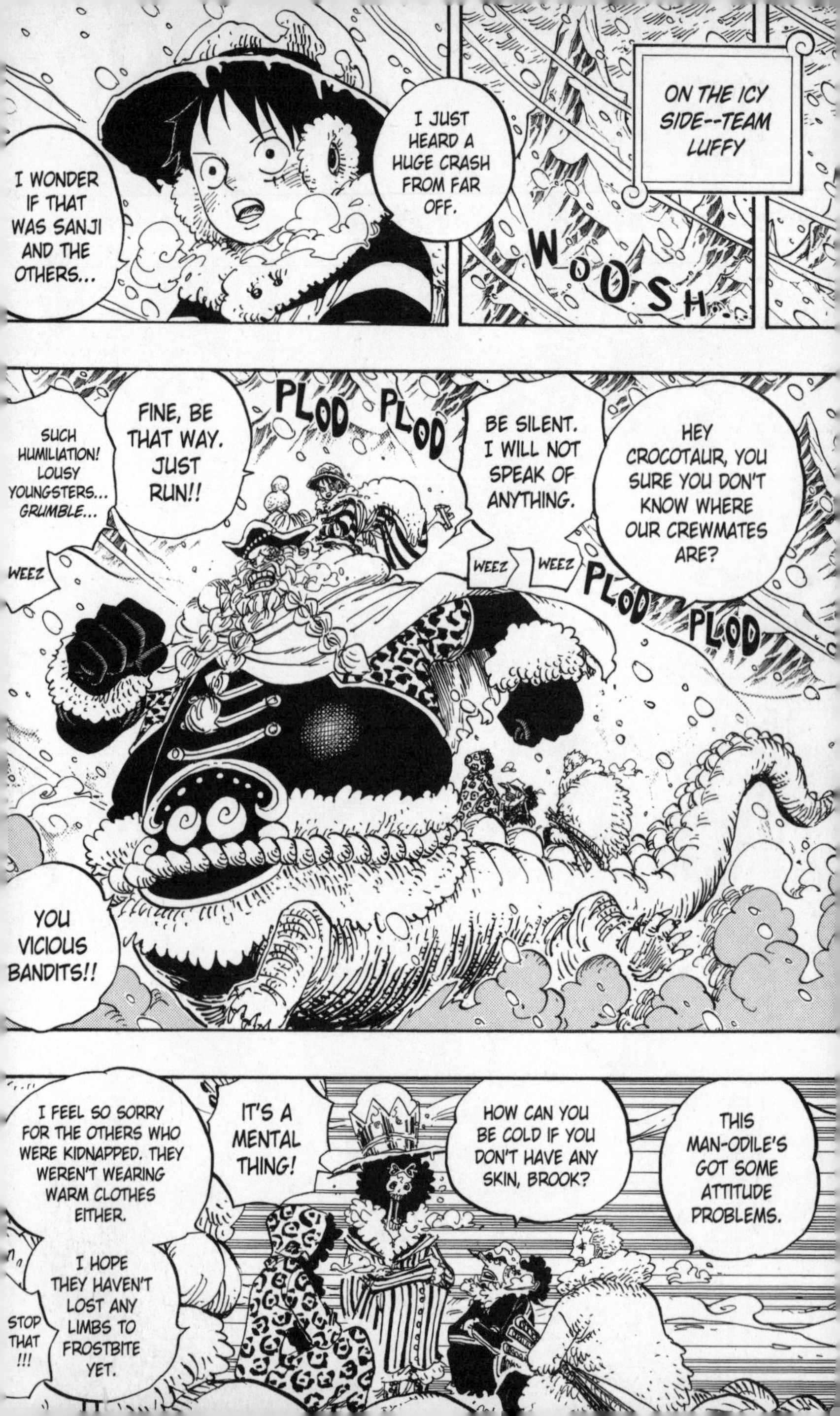
ON THE ICY SIDE--TEAM LUFFY
WOOSH
I JUST HEARD A HUGE CRASH FROM FAR OFF.
I WONDER IF THAT WAS SANJI AND THE OTHERS...
HEY CROCOTAUR, YOU SURE YOU DON'T KNOW WHERE OUR CREWMATES ARE?
PLOD PLOD
BE SILENT. I WILL NOT SPEAK OF ANYTHING.
WEEZ WEEZ
PLOD PLOD
FINE, BE THAT WAY. JUST RUN!!
SUCH HUMILIATION! LOUSY YOUNGSTERS... GRUMBLE...
WEEZ
YOU VICIOUS BANDITS!!
THIS MAN-ODILE'S GOT SOME ATTITUDE PROBLEMS.
HOW CAN YOU BE COLD IF YOU DON'T HAVE ANY SKIN, BROOK?
IT'S A MENTAL THING!
I FEEL SO SORRY FOR THE OTHERS WHO WERE KIDNAPPED. THEY WEREN'T WEARING WARM CLOTHES EITHER.
I HOPE THEY HAVEN'T LOST ANY LIMBS TO FROSTBITE YET.
STOP THAT!!!

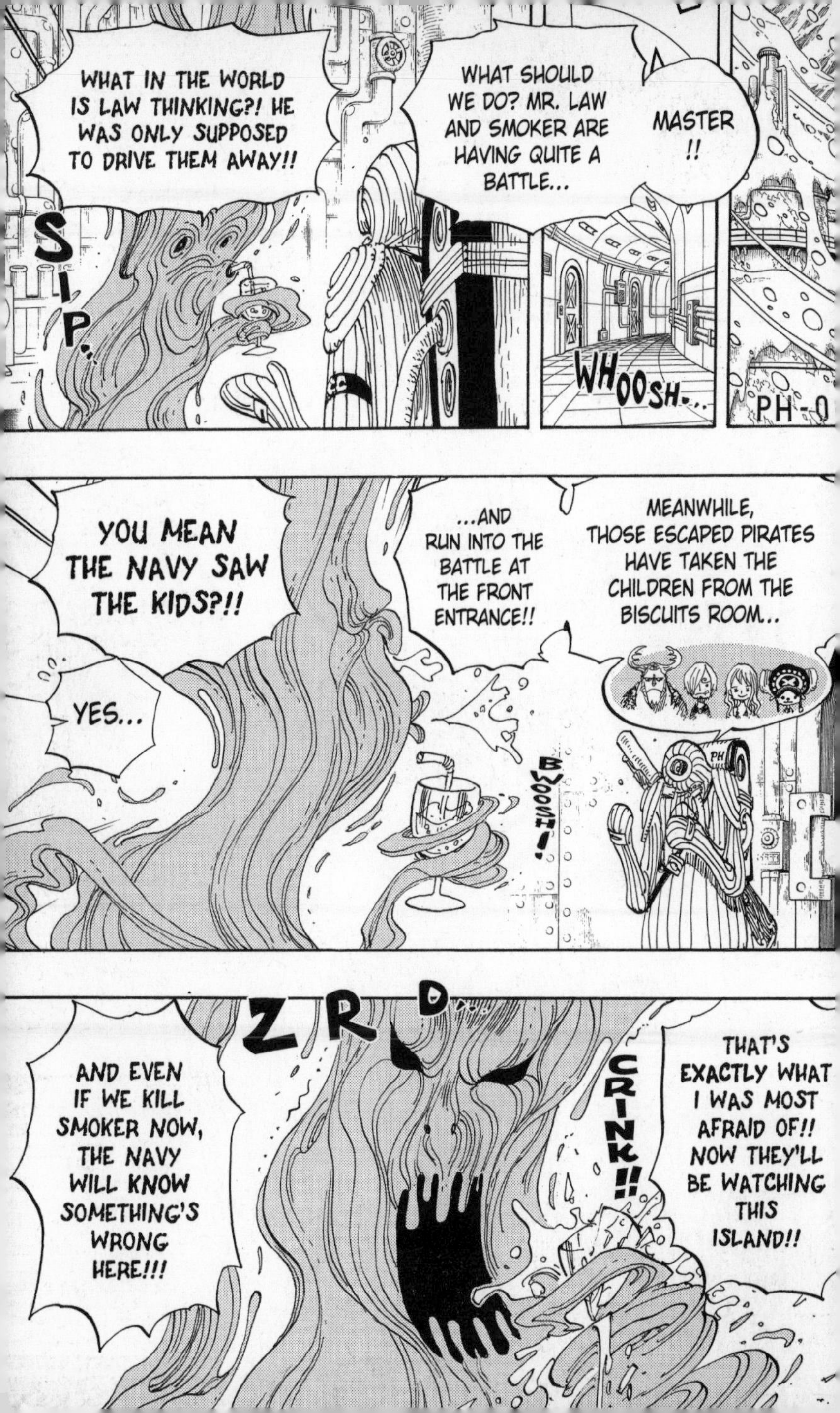
MASTER !!
PH-0
WHOOSH...
WHAT SHOULD WE DO? MR. LAW AND SMOKER ARE HAVING QUITE A BATTLE...
WHAT IN THE WORLD IS LAW THINKING?! HE WAS ONLY SUPPOSED TO DRIVE THEM AWAY!!
SIP..
MEANWHILE, THOSE ESCAPED PIRATES HAVE TAKEN THE CHILDREN FROM THE BISCUITS ROOM..
...AND RUN INTO THE BATTLE AT THE FRONT ENTRANCE!!
BWOOSH!!
YOU MEAN THE NAVY SAW THE KIDS?!!
YES...
THAT'S EXACTLY WHAT I WAS MOST AFRAID OF!! NOW THEY'LL BE WATCHING THIS ISLAND!!
CRINK!!
ZRD...
AND EVEN IF WE KILL SMOKER NOW, THE NAVY WILL KNOW SOMETHING'S WRONG HERE!!!

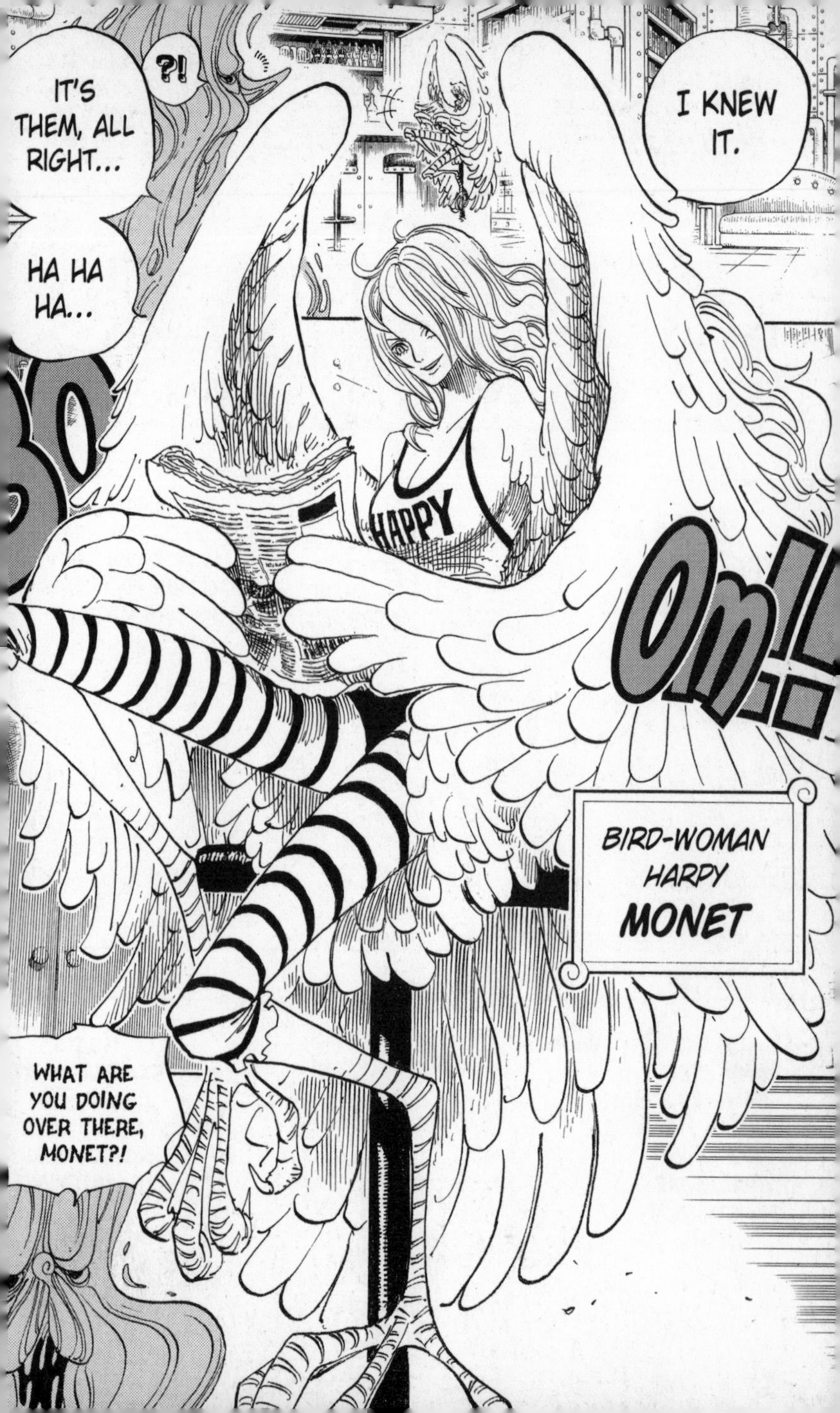
I KNEW IT.
?!
IT'S THEM, ALL RIGHT...
HA HA HA...
BOOM!!
HAPPY
BIRD-WOMAN HARPY MONET
WHAT ARE YOU DOING OVER THERE, MONET?!

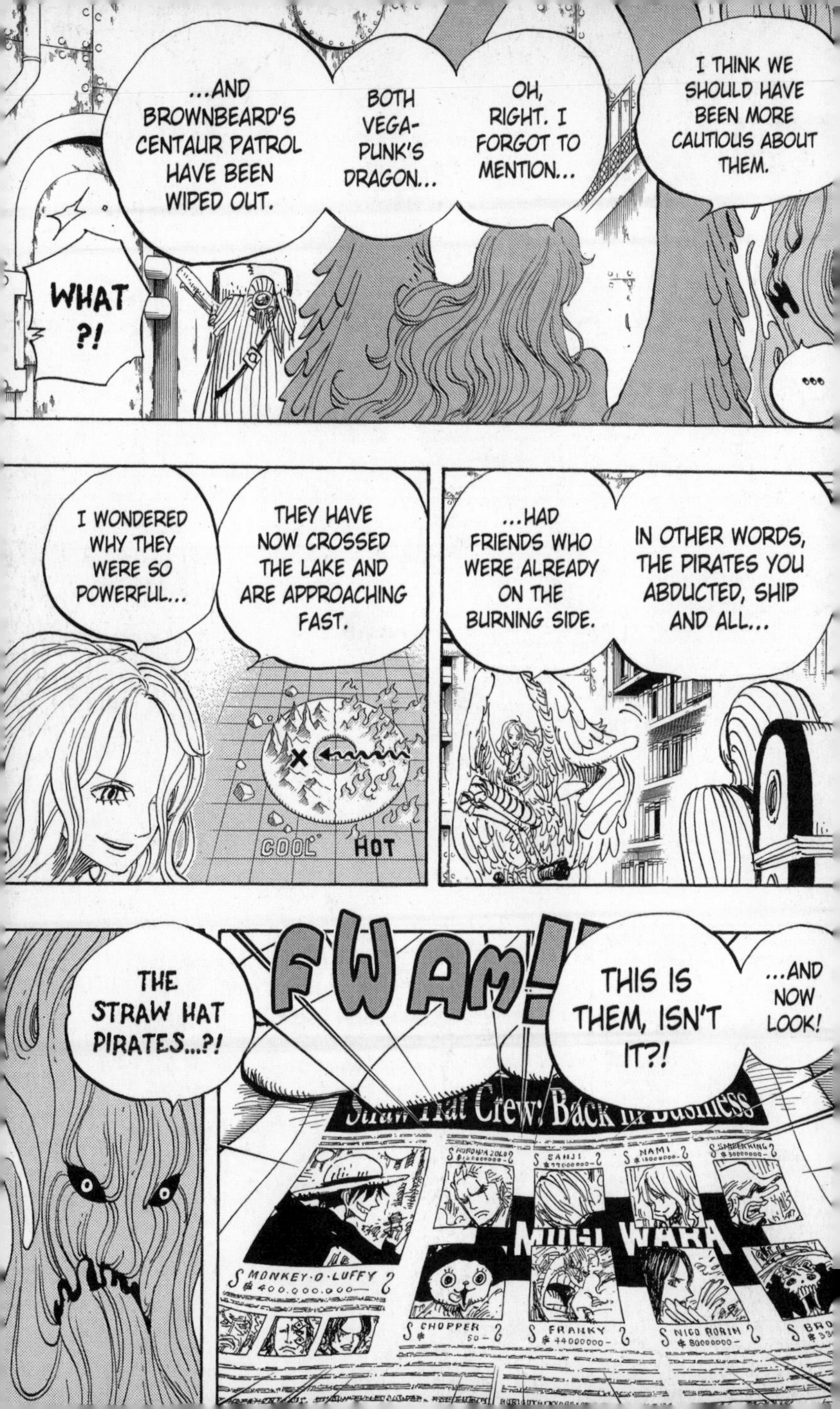
I THINK WE SHOULD HAVE BEEN MORE CAUTIOUS ABOUT THEM.
...
OH, RIGHT. I FORGOT TO MENTION...
BOTH VEGAPUNK'S DRAGON...
...AND BROWNBEARD'S CENTAUR PATROL HAVE BEEN WIPED OUT.
WHAT?!
IN OTHER WORDS, THE PIRATES YOU ABDUCTED, SHIP AND ALL...
...HAD FRIENDS WHO WERE ALREADY ON THE BURNING SIDE.
THEY HAVE NOW CROSSED THE LAKE AND ARE APPROACHING FAST.
I WONDERED WHY THEY WERE SO POWERFUL...
COOL
HOT
...AND NOW LOOK!
FWAM!!
THIS IS THEM, ISN'T IT?!
Straw Hat Crew: Back in Business
MUGI WARA
MONKEY·D·LUFFY
CHOPPER
FRANKY
NICO ROBIN
THE STRAW HAT PIRATES...?!

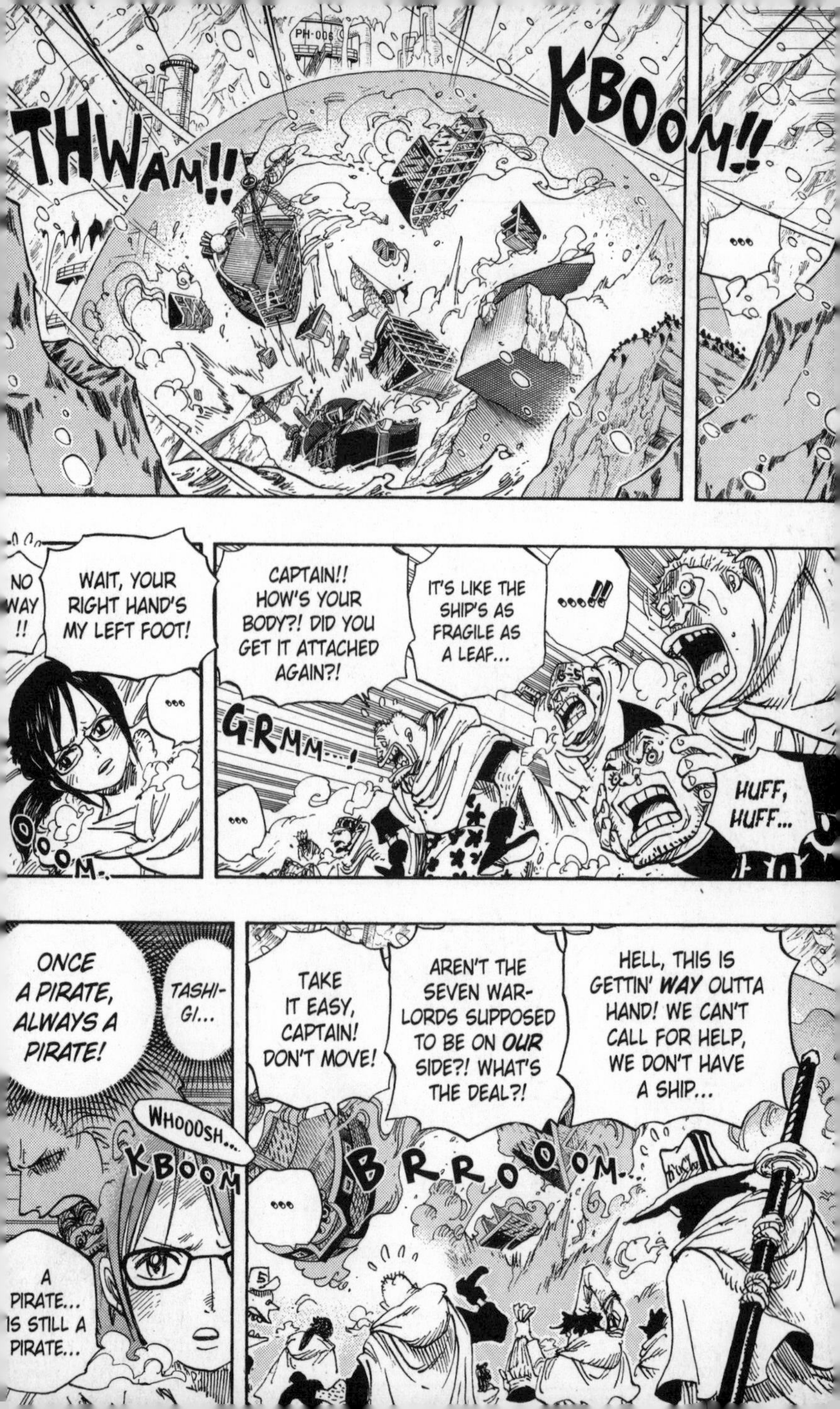
...
KBOOM!!
THWAM!!
...!!
IT'S LIKE THE SHIP'S AS FRAGILE AS A LEAF...
CAPTAIN!! HOW'S YOUR BODY?! DID YOU GET IT ATTACHED AGAIN?!
GRMM...!
HUFF, HUFF...
...
WAIT, YOUR RIGHT HAND'S MY LEFT FOOT!
NO WAY !!
...
OOOM...
HELL, THIS IS GETTIN' *WAY* OUTTA HAND! WE CAN'T CALL FOR HELP, WE DON'T HAVE A SHIP...
AREN'T THE SEVEN WAR-LORDS SUPPOSED TO BE ON *OUR* SIDE?! WHAT'S THE DEAL?!
TAKE IT EASY, CAPTAIN! DON'T MOVE!
BRROOOOM...
...
TASHI-GI...
ONCE A PIRATE, ALWAYS A PIRATE!
WHOOOSH...
KBOOM
A PIRATE... IS STILL A PIRATE...

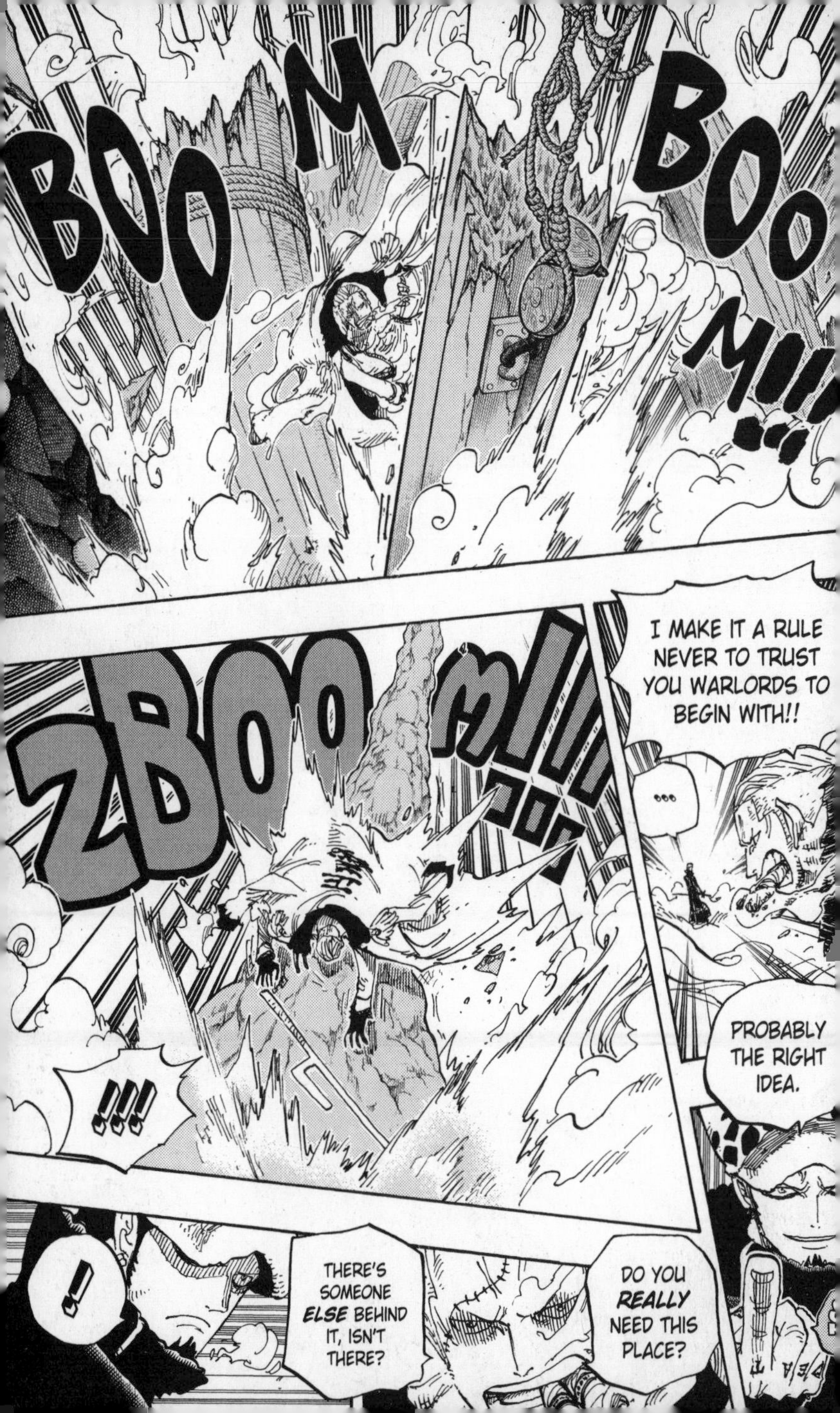
BOOOM!!
BOOM
I MAKE IT A RULE NEVER TO TRUST YOU WARLORDS TO BEGIN WITH!!
...
ZBOOM!!
!!!
PROBABLY THE RIGHT IDEA.
DO YOU REALLY NEED THIS PLACE?
THERE'S SOMEONE ELSE BEHIND IT, ISN'T THERE?
!

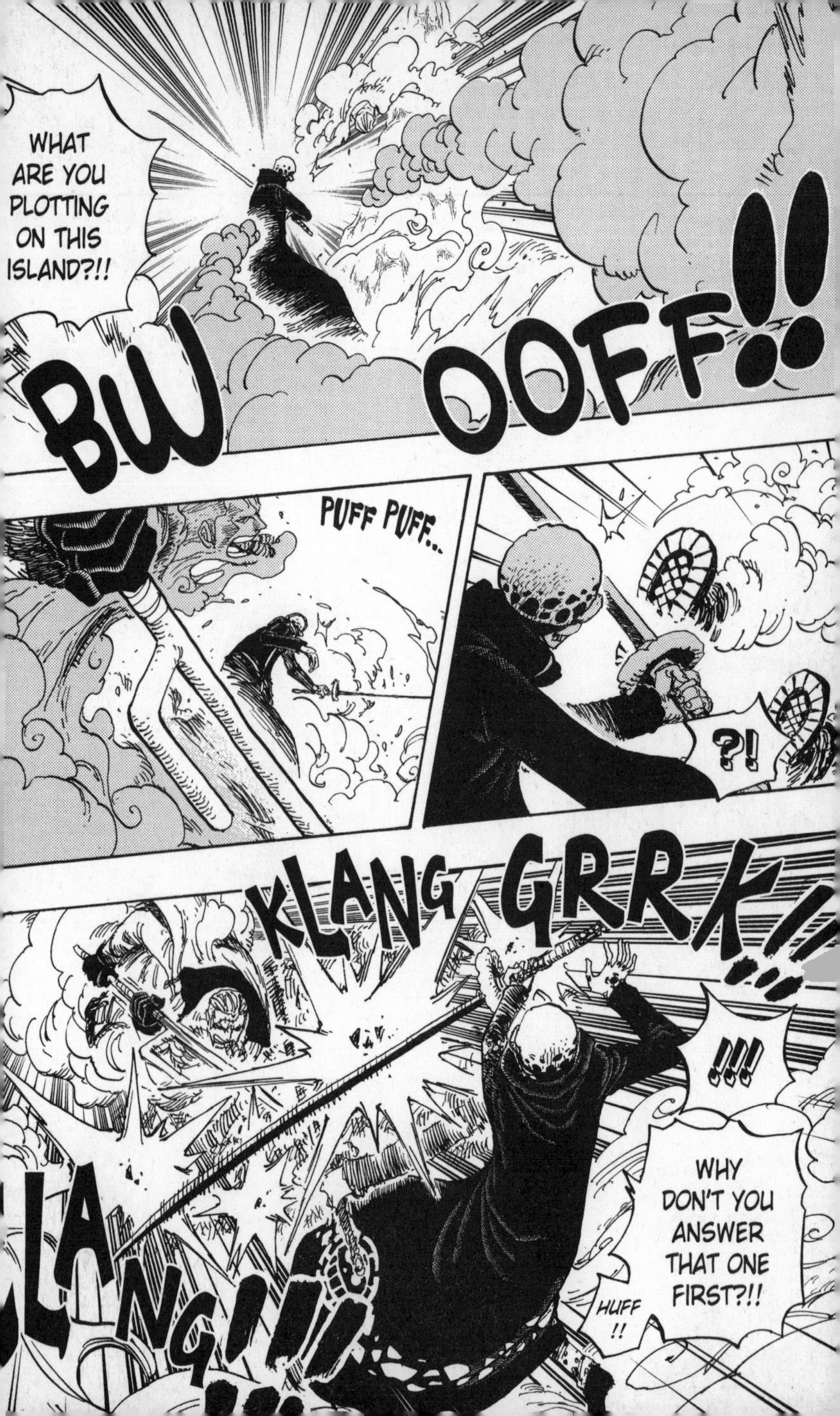

WHAT ARE YOU PLOTTING ON THIS ISLAND?!!
BUW OOFF!!
?!
PUFF PUFF...
KLANG GRRK!!
!!!
WHY DON'T YOU ANSWER THAT ONE FIRST?!!
HUFF !!
LANG!!!

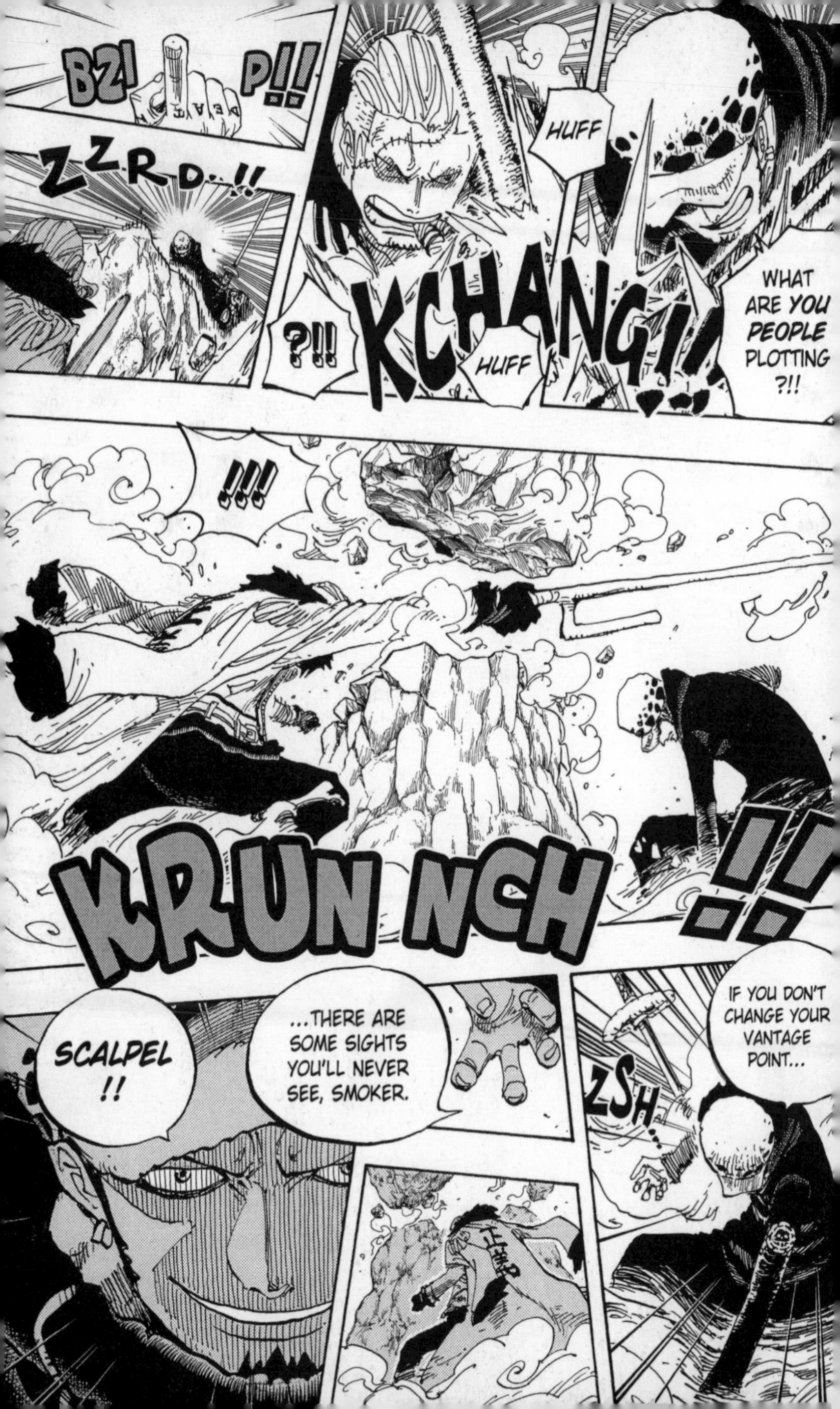
HUFF
WHAT ARE YOU PEOPLE PLOTTING ?!!
KCHANG!!
?!!
HUFF
BZI P!!
ZZRD..!!
!!!
KRUN NCH!!
IF YOU DON'T CHANGE YOUR VANTAGE POINT...
ZSH...
...THERE ARE SOME SIGHTS YOU'LL NEVER SEE, SMOKER.
SCALPEL !!

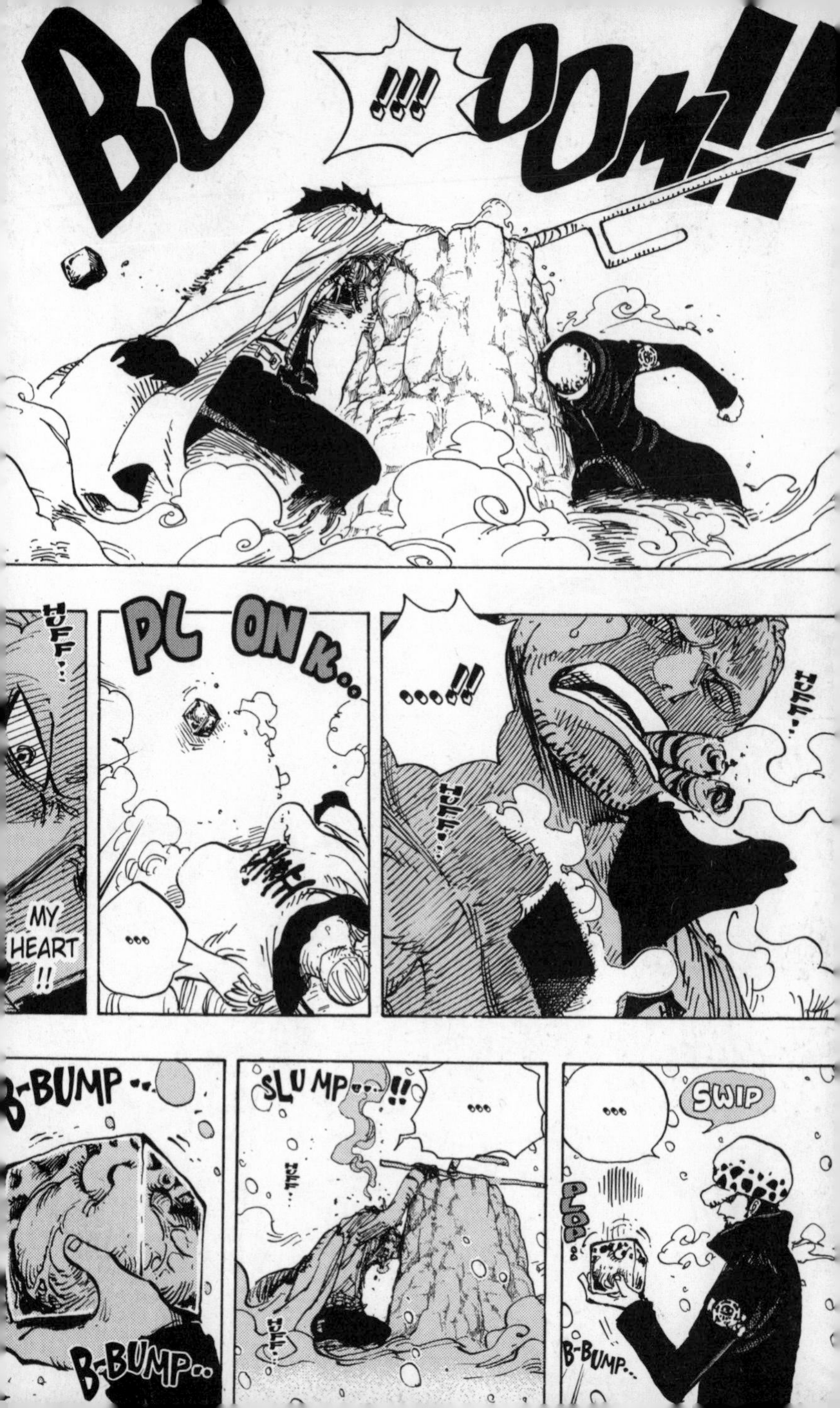
BO OOM!!
!!!
...!!
HUFF..
HUFF...
PLONK...
...
HUFF..
MY HEART!!
SWIP
...
PLOP
B-BUMP...
...
SLUMP...!!
HUFF...
HUFF...
B-BUMP...
B-BUMP..

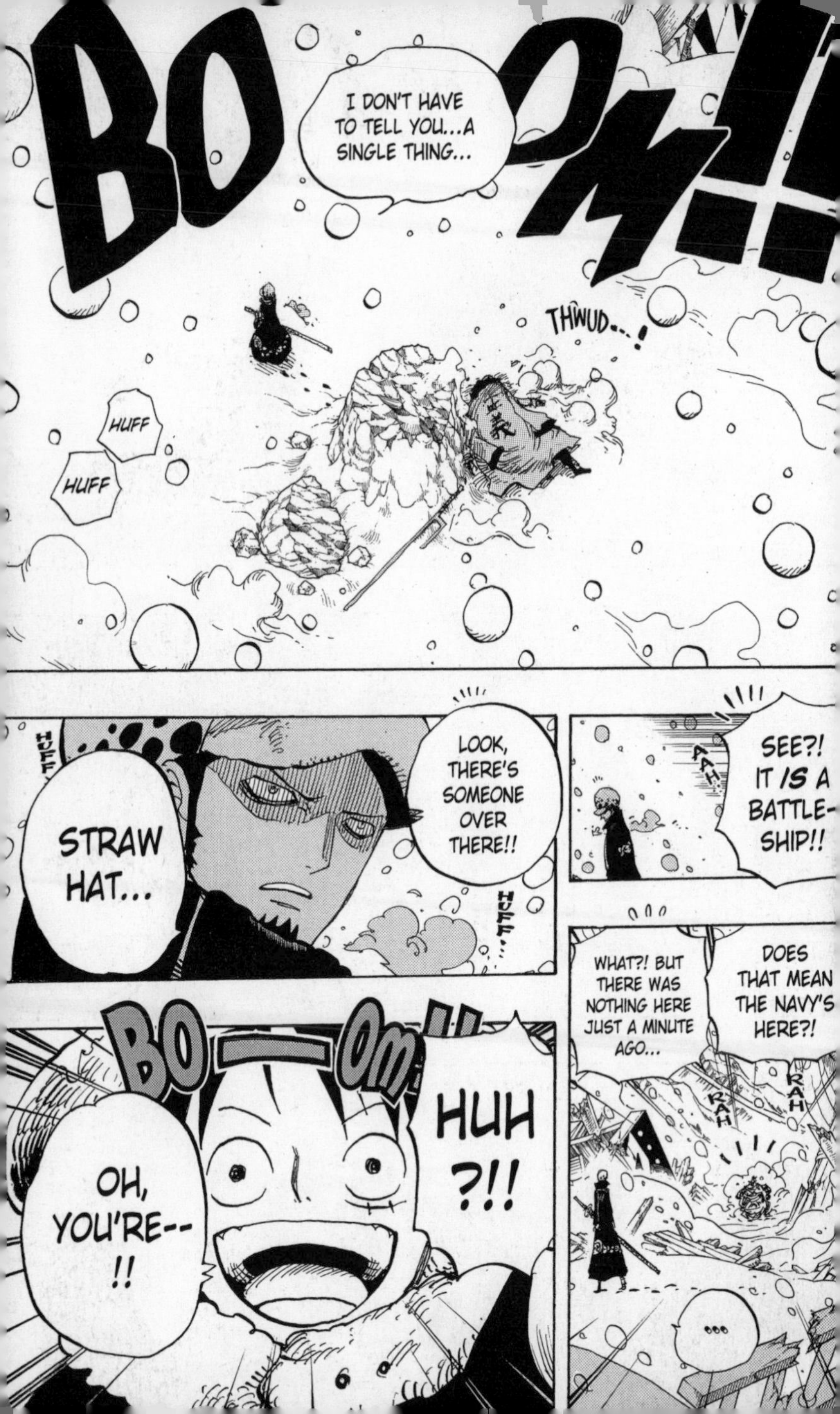
BOOM!!
I DON'T HAVE TO TELL YOU...A SINGLE THING...
THWUD...!
HUFF
HUFF
AAH...
SEE?! IT IS A BATTLESHIP!!
LOOK, THERE'S SOMEONE OVER THERE!!
HUFF
STRAW HAT...
HUFF...
DOES THAT MEAN THE NAVY'S HERE?!
WHAT?! BUT THERE WAS NOTHING HERE JUST A MINUTE AGO...
RAH
RAH
...
BO--OM!!
HUH ?!!
OH, YOU'RE-- !!

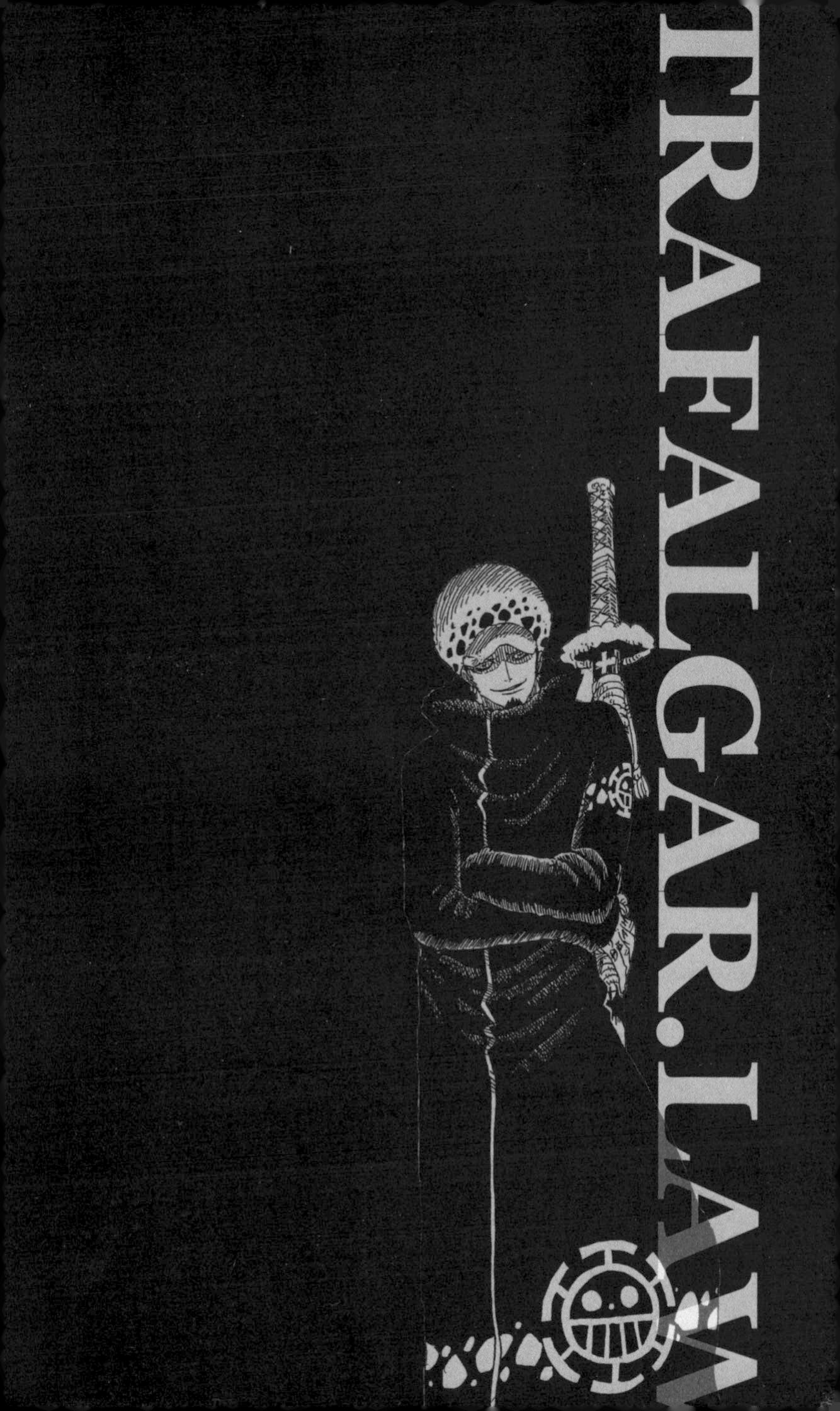
TRAFALGAR.LAW

Chapter 663:
CC

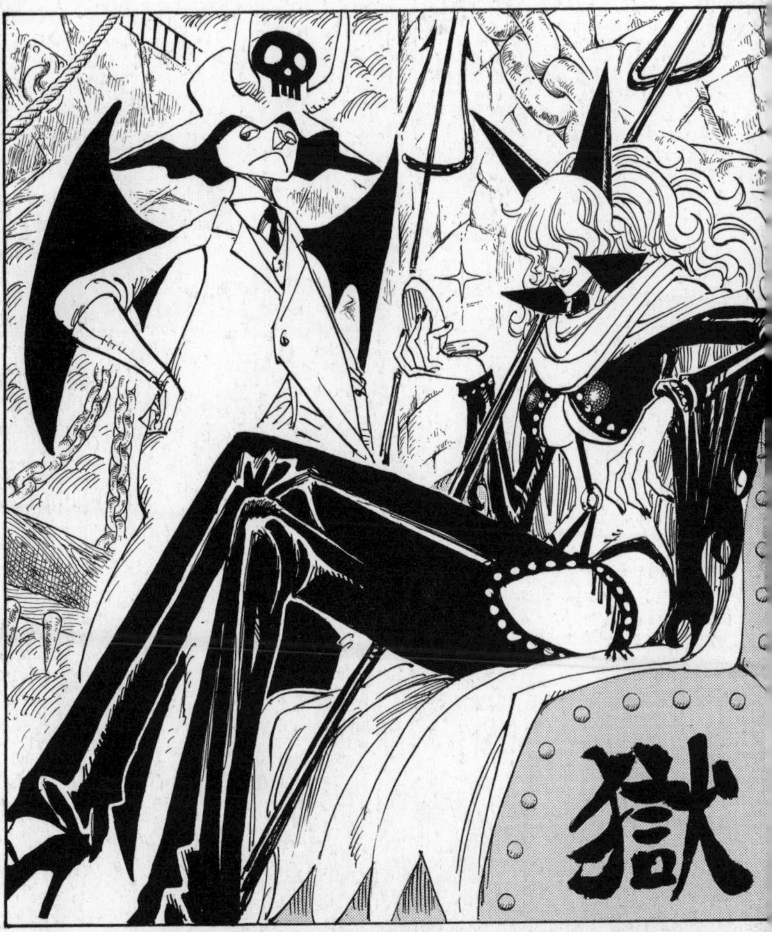
獄

DECKS OF THE WORLD, VOL. 44: "IMPEL DOWN—
SADI'S FALLEN IN LOVE WITH THE NEW VICE WARDEN"

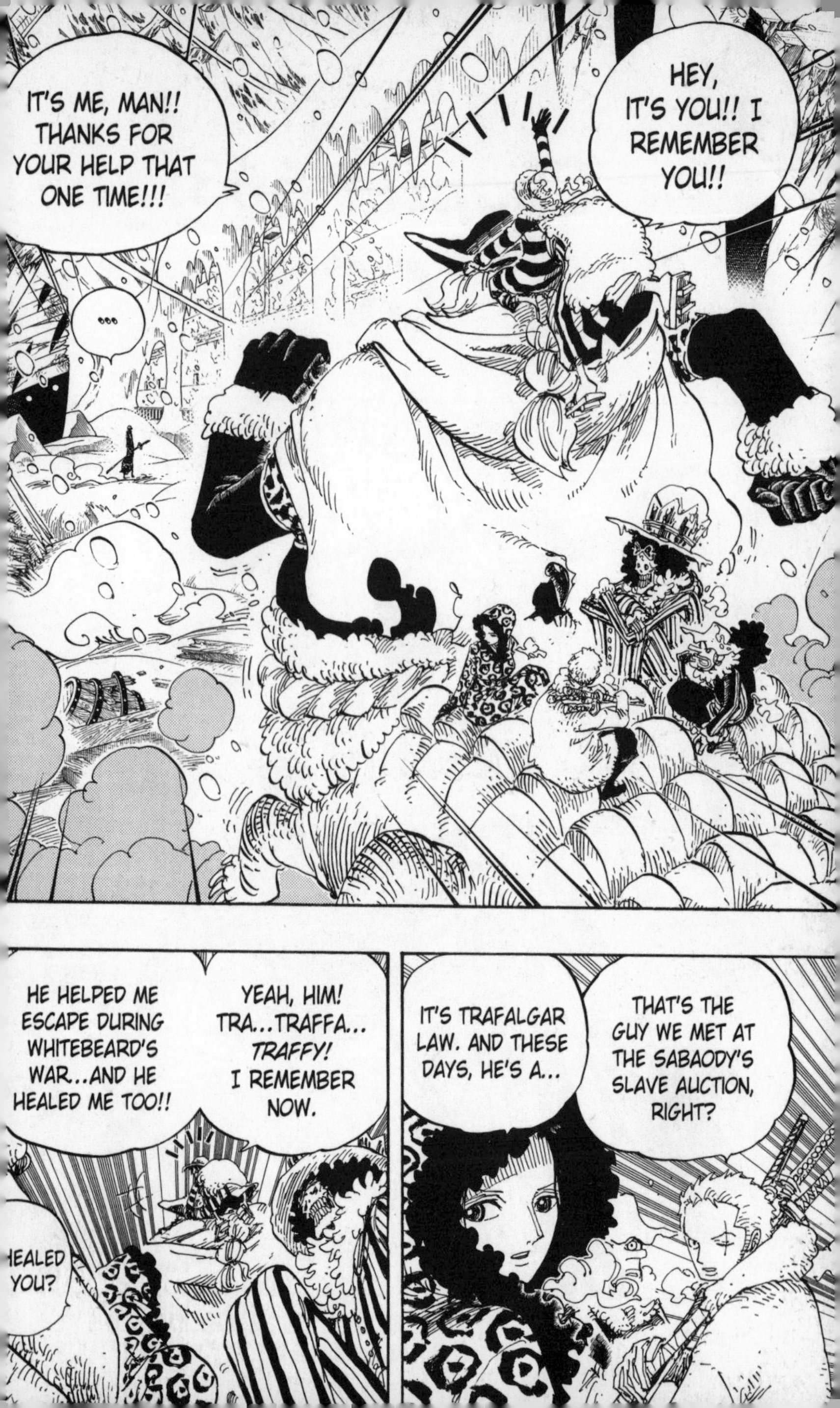
HEY, IT'S YOU!! I REMEMBER YOU!!
IT'S ME, MAN!! THANKS FOR YOUR HELP THAT ONE TIME!!!
...
THAT'S THE GUY WE MET AT THE SABAODY'S SLAVE AUCTION, RIGHT?
IT'S TRAFALGAR LAW. AND THESE DAYS, HE'S A...
YEAH, HIM! TRA...TRAFFA... *TRAFFY!* I REMEMBER NOW.
HE HELPED ME ESCAPE DURING WHITEBEARD'S WAR...AND HE HEALED ME TOO!!
HEALED YOU?

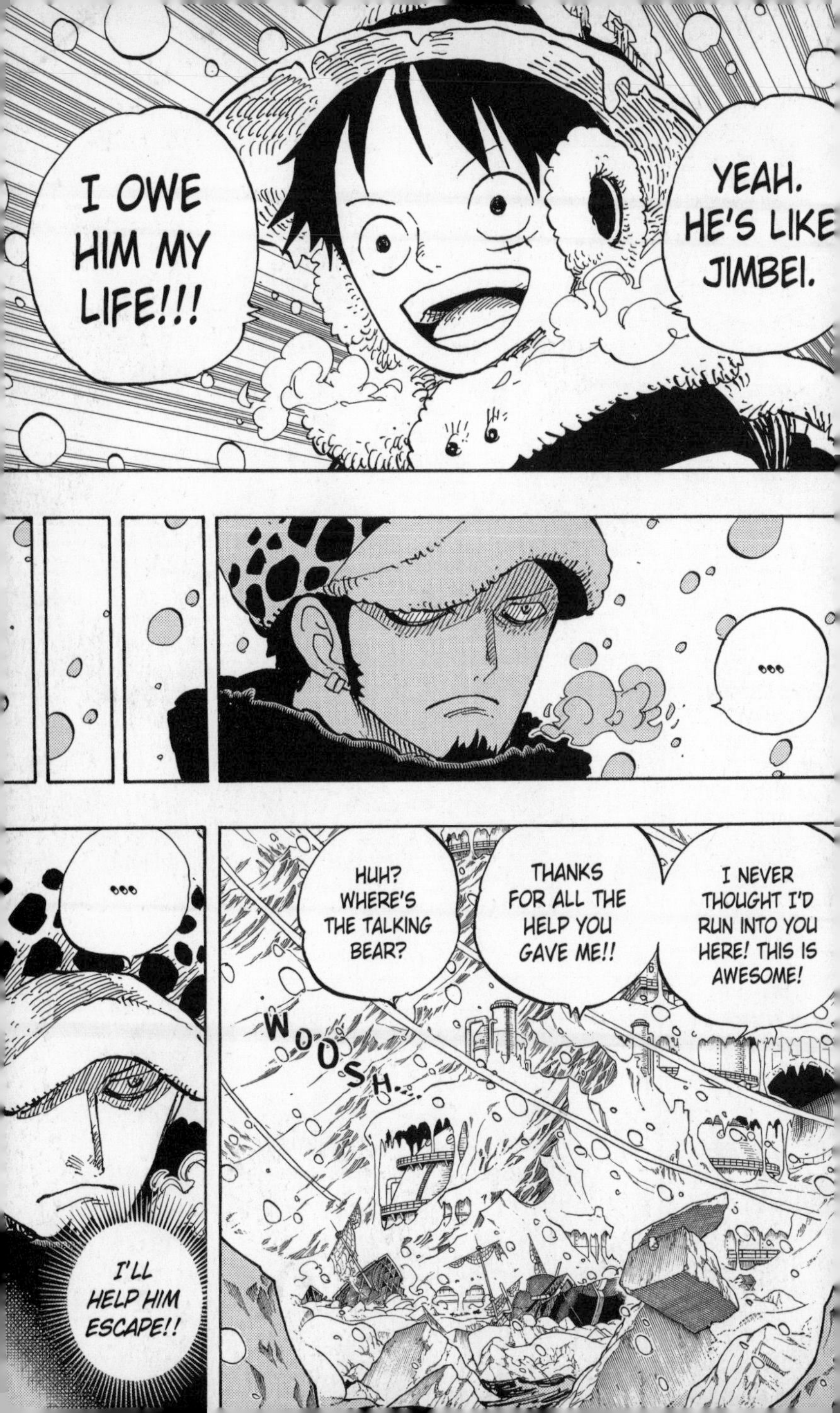
YEAH. HE'S LIKE JIMBEI.
I OWE HIM MY LIFE!!!
...
I NEVER THOUGHT I'D RUN INTO YOU HERE! THIS IS AWESOME!
THANKS FOR ALL THE HELP YOU GAVE ME!!
HUH? WHERE'S THE TALKING BEAR?
WOOSH
...
I'LL HELP HIM ESCAPE!!

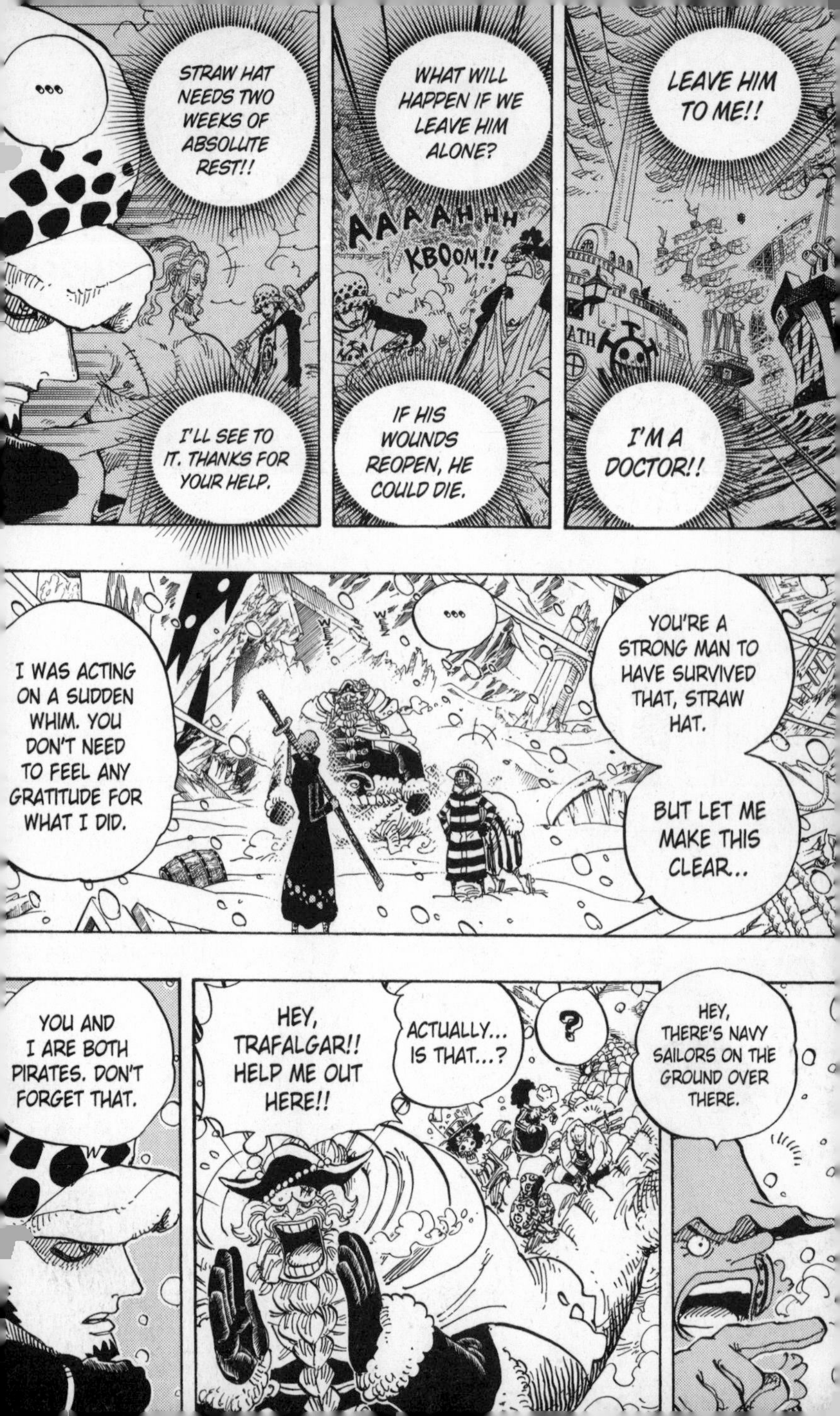

LEAVE HIM TO ME!!
I'M A DOCTOR!!
WHAT WILL HAPPEN IF WE LEAVE HIM ALONE?
AAAAHHH
KBOOM!!
IF HIS WOUNDS REOPEN, HE COULD DIE.
STRAW HAT NEEDS TWO WEEKS OF ABSOLUTE REST!!
...
I'LL SEE TO IT. THANKS FOR YOUR HELP.
YOU'RE A STRONG MAN TO HAVE SURVIVED THAT, STRAW HAT.
BUT LET ME MAKE THIS CLEAR...
...
I WAS ACTING ON A SUDDEN WHIM. YOU DON'T NEED TO FEEL ANY GRATITUDE FOR WHAT I DID.
HEY, THERE'S NAVY SAILORS ON THE GROUND OVER THERE.
?
ACTUALLY... IS THAT...?
HEY, TRAFALGAR!! HELP ME OUT HERE!!
YOU AND I ARE BOTH PIRATES. DON'T FORGET THAT.

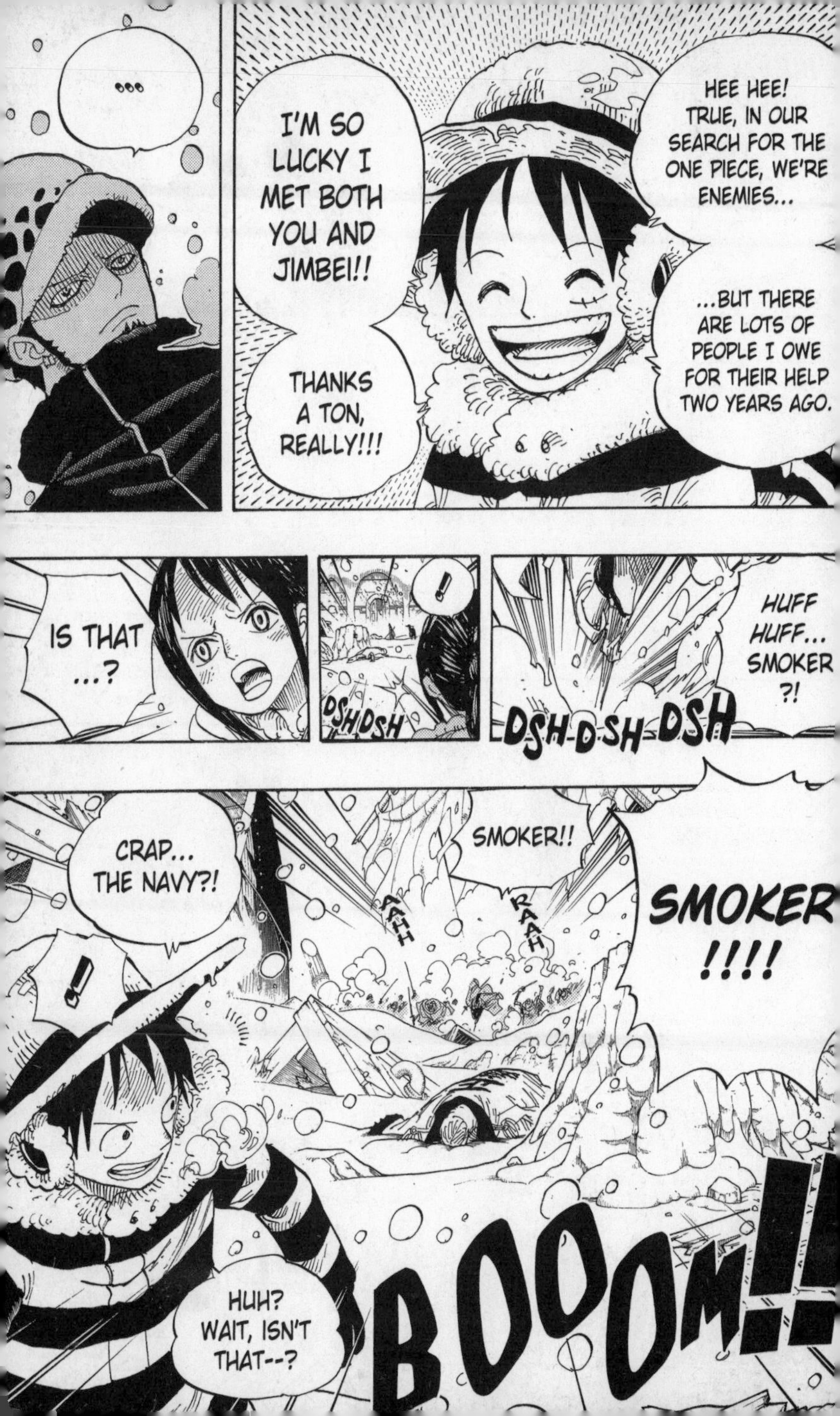
HEE HEE! TRUE, IN OUR SEARCH FOR THE ONE PIECE, WE'RE ENEMIES...
...BUT THERE ARE LOTS OF PEOPLE I OWE FOR THEIR HELP TWO YEARS AGO.
I'M SO LUCKY I MET BOTH YOU AND JIMBEI!!
THANKS A TON, REALLY!!!
...
HUFF HUFF... SMOKER ?!
DSH-DSH-DSH
!
DSHDSH
IS THAT ...?
SMOKER !!!!
SMOKER!!
RAAH
AAHH
CRAP... THE NAVY?!
!
HUH? WAIT, ISN'T THAT--?
BOOOM!!

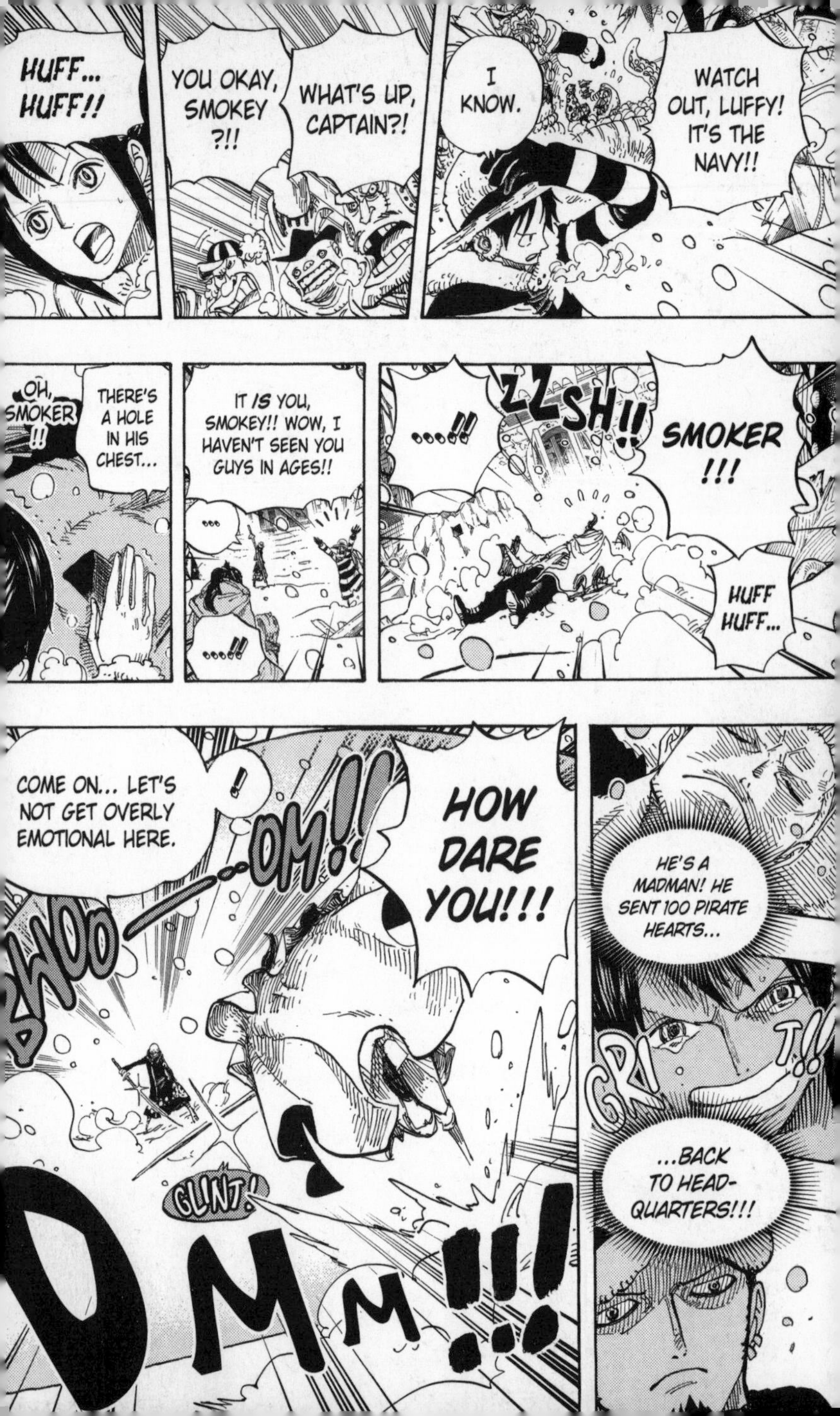
WATCH OUT, LUFFY! IT'S THE NAVY!!
I KNOW.
WHAT'S UP, CAPTAIN?!
YOU OKAY, SMOKEY?!!
HUFF... HUFF!!
SMOKER!!!
ZZSH!!
...!!
HUFF HUFF...
IT IS YOU, SMOKEY!! WOW, I HAVEN'T SEEN YOU GUYS IN AGES!!
...
...!!
THERE'S A HOLE IN HIS CHEST...
OH, SMOKER!!
HE'S A MADMAN! HE SENT 100 PIRATE HEARTS...
GRIT!!
...BACK TO HEAD-QUARTERS!!!
HOW DARE YOU!!!
!
COME ON... LET'S NOT GET OVERLY EMOTIONAL HERE.
BWOO---OM!!
GLINT!
DOMM!!!

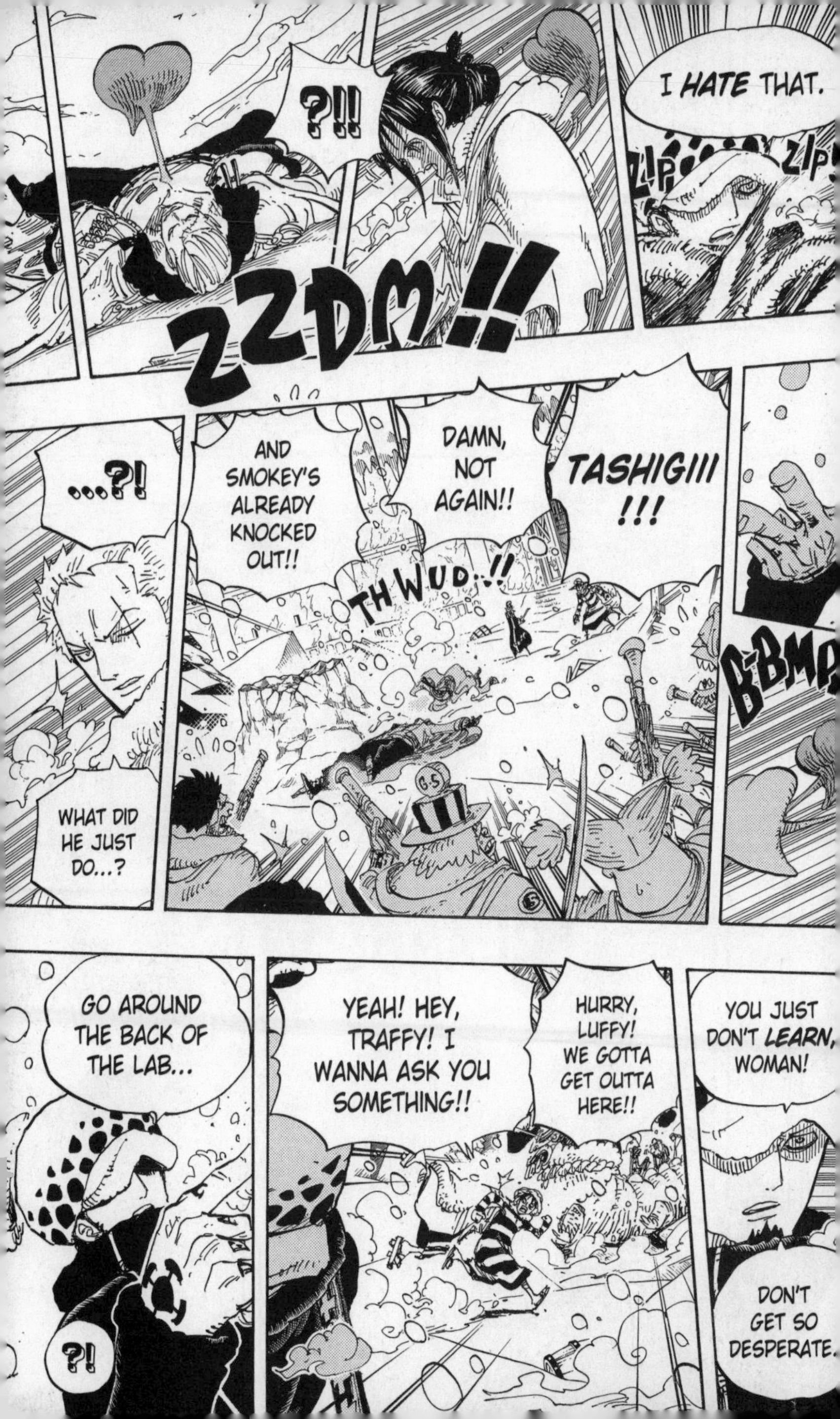
I HATE THAT.
ZIP
ZIP
?!!
ZZDM!!
TASHIGIII!!!
DAMN, NOT AGAIN!!
AND SMOKEY'S ALREADY KNOCKED OUT!!
THWUD..!!
...?!
WHAT DID HE JUST DO...?
YOU JUST DON'T LEARN, WOMAN!
DON'T GET SO DESPERATE.
HURRY, LUFFY! WE GOTTA GET OUTTA HERE!!
YEAH! HEY, TRAFFY! I WANNA ASK YOU SOMETHING!!
GO AROUND THE BACK OF THE LAB...
?!

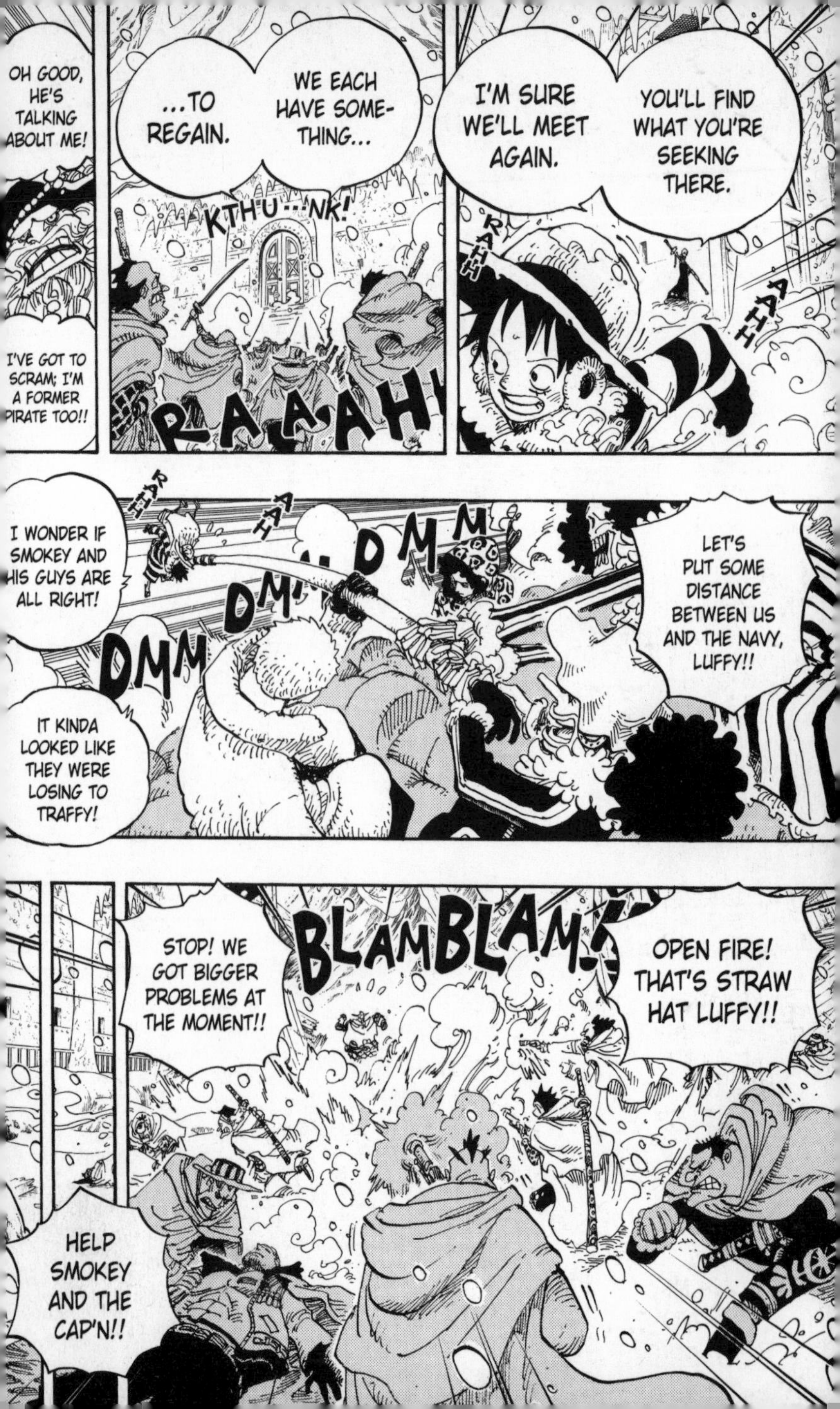
YOU'LL FIND WHAT YOU'RE SEEKING THERE.
I'M SURE WE'LL MEET AGAIN.
RAHHH
AAHH
WE EACH HAVE SOME-THING...
...TO REGAIN.
KTHU...NK!
RAAAH
OH GOOD, HE'S TALKING ABOUT ME!
I'VE GOT TO SCRAM; I'M A FORMER PIRATE TOO!!
LET'S PUT SOME DISTANCE BETWEEN US AND THE NAVY, LUFFY!!
DMM
DMM
DMM
RAHH
AAH
I WONDER IF SMOKEY AND HIS GUYS ARE ALL RIGHT!
IT KINDA LOOKED LIKE THEY WERE LOSING TO TRAFFY!
OPEN FIRE! THAT'S STRAW HAT LUFFY!!
BLAMBLAM!
STOP! WE GOT BIGGER PROBLEMS AT THE MOMENT!!
HELP SMOKEY AND THE CAP'N!!

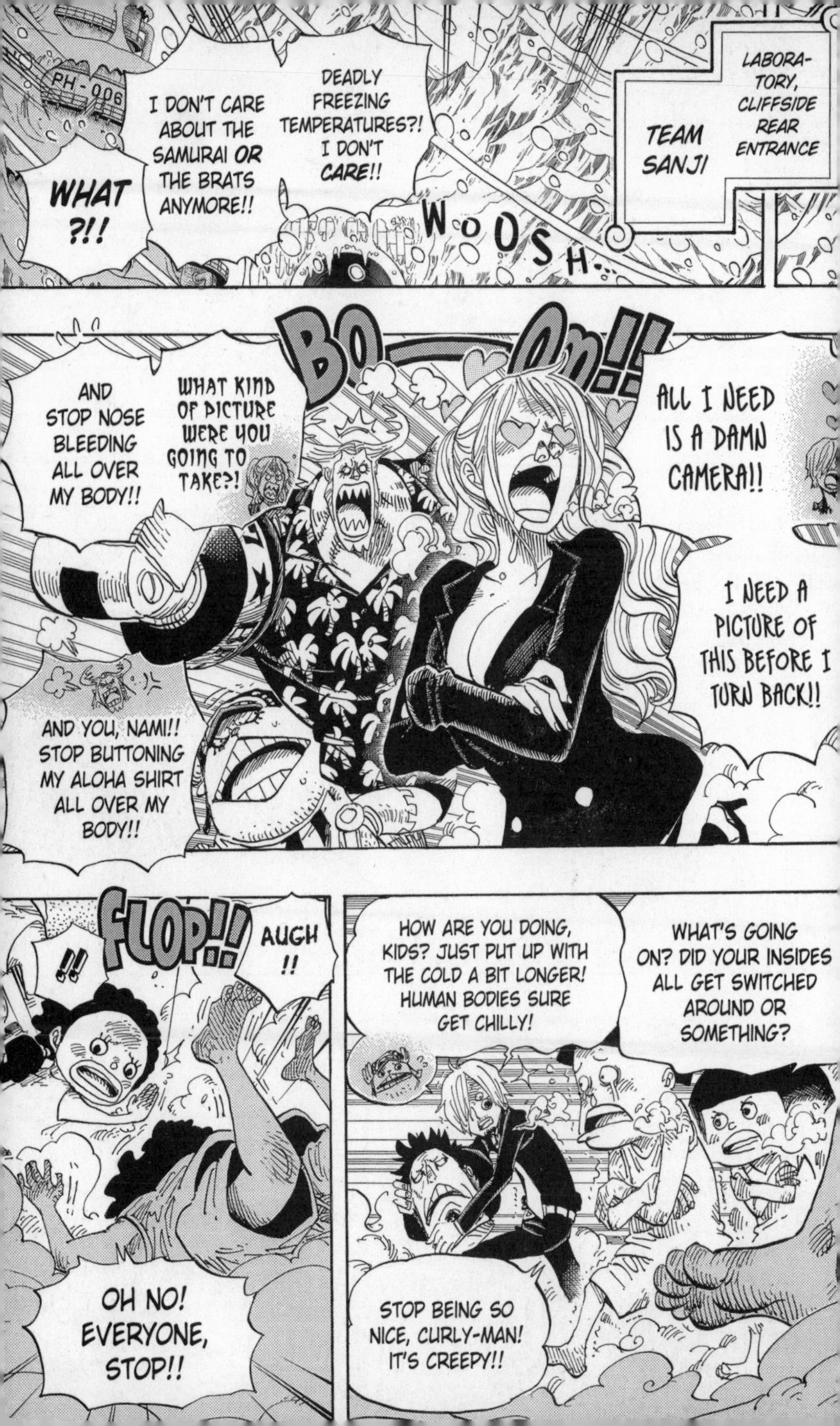
LABORATORY, CLIFFSIDE REAR ENTRANCE
TEAM SANJI
DEADLY FREEZING TEMPERATURES?! I DON'T CARE!!
I DON'T CARE ABOUT THE SAMURAI OR THE BRATS ANYMORE!!
WHAT?!!
WOOSH...
BO—OM!!
ALL I NEED IS A DAMN CAMERA!!
I NEED A PICTURE OF THIS BEFORE I TURN BACK!!
WHAT KIND OF PICTURE WERE YOU GOING TO TAKE?!
AND STOP NOSE BLEEDING ALL OVER MY BODY!!
AND YOU, NAMI!! STOP BUTTONING MY ALOHA SHIRT ALL OVER MY BODY!!
WHAT'S GOING ON? DID YOUR INSIDES ALL GET SWITCHED AROUND OR SOMETHING?
HOW ARE YOU DOING, KIDS? JUST PUT UP WITH THE COLD A BIT LONGER! HUMAN BODIES SURE GET CHILLY!
STOP BEING SO NICE, CURLY-MAN! IT'S CREEPY!!
FLOP!!
AUGH!!
!!
OH NO! EVERYONE, STOP!!

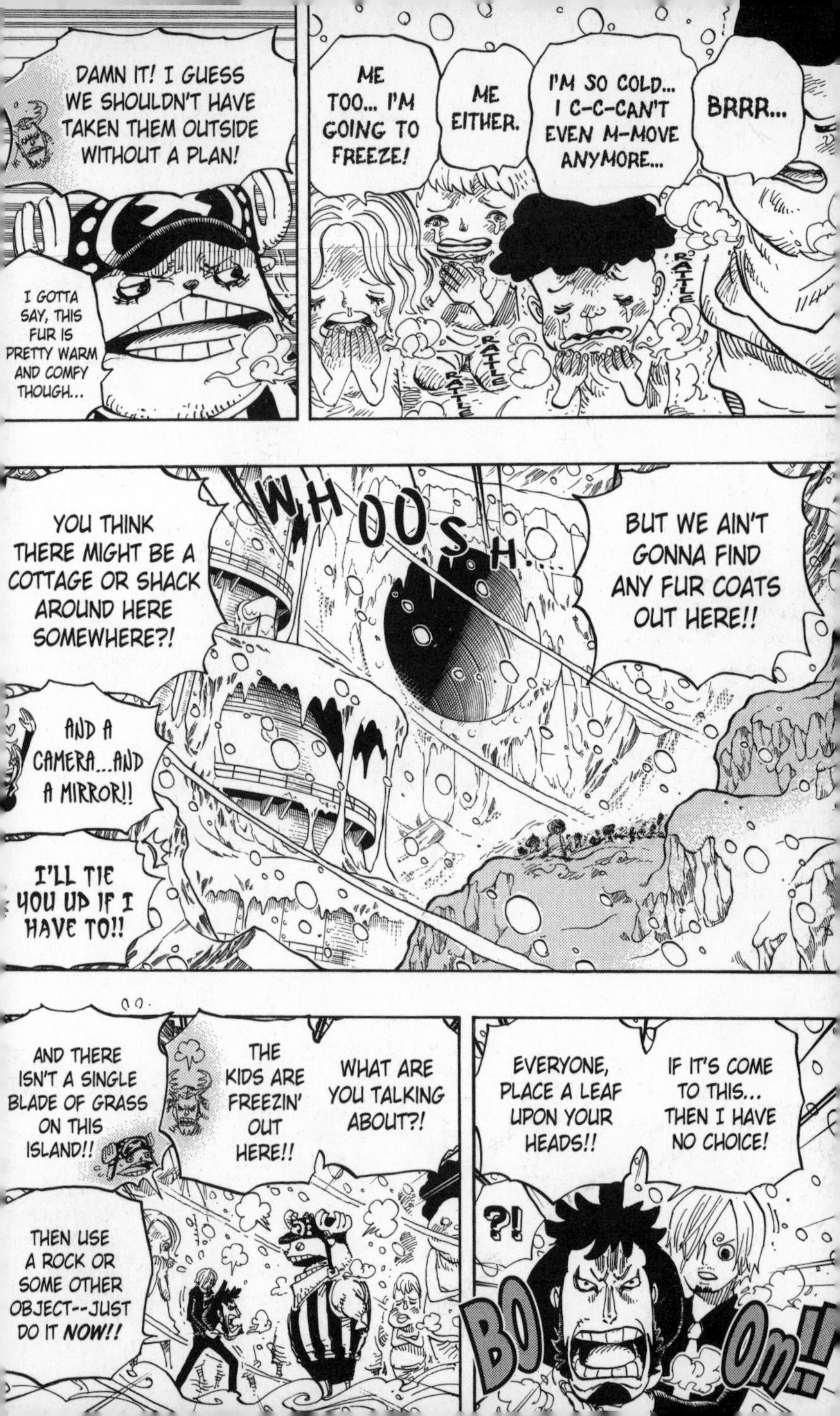
BRRR...
I'M SO COLD... I C-C-CAN'T EVEN M-MOVE ANYMORE...
RATTLE
ME EITHER.
ME TOO... I'M GOING TO FREEZE!
RATTLE
RATTLE
DAMN IT! I GUESS WE SHOULDN'T HAVE TAKEN THEM OUTSIDE WITHOUT A PLAN!
I GOTTA SAY, THIS FUR IS PRETTY WARM AND COMFY THOUGH...
BUT WE AIN'T GONNA FIND ANY FUR COATS OUT HERE!!
WHOOSH...
YOU THINK THERE MIGHT BE A COTTAGE OR SHACK AROUND HERE SOMEWHERE?!
AND A CAMERA...AND A MIRROR!!
I'LL TIE YOU UP IF I HAVE TO!!
IF IT'S COME TO THIS... THEN I HAVE NO CHOICE!
EVERYONE, PLACE A LEAF UPON YOUR HEADS!!
?!
BOOM!!
WHAT ARE YOU TALKING ABOUT?!
THE KIDS ARE FREEZIN' OUT HERE!!
AND THERE ISN'T A SINGLE BLADE OF GRASS ON THIS ISLAND!!
THEN USE A ROCK OR SOME OTHER OBJECT--JUST DO IT NOW!!

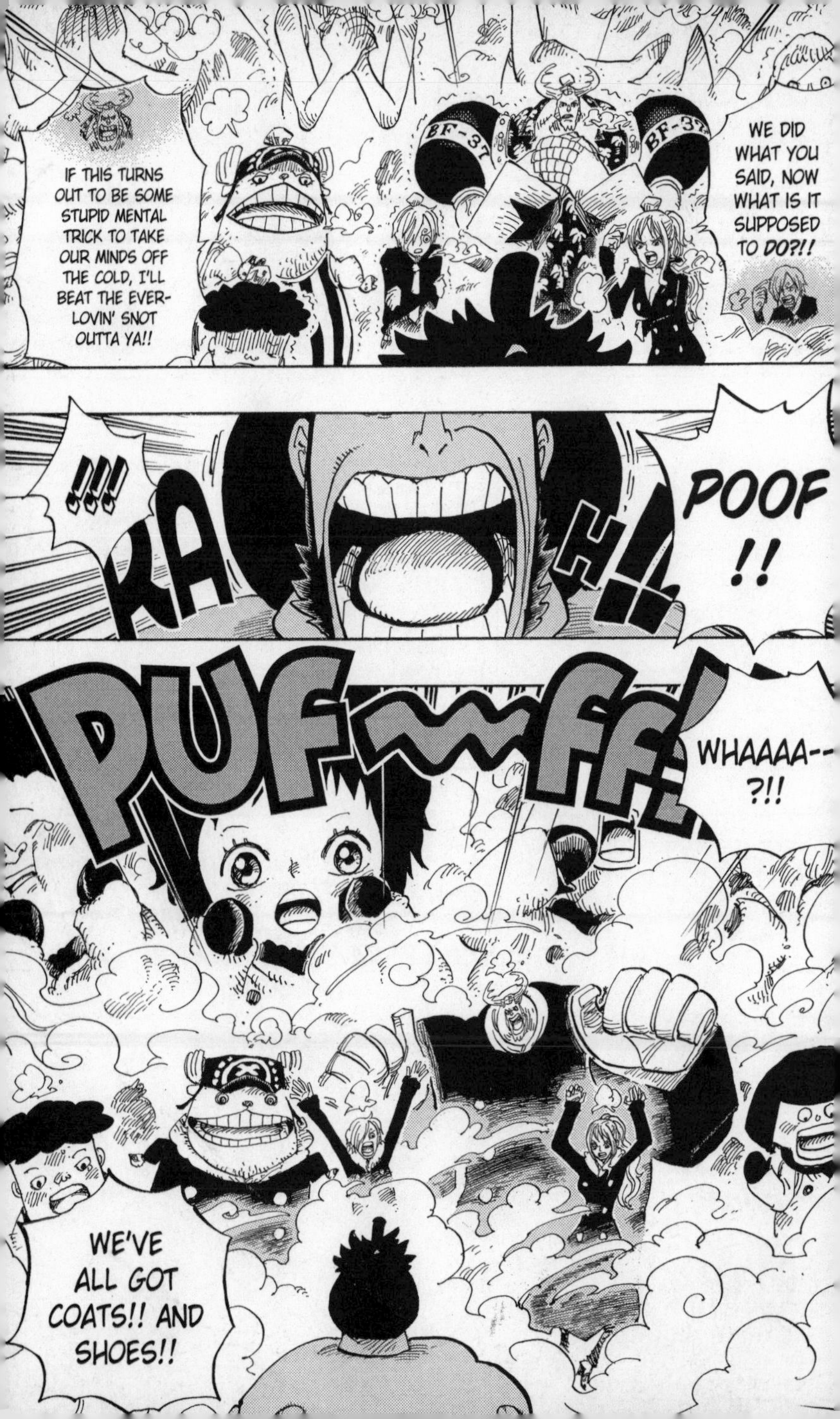
WE DID WHAT YOU SAID, NOW WHAT IS IT SUPPOSED TO DO?!!
IF THIS TURNS OUT TO BE SOME STUPID MENTAL TRICK TO TAKE OUR MINDS OFF THE COLD, I'LL BEAT THE EVER-LOVIN' SNOT OUTTA YA!!
POOF !!
KA H!!
!!!
PUF~~FF
WHAAAA-- ?!!
WE'VE ALL GOT COATS!! AND SHOES!!

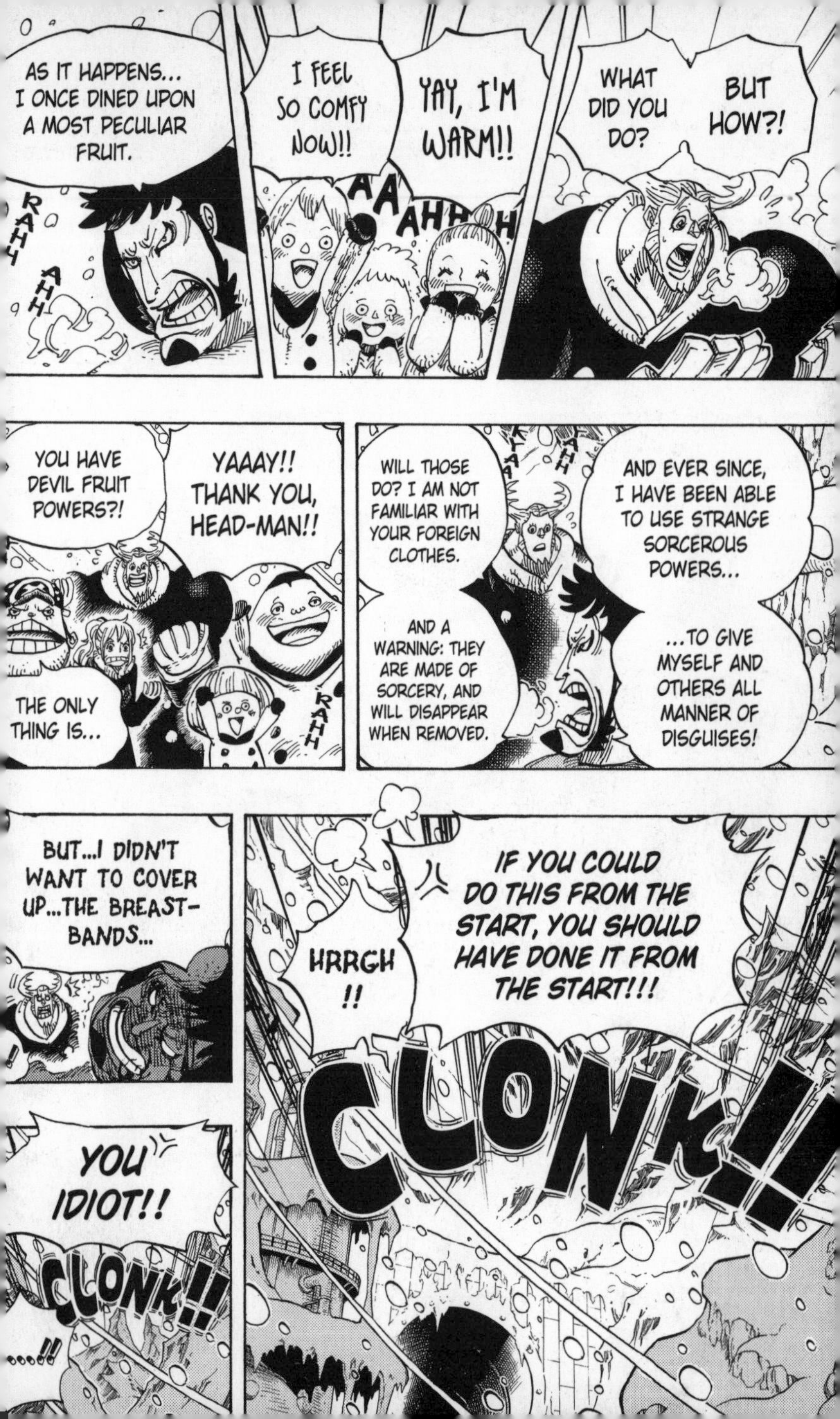

BUT HOW?!
WHAT DID YOU DO?
YAY, I'M WARM!!
I FEEL SO COMFY NOW!!
AS IT HAPPENS... I ONCE DINED UPON A MOST PECULIAR FRUIT.
RAHH
AHH
AND EVER SINCE, I HAVE BEEN ABLE TO USE STRANGE SORCEROUS POWERS...
...TO GIVE MYSELF AND OTHERS ALL MANNER OF DISGUISES!
WILL THOSE DO? I AM NOT FAMILIAR WITH YOUR FOREIGN CLOTHES.
AND A WARNING: THEY ARE MADE OF SORCERY, AND WILL DISAPPEAR WHEN REMOVED.
YAAAY!! THANK YOU, HEAD-MAN!!
YOU HAVE DEVIL FRUIT POWERS?!
THE ONLY THING IS...
RAHH
IF YOU COULD DO THIS FROM THE START, YOU SHOULD HAVE DONE IT FROM THE START!!!
HRRGH !!
CLONK!!
BUT...I DIDN'T WANT TO COVER UP...THE BREAST-BANDS...
YOU IDIOT!!
CLONK!!
...!!

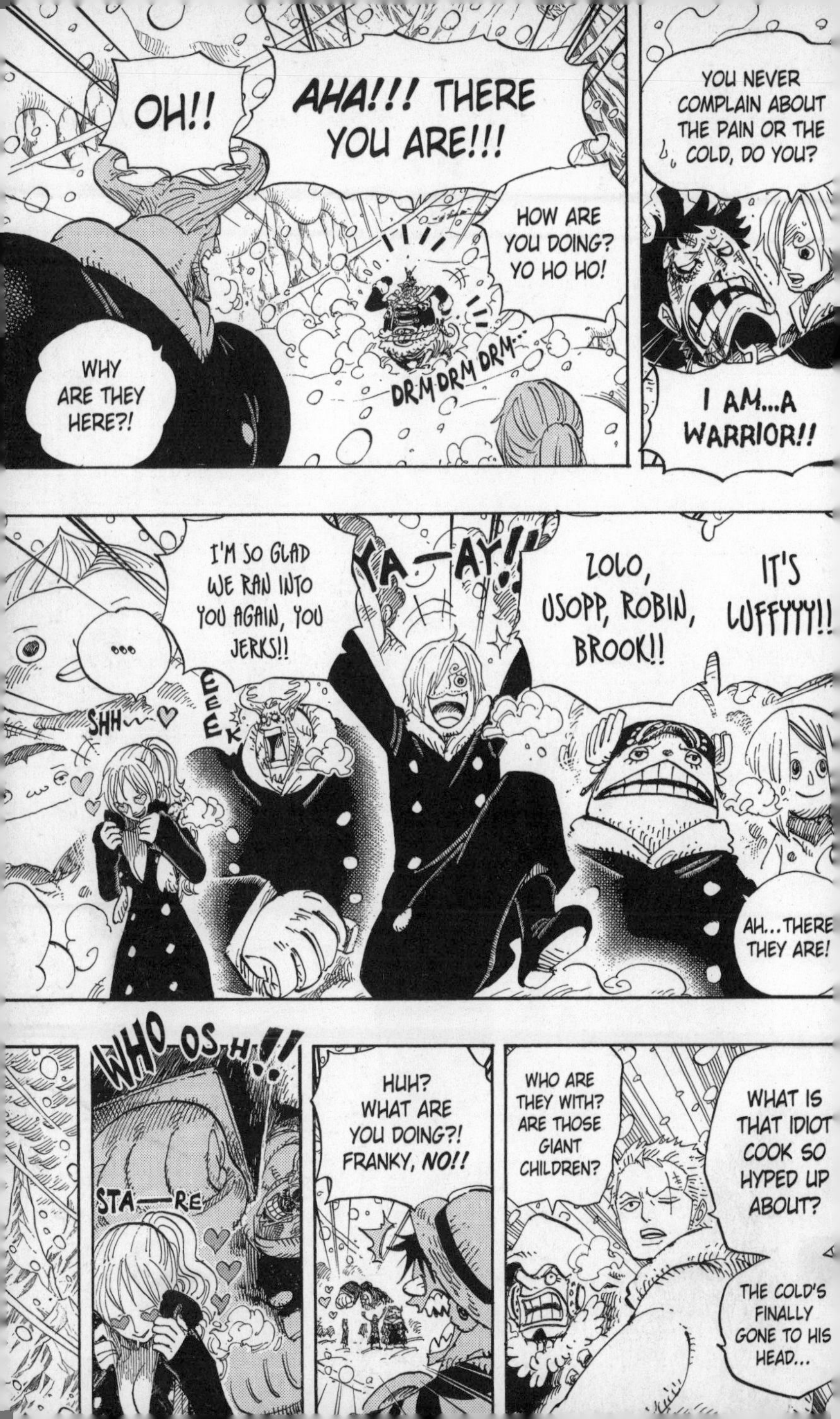
YOU NEVER COMPLAIN ABOUT THE PAIN OR THE COLD, DO YOU?
I AM...A WARRIOR!!
AHA!!! THERE YOU ARE!!!
OH!!
HOW ARE YOU DOING? YO HO HO!
DRM DRM DRM...
WHY ARE THEY HERE?!
IT'S LUFFYYY!!
ZOLO, USOPP, ROBIN, BROOK!!
YA—AY!!
I'M SO GLAD WE RAN INTO YOU AGAIN, YOU JERKS!!
...
EEEK
SHH~♥
AH...THERE THEY ARE!
WHAT IS THAT IDIOT COOK SO HYPED UP ABOUT?
WHO ARE THEY WITH? ARE THOSE GIANT CHILDREN?
THE COLD'S FINALLY GONE TO HIS HEAD...
HUH? WHAT ARE YOU DOING?! FRANKY, NO!!
WHO-OSH!!
STA—RE

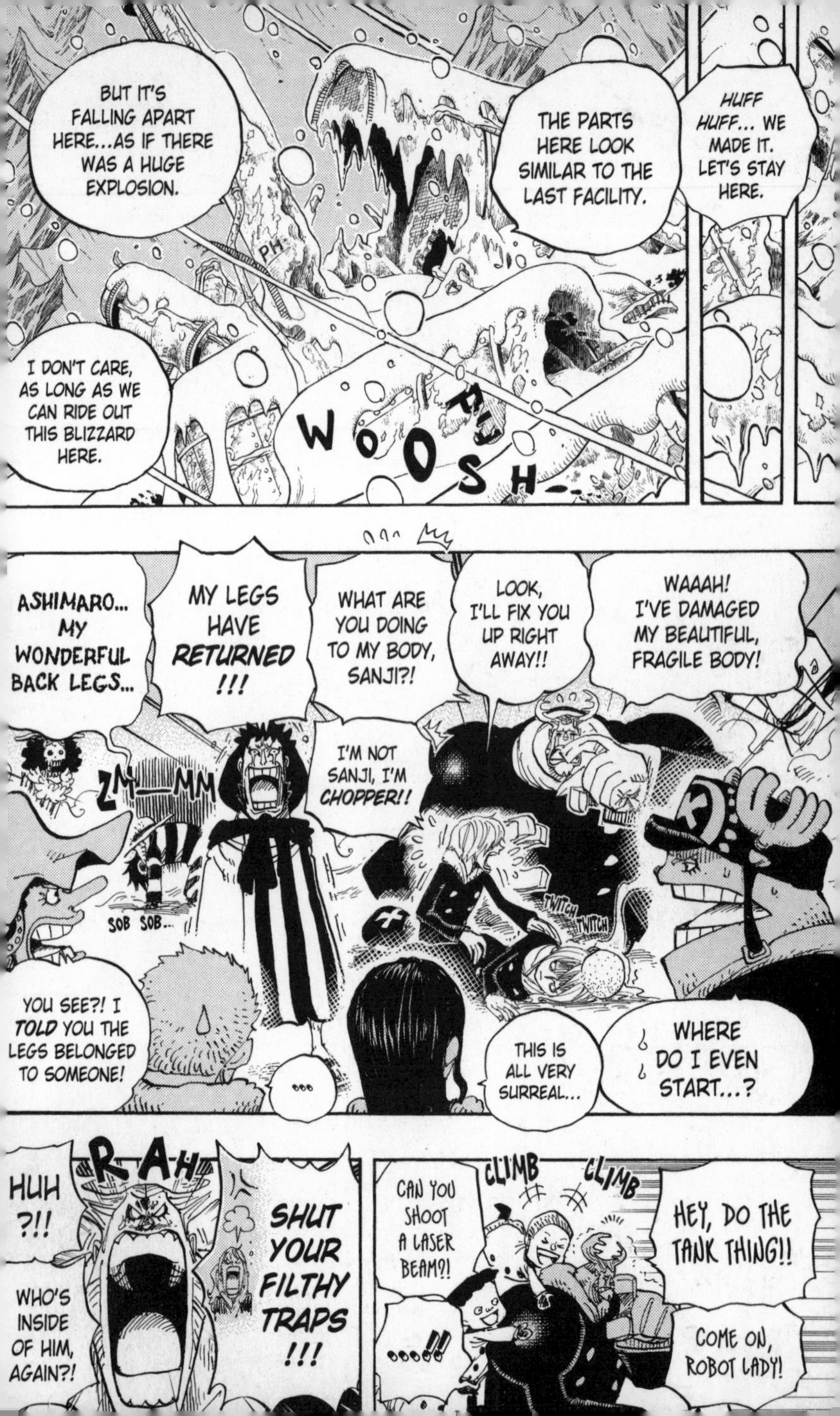
HUFF HUFF... WE MADE IT. LET'S STAY HERE.
THE PARTS HERE LOOK SIMILAR TO THE LAST FACILITY.
BUT IT'S FALLING APART HERE...AS IF THERE WAS A HUGE EXPLOSION.
I DON'T CARE, AS LONG AS WE CAN RIDE OUT THIS BLIZZARD HERE.
WOOSH
WAAAH! I'VE DAMAGED MY BEAUTIFUL, FRAGILE BODY!
LOOK, I'LL FIX YOU UP RIGHT AWAY!!
WHAT ARE YOU DOING TO MY BODY, SANJI?!
I'M NOT SANJI, I'M *CHOPPER!!*
MY LEGS HAVE *RETURNED* !!!
ASHIMARO... MY WONDERFUL BACK LEGS...
ZM—MM
TWITCH TWITCH
WHERE DO I EVEN START...?
THIS IS ALL VERY SURREAL...
SOB SOB...
...
YOU SEE?! I *TOLD* YOU THE LEGS BELONGED TO SOMEONE!
HEY, DO THE TANK THING!!
CLIMB CLIMB
CAN YOU SHOOT A LASER BEAM?!
COME ON, ROBOT LADY!
...!!
SHUT YOUR FILTHY TRAPS !!!
RAH
HUH ?!!
WHO'S INSIDE OF HIM, AGAIN?!

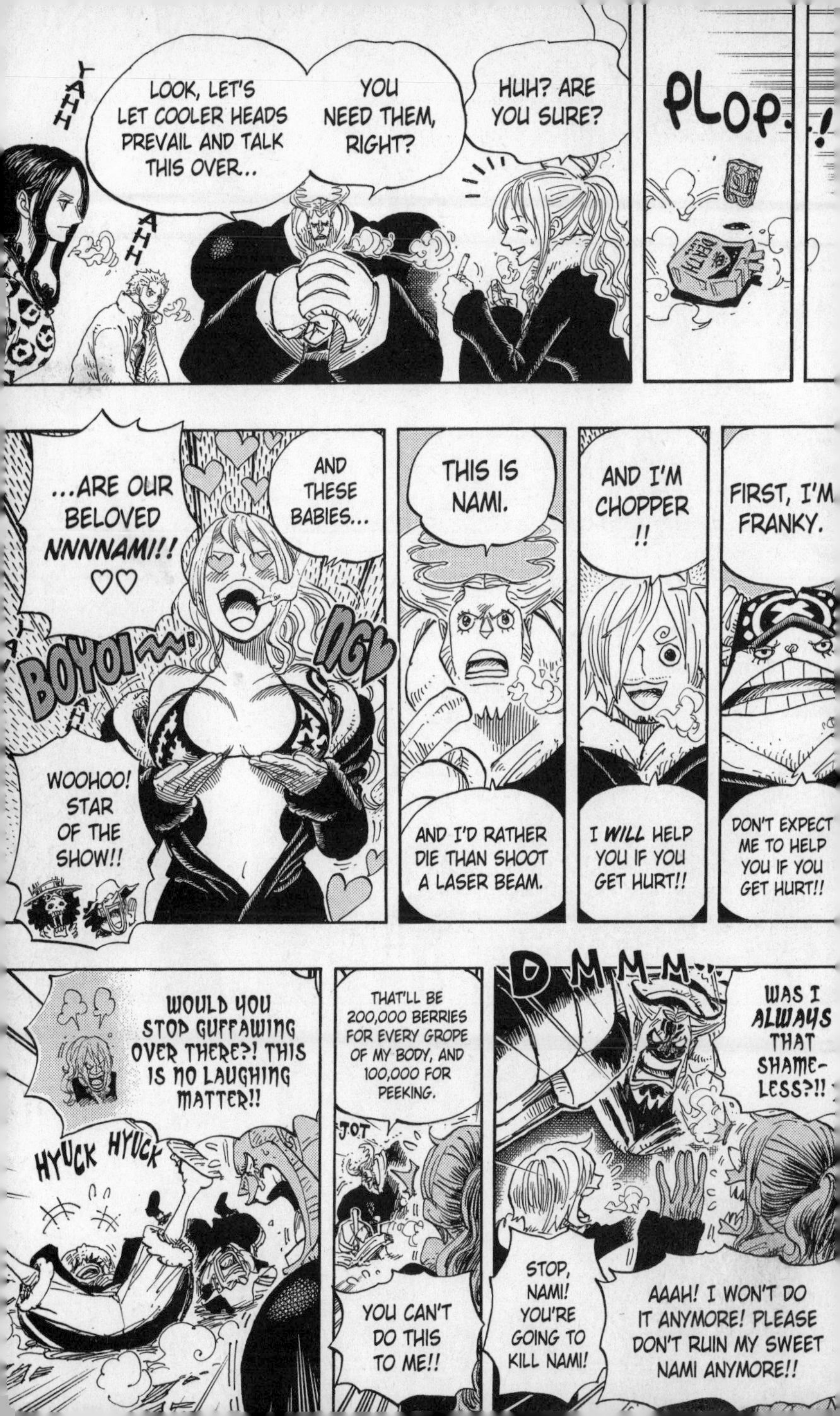
PLOP...!
HUH? ARE YOU SURE?
YOU NEED THEM, RIGHT?
LOOK, LET'S LET COOLER HEADS PREVAIL AND TALK THIS OVER...
YAHH
AHH
FIRST, I'M FRANKY.
DON'T EXPECT ME TO HELP YOU IF YOU GET HURT!!
AND I'M CHOPPER !!
I *WILL* HELP YOU IF YOU GET HURT!!
THIS IS NAMI.
AND I'D RATHER DIE THAN SHOOT A LASER BEAM.
AND THESE BABIES...
...ARE OUR BELOVED *NNNNAMI!!* ♡♡
NGV
BOYOI~~
WOOHOO! STAR OF THE SHOW!!
D M M M
WAS I *ALWAYS* THAT SHAME-LESS?!!
AAAH! I WON'T DO IT ANYMORE! PLEASE DON'T RUIN MY SWEET NAMI ANYMORE!!
STOP, NAMI! YOU'RE GOING TO KILL NAMI!
THAT'LL BE 200,000 BERRIES FOR EVERY GROPE OF MY BODY, AND 100,000 FOR PEEKING.
JOT
YOU CAN'T DO THIS TO ME!!
WOULD YOU STOP GUFFAWING OVER THERE?! THIS IS NO LAUGHING MATTER!!
HYUCK HYUCK

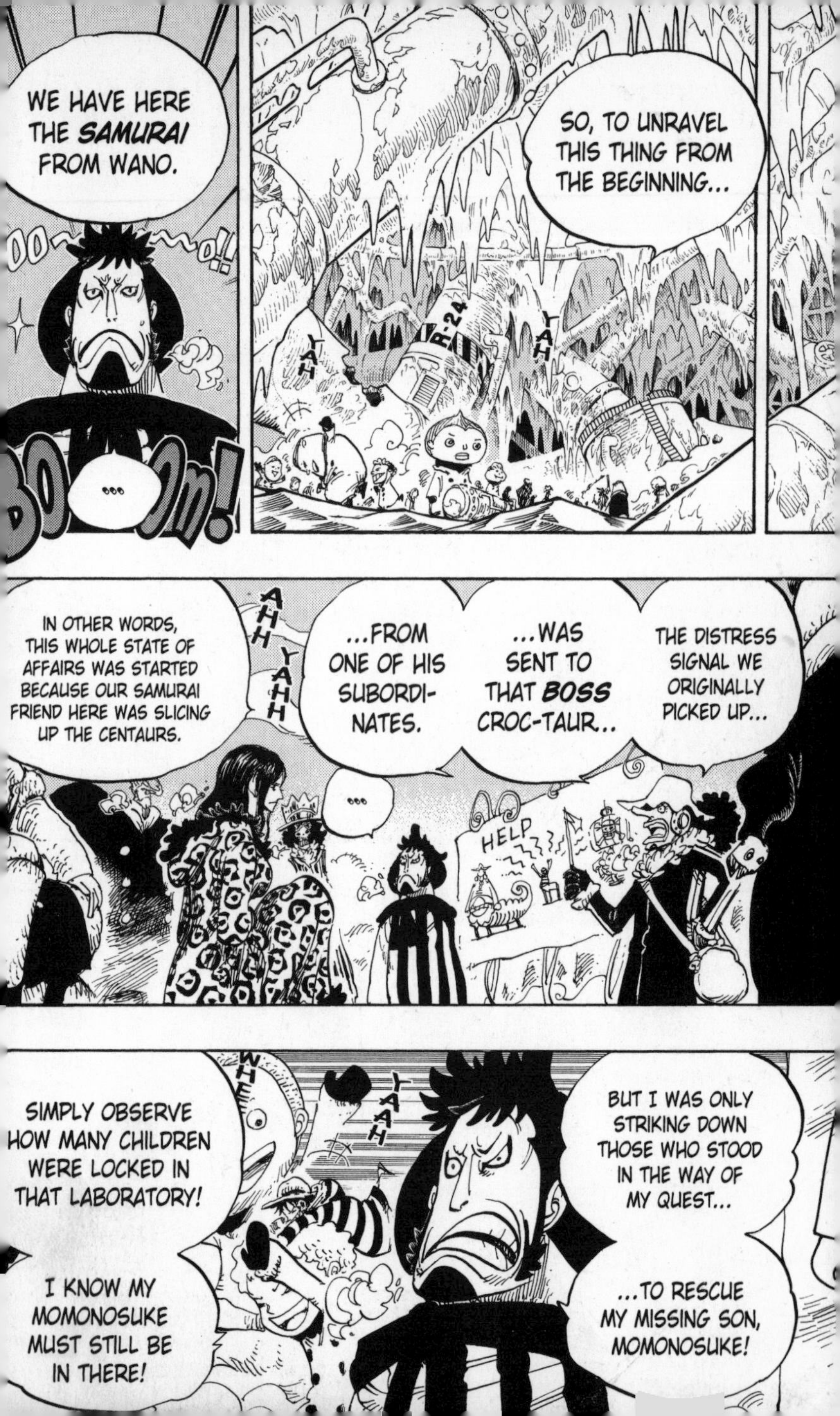
SO, TO UNRAVEL THIS THING FROM THE BEGINNING...
YAH
R-24
YAH
WE HAVE HERE THE SAMURAI FROM WANO.
BOOOM!
...
THE DISTRESS SIGNAL WE ORIGINALLY PICKED UP...
...WAS SENT TO THAT BOSS CROC-TAUR...
...FROM ONE OF HIS SUBORDINATES.
AHH YAHH
IN OTHER WORDS, THIS WHOLE STATE OF AFFAIRS WAS STARTED BECAUSE OUR SAMURAI FRIEND HERE WAS SLICING UP THE CENTAURS.
HELP
...
BUT I WAS ONLY STRIKING DOWN THOSE WHO STOOD IN THE WAY OF MY QUEST...
...TO RESCUE MY MISSING SON, MOMONOSUKE!
YAAH
SIMPLY OBSERVE HOW MANY CHILDREN WERE LOCKED IN THAT LABORATORY!
I KNOW MY MOMONOSUKE MUST STILL BE IN THERE!

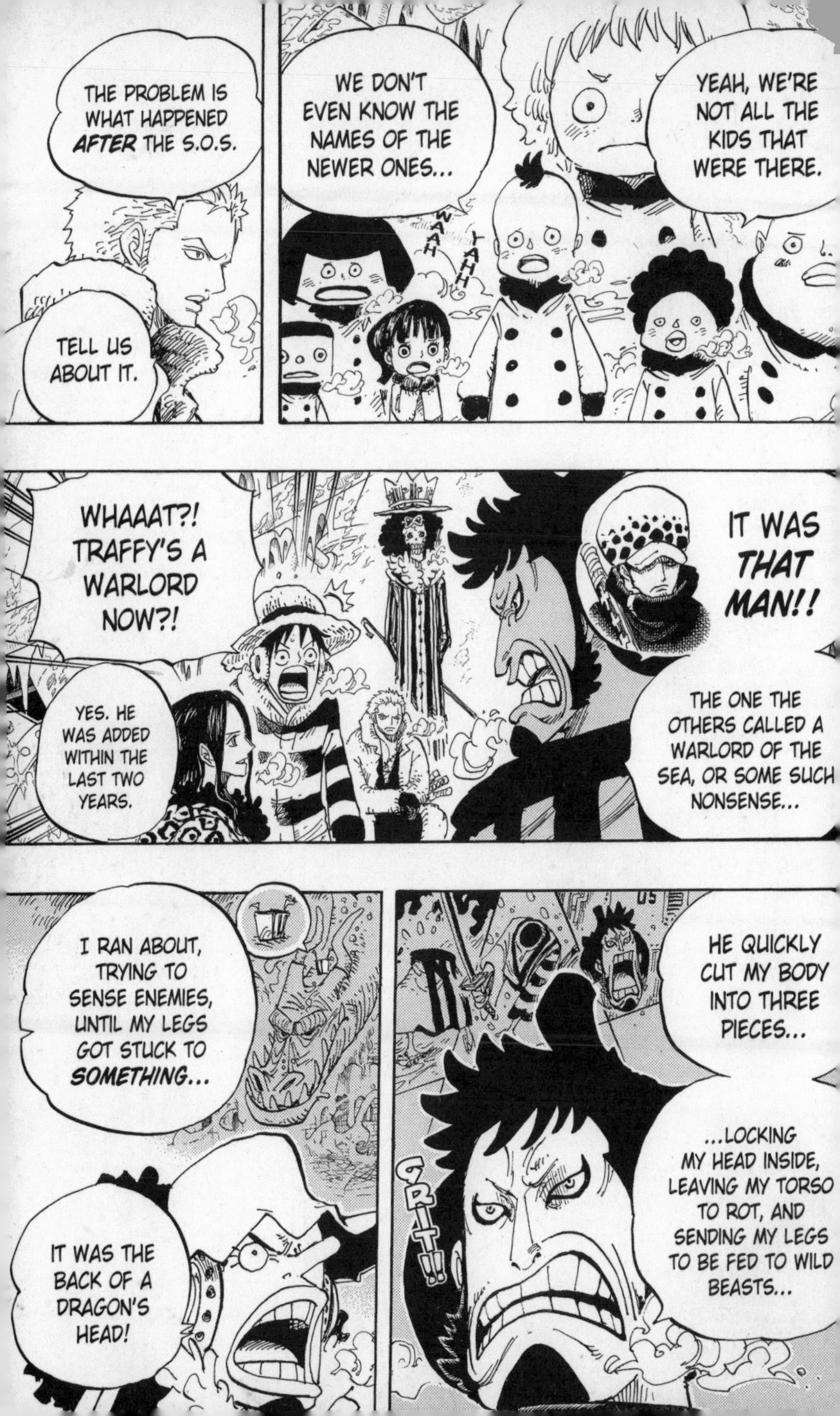
YEAH, WE'RE NOT ALL THE KIDS THAT WERE THERE.
WE DON'T EVEN KNOW THE NAMES OF THE NEWER ONES...
WAAH
YAHH
THE PROBLEM IS WHAT HAPPENED *AFTER* THE S.O.S.
TELL US ABOUT IT.
IT WAS *THAT MAN!!*
THE ONE THE OTHERS CALLED A WARLORD OF THE SEA, OR SOME SUCH NONSENSE...
WHAAAT?! TRAFFY'S A WARLORD NOW?!
YES. HE WAS ADDED WITHIN THE LAST TWO YEARS.
HE QUICKLY CUT MY BODY INTO THREE PIECES...
GRIT!!
...LOCKING MY HEAD INSIDE, LEAVING MY TORSO TO ROT, AND SENDING MY LEGS TO BE FED TO WILD BEASTS...
I RAN ABOUT, TRYING TO SENSE ENEMIES, UNTIL MY LEGS GOT STUCK TO *SOMETHING*...
IT WAS THE BACK OF A DRAGON'S HEAD!

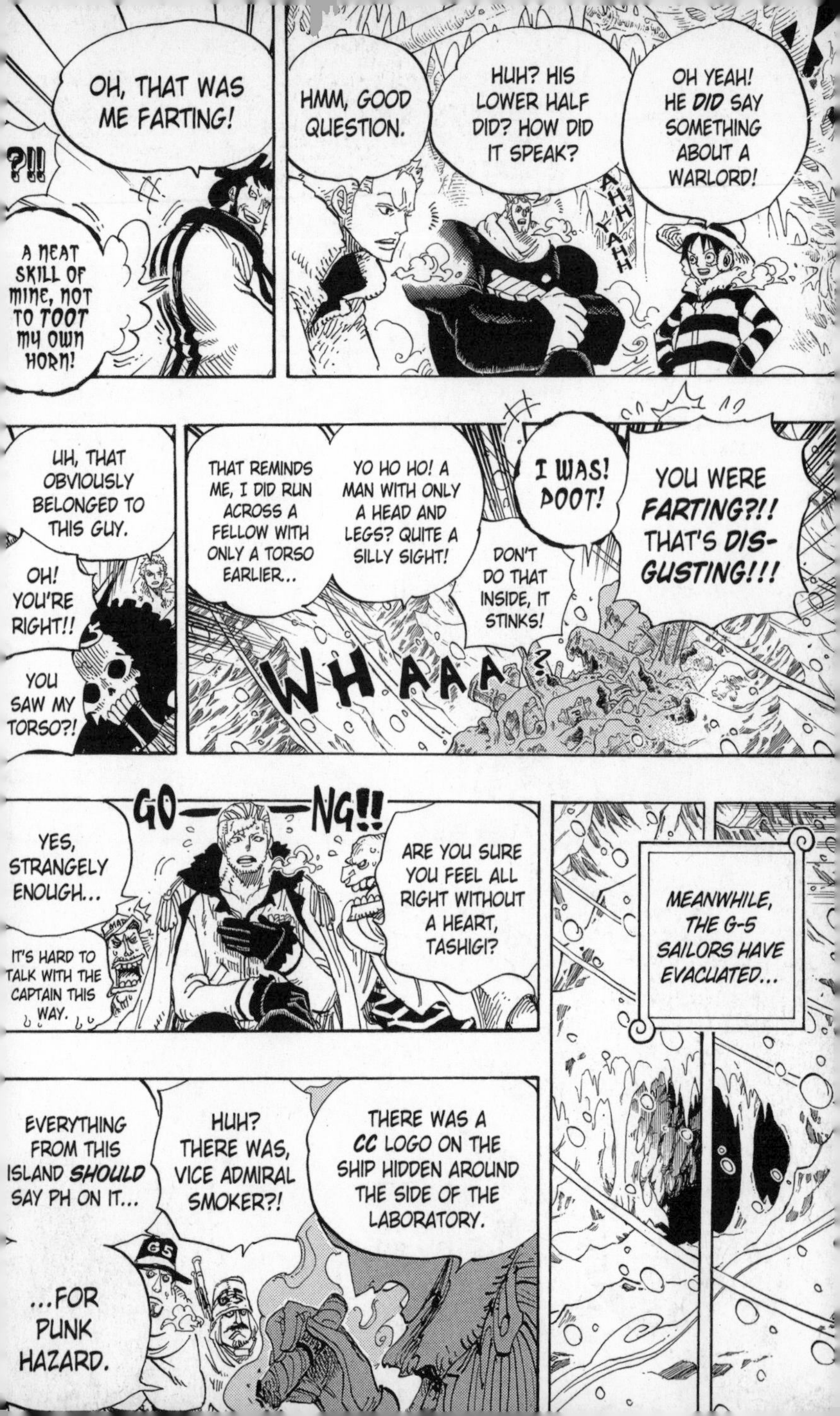
OH YEAH! HE *DID* SAY SOMETHING ABOUT A WARLORD!
AHHYAHH
HUH? HIS LOWER HALF DID? HOW DID IT SPEAK?
HMM, GOOD QUESTION.
?!!
OH, THAT WAS ME FARTING!
A NEAT SKILL OF MINE, NOT TO *TOOT* MY OWN HORN!
YOU WERE *FARTING?!!* THAT'S *DISGUSTING!!!*
I WAS! POOT!
DON'T DO THAT INSIDE, IT STINKS!
WHAAA ?
YO HO HO! A MAN WITH ONLY A HEAD AND LEGS? QUITE A SILLY SIGHT!
THAT REMINDS ME, I DID RUN ACROSS A FELLOW WITH ONLY A TORSO EARLIER...
UH, THAT OBVIOUSLY BELONGED TO THIS GUY.
OH! YOU'RE RIGHT!!
YOU SAW MY TORSO?!
MEANWHILE, THE G-5 SAILORS HAVE EVACUATED...
GO—NG!!
ARE YOU SURE YOU FEEL ALL RIGHT WITHOUT A HEART, TASHIGI?
YES, STRANGELY ENOUGH...
IT'S HARD TO TALK WITH THE CAPTAIN THIS WAY.
THERE WAS A *CC* LOGO ON THE SHIP HIDDEN AROUND THE SIDE OF THE LABORATORY.
HUH? THERE WAS, VICE ADMIRAL SMOKER?!
EVERYTHING FROM THIS ISLAND *SHOULD* SAY PH ON IT...
...FOR PUNK HAZARD.

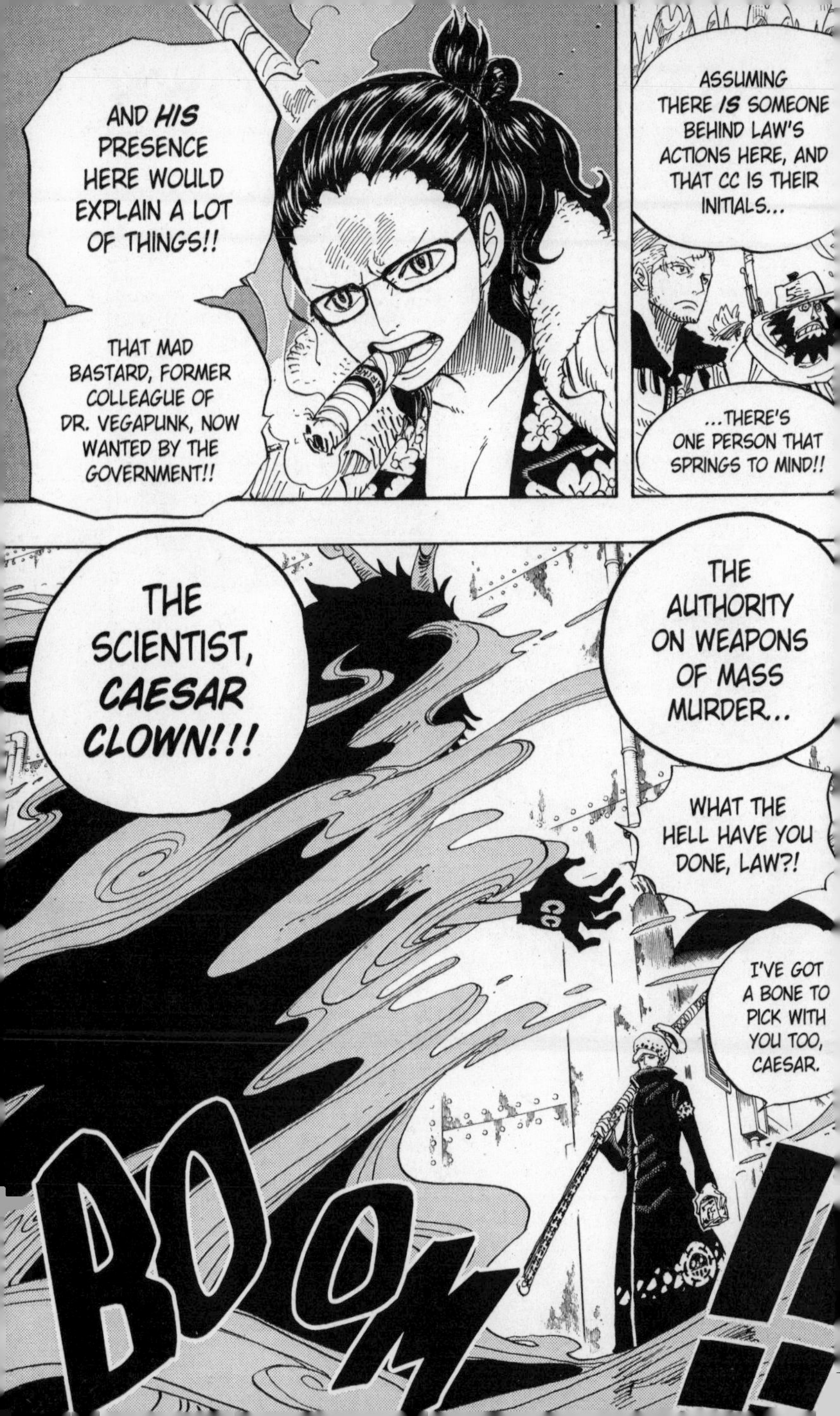

ASSUMING THERE *IS* SOMEONE BEHIND LAW'S ACTIONS HERE, AND THAT CC IS THEIR INITIALS...
...THERE'S ONE PERSON THAT SPRINGS TO MIND!!
AND *HIS* PRESENCE HERE WOULD EXPLAIN A LOT OF THINGS!!
THAT MAD BASTARD, FORMER COLLEAGUE OF DR. VEGAPUNK, NOW WANTED BY THE GOVERNMENT!!
THE AUTHORITY ON WEAPONS OF MASS MURDER...
THE SCIENTIST, *CAESAR CLOWN!!!*
WHAT THE HELL HAVE YOU DONE, LAW?!
I'VE GOT A BONE TO PICK WITH YOU TOO, CAESAR.
BOOM!!

MASTER CAESAR CLOWN

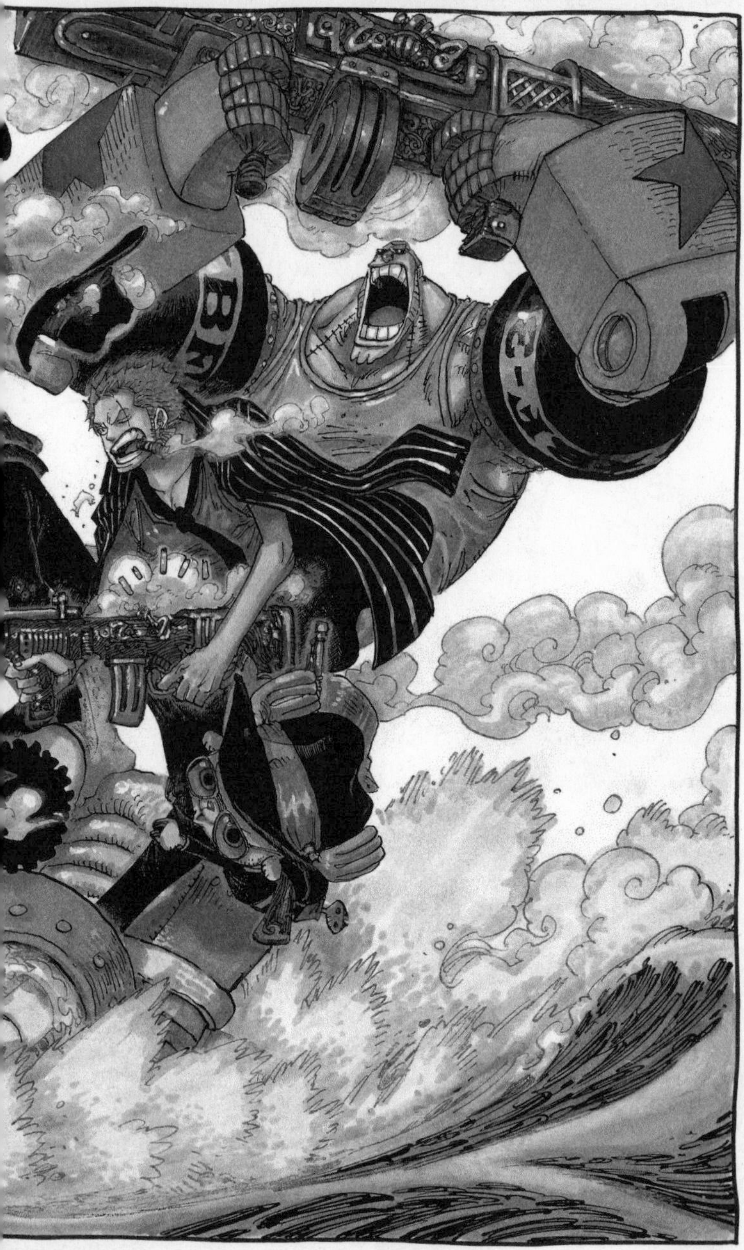

Chapter 664:

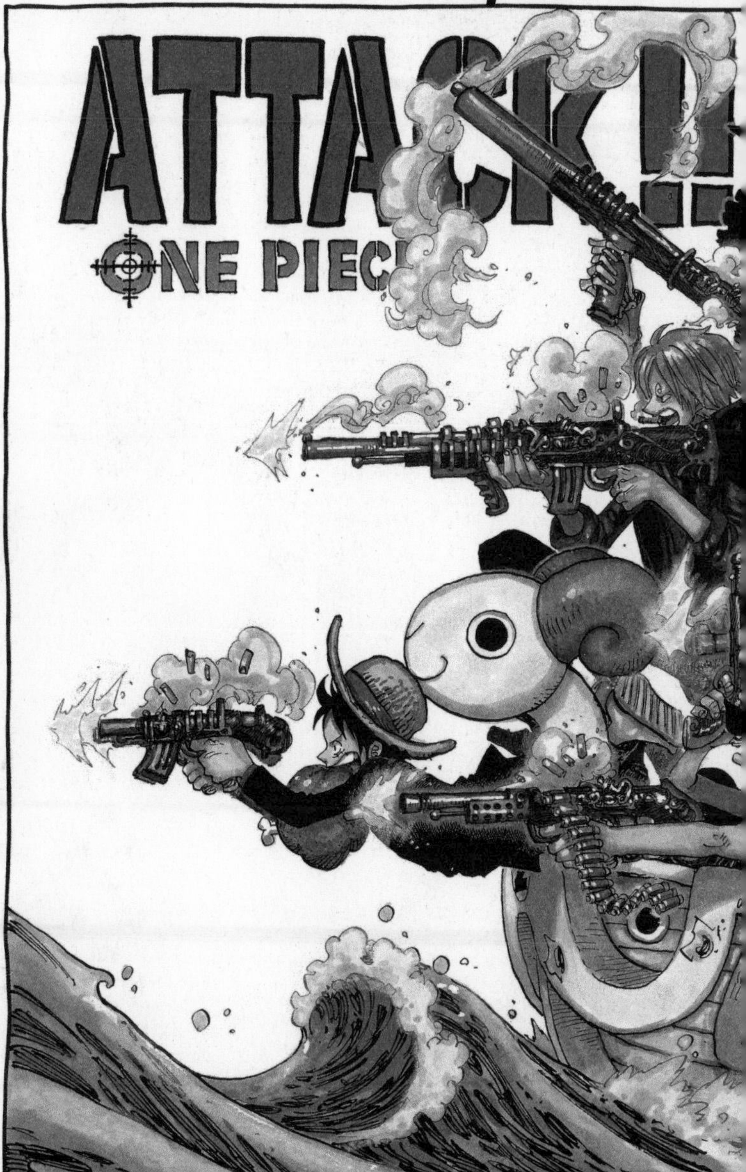
ATTACK!!
ONE PIEC

vol.67
ONE PIECE

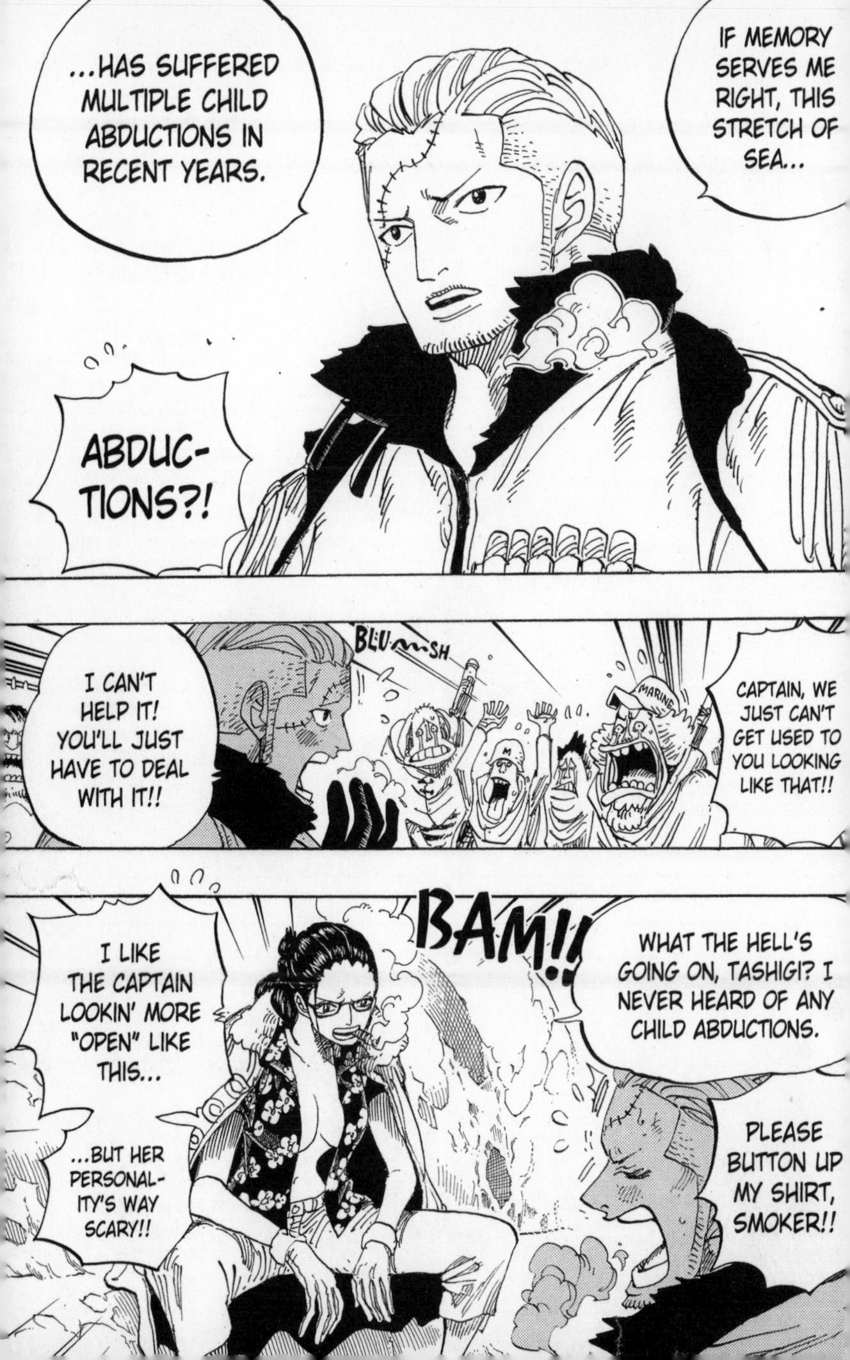

IF MEMORY SERVES ME RIGHT, THIS STRETCH OF SEA...
...HAS SUFFERED MULTIPLE CHILD ABDUCTIONS IN RECENT YEARS.
ABDUC-TIONS?!
CAPTAIN, WE JUST CAN'T GET USED TO YOU LOOKING LIKE THAT!!
BLU~SH
I CAN'T HELP IT! YOU'LL JUST HAVE TO DEAL WITH IT!!
WHAT THE HELL'S GOING ON, TASHIGI? I NEVER HEARD OF ANY CHILD ABDUCTIONS.
PLEASE BUTTON UP MY SHIRT, SMOKER!!
BAM!!
I LIKE THE CAPTAIN LOOKIN' MORE "OPEN" LIKE THIS...
...BUT HER PERSONAL-ITY'S WAY SCARY!!

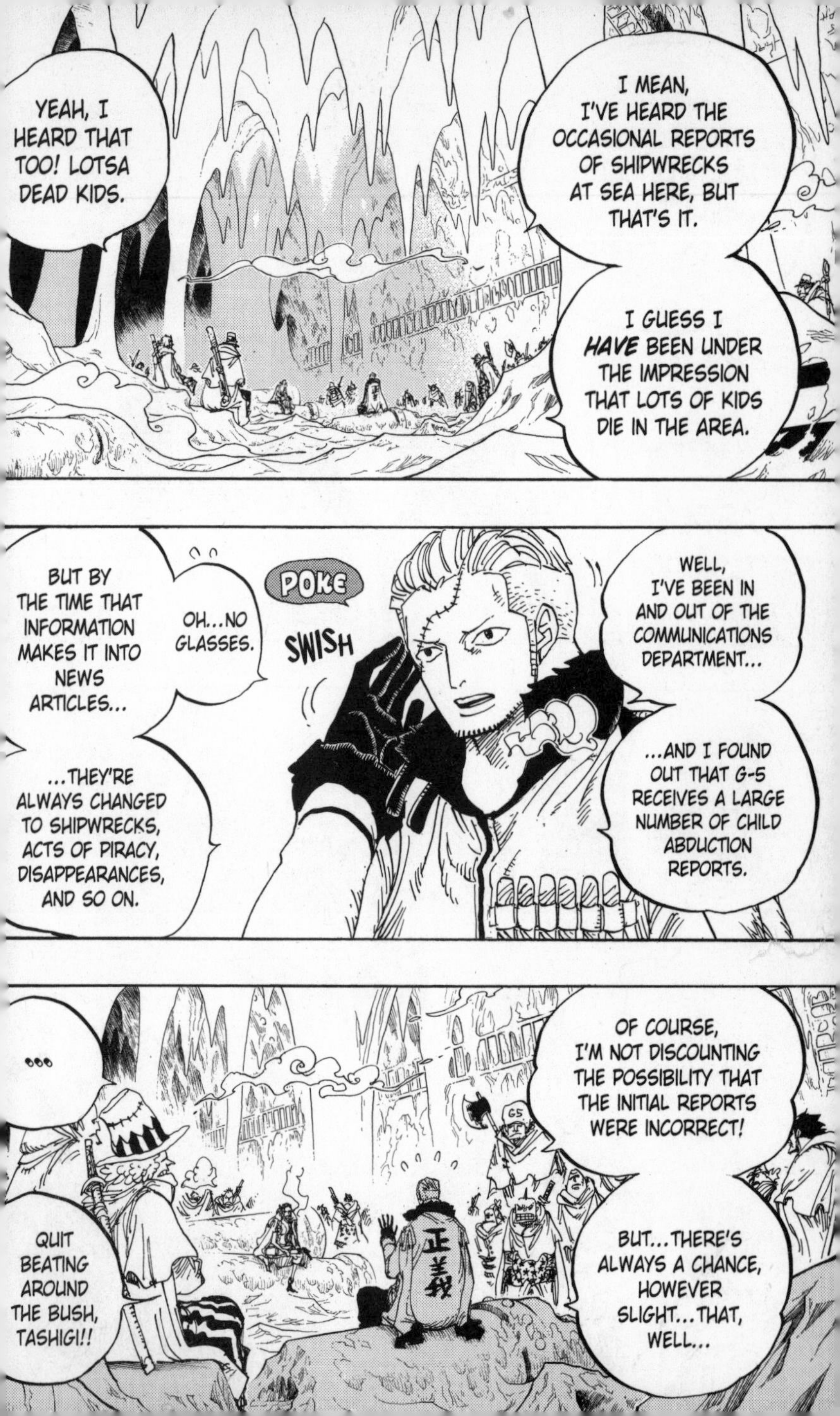
I MEAN, I'VE HEARD THE OCCASIONAL REPORTS OF SHIPWRECKS AT SEA HERE, BUT THAT'S IT.
I GUESS I *HAVE* BEEN UNDER THE IMPRESSION THAT LOTS OF KIDS DIE IN THE AREA.
YEAH, I HEARD THAT TOO! LOTSA DEAD KIDS.
WELL, I'VE BEEN IN AND OUT OF THE COMMUNICATIONS DEPARTMENT...
...AND I FOUND OUT THAT G-5 RECEIVES A LARGE NUMBER OF CHILD ABDUCTION REPORTS.
SWISH
POKE
OH...NO GLASSES.
BUT BY THE TIME THAT INFORMATION MAKES IT INTO NEWS ARTICLES...
...THEY'RE ALWAYS CHANGED TO SHIPWRECKS, ACTS OF PIRACY, DISAPPEARANCES, AND SO ON.
OF COURSE, I'M NOT DISCOUNTING THE POSSIBILITY THAT THE INITIAL REPORTS WERE INCORRECT!
BUT...THERE'S ALWAYS A CHANCE, HOWEVER SLIGHT...THAT, WELL...
...
QUIT BEATING AROUND THE BUSH, TASHIGI!!

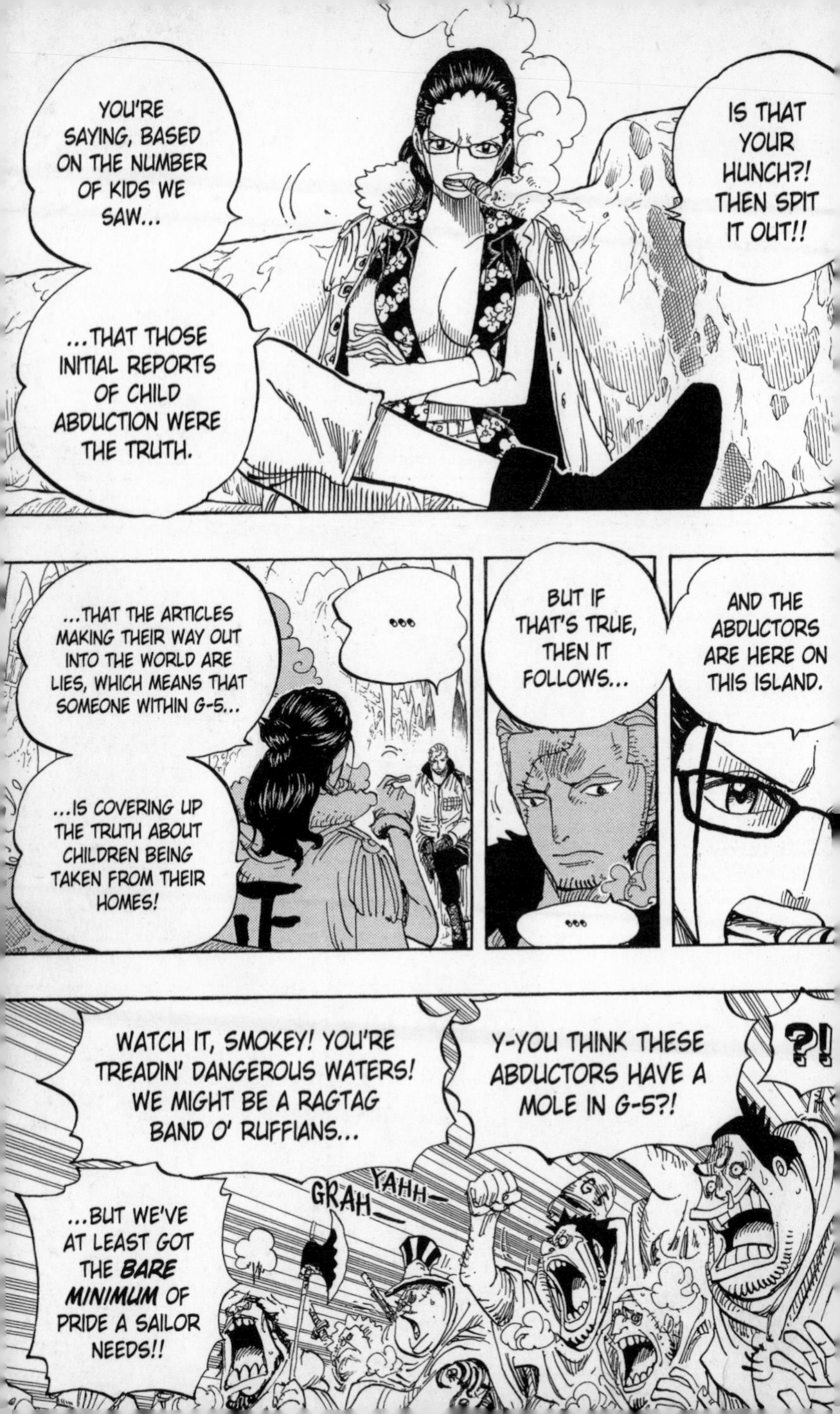
IS THAT YOUR HUNCH?! THEN SPIT IT OUT!!
YOU'RE SAYING, BASED ON THE NUMBER OF KIDS WE SAW...
...THAT THOSE INITIAL REPORTS OF CHILD ABDUCTION WERE THE TRUTH.
AND THE ABDUCTORS ARE HERE ON THIS ISLAND.
BUT IF THAT'S TRUE, THEN IT FOLLOWS...
...
...
...THAT THE ARTICLES MAKING THEIR WAY OUT INTO THE WORLD ARE LIES, WHICH MEANS THAT SOMEONE WITHIN G-5...
...IS COVERING UP THE TRUTH ABOUT CHILDREN BEING TAKEN FROM THEIR HOMES!
?!
Y-YOU THINK THESE ABDUCTORS HAVE A MOLE IN G-5?!
YAHH—
GRAH—
WATCH IT, SMOKEY! YOU'RE TREADIN' DANGEROUS WATERS! WE MIGHT BE A RAGTAG BAND O' RUFFIANS...
...BUT WE'VE AT LEAST GOT THE ***BARE MINIMUM*** OF PRIDE A SAILOR NEEDS!!

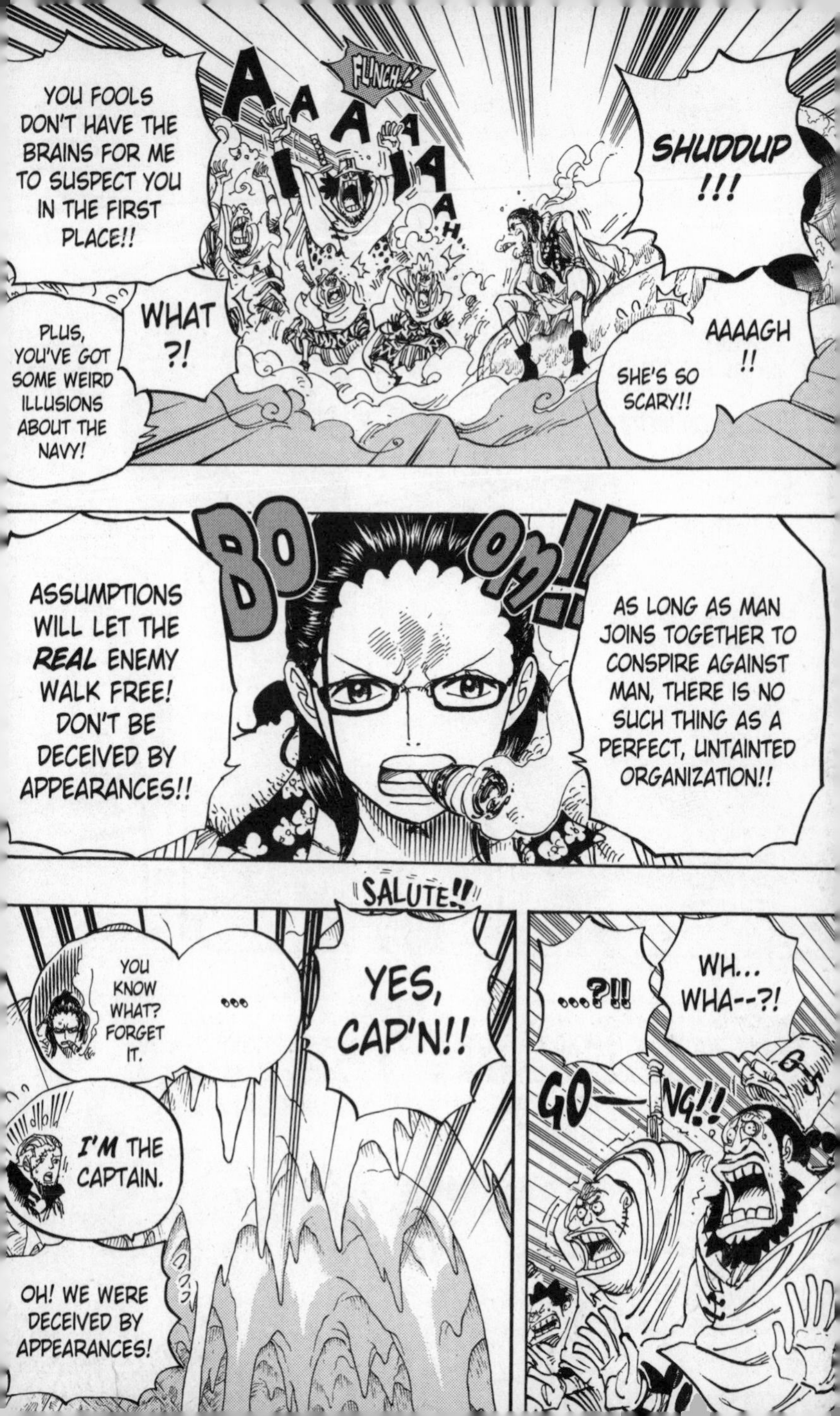
SHUDDUP!!!
FLINCH!!
AAAAGH!! SHE'S SO SCARY!!
YOU FOOLS DON'T HAVE THE BRAINS FOR ME TO SUSPECT YOU IN THE FIRST PLACE!!
WHAT?!
PLUS, YOU'VE GOT SOME WEIRD ILLUSIONS ABOUT THE NAVY!
AS LONG AS MAN JOINS TOGETHER TO CONSPIRE AGAINST MAN, THERE IS NO SUCH THING AS A PERFECT, UNTAINTED ORGANIZATION!!
BOOM!!
ASSUMPTIONS WILL LET THE *REAL* ENEMY WALK FREE! DON'T BE DECEIVED BY APPEARANCES!!
WH... WHA--?!
...?!!
GO—NG!!
SALUTE!!
YES, CAP'N!!
...
YOU KNOW WHAT? FORGET IT.
I'M THE CAPTAIN.
OH! WE WERE DECEIVED BY APPEARANCES!

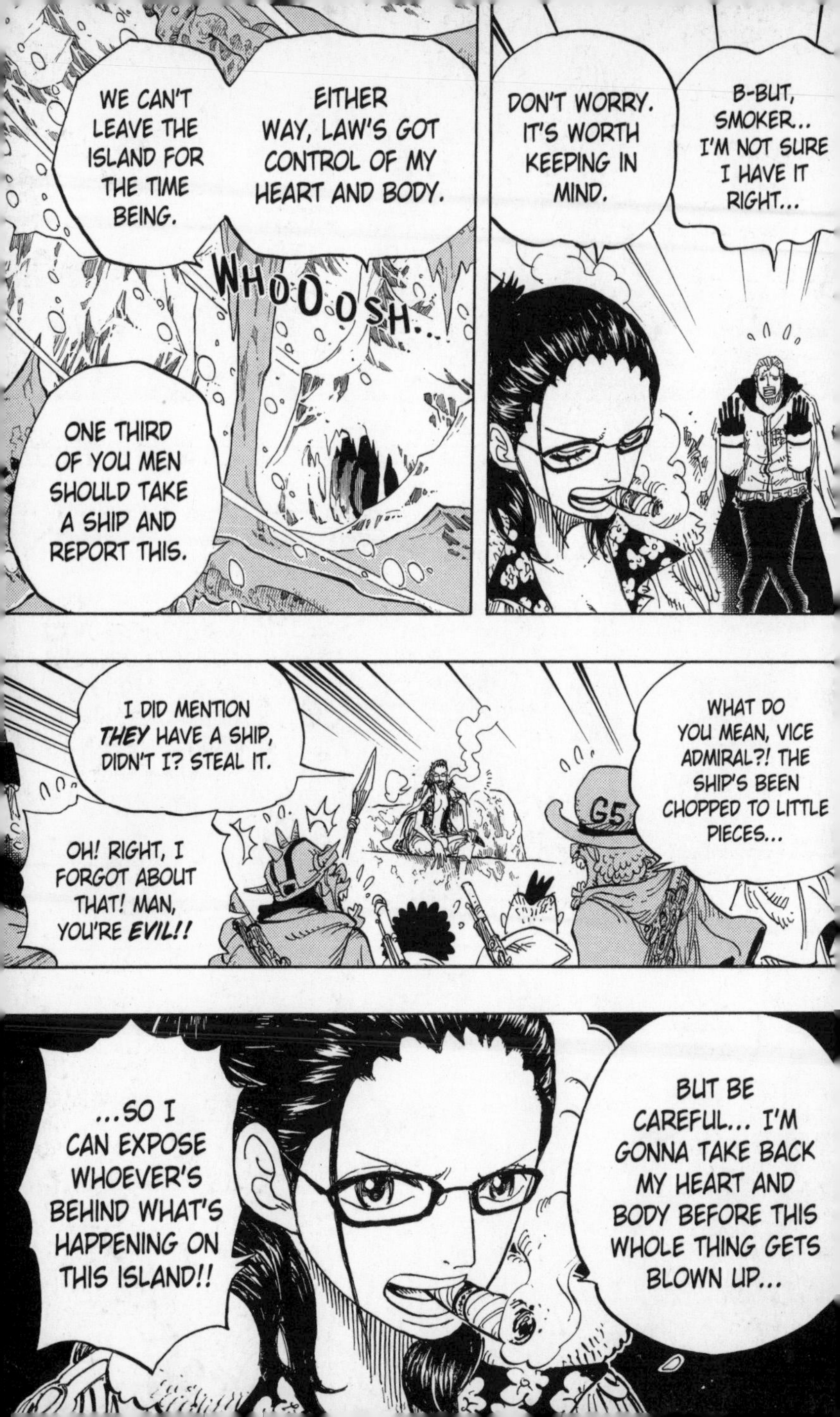
B-BUT, SMOKER... I'M NOT SURE I HAVE IT RIGHT...
DON'T WORRY. IT'S WORTH KEEPING IN MIND.
EITHER WAY, LAW'S GOT CONTROL OF MY HEART AND BODY.
WE CAN'T LEAVE THE ISLAND FOR THE TIME BEING.
WHOOOOSH...
ONE THIRD OF YOU MEN SHOULD TAKE A SHIP AND REPORT THIS.
WHAT DO YOU MEAN, VICE ADMIRAL?! THE SHIP'S BEEN CHOPPED TO LITTLE PIECES...
G5
I DID MENTION *THEY* HAVE A SHIP, DIDN'T I? STEAL IT.
OH! RIGHT, I FORGOT ABOUT THAT! MAN, YOU'RE ***EVIL!!***
BUT BE CAREFUL... I'M GONNA TAKE BACK MY HEART AND BODY BEFORE THIS WHOLE THING GETS BLOWN UP...
...SO I CAN EXPOSE WHOEVER'S BEHIND WHAT'S HAPPENING ON THIS ISLAND!!

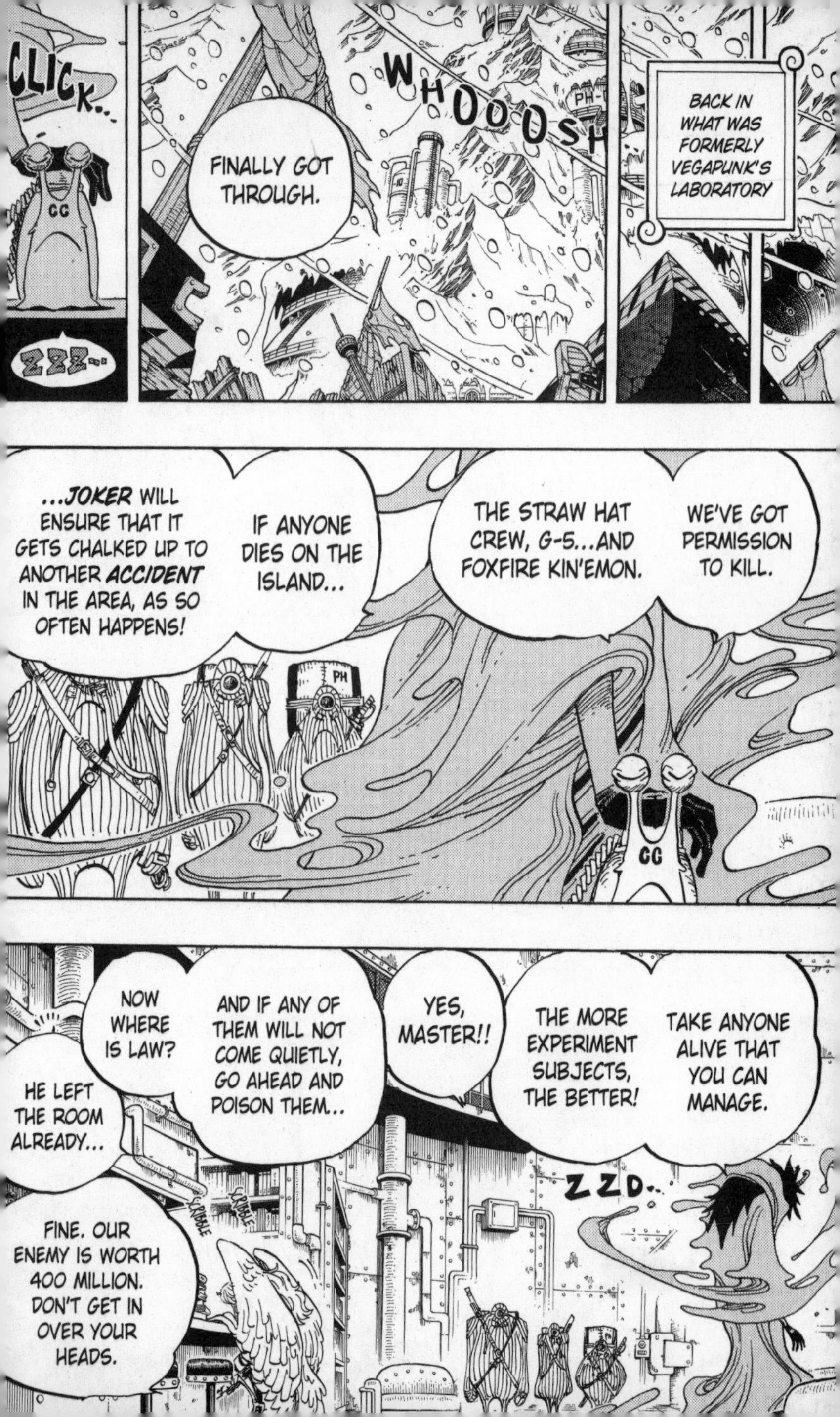
BACK IN WHAT WAS FORMERLY VEGAPUNK'S LABORATORY
WHOOOSH
FINALLY GOT THROUGH.
CLICK...
ZZZ...
WE'VE GOT PERMISSION TO KILL.
THE STRAW HAT CREW, G-5...AND FOXFIRE KIN'EMON.
IF ANYONE DIES ON THE ISLAND...
...JOKER WILL ENSURE THAT IT GETS CHALKED UP TO ANOTHER ACCIDENT IN THE AREA, AS SO OFTEN HAPPENS!
TAKE ANYONE ALIVE THAT YOU CAN MANAGE.
THE MORE EXPERIMENT SUBJECTS, THE BETTER!
YES, MASTER!!
AND IF ANY OF THEM WILL NOT COME QUIETLY, GO AHEAD AND POISON THEM...
ZZD...
NOW WHERE IS LAW?
HE LEFT THE ROOM ALREADY...
SCRIBBLE
SCRIBBLE
FINE. OUR ENEMY IS WORTH 400 MILLION. DON'T GET IN OVER YOUR HEADS.

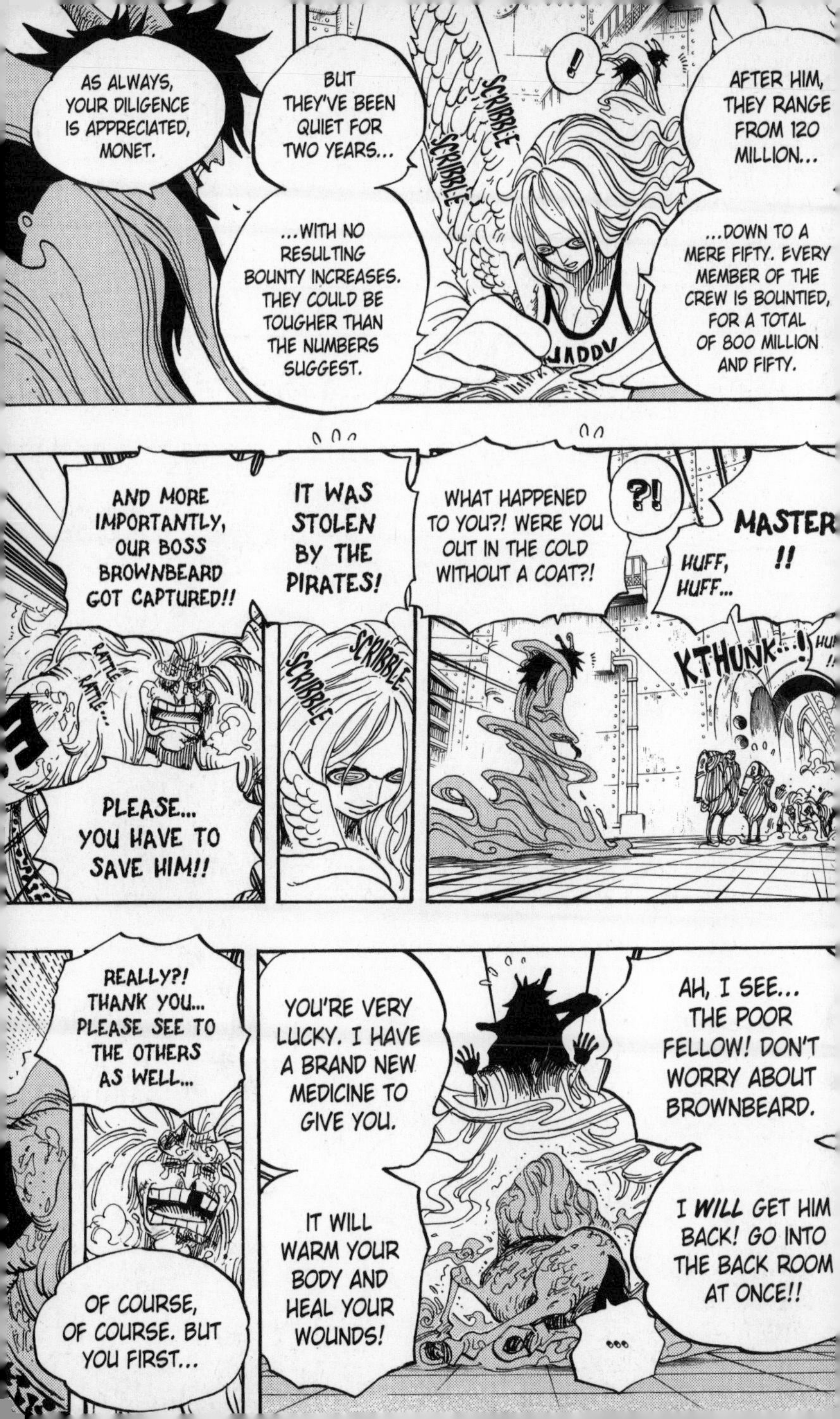
!
AFTER HIM, THEY RANGE FROM 120 MILLION...
...DOWN TO A MERE FIFTY. EVERY MEMBER OF THE CREW IS BOUNTIED, FOR A TOTAL OF 800 MILLION AND FIFTY.
SCRIBBLE SCRIBBLE
BUT THEY'VE BEEN QUIET FOR TWO YEARS...
...WITH NO RESULTING BOUNTY INCREASES. THEY COULD BE TOUGHER THAN THE NUMBERS SUGGEST.
AS ALWAYS, YOUR DILIGENCE IS APPRECIATED, MONET.
KTHUNK...!
HUFF, HUFF...
MASTER!!
?!
WHAT HAPPENED TO YOU?! WERE YOU OUT IN THE COLD WITHOUT A COAT?!
IT WAS STOLEN BY THE PIRATES!
SCRIBBLE SCRIBBLE
AND MORE IMPORTANTLY, OUR BOSS BROWNBEARD GOT CAPTURED!!
RATTLE RATTLE...
PLEASE... YOU HAVE TO SAVE HIM!!
AH, I SEE... THE POOR FELLOW! DON'T WORRY ABOUT BROWNBEARD.
I WILL GET HIM BACK! GO INTO THE BACK ROOM AT ONCE!!
...
YOU'RE VERY LUCKY. I HAVE A BRAND NEW MEDICINE TO GIVE YOU.
IT WILL WARM YOUR BODY AND HEAL YOUR WOUNDS!
REALLY?! THANK YOU... PLEASE SEE TO THE OTHERS AS WELL...
OF COURSE, OF COURSE. BUT YOU FIRST...

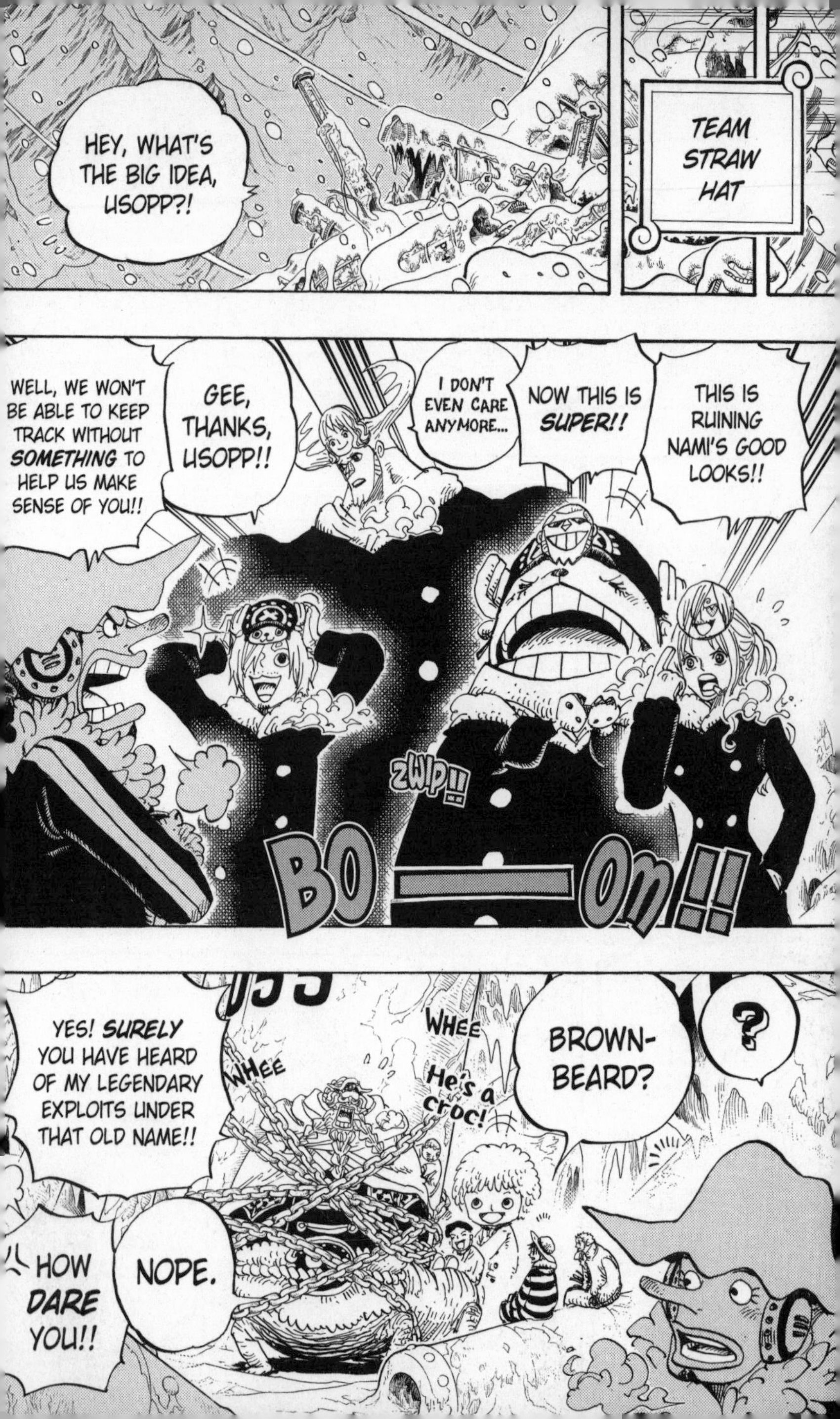
TEAM STRAW HAT
HEY, WHAT'S THE BIG IDEA, USOPP?!
THIS IS RUINING NAMI'S GOOD LOOKS!!
NOW THIS IS SUPER!!
I DON'T EVEN CARE ANYMORE...
GEE, THANKS, USOPP!!
WELL, WE WON'T BE ABLE TO KEEP TRACK WITHOUT SOMETHING TO HELP US MAKE SENSE OF YOU!!
ZWIP!!
BO——OM!!
?
BROWN-BEARD?
WHEE
He's a croc!
WHEE
YES! SURELY YOU HAVE HEARD OF MY LEGENDARY EXPLOITS UNDER THAT OLD NAME!!
NOPE.
HOW DARE YOU!!

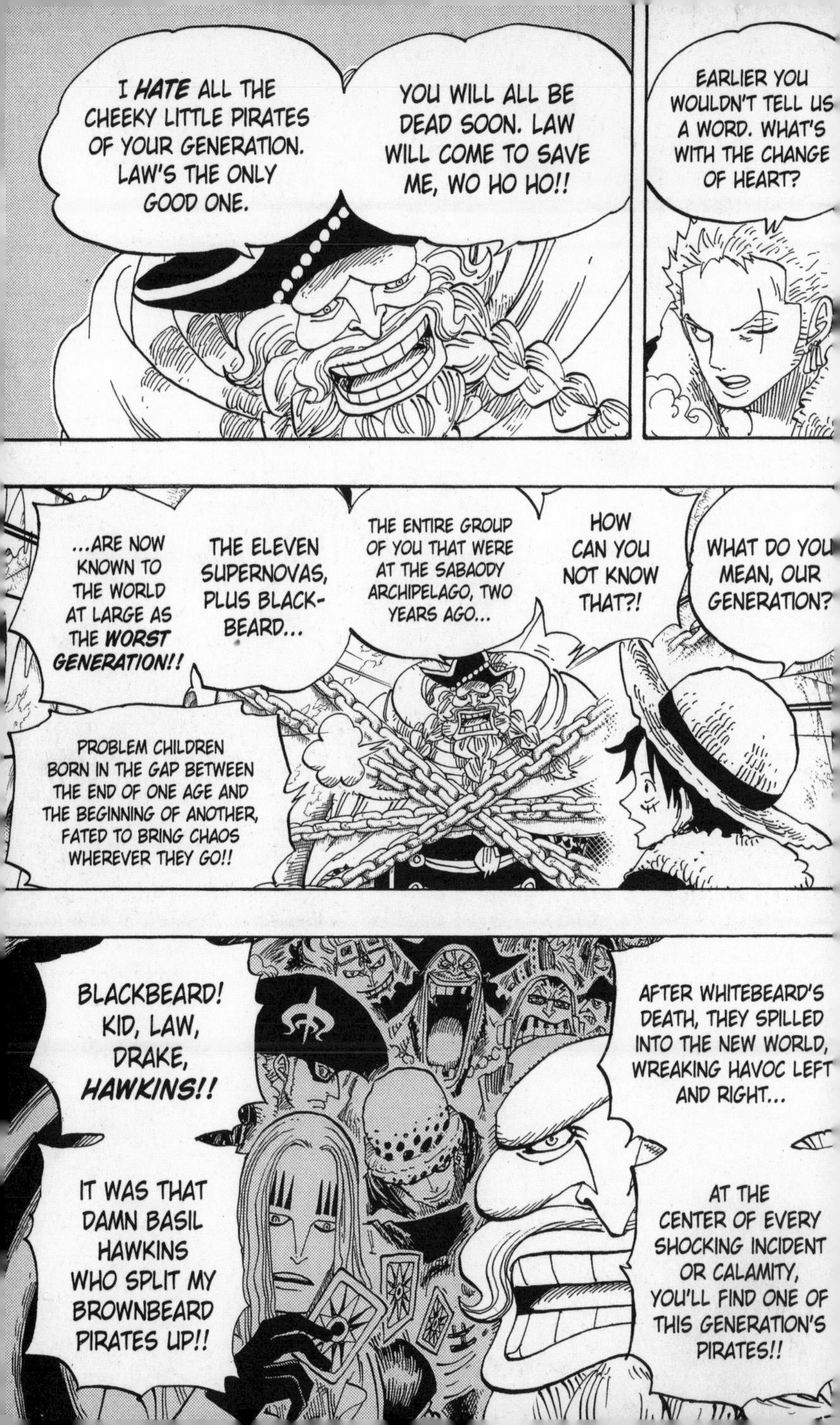
EARLIER YOU WOULDN'T TELL US A WORD. WHAT'S WITH THE CHANGE OF HEART?
YOU WILL ALL BE DEAD SOON. LAW WILL COME TO SAVE ME, WO HO HO!!
I **HATE** ALL THE CHEEKY LITTLE PIRATES OF YOUR GENERATION. LAW'S THE ONLY GOOD ONE.
WHAT DO YOU MEAN, OUR GENERATION?
HOW CAN YOU NOT KNOW THAT?!
THE ENTIRE GROUP OF YOU THAT WERE AT THE SABAODY ARCHIPELAGO, TWO YEARS AGO...
THE ELEVEN SUPERNOVAS, PLUS BLACKBEARD...
...ARE NOW KNOWN TO THE WORLD AT LARGE AS THE ***WORST GENERATION!!***
PROBLEM CHILDREN BORN IN THE GAP BETWEEN THE END OF ONE AGE AND THE BEGINNING OF ANOTHER, FATED TO BRING CHAOS WHEREVER THEY GO!!
AFTER WHITEBEARD'S DEATH, THEY SPILLED INTO THE NEW WORLD, WREAKING HAVOC LEFT AND RIGHT...
BLACKBEARD! KID, LAW, DRAKE, ***HAWKINS!!***
AT THE CENTER OF EVERY SHOCKING INCIDENT OR CALAMITY, YOU'LL FIND ONE OF THIS GENERATION'S PIRATES!!
IT WAS THAT DAMN BASIL HAWKINS WHO SPLIT MY BROWNBEARD PIRATES UP!!

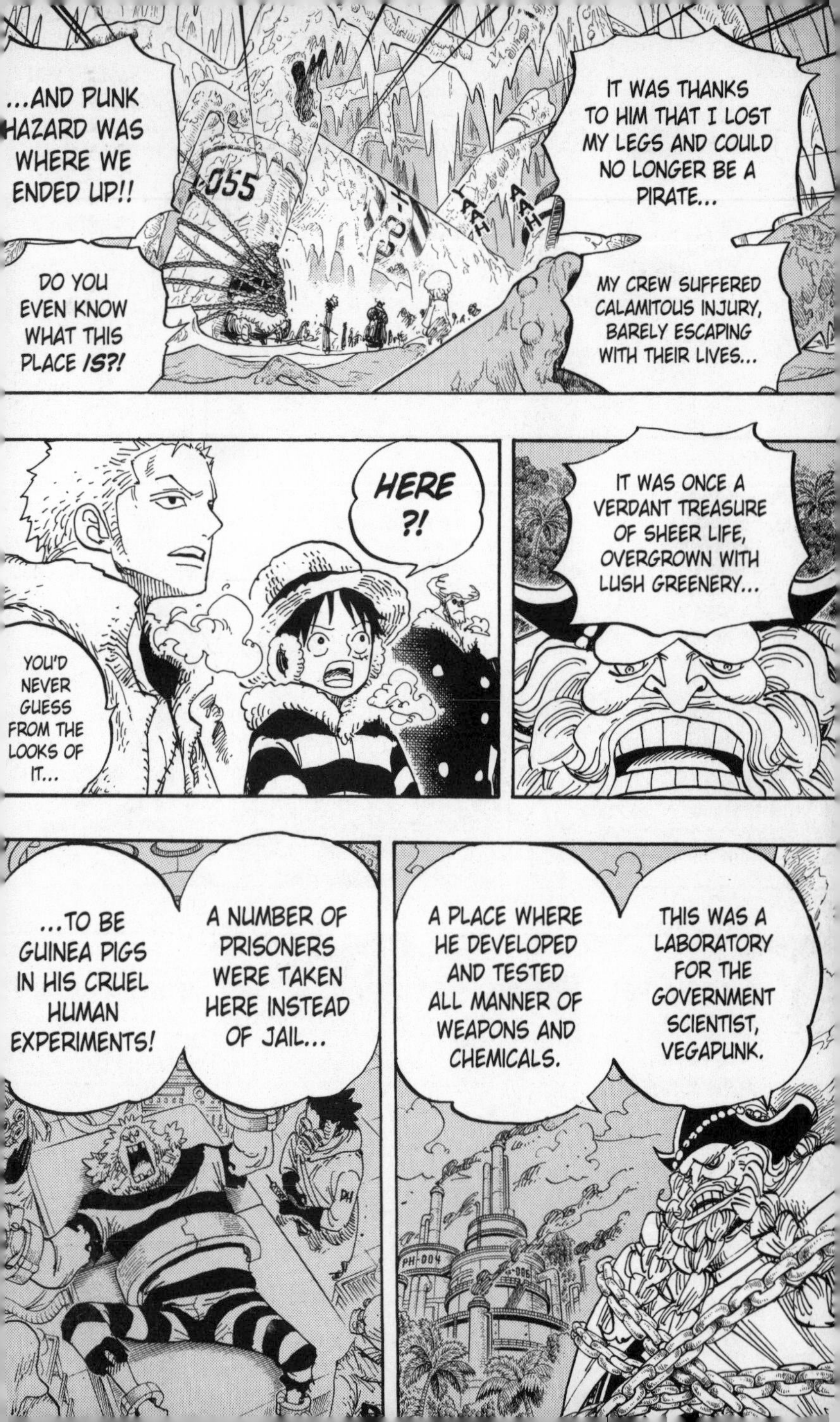
IT WAS THANKS TO HIM THAT I LOST MY LEGS AND COULD NO LONGER BE A PIRATE...
MY CREW SUFFERED CALAMITOUS INJURY, BARELY ESCAPING WITH THEIR LIVES...
AAH
YAAH
...AND PUNK HAZARD WAS WHERE WE ENDED UP!!
DO YOU EVEN KNOW WHAT THIS PLACE *IS*?!
IT WAS ONCE A VERDANT TREASURE OF SHEER LIFE, OVERGROWN WITH LUSH GREENERY...
HERE ?!
YOU'D NEVER GUESS FROM THE LOOKS OF IT...
THIS WAS A LABORATORY FOR THE GOVERNMENT SCIENTIST, VEGAPUNK.
A PLACE WHERE HE DEVELOPED AND TESTED ALL MANNER OF WEAPONS AND CHEMICALS.
PH-004
A NUMBER OF PRISONERS WERE TAKEN HERE INSTEAD OF JAIL...
...TO BE GUINEA PIGS IN HIS CRUEL HUMAN EXPERIMENTS!

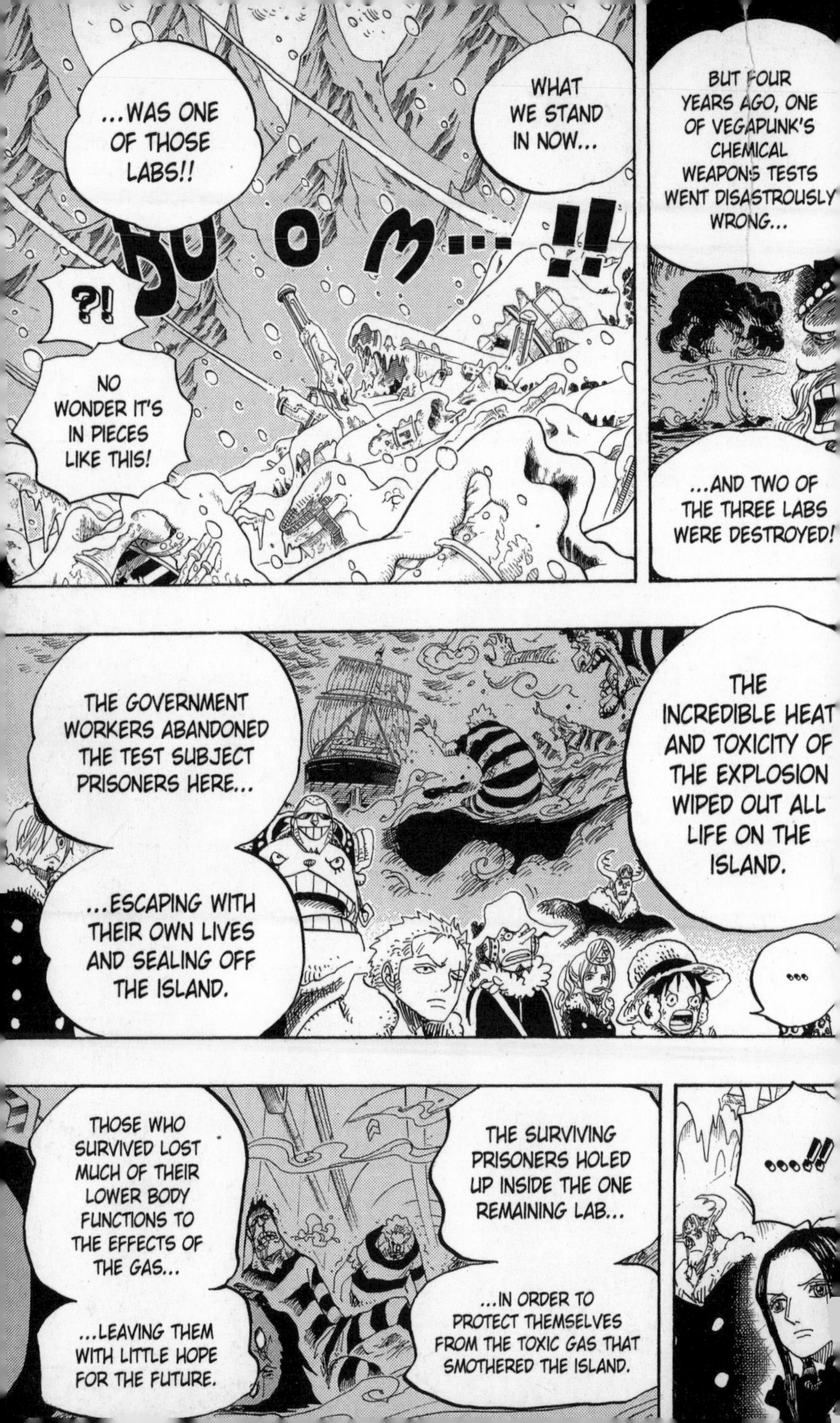

BUT FOUR YEARS AGO, ONE OF VEGAPUNK'S CHEMICAL WEAPONS TESTS WENT DISASTROUSLY WRONG...
...AND TWO OF THE THREE LABS WERE DESTROYED!
WHAT WE STAND IN NOW...
...WAS ONE OF THOSE LABS!!
BOOM...!!
?!
NO WONDER IT'S IN PIECES LIKE THIS!
THE INCREDIBLE HEAT AND TOXICITY OF THE EXPLOSION WIPED OUT ALL LIFE ON THE ISLAND.
...
THE GOVERNMENT WORKERS ABANDONED THE TEST SUBJECT PRISONERS HERE...
...ESCAPING WITH THEIR OWN LIVES AND SEALING OFF THE ISLAND.
.....!!
THE SURVIVING PRISONERS HOLED UP INSIDE THE ONE REMAINING LAB...
...IN ORDER TO PROTECT THEMSELVES FROM THE TOXIC GAS THAT SMOTHERED THE ISLAND.
THOSE WHO SURVIVED LOST MUCH OF THEIR LOWER BODY FUNCTIONS TO THE EFFECTS OF THE GAS...
...LEAVING THEM WITH LITTLE HOPE FOR THE FUTURE.

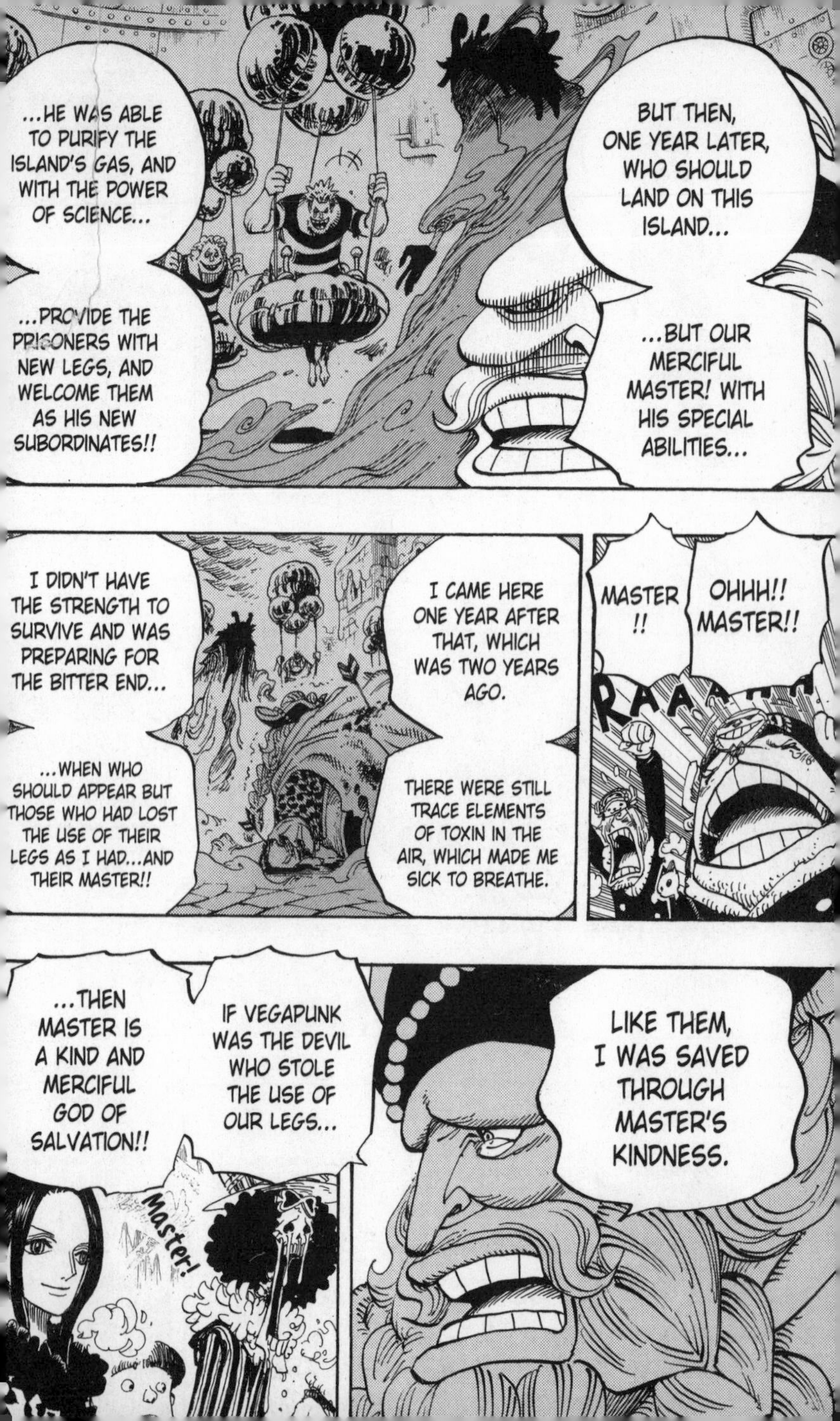

BUT THEN, ONE YEAR LATER, WHO SHOULD LAND ON THIS ISLAND...
...BUT OUR MERCIFUL MASTER! WITH HIS SPECIAL ABILITIES...
...HE WAS ABLE TO PURIFY THE ISLAND'S GAS, AND WITH THE POWER OF SCIENCE...
...PROVIDE THE PRISONERS WITH NEW LEGS, AND WELCOME THEM AS HIS NEW SUBORDINATES!!
OHHH!! MASTER!!
MASTER !!
I CAME HERE ONE YEAR AFTER THAT, WHICH WAS TWO YEARS AGO.
THERE WERE STILL TRACE ELEMENTS OF TOXIN IN THE AIR, WHICH MADE ME SICK TO BREATHE.
I DIDN'T HAVE THE STRENGTH TO SURVIVE AND WAS PREPARING FOR THE BITTER END...
...WHEN WHO SHOULD APPEAR BUT THOSE WHO HAD LOST THE USE OF THEIR LEGS AS I HAD...AND THEIR MASTER!!
LIKE THEM, I WAS SAVED THROUGH MASTER'S KINDNESS.
IF VEGAPUNK WAS THE DEVIL WHO STOLE THE USE OF OUR LEGS...
...THEN MASTER IS A KIND AND MERCIFUL GOD OF SALVATION!!
Master!

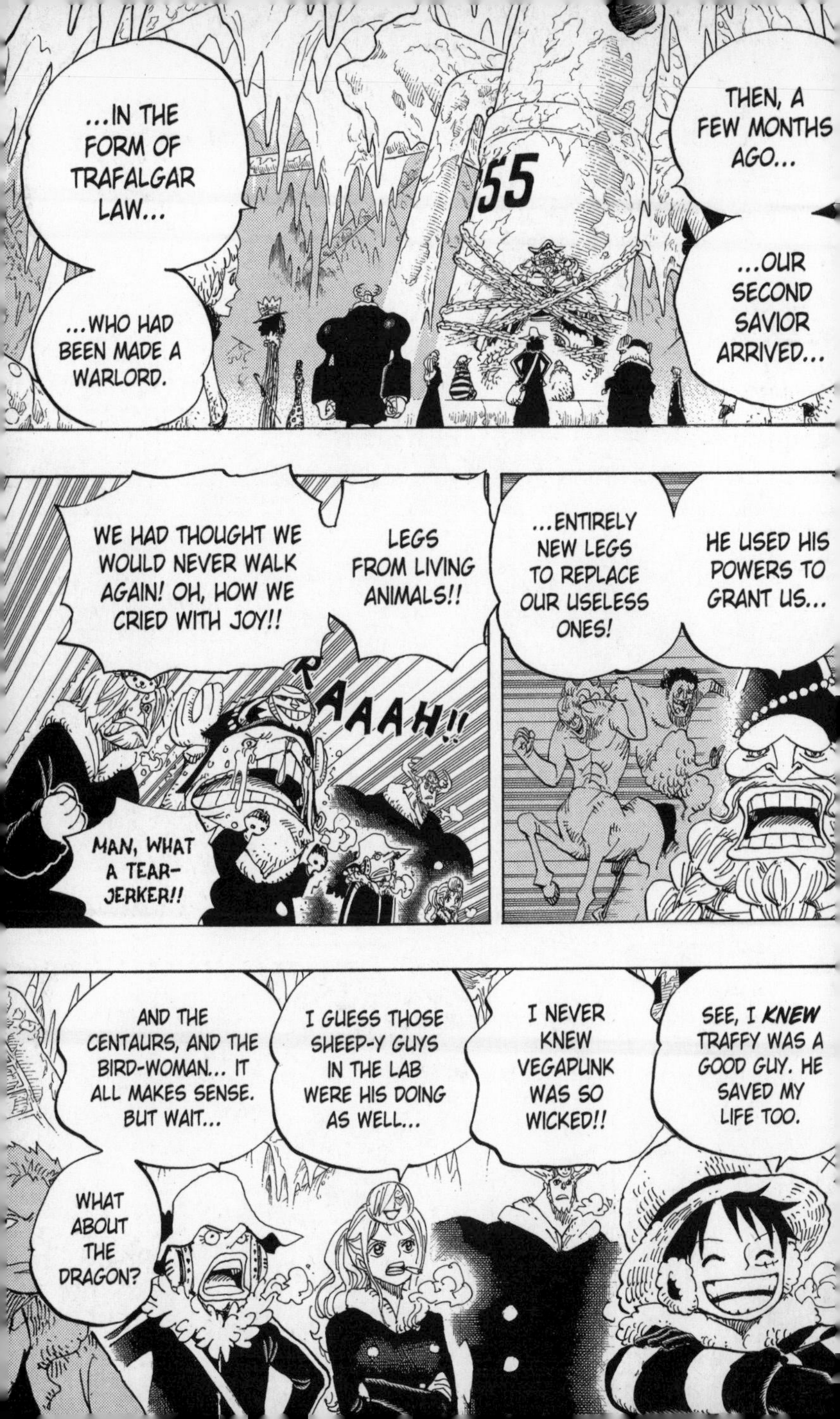
THEN, A FEW MONTHS AGO...
...OUR SECOND SAVIOR ARRIVED...
...IN THE FORM OF TRAFALGAR LAW...
...WHO HAD BEEN MADE A WARLORD.
55
HE USED HIS POWERS TO GRANT US...
...ENTIRELY NEW LEGS TO REPLACE OUR USELESS ONES!
LEGS FROM LIVING ANIMALS!!
WE HAD THOUGHT WE WOULD NEVER WALK AGAIN! OH, HOW WE CRIED WITH JOY!!
RAAAAH!!
MAN, WHAT A TEAR-JERKER!!
SEE, I *KNEW* TRAFFY WAS A GOOD GUY. HE SAVED MY LIFE TOO.
I NEVER KNEW VEGAPUNK WAS SO WICKED!!
I GUESS THOSE SHEEP-Y GUYS IN THE LAB WERE HIS DOING AS WELL...
AND THE CENTAURS, AND THE BIRD-WOMAN... IT ALL MAKES SENSE. BUT WAIT...
WHAT ABOUT THE DRAGON?

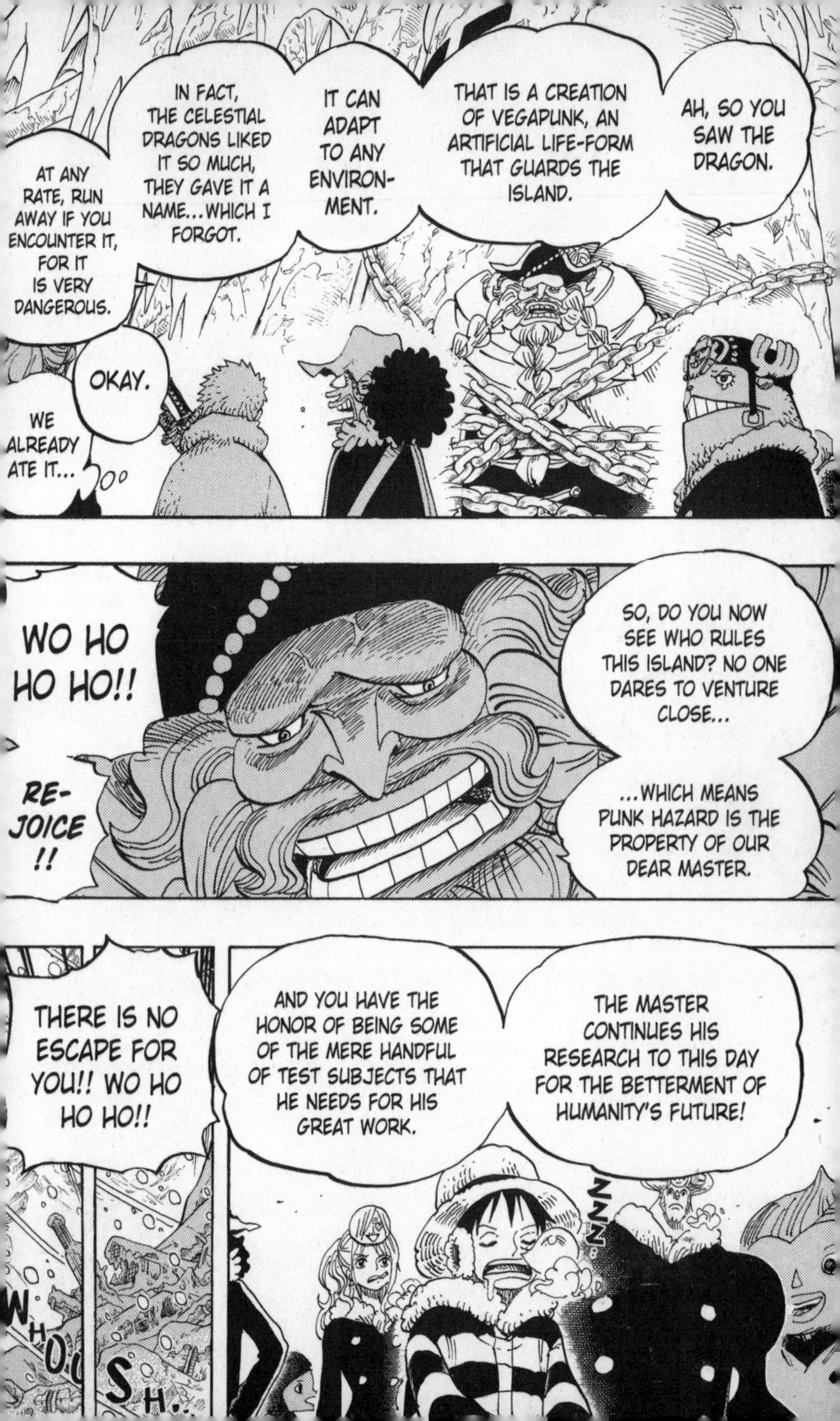
AH, SO YOU SAW THE DRAGON.
THAT IS A CREATION OF VEGAPUNK, AN ARTIFICIAL LIFE-FORM THAT GUARDS THE ISLAND.
IT CAN ADAPT TO ANY ENVIRON-MENT.
IN FACT, THE CELESTIAL DRAGONS LIKED IT SO MUCH, THEY GAVE IT A NAME...WHICH I FORGOT.
AT ANY RATE, RUN AWAY IF YOU ENCOUNTER IT, FOR IT IS VERY DANGEROUS.
OKAY.
WE ALREADY ATE IT...
SO, DO YOU NOW SEE WHO RULES THIS ISLAND? NO ONE DARES TO VENTURE CLOSE...
...WHICH MEANS PUNK HAZARD IS THE PROPERTY OF OUR DEAR MASTER.
WO HO HO HO!!
RE-JOICE!!
THE MASTER CONTINUES HIS RESEARCH TO THIS DAY FOR THE BETTERMENT OF HUMANITY'S FUTURE!
AND YOU HAVE THE HONOR OF BEING SOME OF THE MERE HANDFUL OF TEST SUBJECTS THAT HE NEEDS FOR HIS GREAT WORK.
ZZZ
THERE IS NO ESCAPE FOR YOU!! WO HO HO HO!!
WHOOSH..

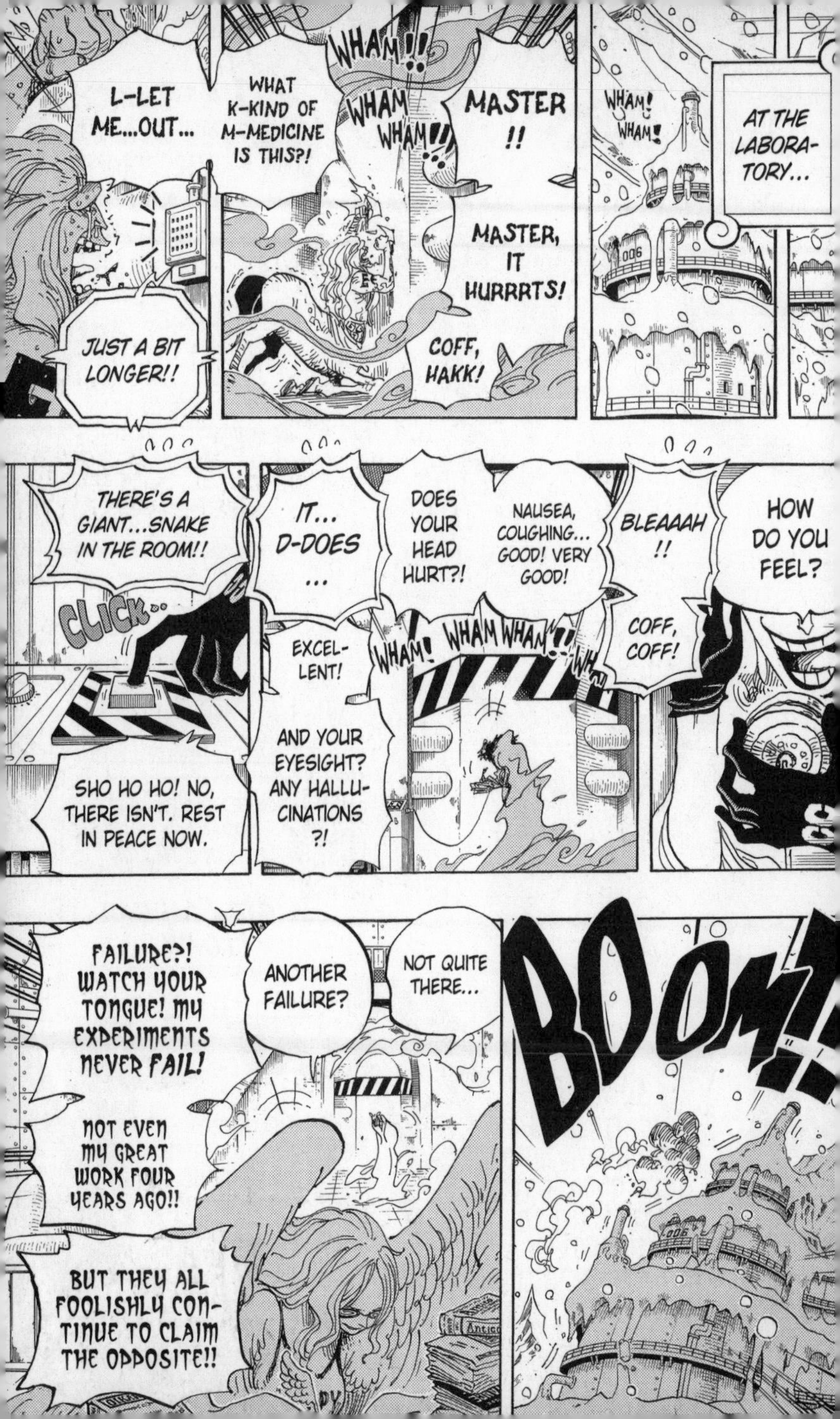
AT THE LABORATORY...
WHAM! WHAM!
WHAM!!
WHAM WHAM!!
MASTER!!
WHAT K-KIND OF M-MEDICINE IS THIS?!
MASTER, IT HURRRTS!
COFF, HAKK!
L-LET ME...OUT...
JUST A BIT LONGER!!
HOW DO YOU FEEL?
BLEAAAH!!
COFF, COFF!
NAUSEA, COUGHING... GOOD! VERY GOOD!
DOES YOUR HEAD HURT?!
IT... D-DOES...
WHAM! WHAM WHAM!!
EXCEL-LENT!
AND YOUR EYESIGHT? ANY HALLU-CINATIONS?!
THERE'S A GIANT...SNAKE IN THE ROOM!!
CLICK..
SHO HO HO! NO, THERE ISN'T. REST IN PEACE NOW.
BOOM!!
NOT QUITE THERE...
ANOTHER FAILURE?
FAILURE?! WATCH YOUR TONGUE! MY EXPERIMENTS NEVER FAIL!
NOT EVEN MY GREAT WORK FOUR YEARS AGO!!
BUT THEY ALL FOOLISHLY CON-TINUE TO CLAIM THE OPPOSITE!!

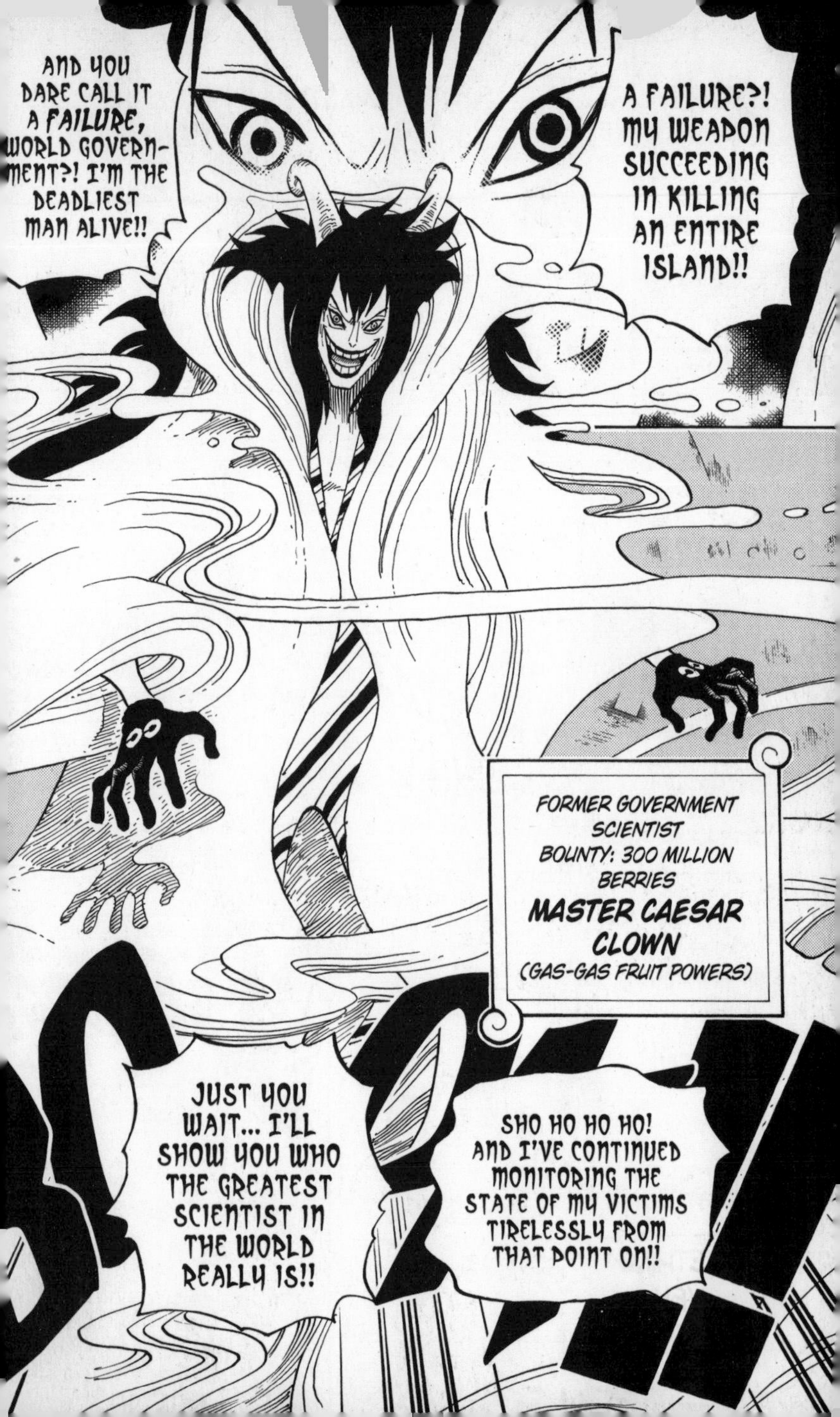
A FAILURE?! MY WEAPON SUCCEEDING IN KILLING AN ENTIRE ISLAND!!
AND YOU DARE CALL IT A *FAILURE*, WORLD GOVERNMENT?! I'M THE DEADLIEST MAN ALIVE!!
FORMER GOVERNMENT SCIENTIST BOUNTY: 300 MILLION BERRIES
MASTER CAESAR CLOWN
(GAS-GAS FRUIT POWERS)
SHO HO HO HO! AND I'VE CONTINUED MONITORING THE STATE OF MY VICTIMS TIRELESSLY FROM THAT POINT ON!!
JUST YOU WAIT... I'LL SHOW YOU WHO THE GREATEST SCIENTIST IN THE WORLD REALLY IS!!

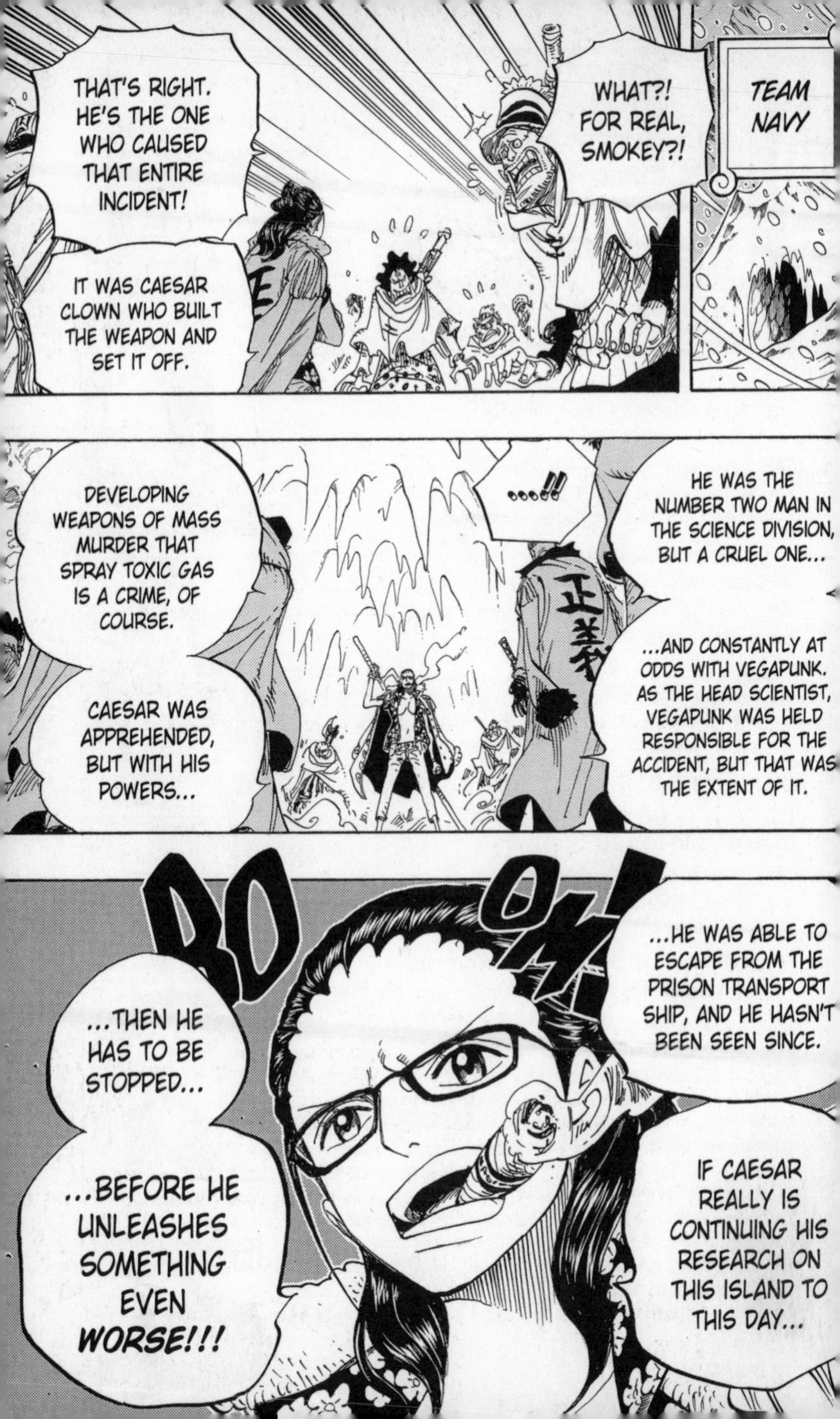
TEAM NAVY
WHAT?! FOR REAL, SMOKEY?!
THAT'S RIGHT. HE'S THE ONE WHO CAUSED THAT ENTIRE INCIDENT!
IT WAS CAESAR CLOWN WHO BUILT THE WEAPON AND SET IT OFF.
HE WAS THE NUMBER TWO MAN IN THE SCIENCE DIVISION, BUT A CRUEL ONE...
....!!
...AND CONSTANTLY AT ODDS WITH VEGAPUNK. AS THE HEAD SCIENTIST, VEGAPUNK WAS HELD RESPONSIBLE FOR THE ACCIDENT, BUT THAT WAS THE EXTENT OF IT.
DEVELOPING WEAPONS OF MASS MURDER THAT SPRAY TOXIC GAS IS A CRIME, OF COURSE.
CAESAR WAS APPREHENDED, BUT WITH HIS POWERS...
BOOM!
...HE WAS ABLE TO ESCAPE FROM THE PRISON TRANSPORT SHIP, AND HE HASN'T BEEN SEEN SINCE.
IF CAESAR REALLY IS CONTINUING HIS RESEARCH ON THIS ISLAND TO THIS DAY...
...THEN HE HAS TO BE STOPPED...
...BEFORE HE UNLEASHES SOMETHING EVEN *WORSE!!!*

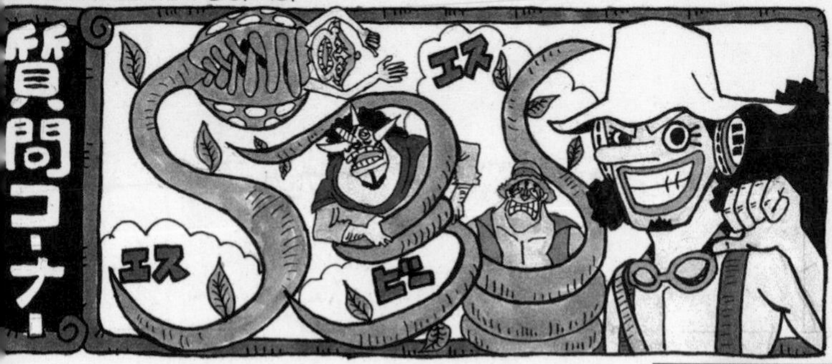
質問コーナー
エス
エス
ビー

(Patrick, Osaka)

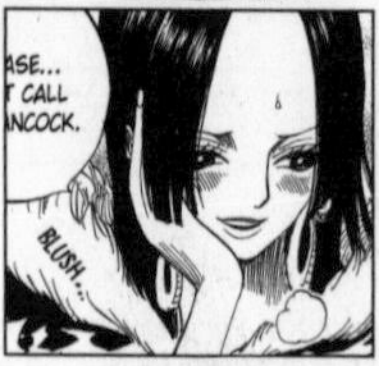
BLUSH...

Q: I think I have a crush on someone!♡♡ How should I put the moves on them?! Mr. Oda, give me some advice!!

--I Can Do It

A: Personally, I think a nice, powerful move like Gum-Gum Bazooka should do the trick! I hope you beat up that special someone! (^ ^)

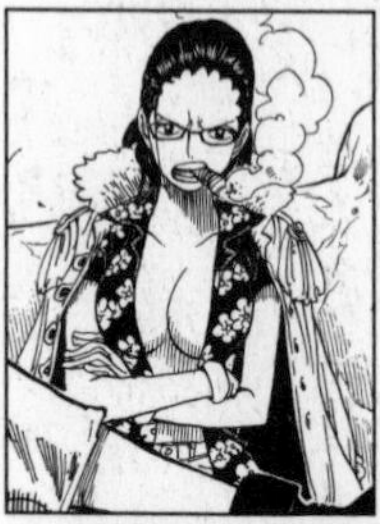

Q: I couldn't help but notice that when Smokey was inside Tashigi, she wasn't wearing a bra. Did he take it off, or was she (gasp!♡) not wearing one to begin with? You gotta tell me, or I won't be able to get to sleep!!

--Kumakoro

Q: True, she's got nothing on!♡ So what is the truth? Let's call Smoker over and ask him. Vice Admiral Smoker! Give us an answer!

Smoker: **I ripped it off. What's it to ya?**

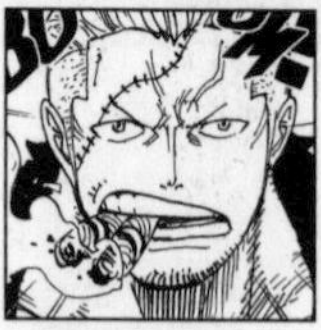

A: Uh... ...I... I see. Thank you for the answer. Well, there you have it!!

Q: Nice to meet you, Odacchi! Heso!! So, I wanted to ask you something about a policy (I think?) of yours that I noticed!! You don't ever write side comments inside or outside of the speech bubbles, do you?! Some other manga artists seem to do it a lot… What's up with that?!

--Myari

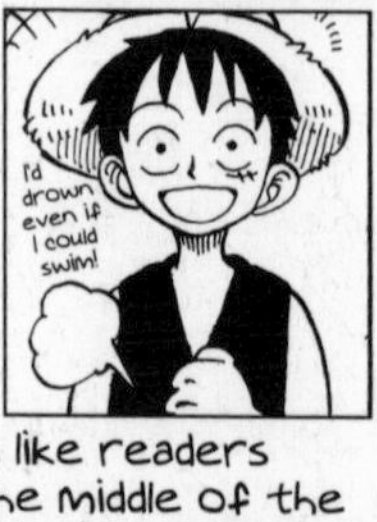
I'd drown even if I could swim!

A: Ah, yes. You see handwritten lines of dialogue in and around bubbles a lot, don't you? I tried it a bit myself when I was just breaking into the business, and fairly early on, I decided to myself that I wouldn't do it anymore. That's not meant to be a comment on other artists in any way. I stopped doing it because it felt to me like readers coming across my own handwritten words in the middle of the manga experience would be taken out of the story and forced to envision the author himself, writing that comment. Does that make sense? In other words, I don't want you to notice me while reading One Piece, I just want you to focus on the manga.

Chapter 665:
CANDY

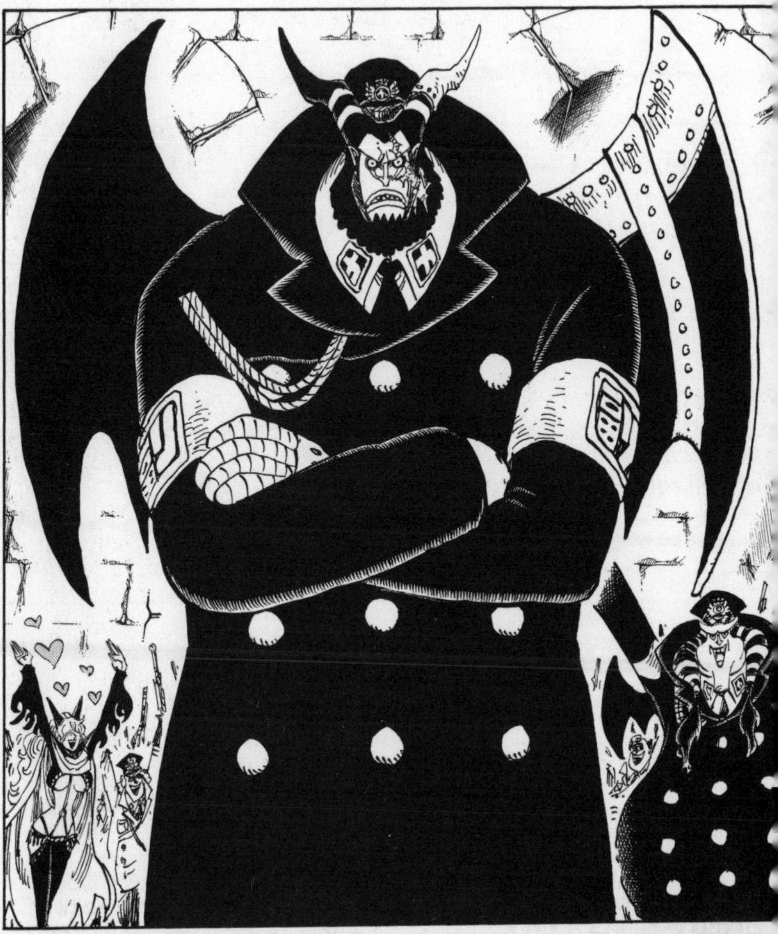

DECKS OF THE WORLD, VOL. 45: "IMPEL DOWN—THE MOST TRUSTWORTHY MAN IN HELL, NEW VICE WARDEN MAGELLAN"

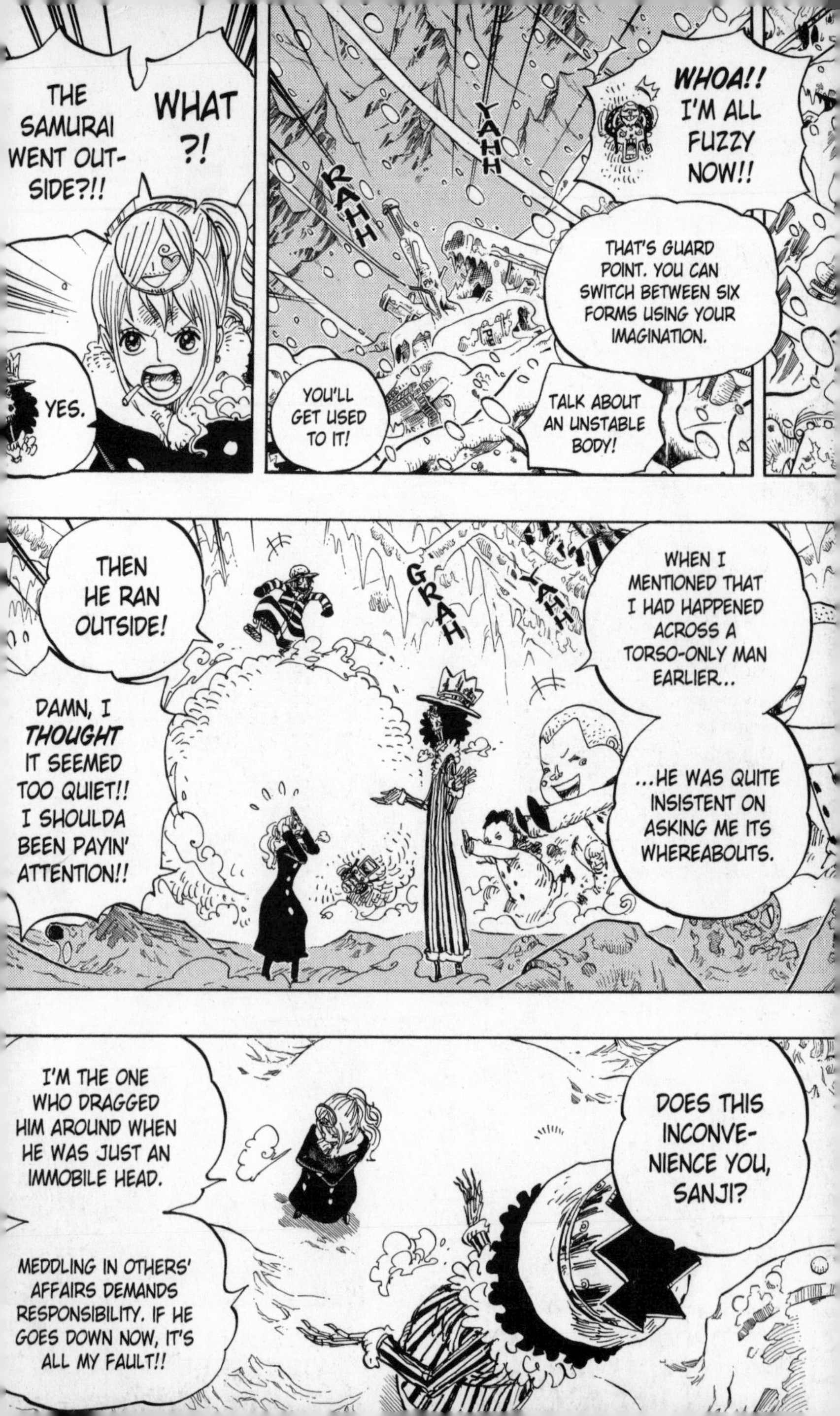
WHOA!! I'M ALL FUZZY NOW!!
THAT'S GUARD POINT. YOU CAN SWITCH BETWEEN SIX FORMS USING YOUR IMAGINATION.
YAHH
RAHH
TALK ABOUT AN UNSTABLE BODY!
YOU'LL GET USED TO IT!
WHAT ?!
THE SAMURAI WENT OUT-SIDE?!!
YES.
WHEN I MENTIONED THAT I HAD HAPPENED ACROSS A TORSO-ONLY MAN EARLIER...
...HE WAS QUITE INSISTENT ON ASKING ME ITS WHEREABOUTS.
YAHH
GRAH
THEN HE RAN OUTSIDE!
DAMN, I *THOUGHT* IT SEEMED TOO QUIET!! I SHOULDA BEEN PAYIN' ATTENTION!!
DOES THIS INCONVE-NIENCE YOU, SANJI?
I'M THE ONE WHO DRAGGED HIM AROUND WHEN HE WAS JUST AN IMMOBILE HEAD.
MEDDLING IN OTHERS' AFFAIRS DEMANDS RESPONSIBILITY. IF HE GOES DOWN NOW, IT'S ALL MY FAULT!!

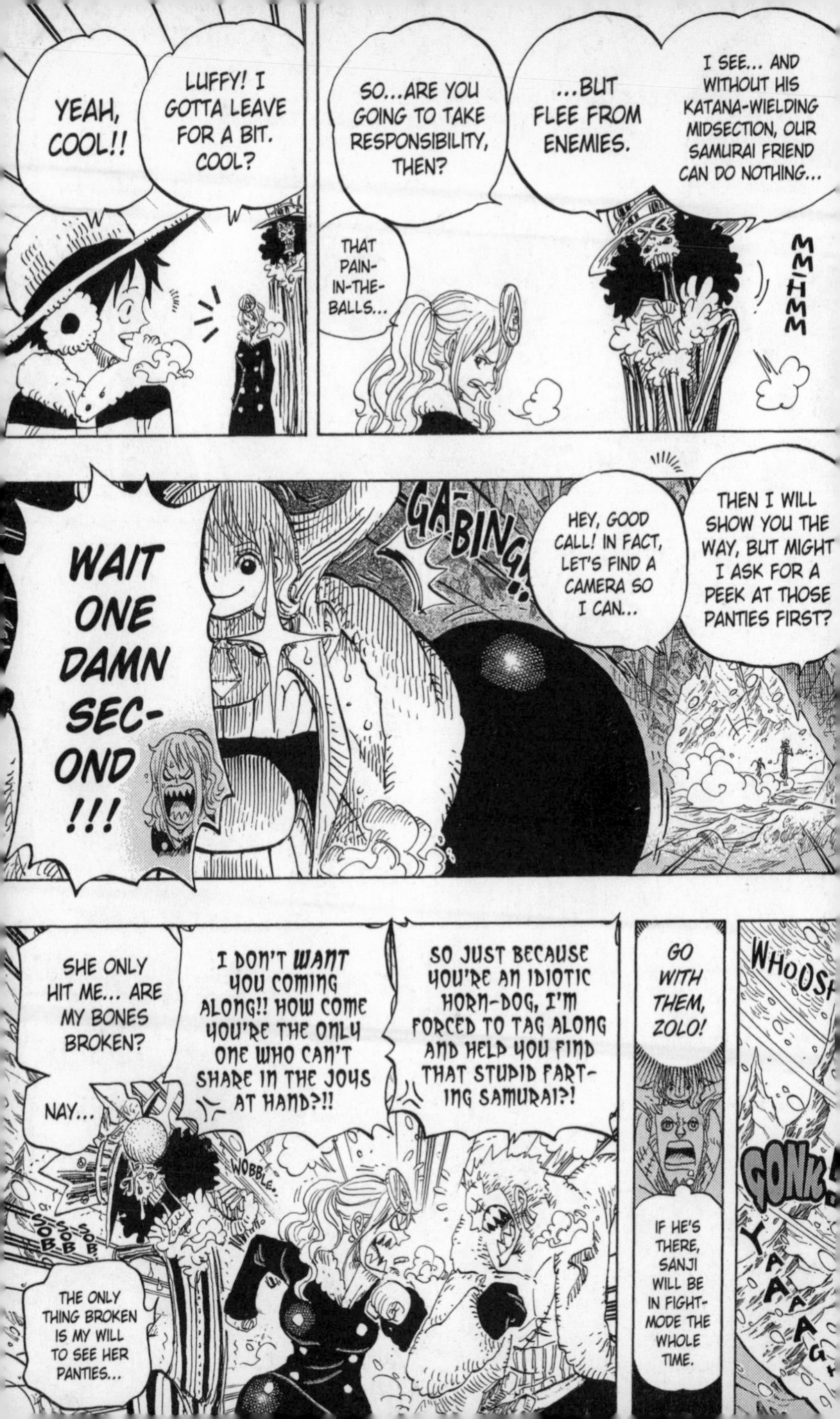
I SEE... AND WITHOUT HIS KATANA-WIELDING MIDSECTION, OUR SAMURAI FRIEND CAN DO NOTHING...
...BUT FLEE FROM ENEMIES.
MMHMM
SO...ARE YOU GOING TO TAKE RESPONSIBILITY, THEN?
THAT PAIN-IN-THE-BALLS...
LUFFY! I GOTTA LEAVE FOR A BIT. COOL?
YEAH, COOL!!
THEN I WILL SHOW YOU THE WAY, BUT MIGHT I ASK FOR A PEEK AT THOSE PANTIES FIRST?
HEY, GOOD CALL! IN FACT, LET'S FIND A CAMERA SO I CAN...
GA-BING!!
WAIT ONE DAMN SEC-OND!!!
WHOOSH
GONK
YAAAAG
GO WITH THEM, ZOLO!
IF HE'S THERE, SANJI WILL BE IN FIGHT-MODE THE WHOLE TIME.
SO JUST BECAUSE YOU'RE AN IDIOTIC HORN-DOG, I'M FORCED TO TAG ALONG AND HELP YOU FIND THAT STUPID FART-ING SAMURAI?!
I DON'T WANT YOU COMING ALONG!! HOW COME YOU'RE THE ONLY ONE WHO CAN'T SHARE IN THE JOYS AT HAND?!!
WOBBLE
SHE ONLY HIT ME... ARE MY BONES BROKEN?
NAY...
SOB SOB SOB
THE ONLY THING BROKEN IS MY WILL TO SEE HER PANTIES...

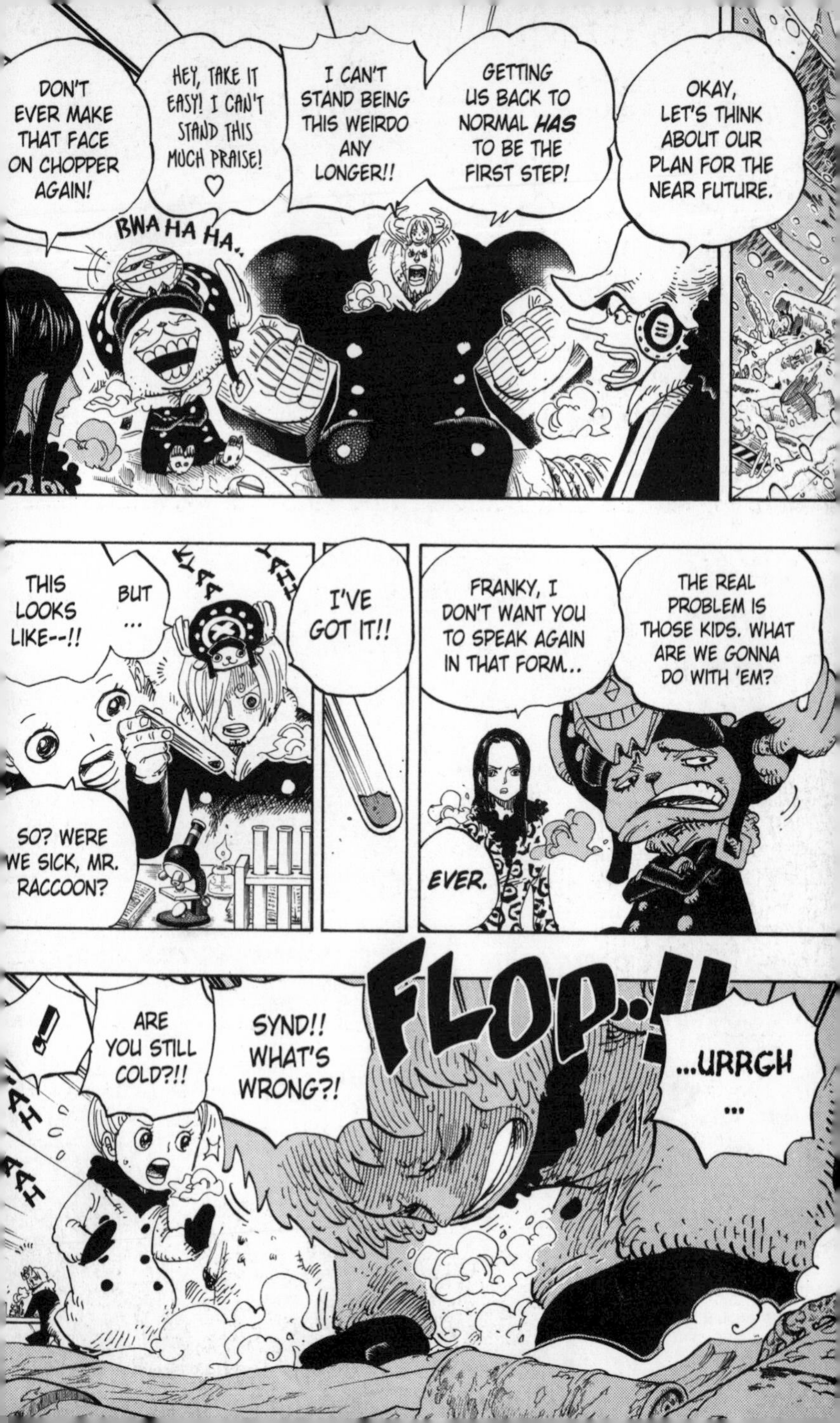
OKAY, LET'S THINK ABOUT OUR PLAN FOR THE NEAR FUTURE.
GETTING US BACK TO NORMAL HAS TO BE THE FIRST STEP!
I CAN'T STAND BEING THIS WEIRDO ANY LONGER!!
HEY, TAKE IT EASY! I CAN'T STAND THIS MUCH PRAISE! ♡
BWA HA HA..
DON'T EVER MAKE THAT FACE ON CHOPPER AGAIN!
THE REAL PROBLEM IS THOSE KIDS. WHAT ARE WE GONNA DO WITH 'EM?
FRANKY, I DON'T WANT YOU TO SPEAK AGAIN IN THAT FORM...
EVER.
I'VE GOT IT!!
BUT ...
THIS LOOKS LIKE--!!
SO? WERE WE SICK, MR. RACCOON?
...URRGH ...
FLOP..!!
SYND!! WHAT'S WRONG?!
ARE YOU STILL COLD?!!
!

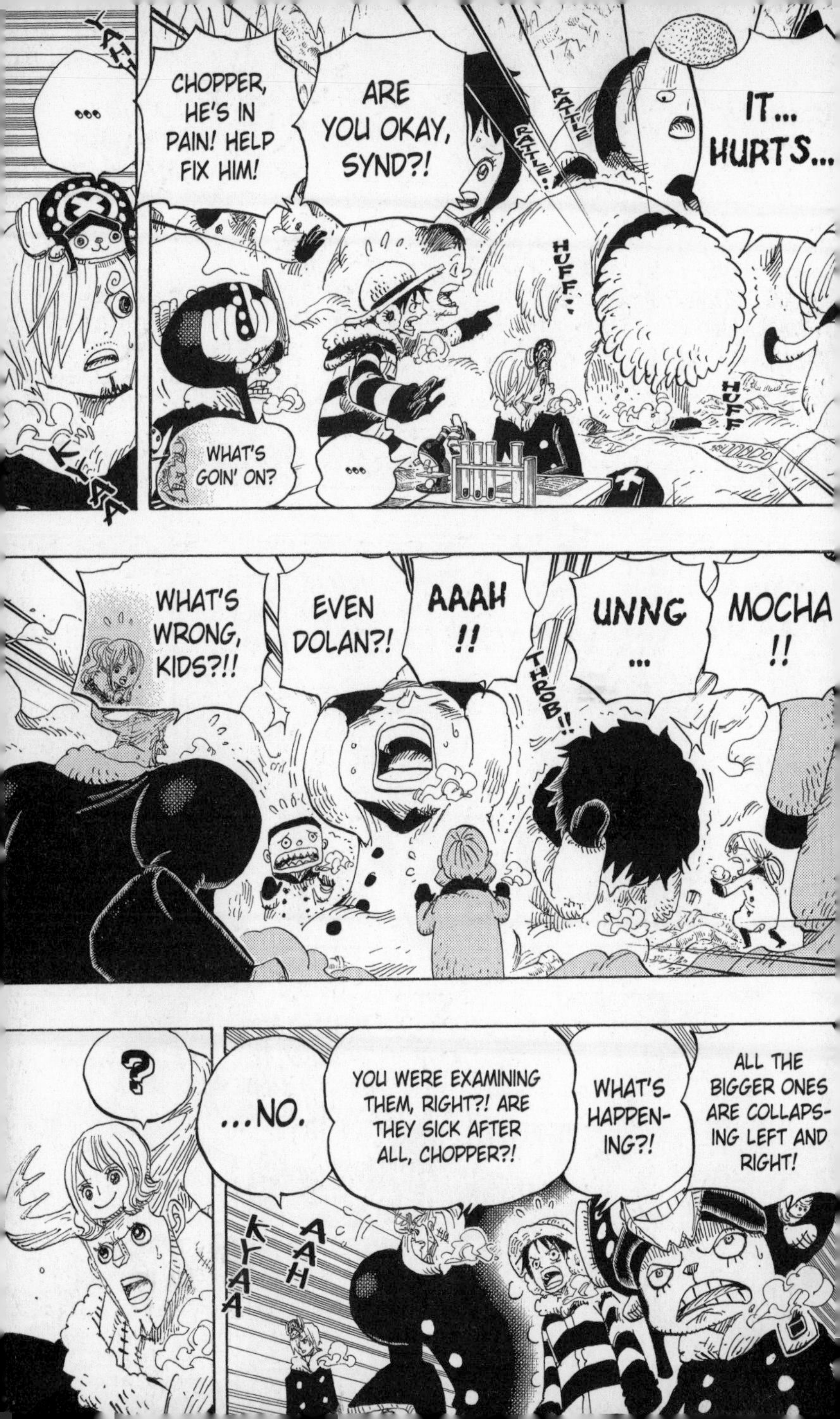
IT... HURTS...
RATTLE
RATTLE..
ARE YOU OKAY, SYND?!
CHOPPER, HE'S IN PAIN! HELP FIX HIM!
HUFF..
HUFF
...
WHAT'S GOIN' ON?
YAHH
...
KYAA
MOCHA !!
UNNG ...
THROB!!
AAAH !!
EVEN DOLAN?!
WHAT'S WRONG, KIDS?!!
ALL THE BIGGER ONES ARE COLLAPSING LEFT AND RIGHT!
WHAT'S HAPPENING?!
YOU WERE EXAMINING THEM, RIGHT?! ARE THEY SICK AFTER ALL, CHOPPER?!
...NO.
AAH
KYAA
?

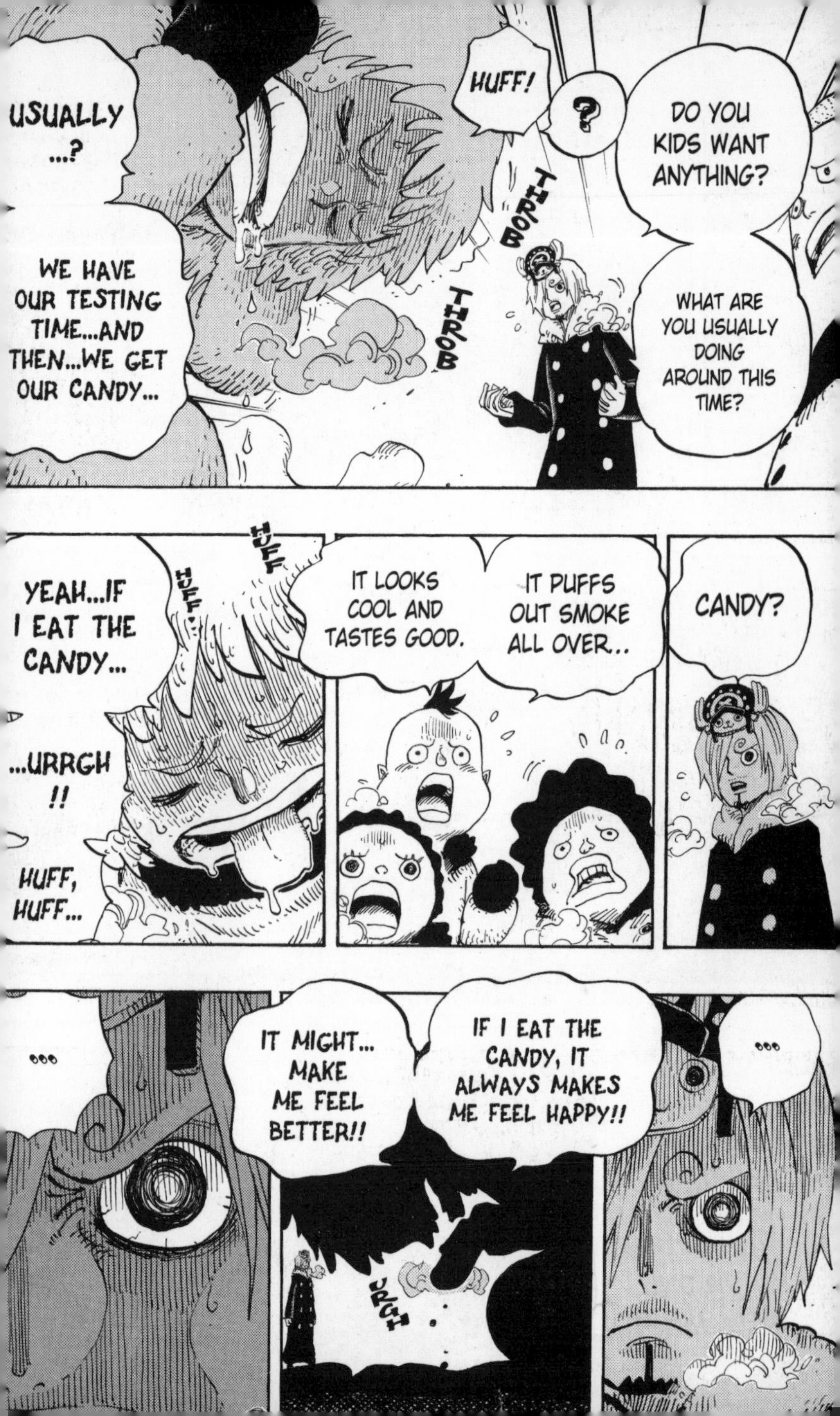
DO YOU KIDS WANT ANYTHING?
?
HUFF!
THROB
WHAT ARE YOU USUALLY DOING AROUND THIS TIME?
THROB
USUALLY ...?
WE HAVE OUR TESTING TIME...AND THEN...WE GET OUR CANDY...
CANDY?
IT PUFFS OUT SMOKE ALL OVER..
IT LOOKS COOL AND TASTES GOOD.
HUFF
HUFF
YEAH...IF I EAT THE CANDY...
...URRGH !!
HUFF, HUFF...
...
IF I EAT THE CANDY, IT ALWAYS MAKES ME FEEL HAPPY!!
IT MIGHT... MAKE ME FEEL BETTER!!
URGH
...

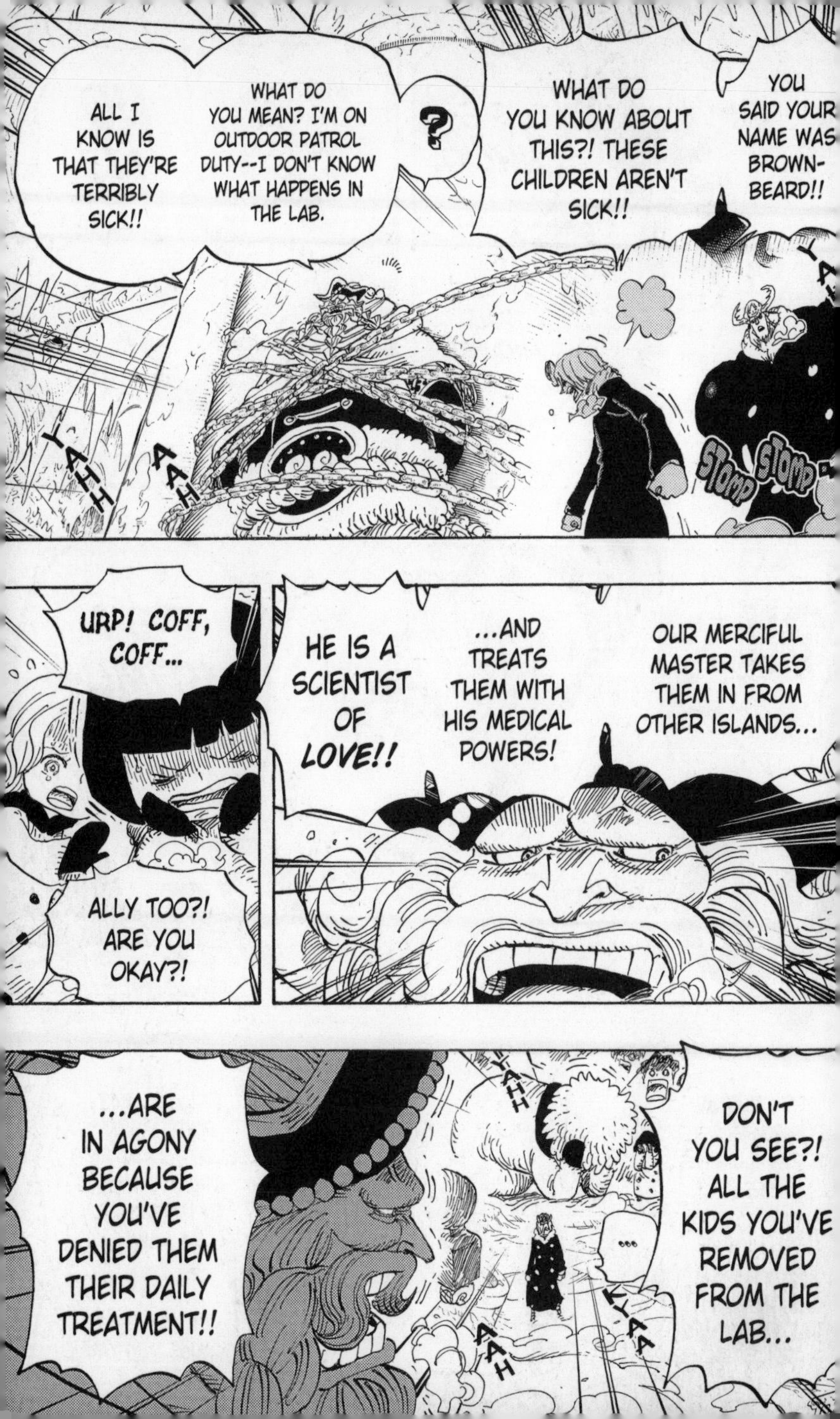

YOU SAID YOUR NAME WAS BROWN-BEARD!!
WHAT DO YOU KNOW ABOUT THIS?! THESE CHILDREN AREN'T SICK!!
?
WHAT DO YOU MEAN? I'M ON OUTDOOR PATROL DUTY--I DON'T KNOW WHAT HAPPENS IN THE LAB.
ALL I KNOW IS THAT THEY'RE TERRIBLY SICK!!
STOMP
STOMP
AAH
YAHH
OUR MERCIFUL MASTER TAKES THEM IN FROM OTHER ISLANDS...
...AND TREATS THEM WITH HIS MEDICAL POWERS!
HE IS A SCIENTIST OF *LOVE!!*
URP! COFF, COFF...
ALLY TOO?! ARE YOU OKAY?!
DON'T YOU SEE?! ALL THE KIDS YOU'VE REMOVED FROM THE LAB...
YAHH
...
KYAA
AAH
...ARE IN AGONY BECAUSE YOU'VE DENIED THEM THEIR DAILY TREATMENT!!

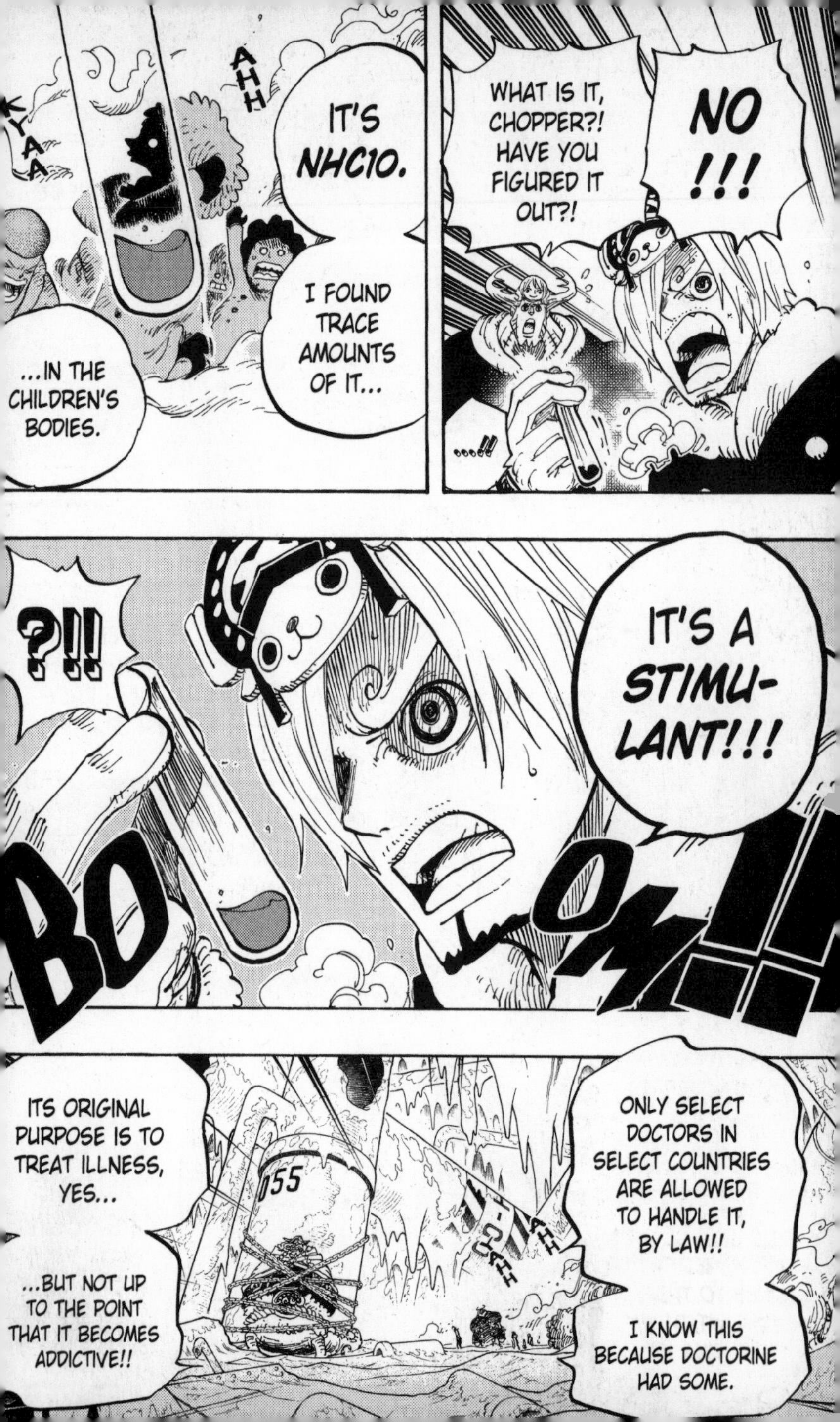
NO!!!
WHAT IS IT, CHOPPER?! HAVE YOU FIGURED IT OUT?!
....!!
IT'S NHC10.
I FOUND TRACE AMOUNTS OF IT...
AHH
KYAA
...IN THE CHILDREN'S BODIES.
IT'S A STIMU-LANT!!!
?!!
BOOM!!
ONLY SELECT DOCTORS IN SELECT COUNTRIES ARE ALLOWED TO HANDLE IT, BY LAW!!
I KNOW THIS BECAUSE DOCTORINE HAD SOME.
055
ITS ORIGINAL PURPOSE IS TO TREAT ILLNESS, YES...
...BUT NOT UP TO THE POINT THAT IT BECOMES ADDICTIVE!!

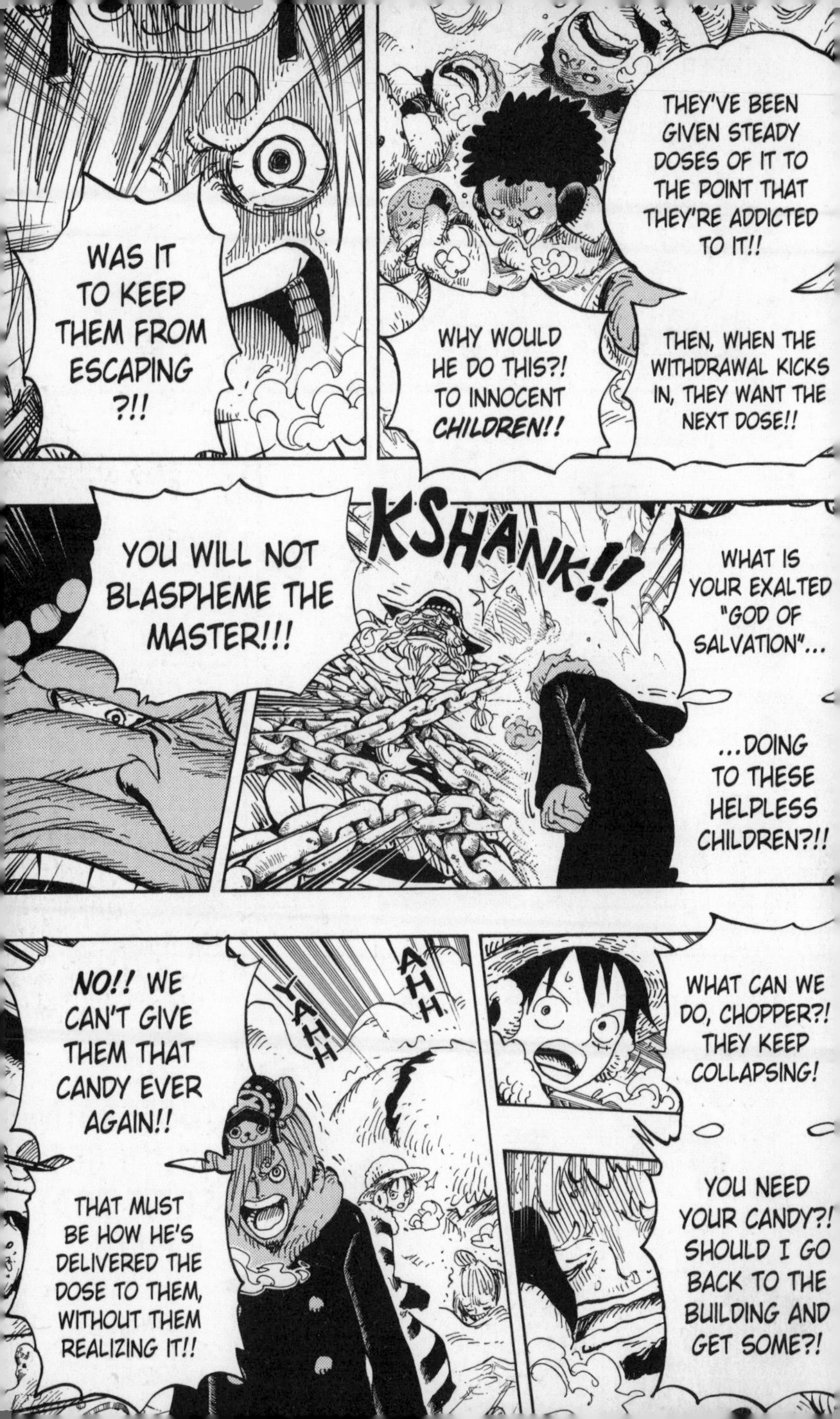
THEY'VE BEEN GIVEN STEADY DOSES OF IT TO THE POINT THAT THEY'RE ADDICTED TO IT!!
THEN, WHEN THE WITHDRAWAL KICKS IN, THEY WANT THE NEXT DOSE!!
WHY WOULD HE DO THIS?! TO INNOCENT CHILDREN!!
WAS IT TO KEEP THEM FROM ESCAPING ?!!
WHAT IS YOUR EXALTED "GOD OF SALVATION"...
...DOING TO THESE HELPLESS CHILDREN?!!
KSHANK!!
YOU WILL NOT BLASPHEME THE MASTER!!!
WHAT CAN WE DO, CHOPPER?! THEY KEEP COLLAPSING!
YOU NEED YOUR CANDY?! SHOULD I GO BACK TO THE BUILDING AND GET SOME?!
AHH
YAHH
NO!! WE CAN'T GIVE THEM THAT CANDY EVER AGAIN!!
THAT MUST BE HOW HE'S DELIVERED THE DOSE TO THEM, WITHOUT THEM REALIZING IT!!

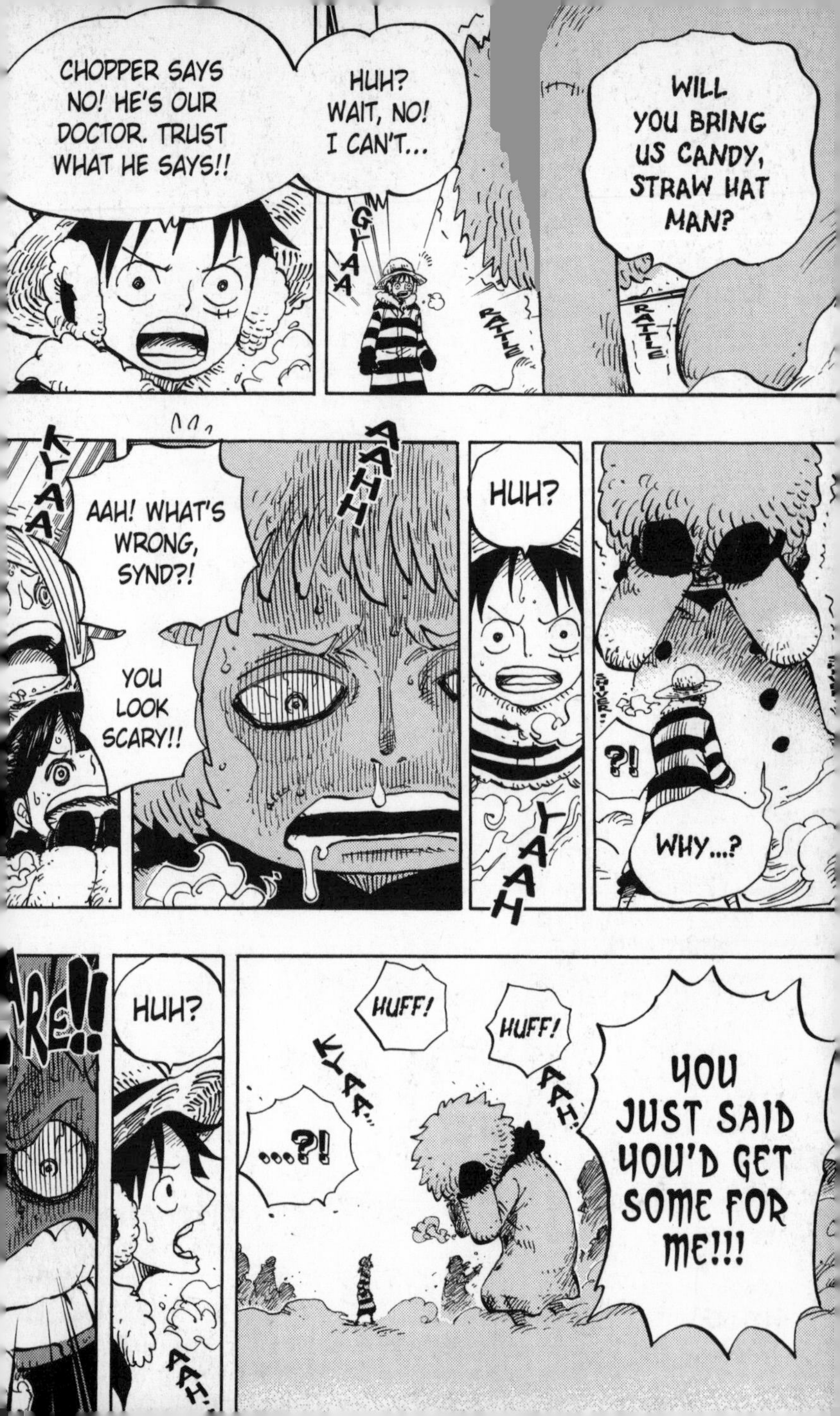
WILL YOU BRING US CANDY, STRAW HAT MAN?
RATTLE
HUH? WAIT, NO! I CAN'T...
GYAA
RATTLE
CHOPPER SAYS NO! HE'S OUR DOCTOR. TRUST WHAT HE SAYS!!
SHIVER...
?!
WHY...?
HUH?
YAAAH
AAHH
KYAAA
AAH! WHAT'S WRONG, SYND?!
YOU LOOK SCARY!!
YOU JUST SAID YOU'D GET SOME FOR ME!!!
HUFF!
AAH!
HUFF!
KYAA...
...?!
HUH?
AAH!
RE!!

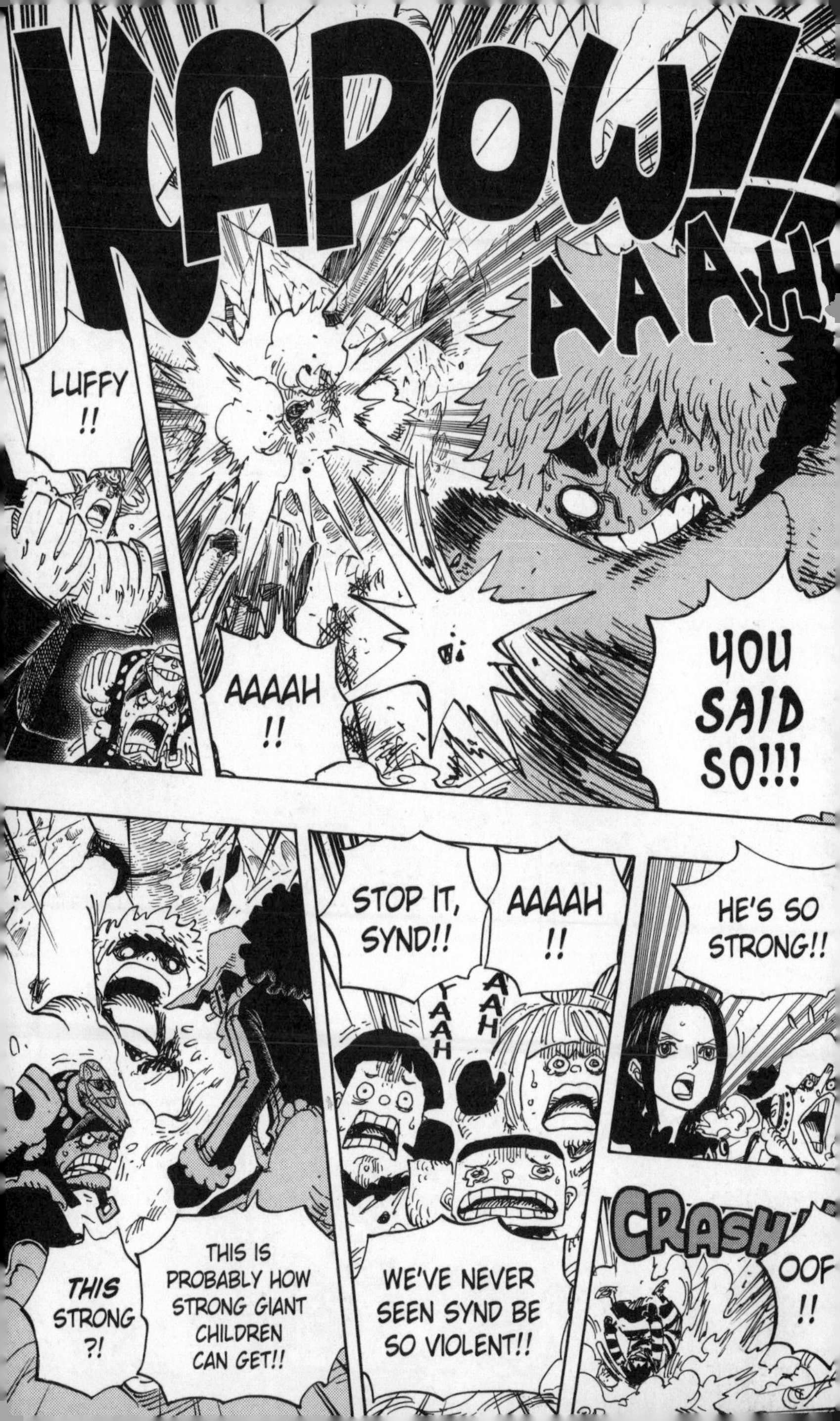
KAPOW!!!
AAAH!!
YOU SAID SO!!!
AAAAH !!
LUFFY !!
HE'S SO STRONG!!
CRASH
OOF !!
AAAAH !!
STOP IT, SYND!!
AAAH
FAAAH
WE'VE NEVER SEEN SYND BE SO VIOLENT!!
THIS IS PROBABLY HOW STRONG GIANT CHILDREN CAN GET!!
THIS STRONG ?!

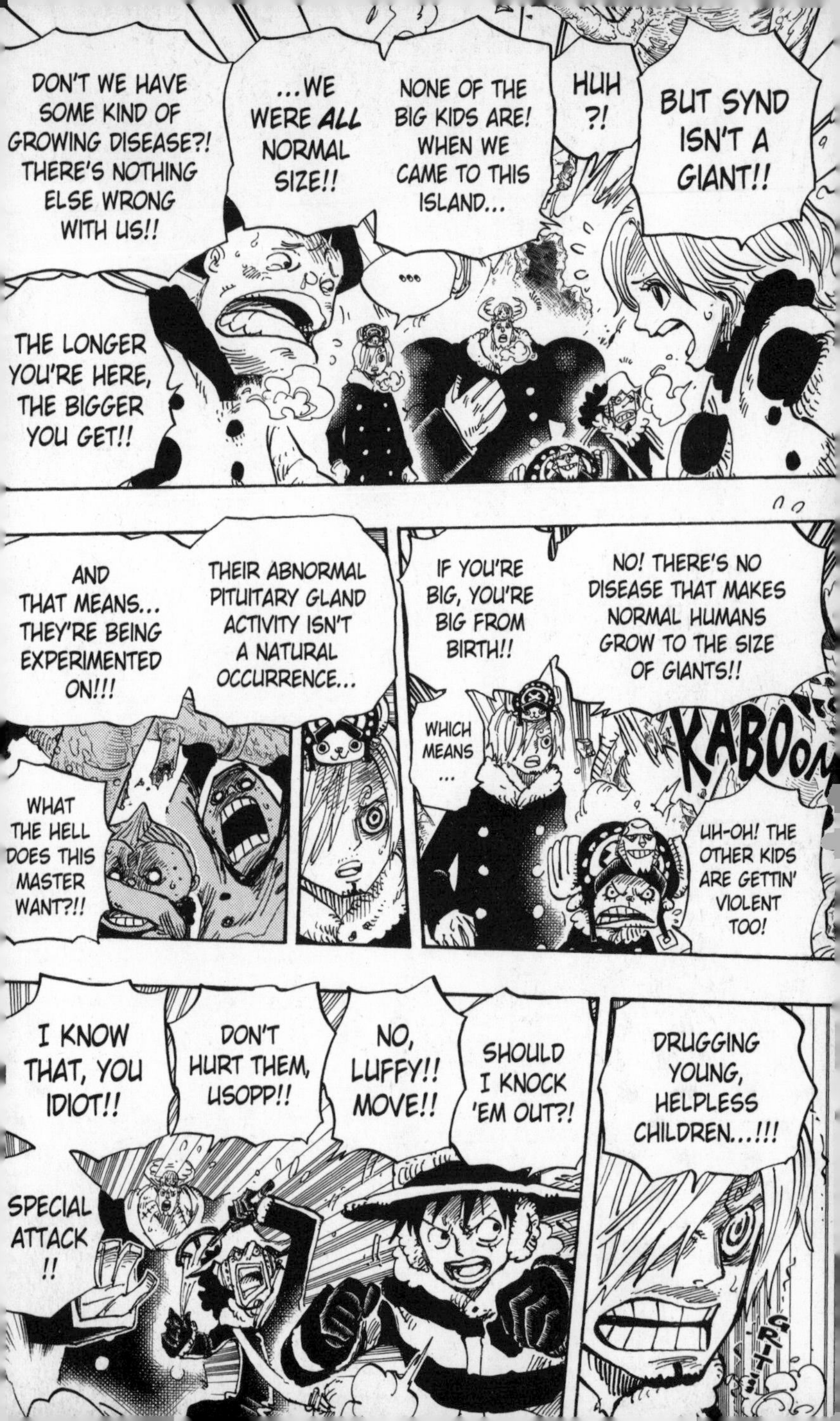
BUT SYND ISN'T A GIANT!!
HUH ?!
NONE OF THE BIG KIDS ARE! WHEN WE CAME TO THIS ISLAND...
...WE WERE ALL NORMAL SIZE!!
DON'T WE HAVE SOME KIND OF GROWING DISEASE?! THERE'S NOTHING ELSE WRONG WITH US!!
...
THE LONGER YOU'RE HERE, THE BIGGER YOU GET!!
NO! THERE'S NO DISEASE THAT MAKES NORMAL HUMANS GROW TO THE SIZE OF GIANTS!!
IF YOU'RE BIG, YOU'RE BIG FROM BIRTH!!
KABOOM
WHICH MEANS ...
UH-OH! THE OTHER KIDS ARE GETTIN' VIOLENT TOO!
THEIR ABNORMAL PITUITARY GLAND ACTIVITY ISN'T A NATURAL OCCURRENCE...
AND THAT MEANS... THEY'RE BEING EXPERIMENTED ON!!!
WHAT THE HELL DOES THIS MASTER WANT?!!
DRUGGING YOUNG, HELPLESS CHILDREN...!!!
GRIT
SHOULD I KNOCK 'EM OUT?!
NO, LUFFY!! MOVE!!
DON'T HURT THEM, USOPP!!
I KNOW THAT, YOU IDIOT!!
SPECIAL ATTACK !!

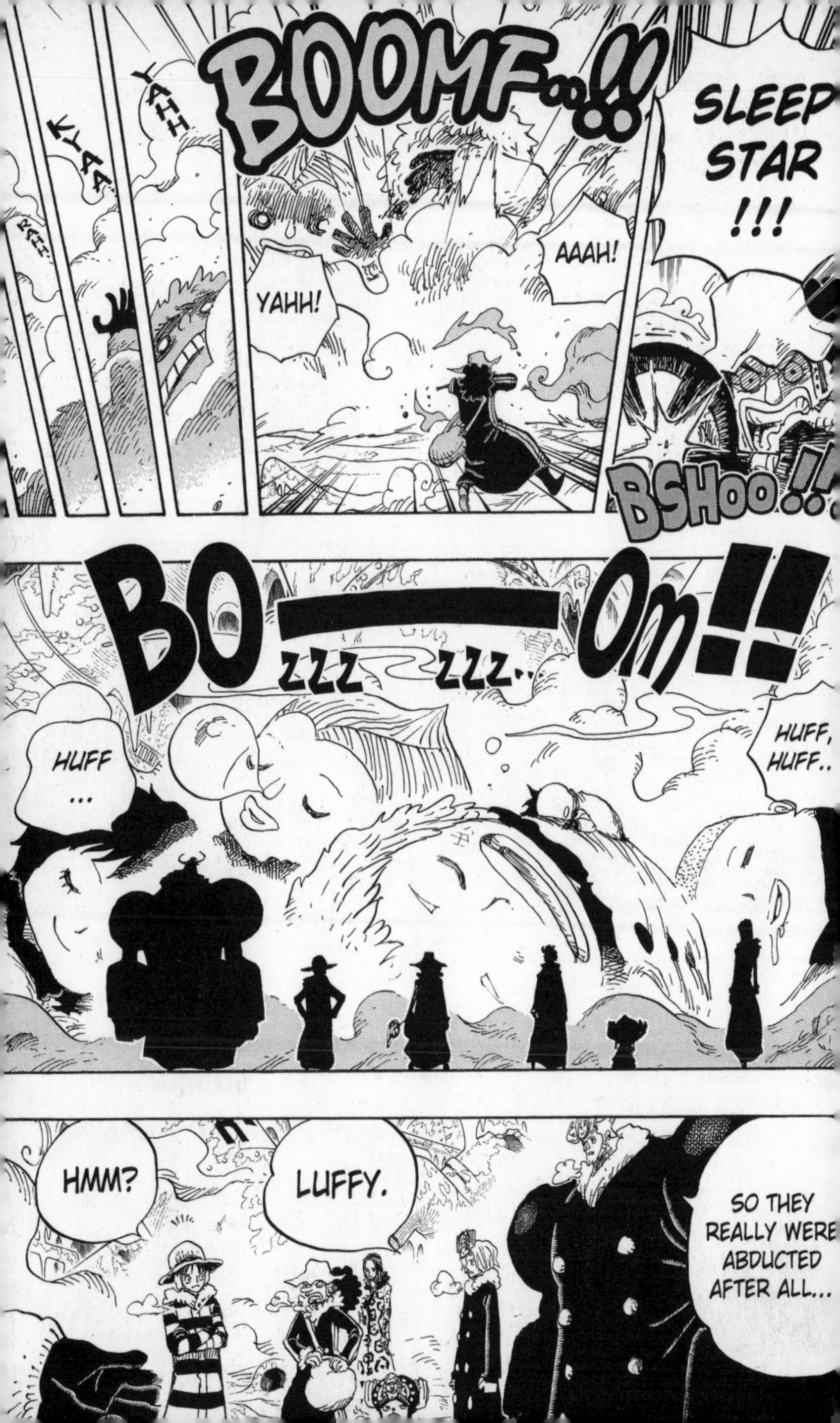
SLEEP STAR !!!
BSHOO!!!
BOOMF..!!
AAAH!
YAHH!
YAHH
KYAA
RAHH
BO——OM!!
ZZZ ZZZ..
HUFF, HUFF..
HUFF ...
SO THEY REALLY WERE ABDUCTED AFTER ALL...
LUFFY.
HMM?

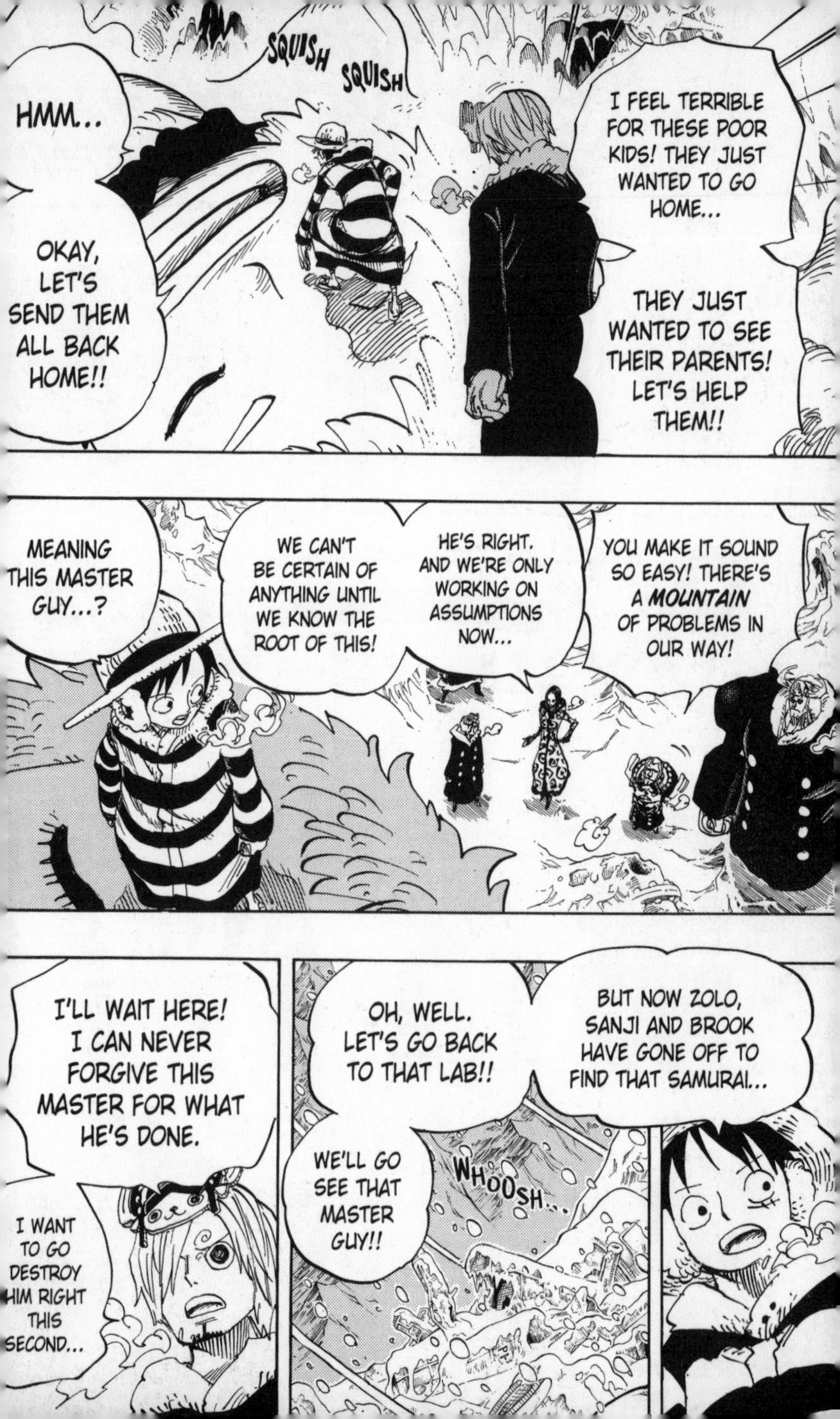
I FEEL TERRIBLE FOR THESE POOR KIDS! THEY JUST WANTED TO GO HOME...
THEY JUST WANTED TO SEE THEIR PARENTS! LET'S HELP THEM!!
SQUISH
SQUISH
HMM...
OKAY, LET'S SEND THEM ALL BACK HOME!!
YOU MAKE IT SOUND SO EASY! THERE'S A *MOUNTAIN* OF PROBLEMS IN OUR WAY!
HE'S RIGHT. AND WE'RE ONLY WORKING ON ASSUMPTIONS NOW...
WE CAN'T BE CERTAIN OF ANYTHING UNTIL WE KNOW THE ROOT OF THIS!
MEANING THIS MASTER GUY...?
BUT NOW ZOLO, SANJI AND BROOK HAVE GONE OFF TO FIND THAT SAMURAI...
OH, WELL. LET'S GO BACK TO THAT LAB!!
WE'LL GO SEE THAT MASTER GUY!!
WHOOSH...
I'LL WAIT HERE! I CAN NEVER FORGIVE THIS MASTER FOR WHAT HE'S DONE.
I WANT TO GO DESTROY HIM RIGHT THIS SECOND...

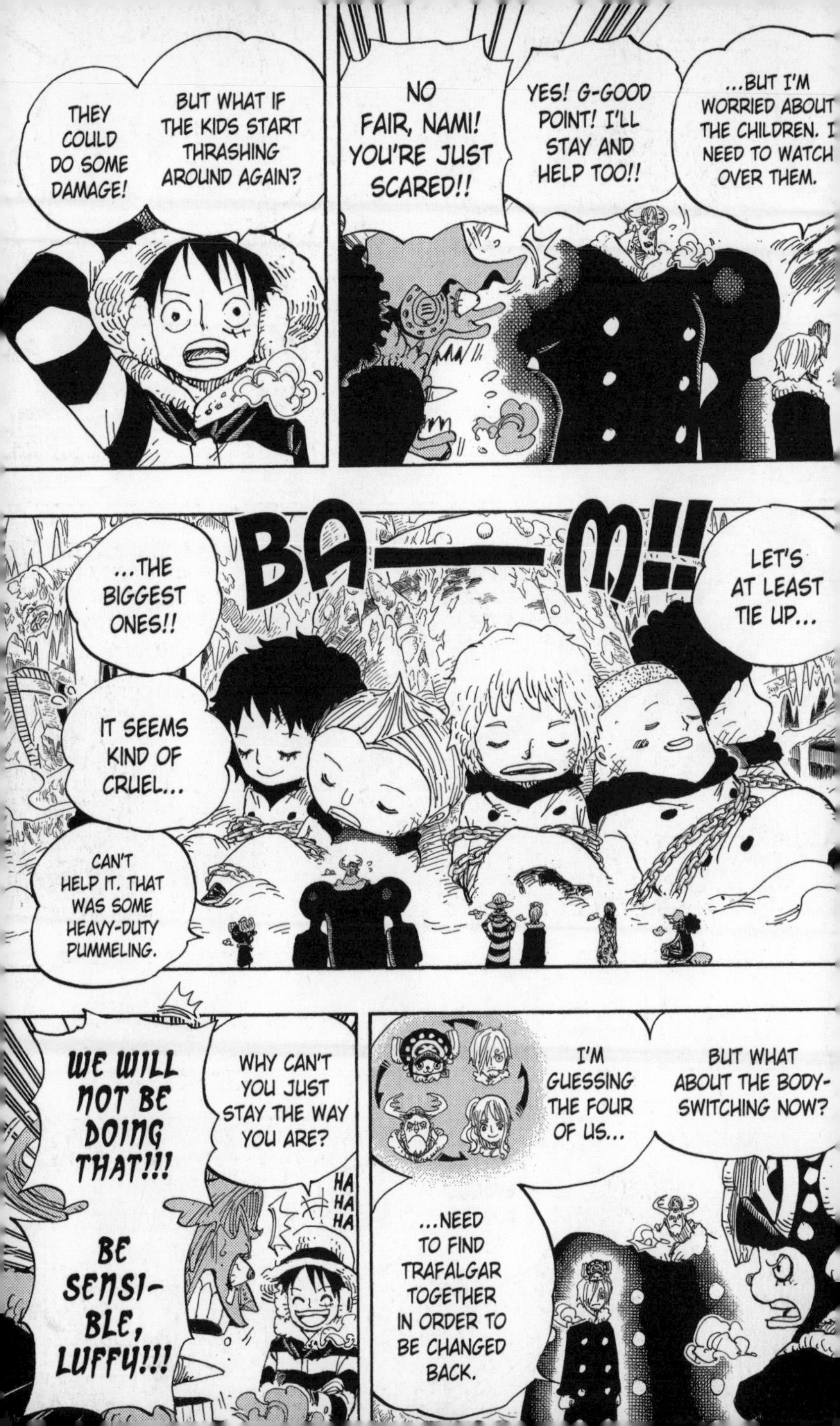
...BUT I'M WORRIED ABOUT THE CHILDREN. I NEED TO WATCH OVER THEM.
YES! G-GOOD POINT! I'LL STAY AND HELP TOO!!
NO FAIR, NAMI! YOU'RE JUST SCARED!!
BUT WHAT IF THE KIDS START THRASHING AROUND AGAIN?
THEY COULD DO SOME DAMAGE!
BA—M!!
LET'S AT LEAST TIE UP...
...THE BIGGEST ONES!!
IT SEEMS KIND OF CRUEL...
CAN'T HELP IT. THAT WAS SOME HEAVY-DUTY PUMMELING.
BUT WHAT ABOUT THE BODY-SWITCHING NOW?
I'M GUESSING THE FOUR OF US...
...NEED TO FIND TRAFALGAR TOGETHER IN ORDER TO BE CHANGED BACK.
WHY CAN'T YOU JUST STAY THE WAY YOU ARE?
HA HA HA
WE WILL NOT BE DOING THAT!!!
BE SENSI-BLE, LUFFY!!!

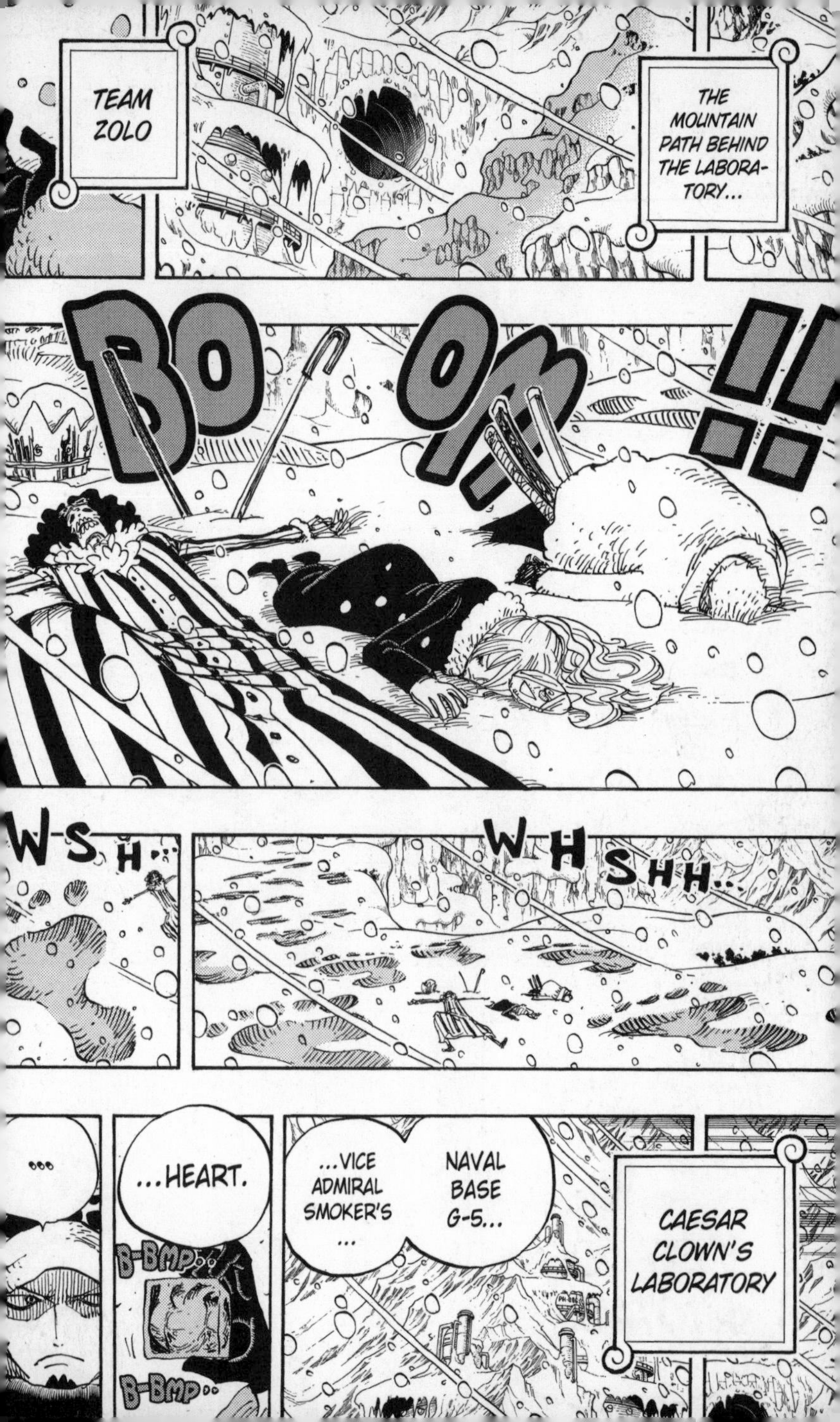
THE MOUNTAIN PATH BEHIND THE LABORATORY...
TEAM ZOLO
BOOM!!
WHSHH...
WSH
CAESAR CLOWN'S LABORATORY
NAVAL BASE G-5...
...VICE ADMIRAL SMOKER'S ...
...HEART.
B-BMP
B-BMP
...

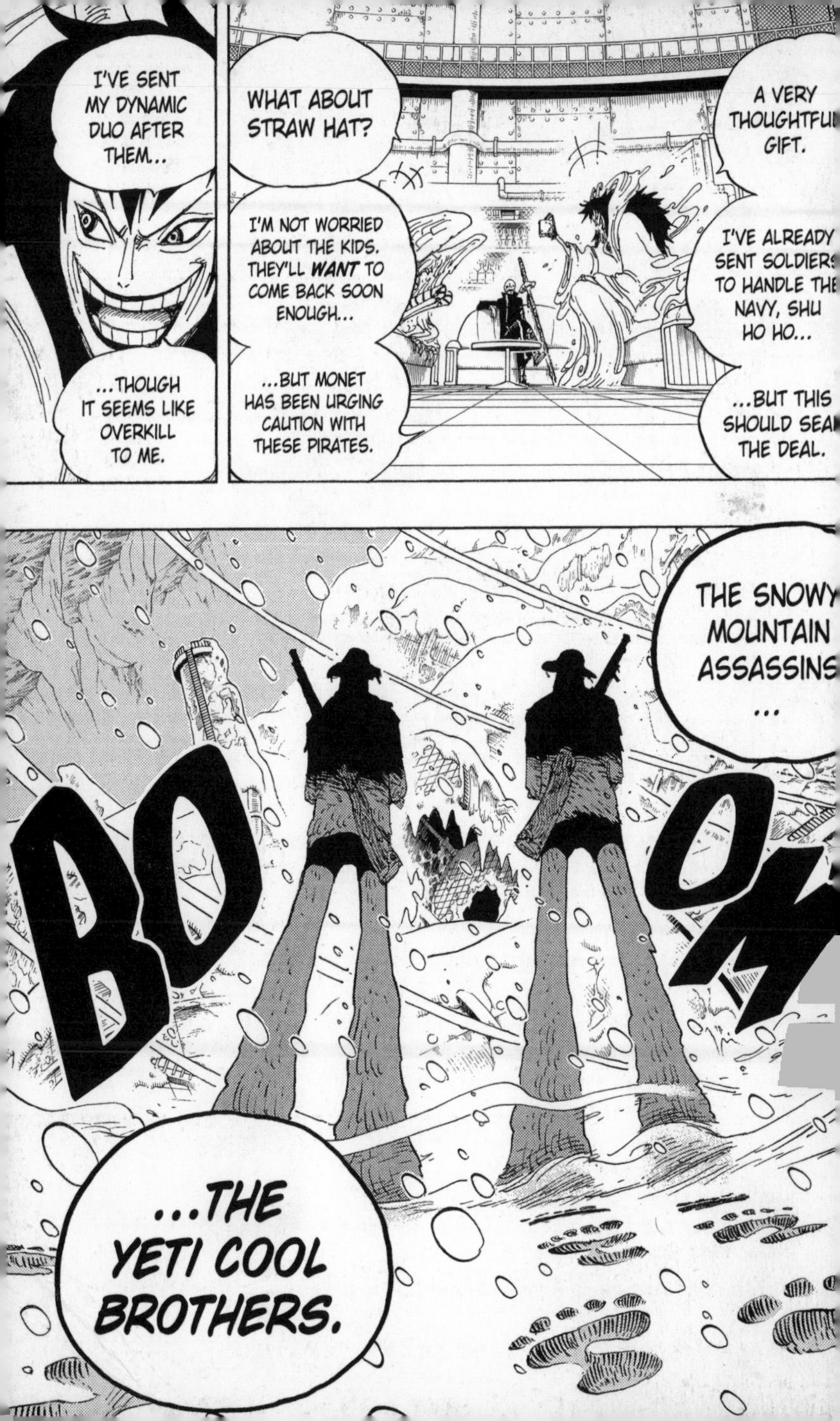
A VERY THOUGHTFUL GIFT.
I'VE ALREADY SENT SOLDIERS TO HANDLE THE NAVY, SHU HO HO...
...BUT THIS SHOULD SEAL THE DEAL.
WHAT ABOUT STRAW HAT?
I'M NOT WORRIED ABOUT THE KIDS. THEY'LL *WANT* TO COME BACK SOON ENOUGH...
...BUT MONET HAS BEEN URGING CAUTION WITH THESE PIRATES.
I'VE SENT MY DYNAMIC DUO AFTER THEM...
...THOUGH IT SEEMS LIKE OVERKILL TO ME.
THE SNOWY MOUNTAIN ASSASSINS ...
BOOM
...THE YETI COOL BROTHERS.

SBS Question Corner

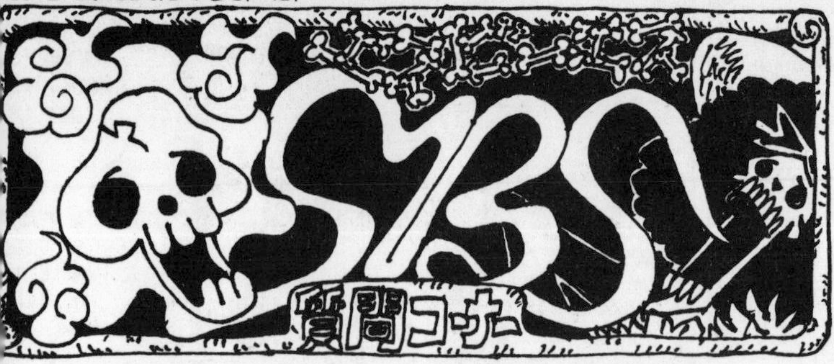
SBS
質問コーナー

(Tomoya Hino, Aichi)

Q: In Chapter 654, Chopper refused to join Nami in the bath because "he wiped his body clean two days ago." Is it because he's a boy, or because he has Devil Fruit Powers? Or because he's an animal?? Can you tell us more about the bathing situation on the *Sunny?*

--Katana★Romance

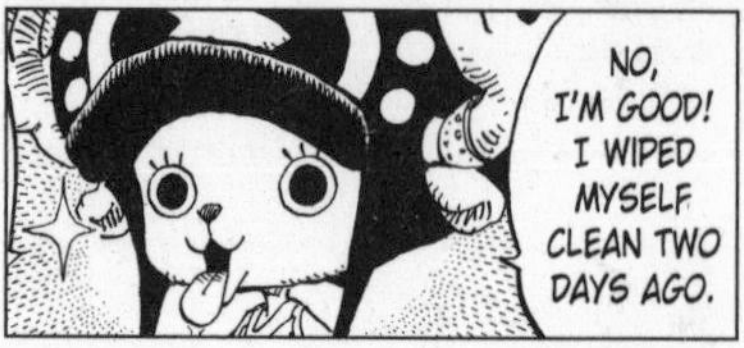
NO, I'M GOOD! I WIPED MYSELF CLEAN TWO DAYS AGO.

A: Well, in Chopper's case, the animal part might explain a lot of it, especially since apparently just wiping yourself counts as "bathing" to him.

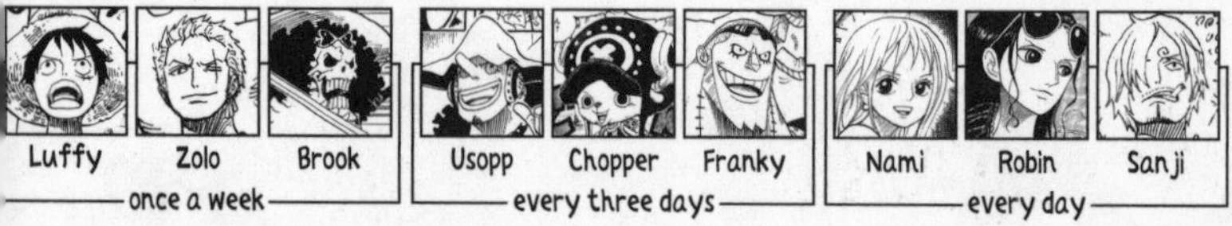
Luffy
Zolo
Brook
once a week
Usopp
Chopper
Franky
every three days
Nami
Robin
Sanji
every day

Sometimes the entire male team gets together for a big fun romp in the bath. The women like to invite Chopper to join them, but he seems to prefer it with the guys.

Q: Hello, Eiichiro. My little sister said, "What's up with Nico Robin always showin' off her boobies? Does she like trotting them out for everyone?" And you know what I told her? "Naw, naw, it's that Oda guy who draws *One Piece* that loves them boobies, he's the one who always makes it like that." Was that the right answer? *Poke, poke poke.*

--I Love Oda

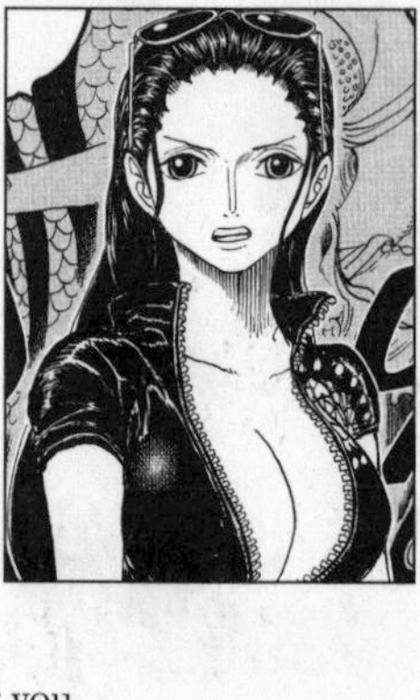

A: So, as you can see, I just received this incredibly rude postcard.
Of course I love drawing them!!
How dare you doubt me!!

Q: Well, if you're not going to wrap this up, I'll do it for you.

--Unagi Now

A: Okay, that's it for this volume! See you next time!

Chapter 666: YETI COOL BROTHERS

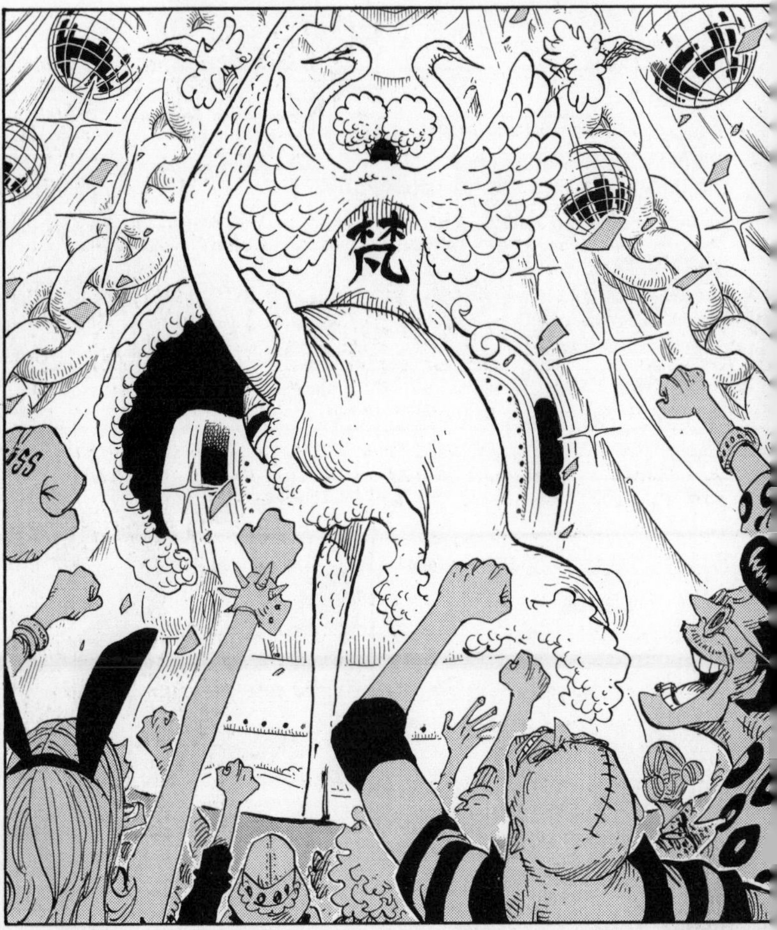

DECKS OF THE WORLD, VOL. 46: "IMPEL DOWN, LEVEL 5.5—ALL HAIL BON, NEW QUEEN OF NEWKAMA LAND"

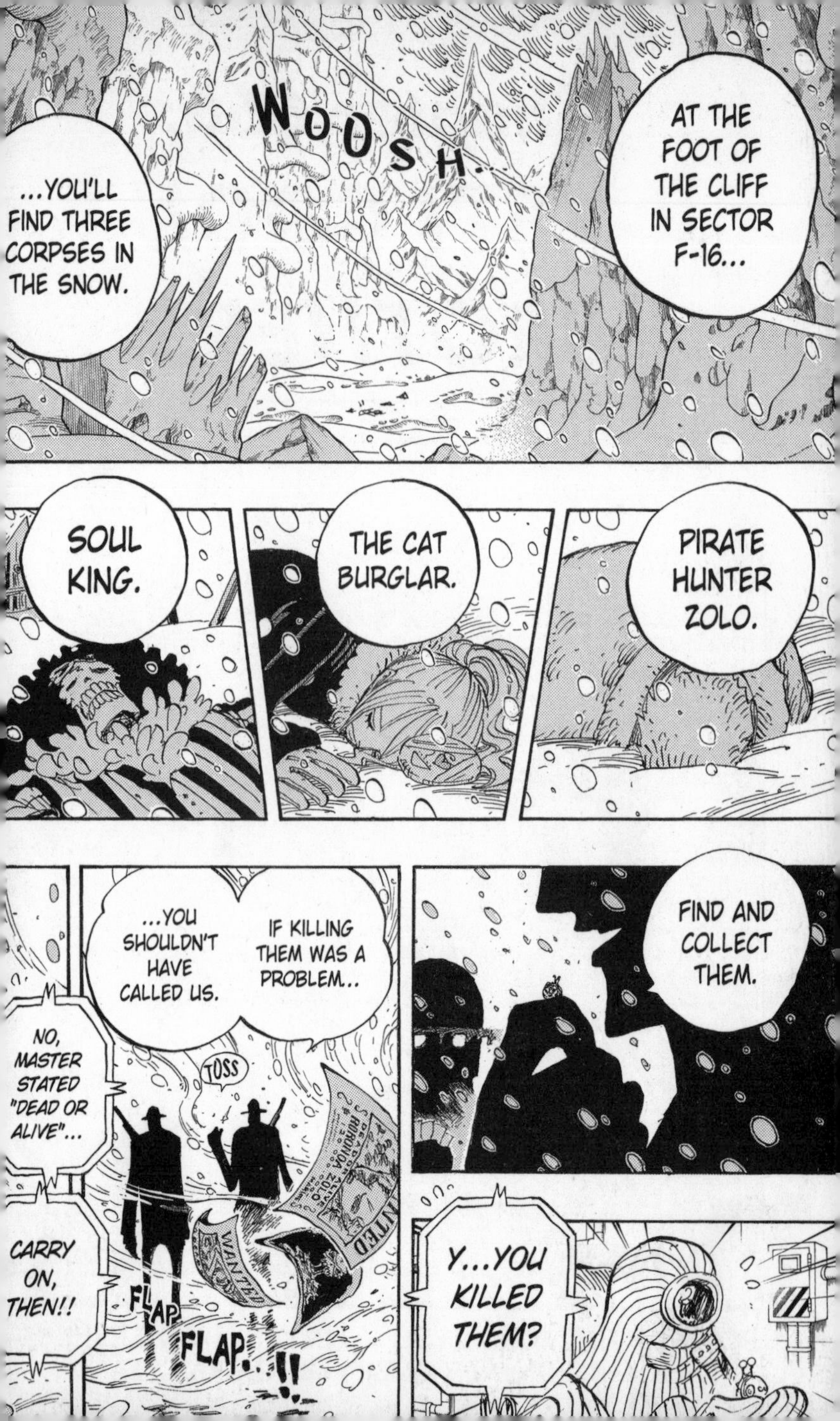
AT THE FOOT OF THE CLIFF IN SECTOR F-16...
WOOSH
...YOU'LL FIND THREE CORPSES IN THE SNOW.
PIRATE HUNTER ZOLO.
THE CAT BURGLAR.
SOUL KING.
FIND AND COLLECT THEM.
Y...YOU KILLED THEM?
IF KILLING THEM WAS A PROBLEM...
...YOU SHOULDN'T HAVE CALLED US.
TOSS
NO, MASTER STATED "DEAD OR ALIVE"...
CARRY ON, THEN!!
WANTED
FLAP
FLAP
!!

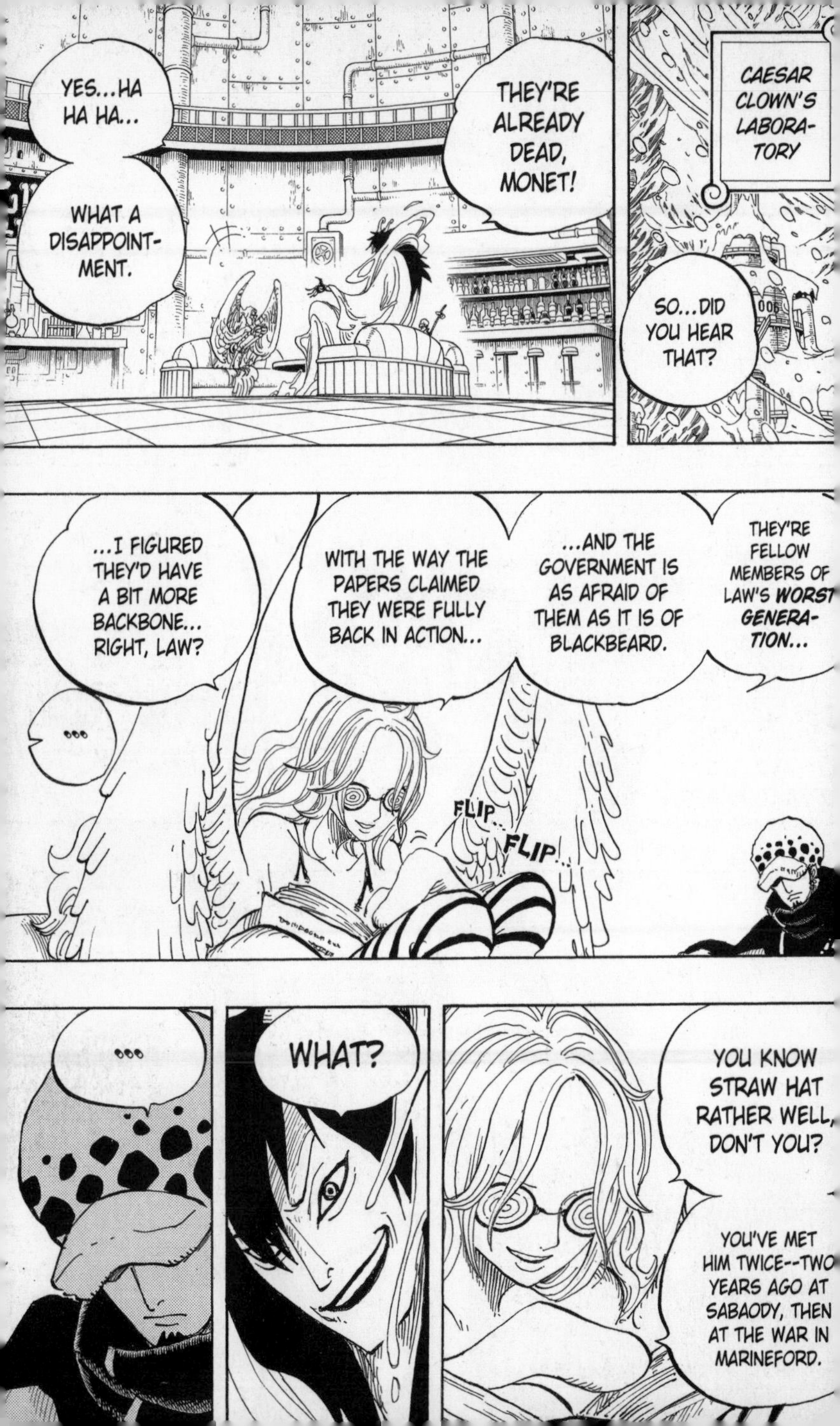
CAESAR CLOWN'S LABORATORY
SO...DID YOU HEAR THAT?
THEY'RE ALREADY DEAD, MONET!
YES...HA HA HA...
WHAT A DISAPPOINTMENT.
THEY'RE FELLOW MEMBERS OF LAW'S **WORST GENERATION**...
...AND THE GOVERNMENT IS AS AFRAID OF THEM AS IT IS OF BLACKBEARD.
WITH THE WAY THE PAPERS CLAIMED THEY WERE FULLY BACK IN ACTION...
...I FIGURED THEY'D HAVE A BIT MORE BACKBONE... RIGHT, LAW?
...
FLIP... FLIP...
YOU KNOW STRAW HAT RATHER WELL, DON'T YOU?
YOU'VE MET HIM TWICE--TWO YEARS AGO AT SABAODY, THEN AT THE WAR IN MARINEFORD.
WHAT?
...

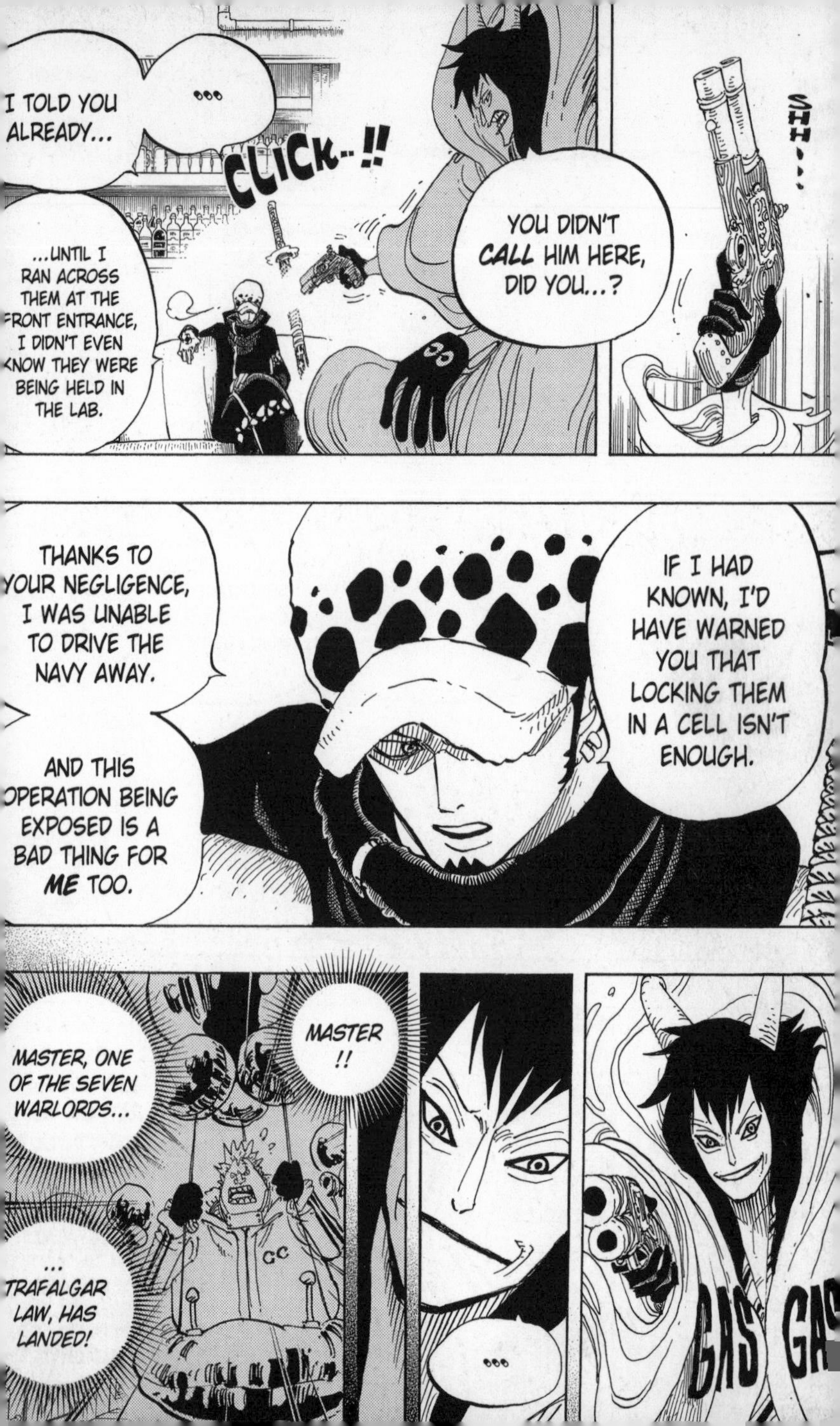
SHH...
YOU DIDN'T CALL HIM HERE, DID YOU...?
CLICK..!!
...
I TOLD YOU ALREADY...
...UNTIL I RAN ACROSS THEM AT THE FRONT ENTRANCE, I DIDN'T EVEN KNOW THEY WERE BEING HELD IN THE LAB.
IF I HAD KNOWN, I'D HAVE WARNED YOU THAT LOCKING THEM IN A CELL ISN'T ENOUGH.
THANKS TO YOUR NEGLIGENCE, I WAS UNABLE TO DRIVE THE NAVY AWAY.
AND THIS OPERATION BEING EXPOSED IS A BAD THING FOR ME TOO.
GAS GA
...
MASTER !!
MASTER, ONE OF THE SEVEN WARLORDS...
...TRAFALGAR LAW, HAS LANDED!

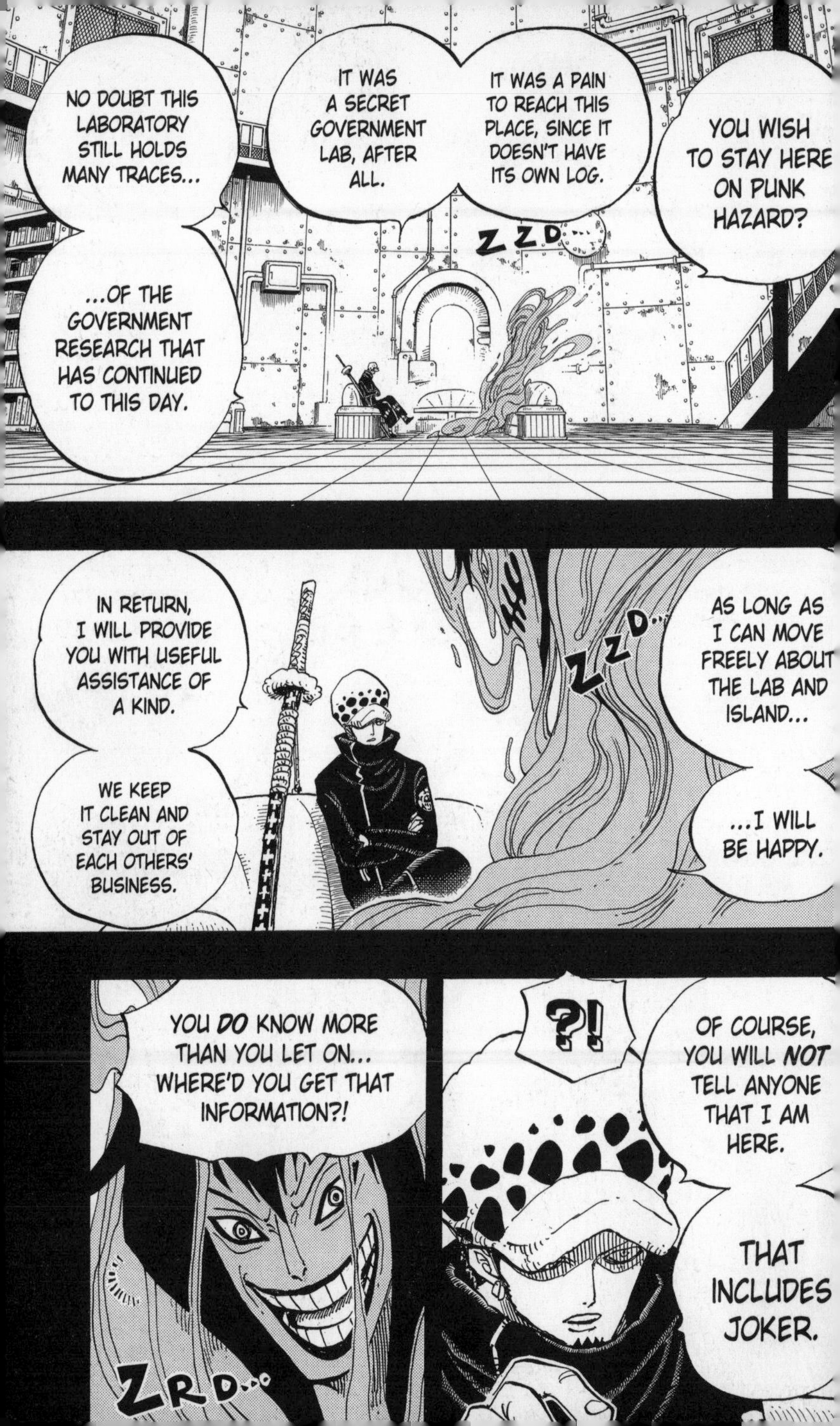
YOU WISH TO STAY HERE ON PUNK HAZARD?
IT WAS A PAIN TO REACH THIS PLACE, SINCE IT DOESN'T HAVE ITS OWN LOG.
IT WAS A SECRET GOVERNMENT LAB, AFTER ALL.
ZZD...
NO DOUBT THIS LABORATORY STILL HOLDS MANY TRACES...
...OF THE GOVERNMENT RESEARCH THAT HAS CONTINUED TO THIS DAY.
AS LONG AS I CAN MOVE FREELY ABOUT THE LAB AND ISLAND...
...I WILL BE HAPPY.
ZZD...
IN RETURN, I WILL PROVIDE YOU WITH USEFUL ASSISTANCE OF A KIND.
WE KEEP IT CLEAN AND STAY OUT OF EACH OTHERS' BUSINESS.
OF COURSE, YOU WILL *NOT* TELL ANYONE THAT I AM HERE.
THAT INCLUDES JOKER.
?!
YOU *DO* KNOW MORE THAN YOU LET ON... WHERE'D YOU GET THAT INFORMATION?!
ZRD...

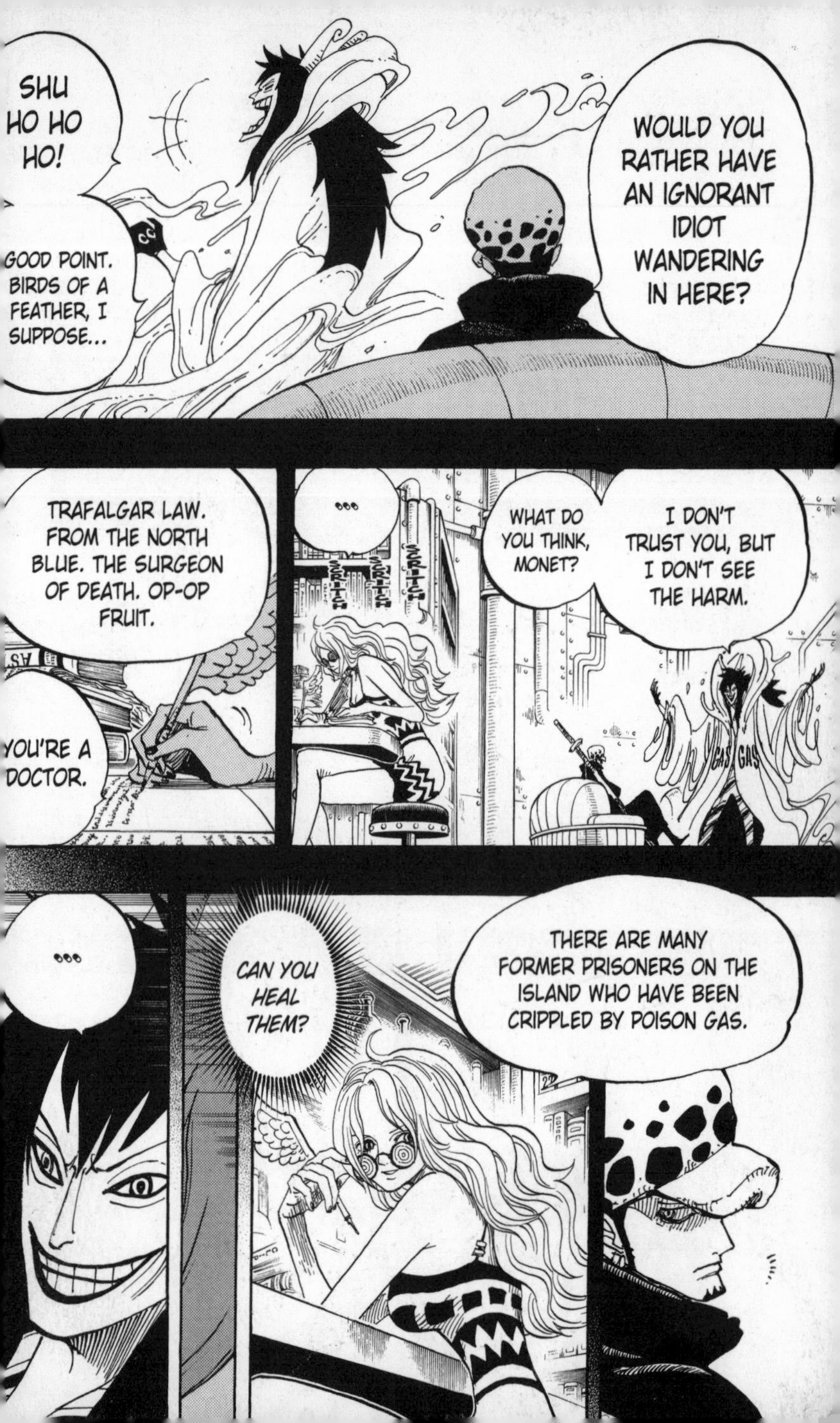
WOULD YOU RATHER HAVE AN IGNORANT IDIOT WANDERING IN HERE?
SHU HO HO HO!
GOOD POINT. BIRDS OF A FEATHER, I SUPPOSE...
I DON'T TRUST YOU, BUT I DON'T SEE THE HARM.
WHAT DO YOU THINK, MONET?
GAS GAS
...
SCRITCH SCRITCH SCRITCH
TRAFALGAR LAW. FROM THE NORTH BLUE. THE SURGEON OF DEATH. OP-OP FRUIT.
YOU'RE A DOCTOR.
THERE ARE MANY FORMER PRISONERS ON THE ISLAND WHO HAVE BEEN CRIPPLED BY POISON GAS.
CAN YOU HEAL THEM?
...

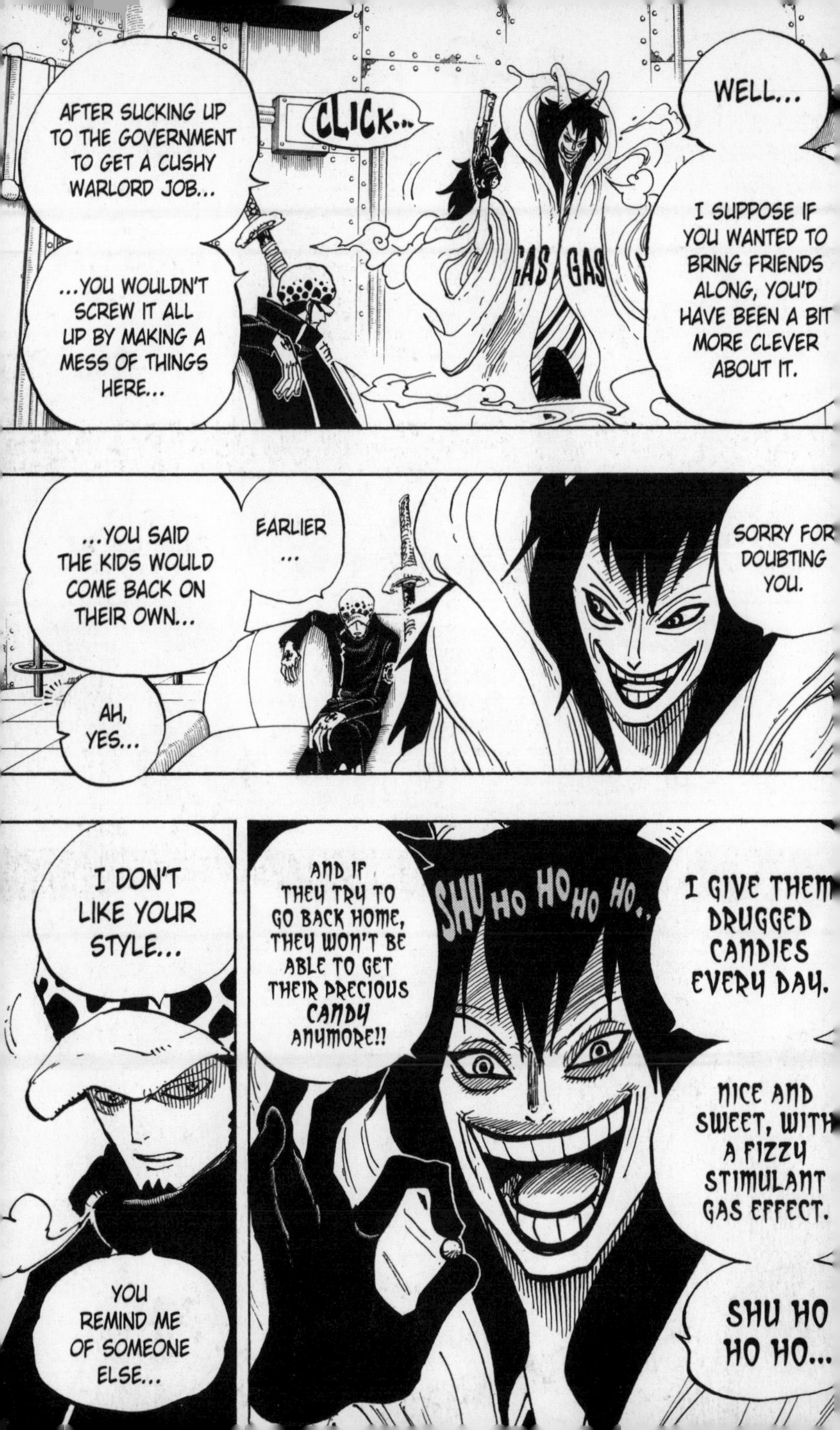
WELL...
I SUPPOSE IF YOU WANTED TO BRING FRIENDS ALONG, YOU'D HAVE BEEN A BIT MORE CLEVER ABOUT IT.
CLICK...
AFTER SUCKING UP TO THE GOVERNMENT TO GET A CUSHY WARLORD JOB...
...YOU WOULDN'T SCREW IT ALL UP BY MAKING A MESS OF THINGS HERE...
GAS GAS
SORRY FOR DOUBTING YOU.
EARLIER ...
...YOU SAID THE KIDS WOULD COME BACK ON THEIR OWN...
AH, YES...
I GIVE THEM DRUGGED CANDIES EVERY DAY.
SHU HO HO HO HO..
AND IF THEY TRY TO GO BACK HOME, THEY WON'T BE ABLE TO GET THEIR PRECIOUS CANDY ANYMORE!!
NICE AND SWEET, WITH A FIZZY STIMULANT GAS EFFECT.
SHU HO HO HO...
I DON'T LIKE YOUR STYLE...
YOU REMIND ME OF SOMEONE ELSE...

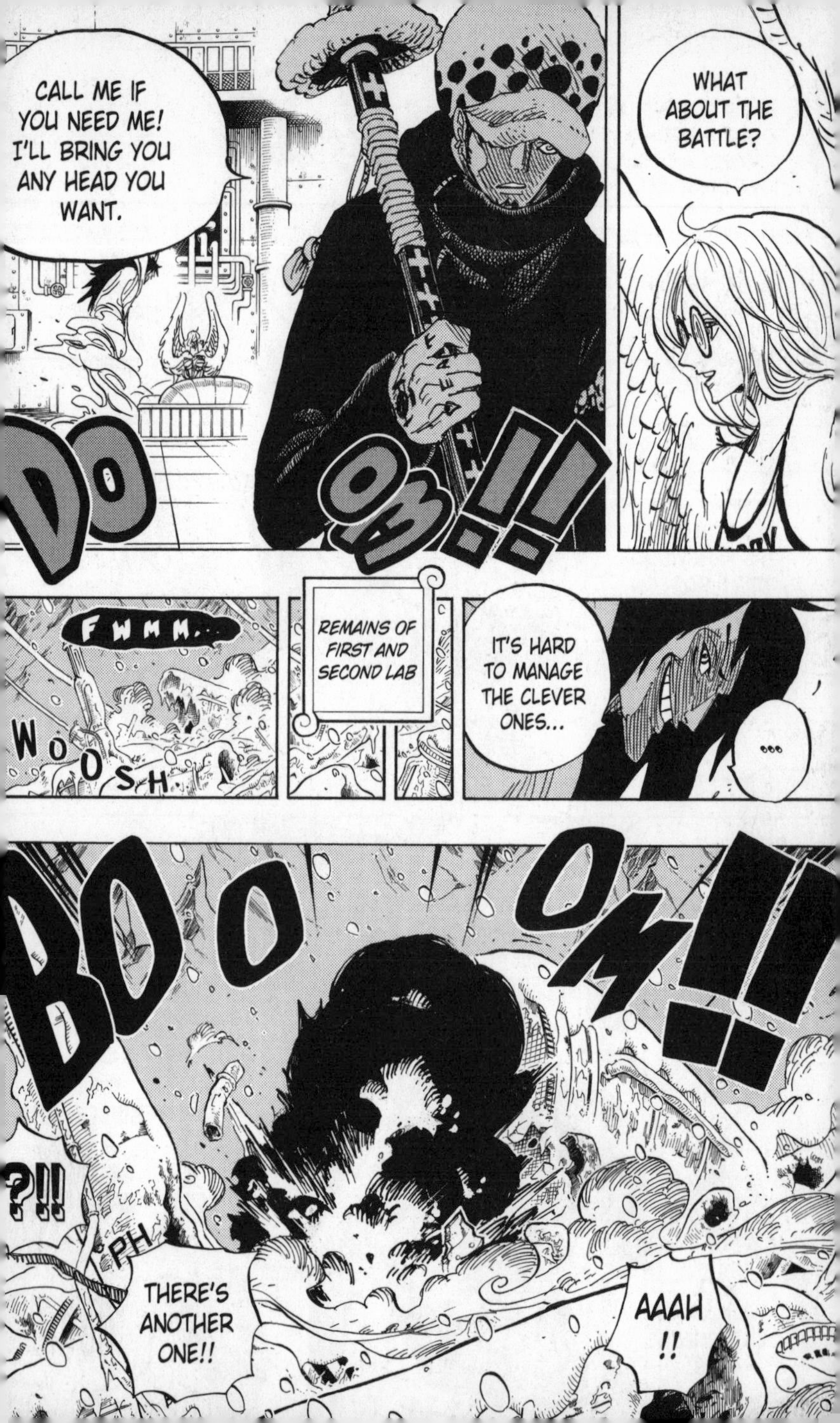
WHAT ABOUT THE BATTLE?
CALL ME IF YOU NEED ME! I'LL BRING YOU ANY HEAD YOU WANT.
DOOM!!
IT'S HARD TO MANAGE THE CLEVER ONES...
...
REMAINS OF FIRST AND SECOND LAB
FWMM...
WOOSH
BOOOM!!
AAAH!!
?!!
PH
THERE'S ANOTHER ONE!!

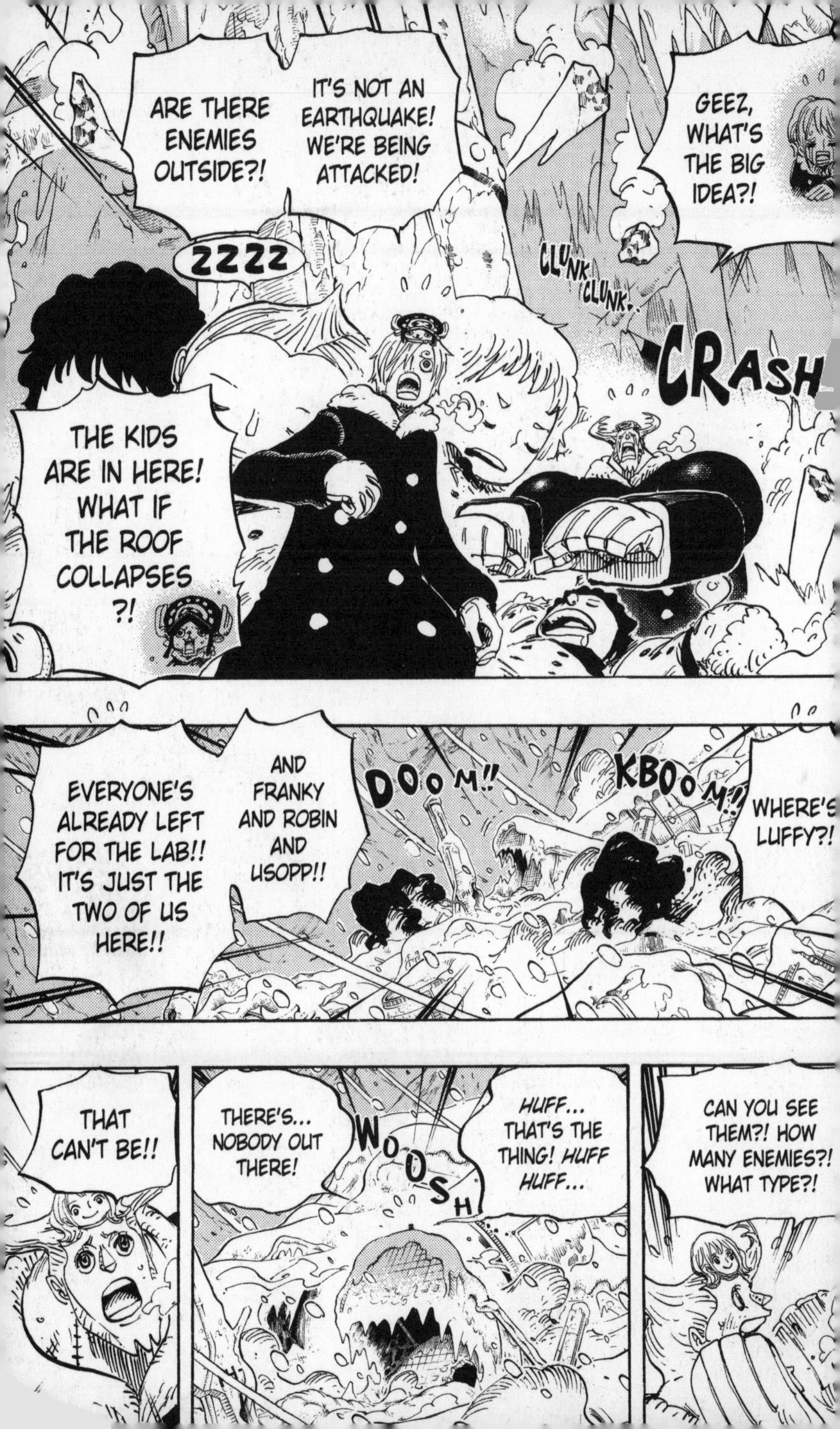
GEEZ, WHAT'S THE BIG IDEA?!
CLUNK CLUNK..
CRASH
IT'S NOT AN EARTHQUAKE! WE'RE BEING ATTACKED!
ARE THERE ENEMIES OUTSIDE?!
ZZZZ
THE KIDS ARE IN HERE! WHAT IF THE ROOF COLLAPSES?!
WHERE'S LUFFY?!
KBOOM!!
DOOM!!
AND FRANKY AND ROBIN AND USOPP!!
EVERYONE'S ALREADY LEFT FOR THE LAB!! IT'S JUST THE TWO OF US HERE!!
CAN YOU SEE THEM?! HOW MANY ENEMIES?! WHAT TYPE?!
HUFF... THAT'S THE THING! HUFF HUFF...
WOOSH
THERE'S... NOBODY OUT THERE!
THAT CAN'T BE!!

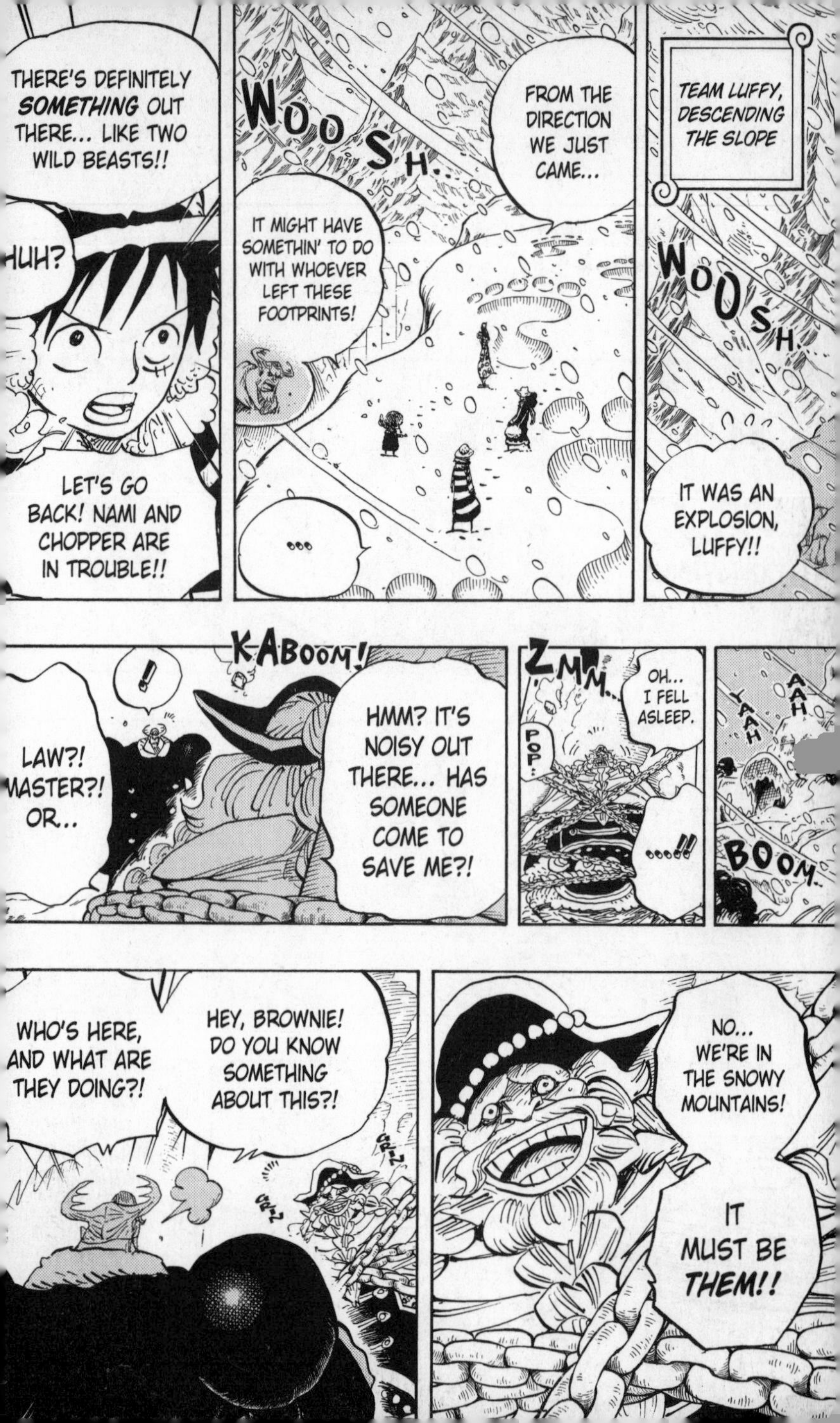
TEAM LUFFY, DESCENDING THE SLOPE
WOOSH
IT WAS AN EXPLOSION, LUFFY!!
FROM THE DIRECTION WE JUST CAME...
WOOSH
IT MIGHT HAVE SOMETHIN' TO DO WITH WHOEVER LEFT THESE FOOTPRINTS!
...
THERE'S DEFINITELY *SOMETHING* OUT THERE... LIKE TWO WILD BEASTS!!
HUH?
LET'S GO BACK! NAMI AND CHOPPER ARE IN TROUBLE!!
YAAH
AAH
BOOM
ZMMM...
OH... I FELL ASLEEP.
POP...
...!!
KABOOM!
HMM? IT'S NOISY OUT THERE... HAS SOMEONE COME TO SAVE ME?!
!
LAW?! MASTER?! OR...
NO... WE'RE IN THE SNOWY MOUNTAINS!
IT MUST BE *THEM!!*
HEY, BROWNIE! DO YOU KNOW SOMETHING ABOUT THIS?!
WHO'S HERE, AND WHAT ARE THEY DOING?!
GRIN
GRIN

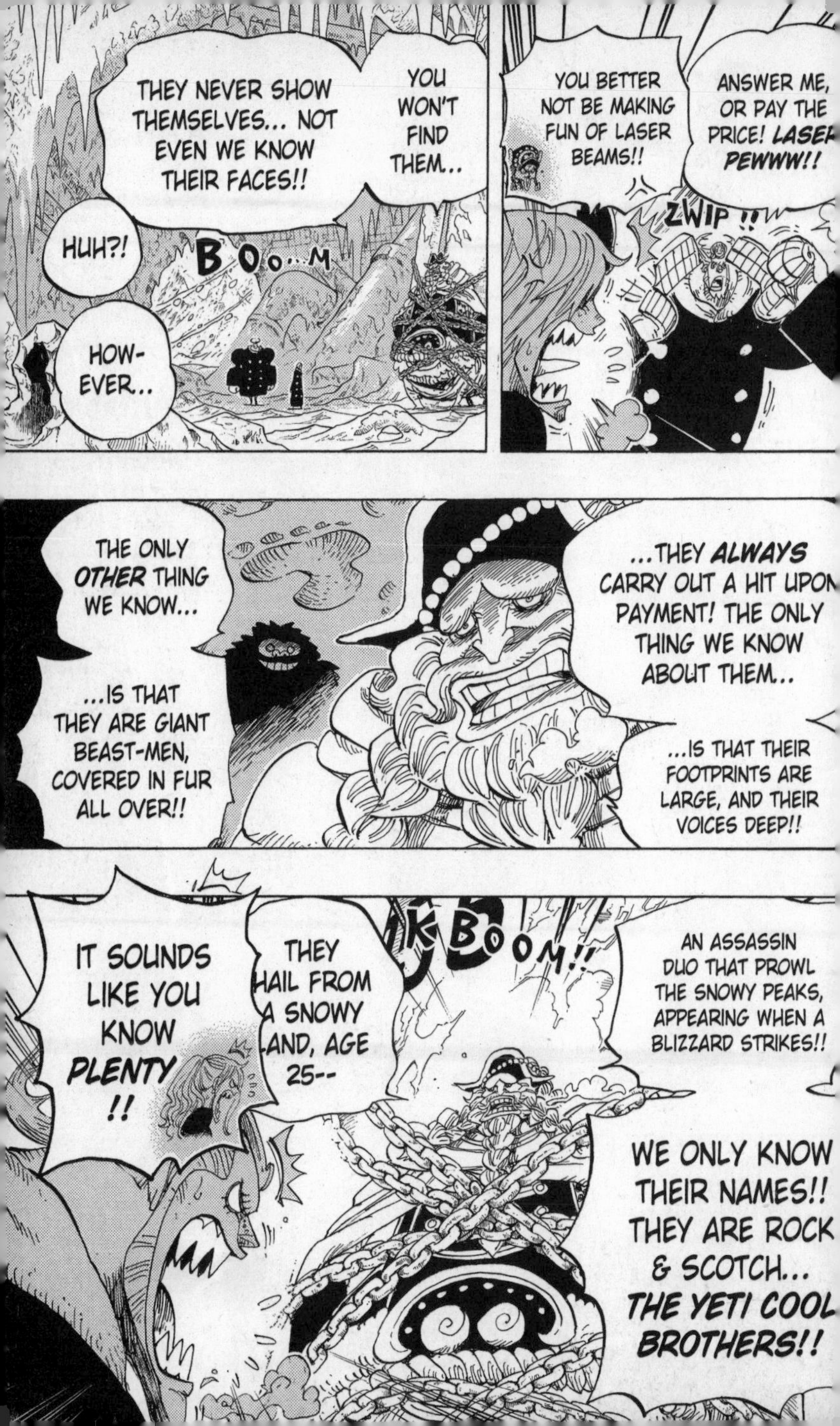
ANSWER ME, OR PAY THE PRICE! LASER PEWWW!!
YOU BETTER NOT BE MAKING FUN OF LASER BEAMS!!
ZWIP!!
YOU WON'T FIND THEM...
THEY NEVER SHOW THEMSELVES... NOT EVEN WE KNOW THEIR FACES!!
HUH?!
BOO...M
HOW-EVER...
...THEY ALWAYS CARRY OUT A HIT UPON PAYMENT! THE ONLY THING WE KNOW ABOUT THEM...
...IS THAT THEIR FOOTPRINTS ARE LARGE, AND THEIR VOICES DEEP!!
THE ONLY OTHER THING WE KNOW...
...IS THAT THEY ARE GIANT BEAST-MEN, COVERED IN FUR ALL OVER!!
AN ASSASSIN DUO THAT PROWL THE SNOWY PEAKS, APPEARING WHEN A BLIZZARD STRIKES!!
KBOOM!!
THEY HAIL FROM A SNOWY LAND, AGE 25--
IT SOUNDS LIKE YOU KNOW PLENTY!!
WE ONLY KNOW THEIR NAMES!! THEY ARE ROCK & SCOTCH... THE YETI COOL BROTHERS!!

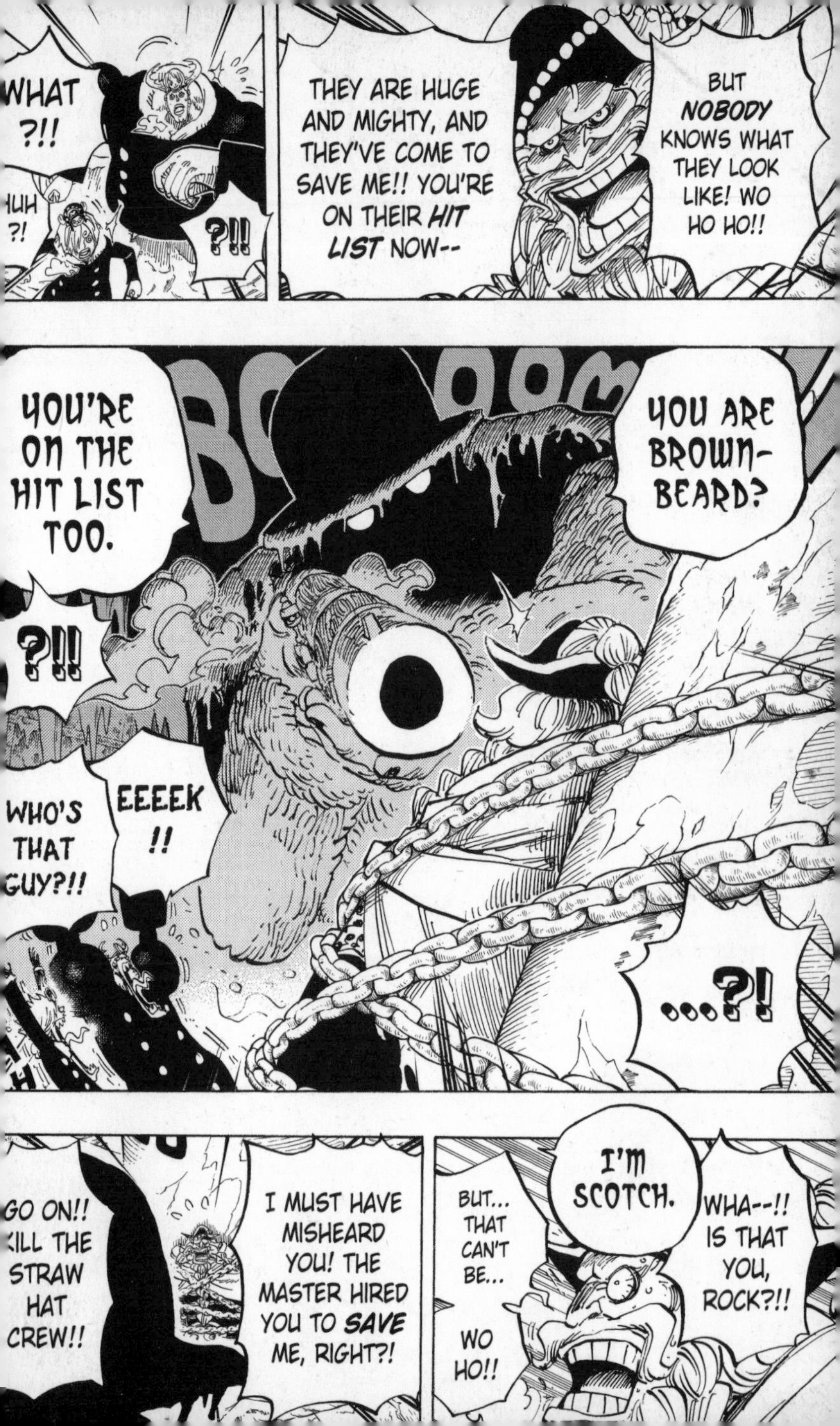
THEY ARE HUGE AND MIGHTY, AND THEY'VE COME TO SAVE ME!! YOU'RE ON THEIR *HIT LIST* NOW--
BUT *NOBODY* KNOWS WHAT THEY LOOK LIKE! WO HO HO!!
WHAT ?!!
?!!
HUH ?!
YOU ARE BROWN-BEARD?
YOU'RE ON THE HIT LIST TOO.
...?!
?!!
EEEEK !!
WHO'S THAT GUY?!!
WHA--!! IS THAT YOU, ROCK?!!
I'M SCOTCH.
BUT... THAT CAN'T BE...
WO HO!!
I MUST HAVE MISHEARD YOU! THE MASTER HIRED YOU TO *SAVE* ME, RIGHT?!
GO ON!! KILL THE STRAW HAT CREW!!

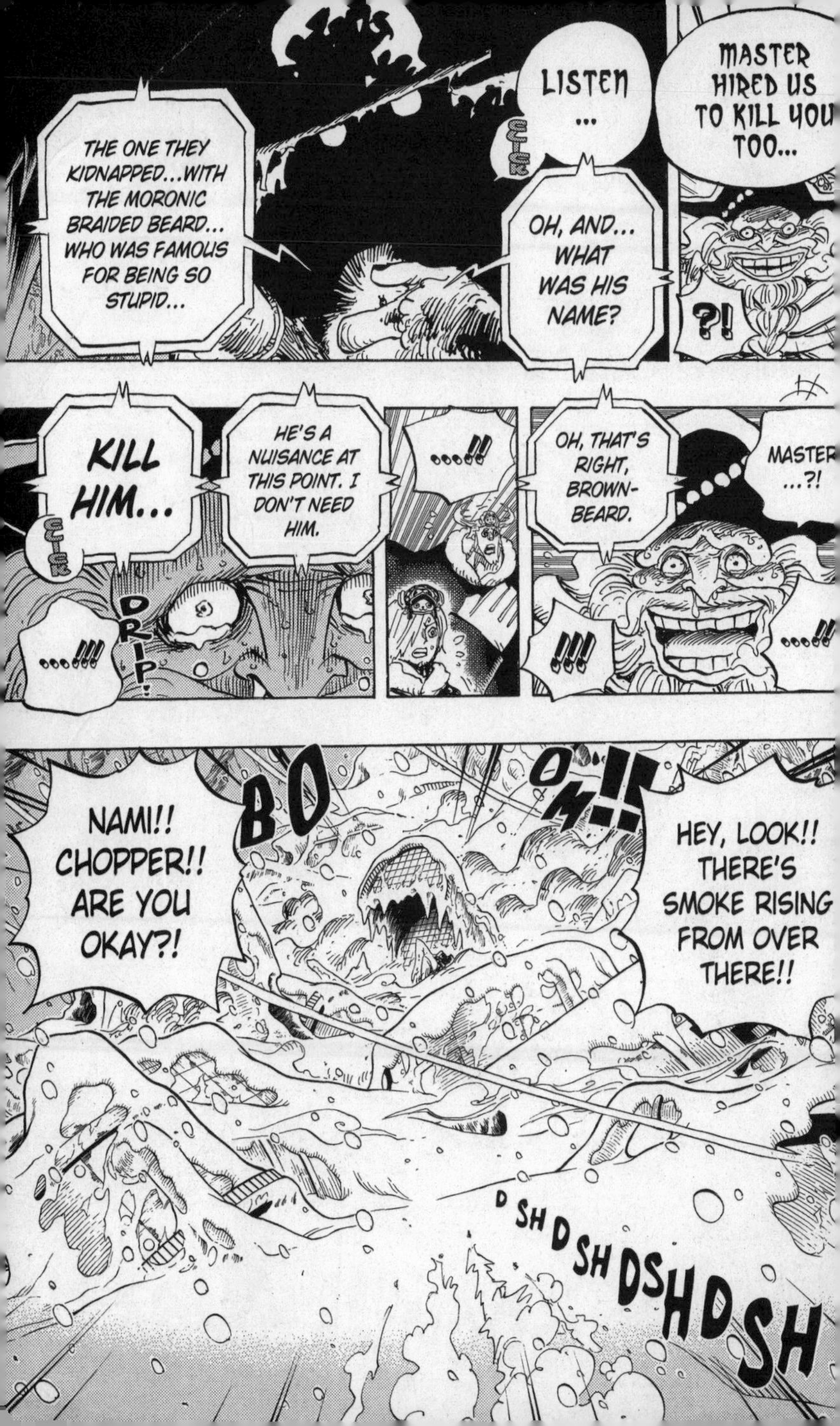
MASTER HIRED US TO KILL YOU TOO...
?!
LISTEN...
CLICK
OH, AND... WHAT WAS HIS NAME?
THE ONE THEY KIDNAPPED...WITH THE MORONIC BRAIDED BEARD... WHO WAS FAMOUS FOR BEING SO STUPID...
MASTER ...?!
...!!
OH, THAT'S RIGHT, BROWN-BEARD.
!!!
...!!
HE'S A NUISANCE AT THIS POINT. I DON'T NEED HIM.
KILL HIM...
CLICK
DRIP!
...!!!
HEY, LOOK!! THERE'S SMOKE RISING FROM OVER THERE!!
BOOM!!
NAMI!! CHOPPER!! ARE YOU OKAY?!
DSHDSHDSHDSH

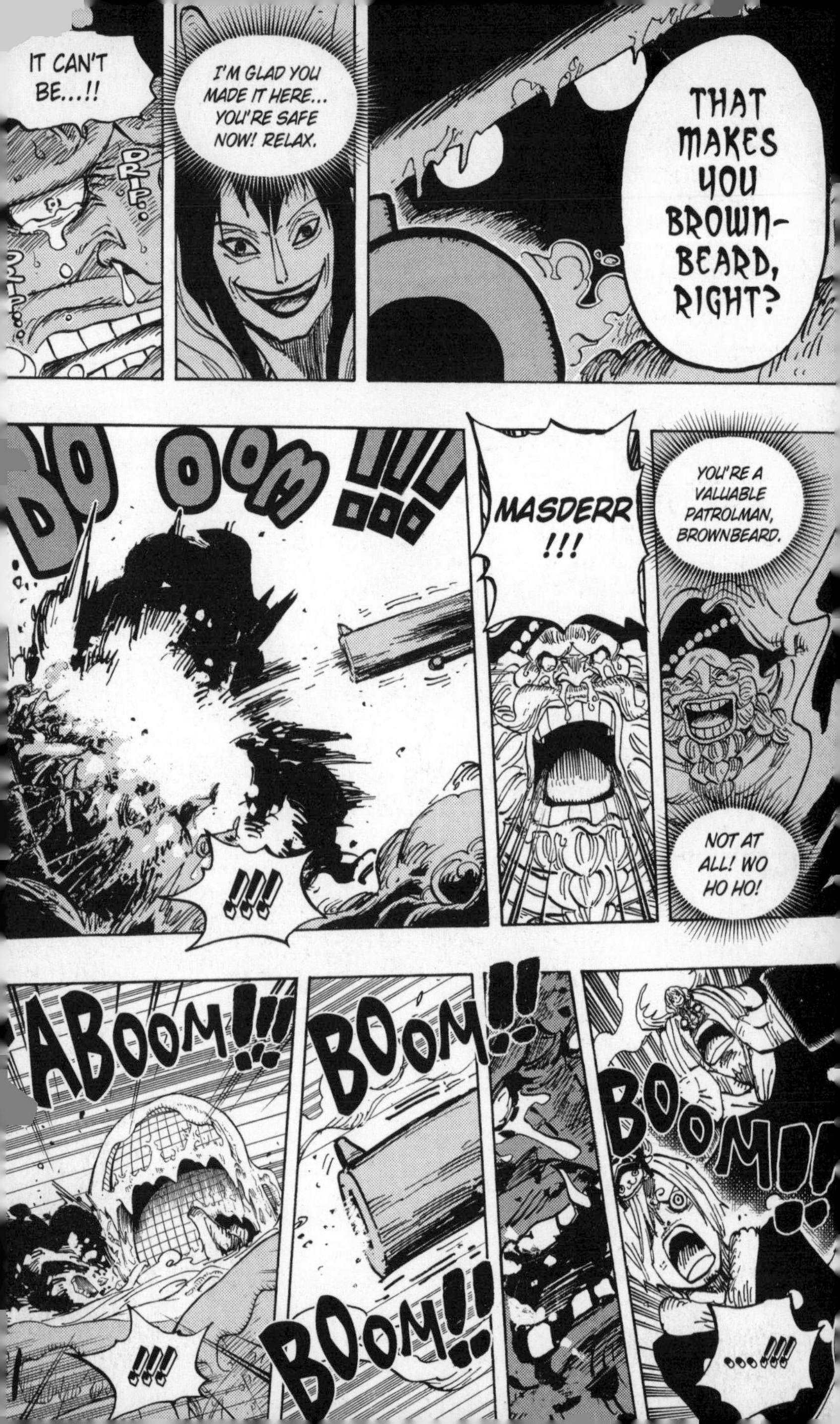
THAT MAKES YOU BROWN-BEARD, RIGHT?
I'M GLAD YOU MADE IT HERE... YOU'RE SAFE NOW! RELAX.
IT CAN'T BE...!!
DRIP
YOU'RE A VALUABLE PATROLMAN, BROWNBEARD.
NOT AT ALL! WO HO HO!
MASDERR !!!
BOOOM!!!
!!!
BOOM!!
...!!!
BOOM!!
BOOM!!
ABOOM!!!
!!!

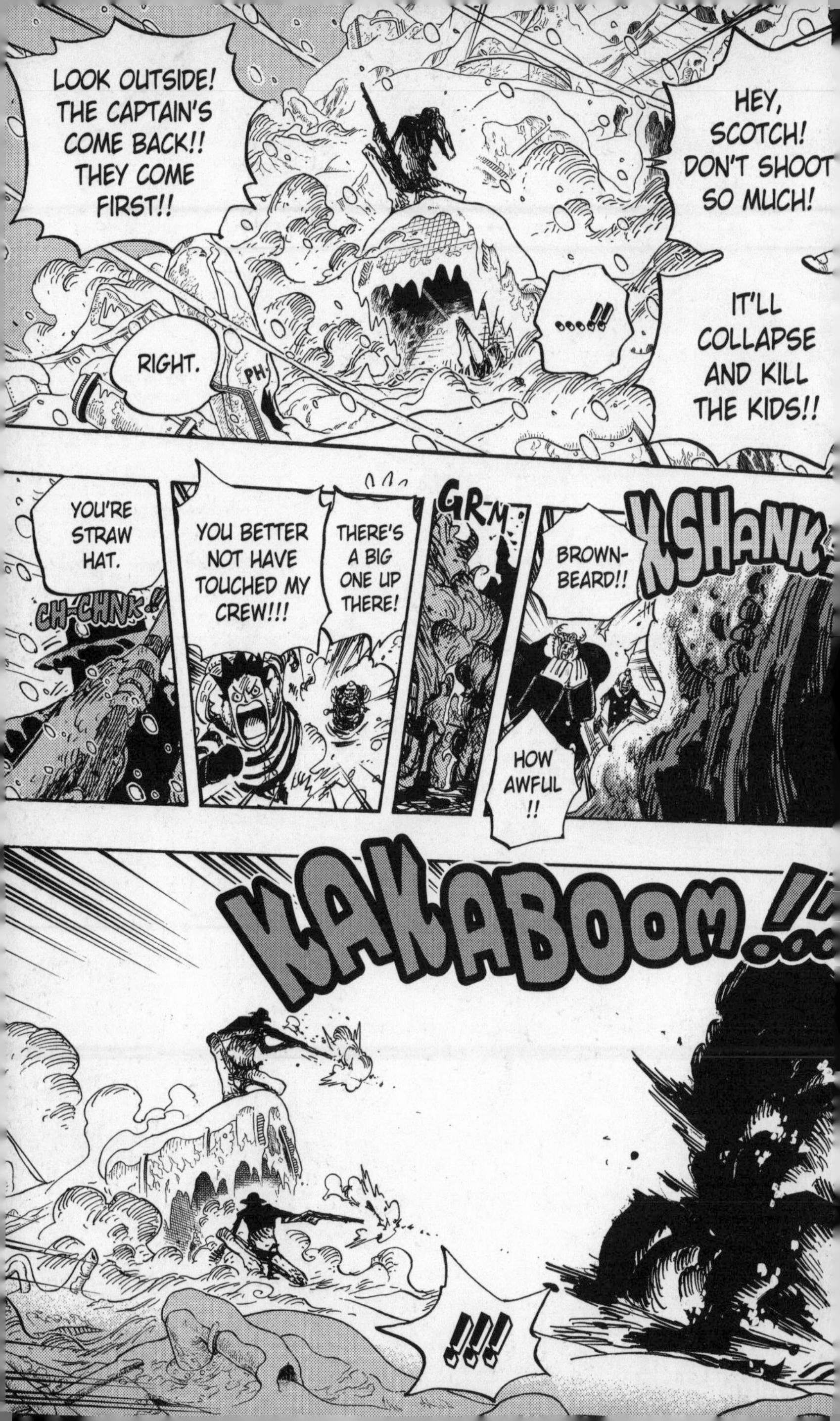
HEY, SCOTCH! DON'T SHOOT SO MUCH!
IT'LL COLLAPSE AND KILL THE KIDS!!
....!!
LOOK OUTSIDE! THE CAPTAIN'S COME BACK!! THEY COME FIRST!!
RIGHT.
PH
KSHANK
BROWN-BEARD!!
HOW AWFUL !!
GR-M
THERE'S A BIG ONE UP THERE!
YOU BETTER NOT HAVE TOUCHED MY CREW!!!
YOU'RE STRAW HAT.
CH-CHNK!!
KAKABOOM!!
!!!

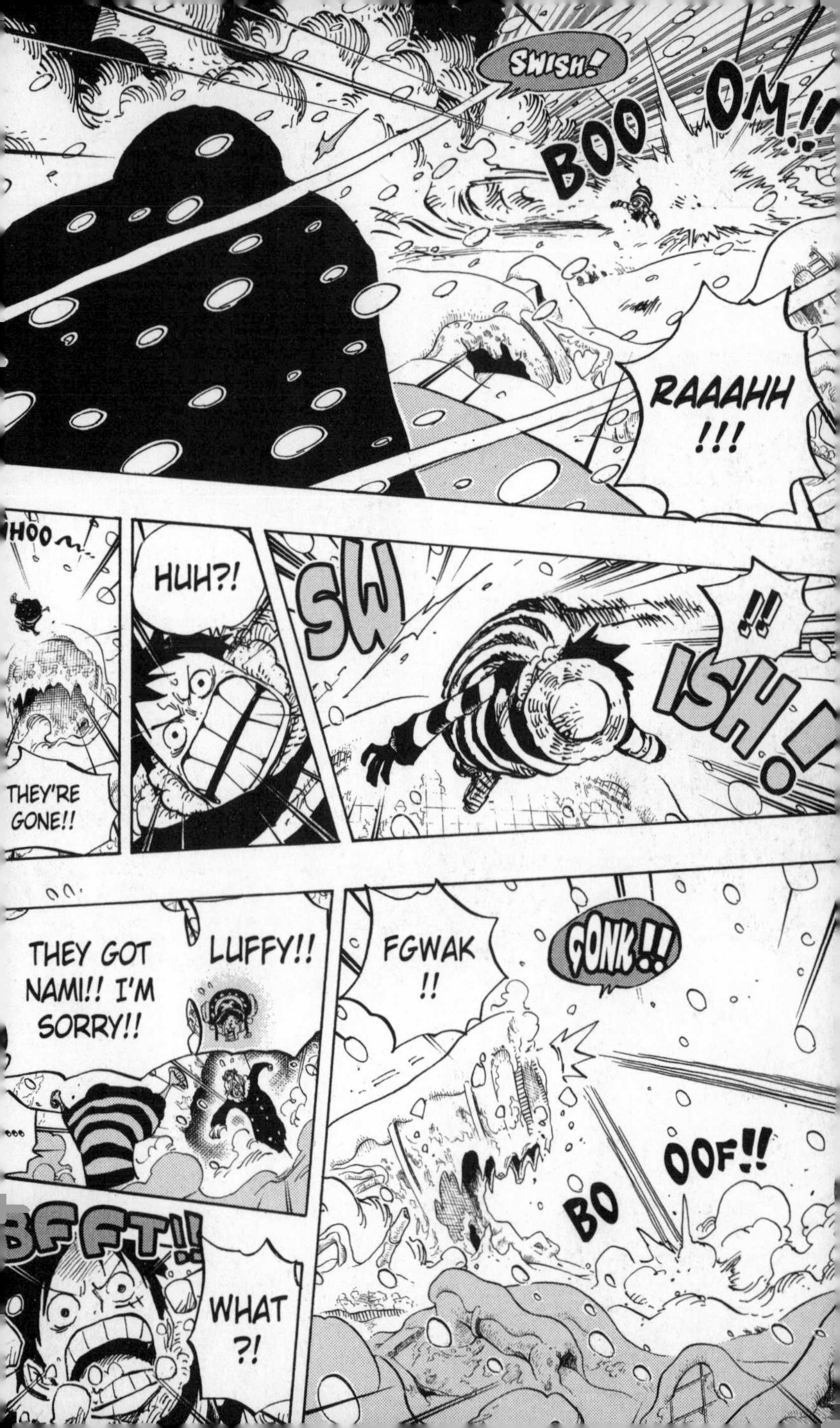
SWISH!
BOO OM!!
RAAAHH !!!
!!
SW ISH!!
HUH?!
HOO~!
THEY'RE GONE!!
GONK!!
FGWAK !!
BO OOF!!
LUFFY!!
THEY GOT NAMI!! I'M SORRY!!
...
BFFT!!
WHAT ?!

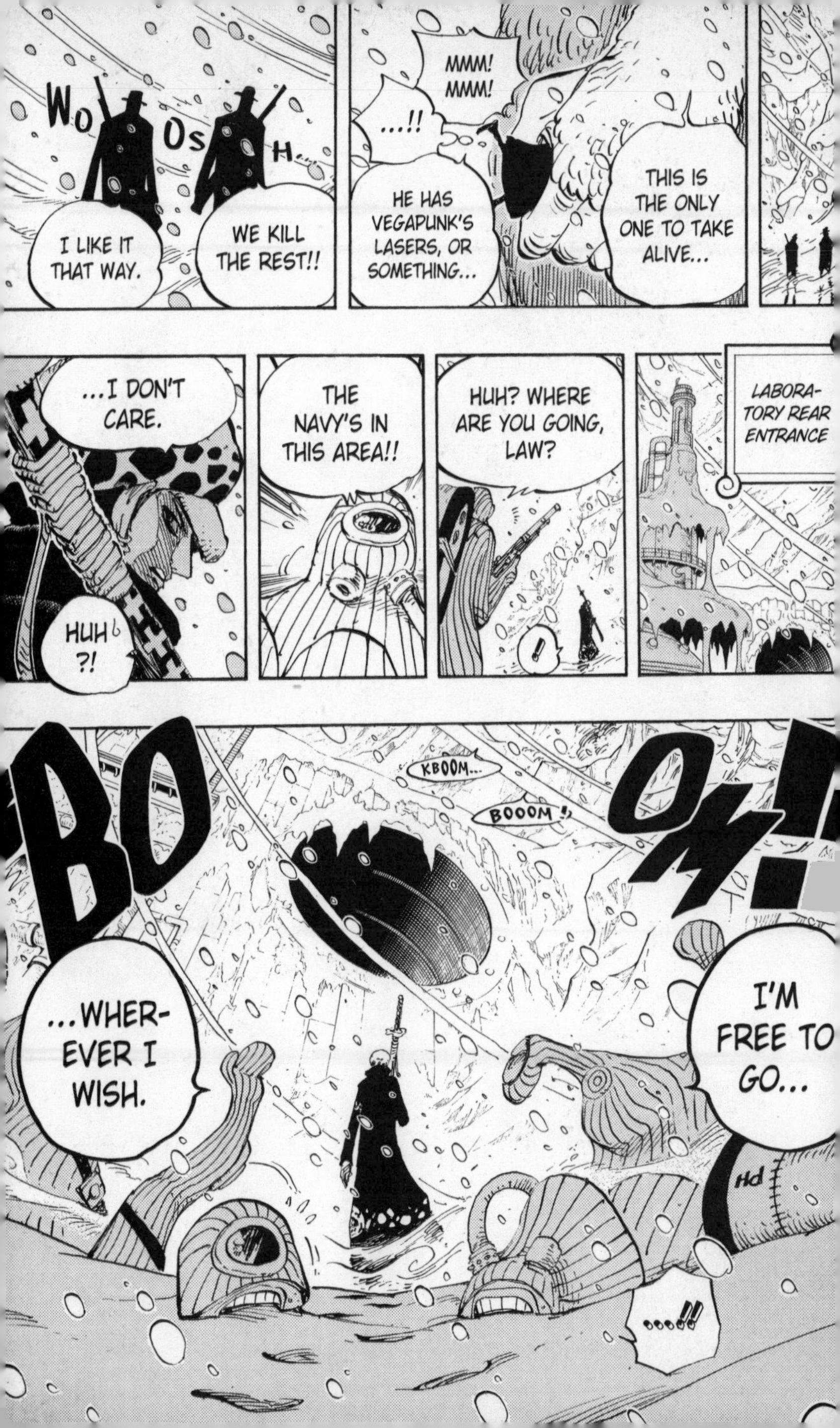
MMM! MMM!
THIS IS THE ONLY ONE TO TAKE ALIVE...
...!!
HE HAS VEGAPUNK'S LASERS, OR SOMETHING...
WOOSH...
WE KILL THE REST!!
I LIKE IT THAT WAY.
LABORA-TORY REAR ENTRANCE
HUH? WHERE ARE YOU GOING, LAW?
!
THE NAVY'S IN THIS AREA!!
...I DON'T CARE.
HUH?!
BOOM!!
KBOOM...
BOOOM!
I'M FREE TO GO...
...WHER-EVER I WISH.
....!!

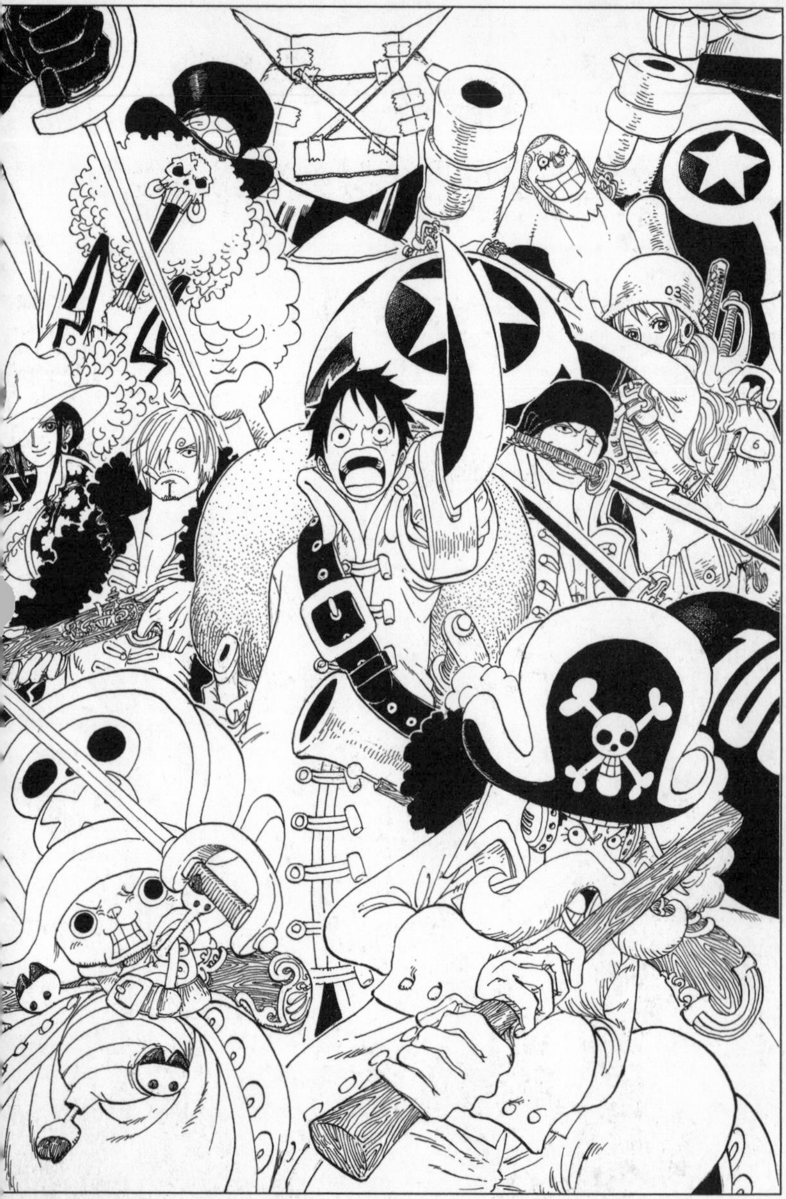
03
6

Chapter 667:
COOL FIGHT

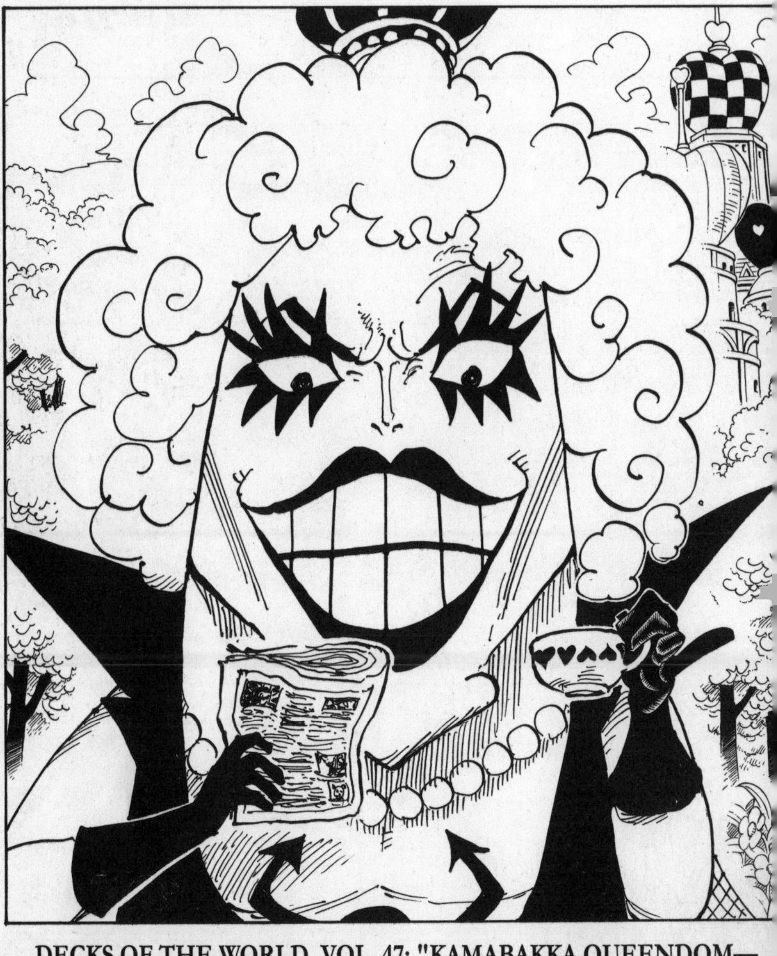

DECKS OF THE WORLD, VOL. 47: "KAMABAKKA QUEENDOM—
THE KING OF THE QUEENS FOLLOWS STRAW BOY'S TRAVELS"

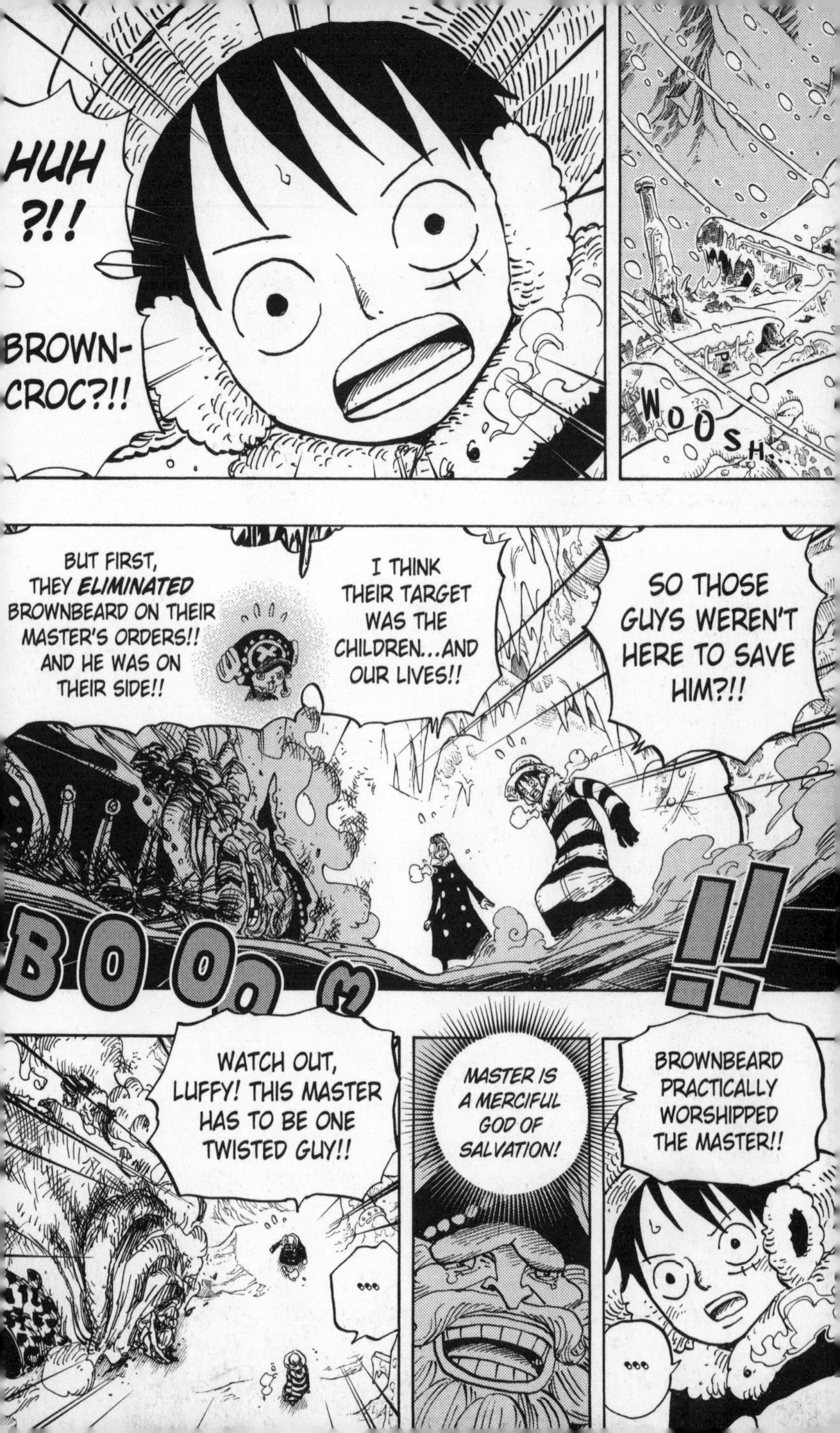
WOOSH...
HUH ?!!
BROWN-CROC?!!
SO THOSE GUYS WEREN'T HERE TO SAVE HIM?!!
I THINK THEIR TARGET WAS THE CHILDREN...AND OUR LIVES!!
BUT FIRST, THEY *ELIMINATED* BROWNBEARD ON THEIR MASTER'S ORDERS!! AND HE WAS ON THEIR SIDE!!
!!
BOOOOM
BROWNBEARD PRACTICALLY WORSHIPPED THE MASTER!!
...
MASTER IS A MERCIFUL GOD OF SALVATION!
WATCH OUT, LUFFY! THIS MASTER HAS TO BE ONE TWISTED GUY!!
...

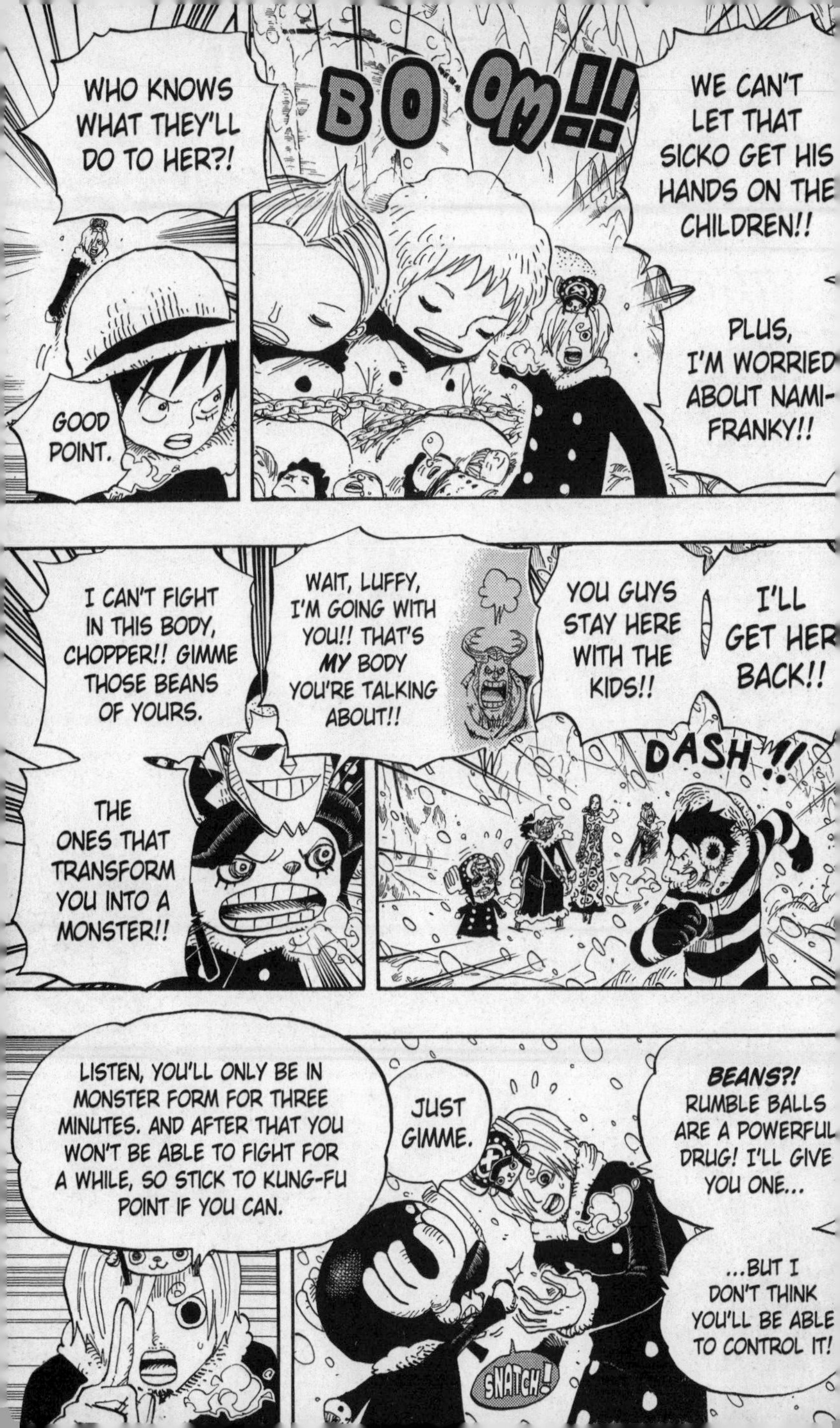

WE CAN'T LET THAT SICKO GET HIS HANDS ON THE CHILDREN!!
BOOM!!
PLUS, I'M WORRIED ABOUT NAMI-FRANKY!!
WHO KNOWS WHAT THEY'LL DO TO HER?!
GOOD POINT.
I'LL GET HER BACK!!
YOU GUYS STAY HERE WITH THE KIDS!!
DASH!!
WAIT, LUFFY, I'M GOING WITH YOU!! THAT'S *MY* BODY YOU'RE TALKING ABOUT!!
I CAN'T FIGHT IN THIS BODY, CHOPPER!! GIMME THOSE BEANS OF YOURS.
THE ONES THAT TRANSFORM YOU INTO A MONSTER!!
BEANS?! RUMBLE BALLS ARE A POWERFUL DRUG! I'LL GIVE YOU ONE...
...BUT I DON'T THINK YOU'LL BE ABLE TO CONTROL IT!
JUST GIMME.
SNATCH!
LISTEN, YOU'LL ONLY BE IN MONSTER FORM FOR THREE MINUTES. AND AFTER THAT YOU WON'T BE ABLE TO FIGHT FOR A WHILE, SO STICK TO KUNG-FU POINT IF YOU CAN.

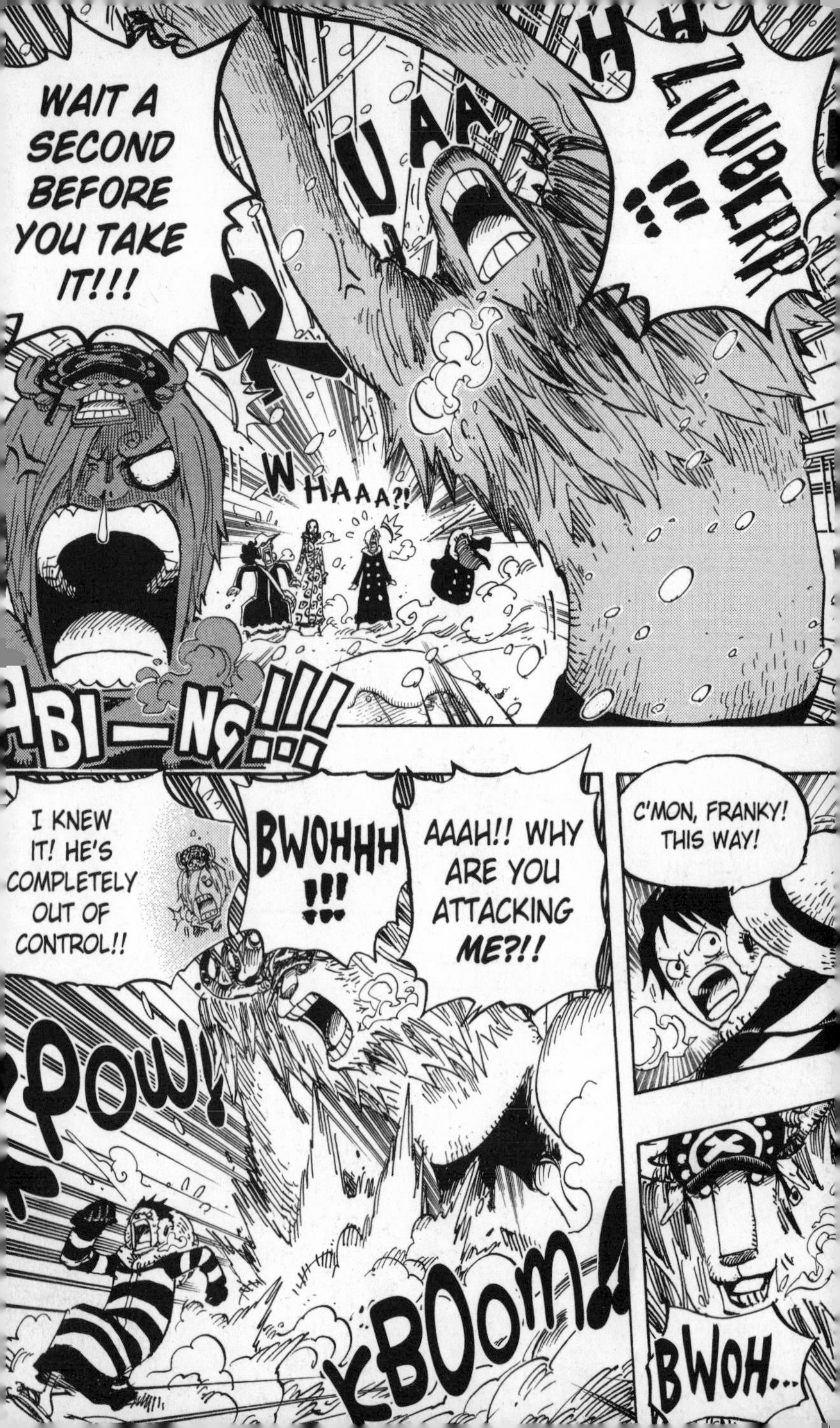
ZUUBERR!!!
WAIT A SECOND BEFORE YOU TAKE IT!!!
WHAAA?!
C'MON, FRANKY! THIS WAY!
AAAH!! WHY ARE YOU ATTACKING ME?!!
BWOHHH!!!
I KNEW IT! HE'S COMPLETELY OUT OF CONTROL!!
POW!
BWOH...
KBOOM!!

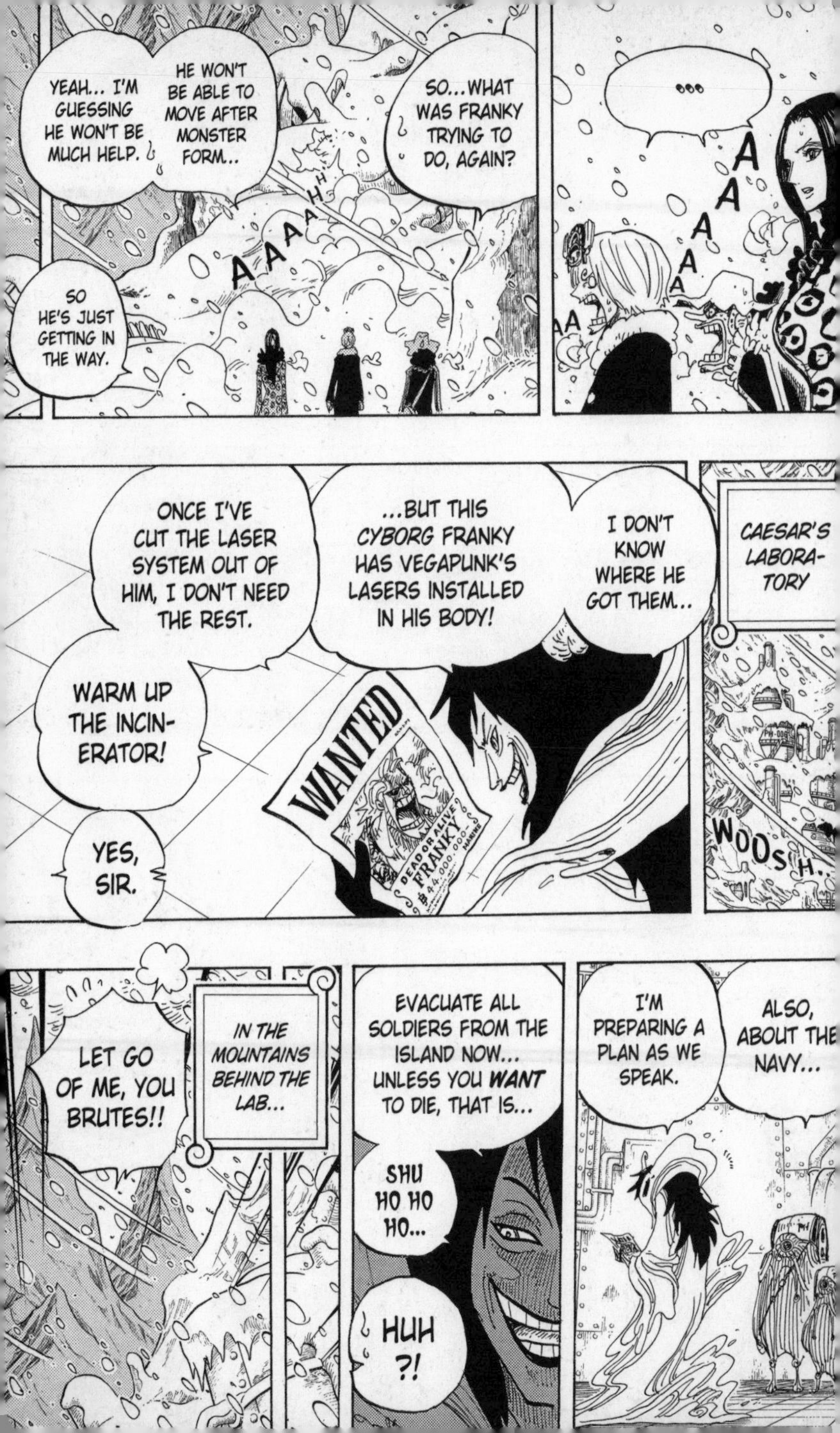
...
AAAAAAA
SO...WHAT WAS FRANKY TRYING TO DO, AGAIN?
HE WON'T BE ABLE TO MOVE AFTER MONSTER FORM...
YEAH... I'M GUESSING HE WON'T BE MUCH HELP.
AAAAAH
SO HE'S JUST GETTING IN THE WAY.
CAESAR'S LABORATORY
WOOSH...
I DON'T KNOW WHERE HE GOT THEM...
...BUT THIS CYBORG FRANKY HAS VEGAPUNK'S LASERS INSTALLED IN HIS BODY!
ONCE I'VE CUT THE LASER SYSTEM OUT OF HIM, I DON'T NEED THE REST.
WANTED
DEAD OR ALIVE
FRANKY
฿44,000,000-
MARINE
WARM UP THE INCIN-ERATOR!
YES, SIR.
ALSO, ABOUT THE NAVY...
I'M PREPARING A PLAN AS WE SPEAK.
EVACUATE ALL SOLDIERS FROM THE ISLAND NOW... UNLESS YOU *WANT* TO DIE, THAT IS...
SHU HO HO HO...
HUH ?!
IN THE MOUNTAINS BEHIND THE LAB...
LET GO OF ME, YOU BRUTES!!

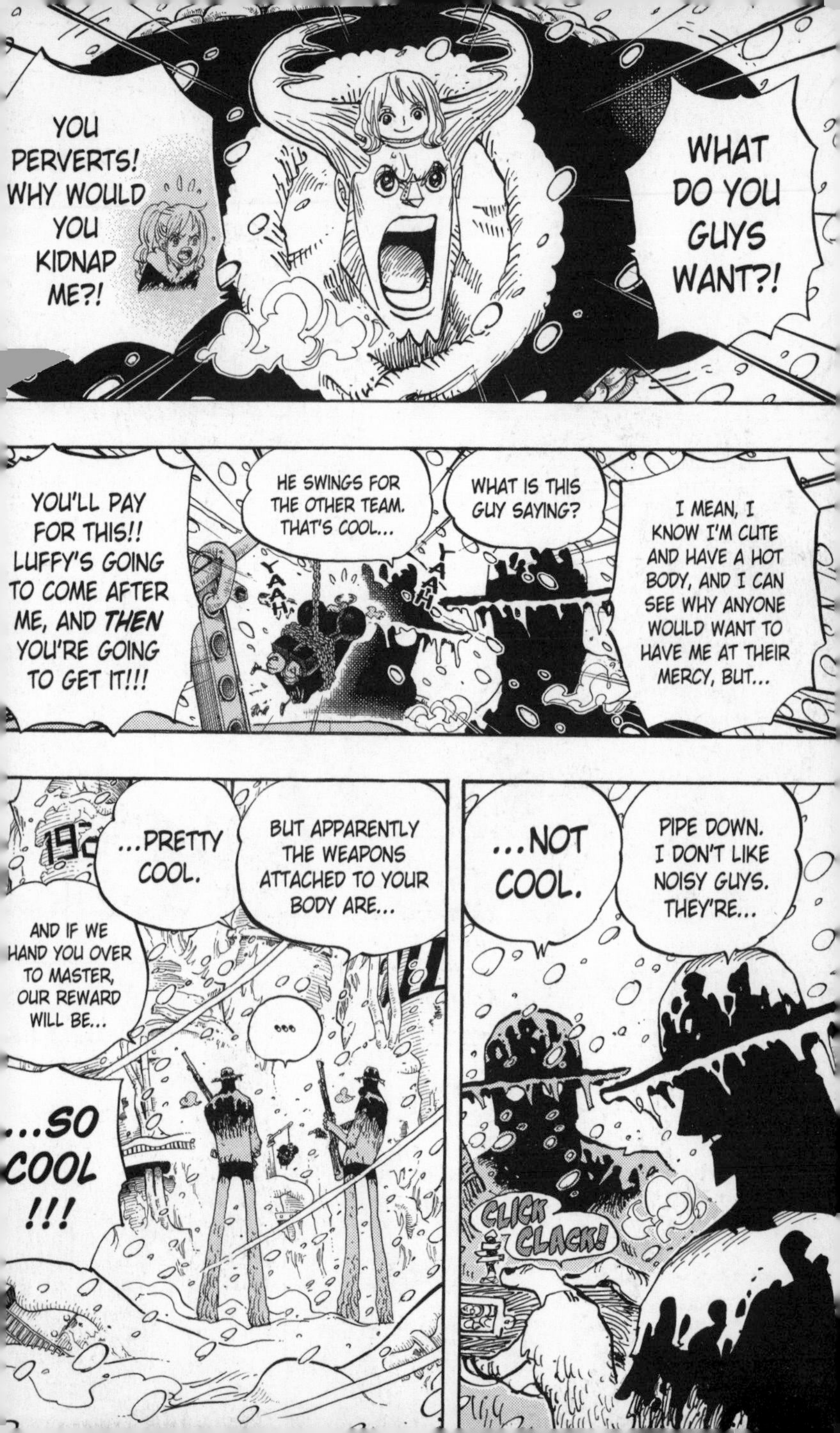
WHAT DO YOU GUYS WANT?!
YOU PERVERTS! WHY WOULD YOU KIDNAP ME?!
I MEAN, I KNOW I'M CUTE AND HAVE A HOT BODY, AND I CAN SEE WHY ANYONE WOULD WANT TO HAVE ME AT THEIR MERCY, BUT...
WHAT IS THIS GUY SAYING?
YAAAH
HE SWINGS FOR THE OTHER TEAM. THAT'S COOL...
YAAAH
YOU'LL PAY FOR THIS!! LUFFY'S GOING TO COME AFTER ME, AND THEN YOU'RE GOING TO GET IT!!!
PIPE DOWN. I DON'T LIKE NOISY GUYS. THEY'RE...
...NOT COOL.
CLICK CLACK!
BUT APPARENTLY THE WEAPONS ATTACHED TO YOUR BODY ARE...
...PRETTY COOL.
AND IF WE HAND YOU OVER TO MASTER, OUR REWARD WILL BE...
...
...SO COOL!!!

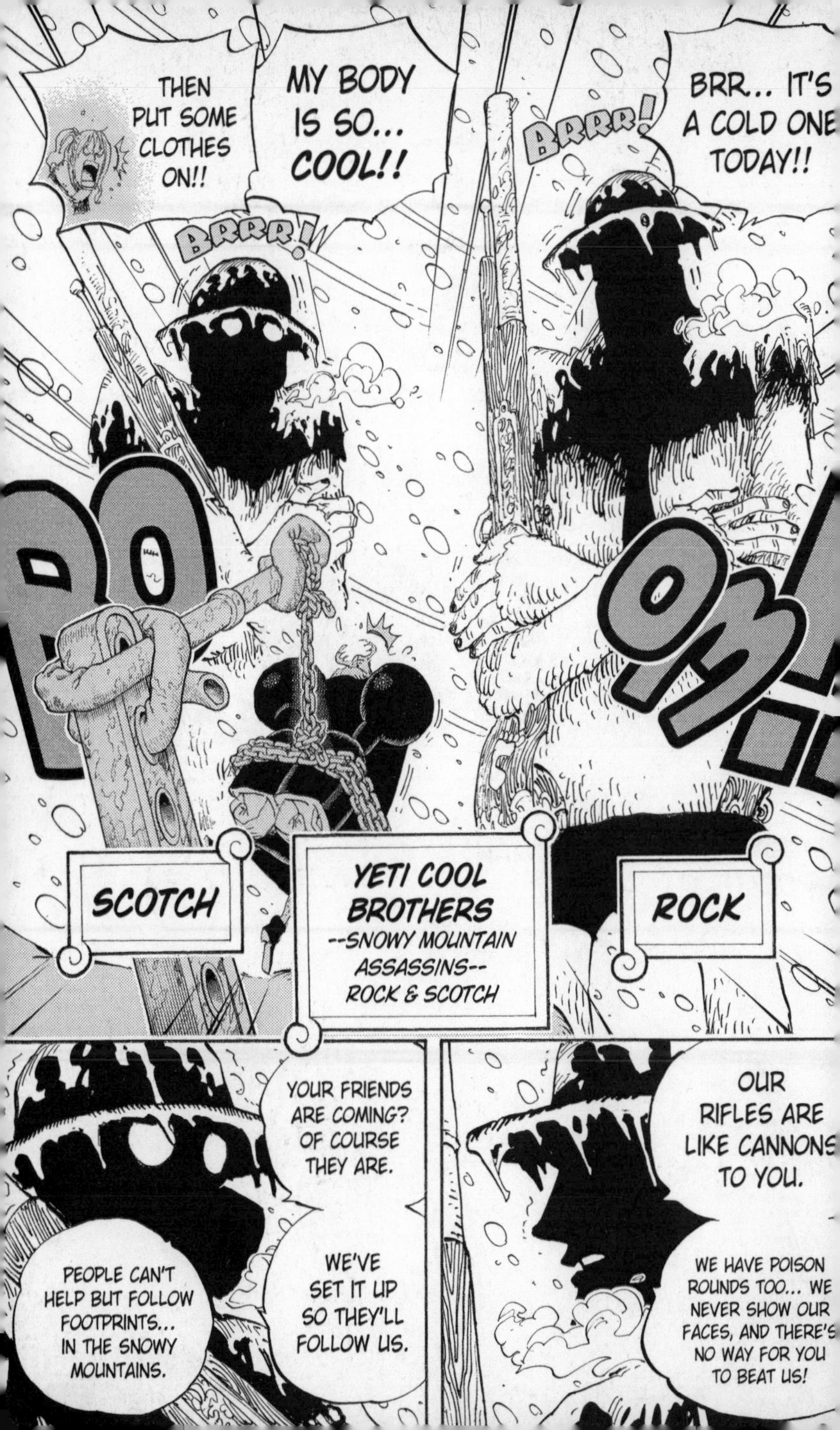
BRRR!
BRR... IT'S A COLD ONE TODAY!!
MY BODY IS SO... COOL!!
BRRR!
THEN PUT SOME CLOTHES ON!!
BOOM!!
ROCK
YETI COOL BROTHERS --SNOWY MOUNTAIN ASSASSINS-- ROCK & SCOTCH
SCOTCH
OUR RIFLES ARE LIKE CANNONS TO YOU.
WE HAVE POISON ROUNDS TOO... WE NEVER SHOW OUR FACES, AND THERE'S NO WAY FOR YOU TO BEAT US!
YOUR FRIENDS ARE COMING? OF COURSE THEY ARE.
WE'VE SET IT UP SO THEY'LL FOLLOW US.
PEOPLE CAN'T HELP BUT FOLLOW FOOTPRINTS... IN THE SNOWY MOUNTAINS.

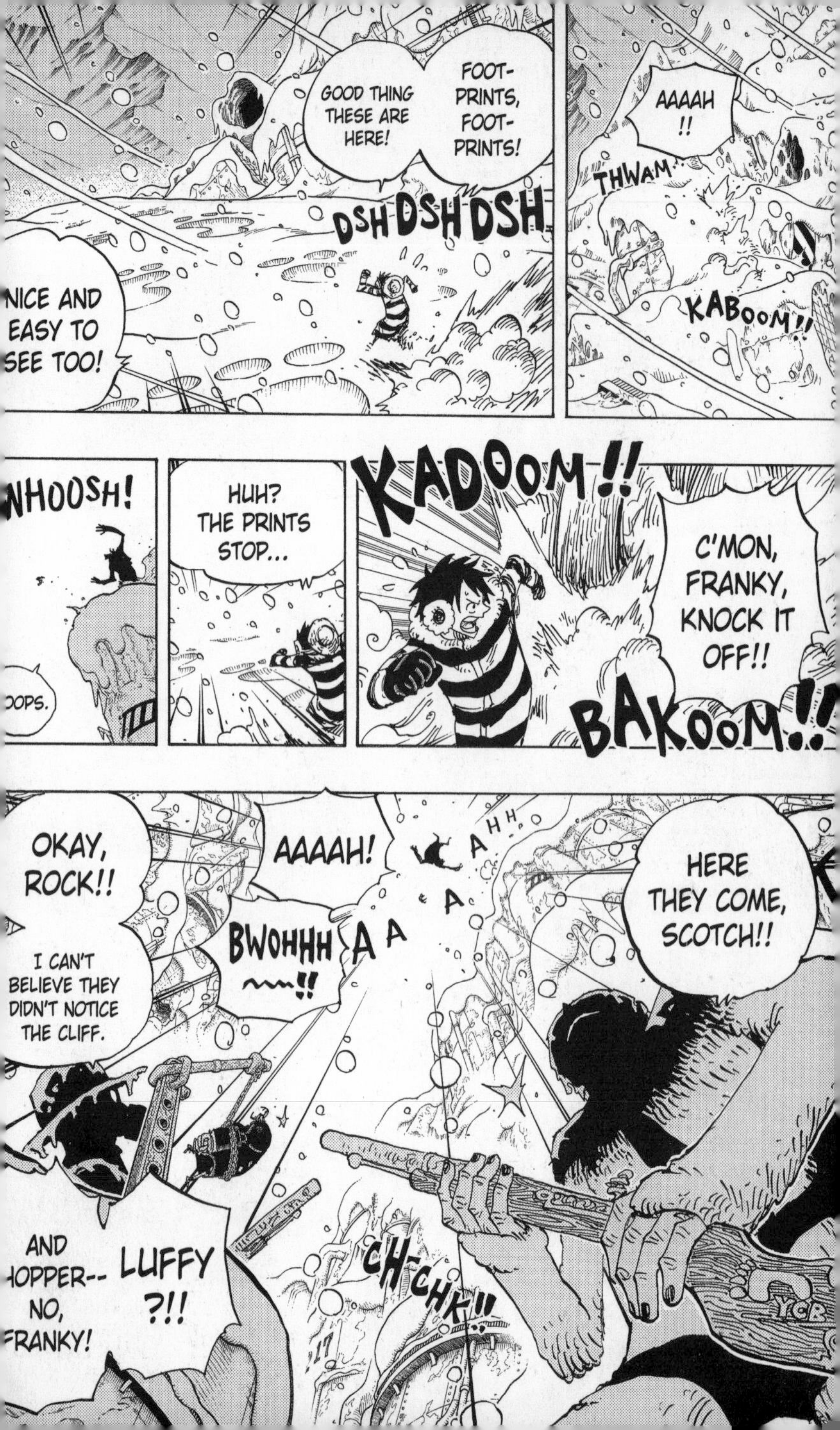
AAAAH !!
THWAM
KABOOM!!
FOOT-PRINTS, FOOT-PRINTS!
GOOD THING THESE ARE HERE!
DSH DSH DSH
NICE AND EASY TO SEE TOO!
KADOOM!!
C'MON, FRANKY, KNOCK IT OFF!!
BAKOOM!!
HUH? THE PRINTS STOP...
WHOOSH!
OOPS.
HERE THEY COME, SCOTCH!!
AAAAH!
A H H A A A A
BWOHHH ~~~!!
OKAY, ROCK!!
I CAN'T BELIEVE THEY DIDN'T NOTICE THE CLIFF.
CH-CHK!!
LUFFY ?!!
AND HOPPER-- NO, FRANKY!

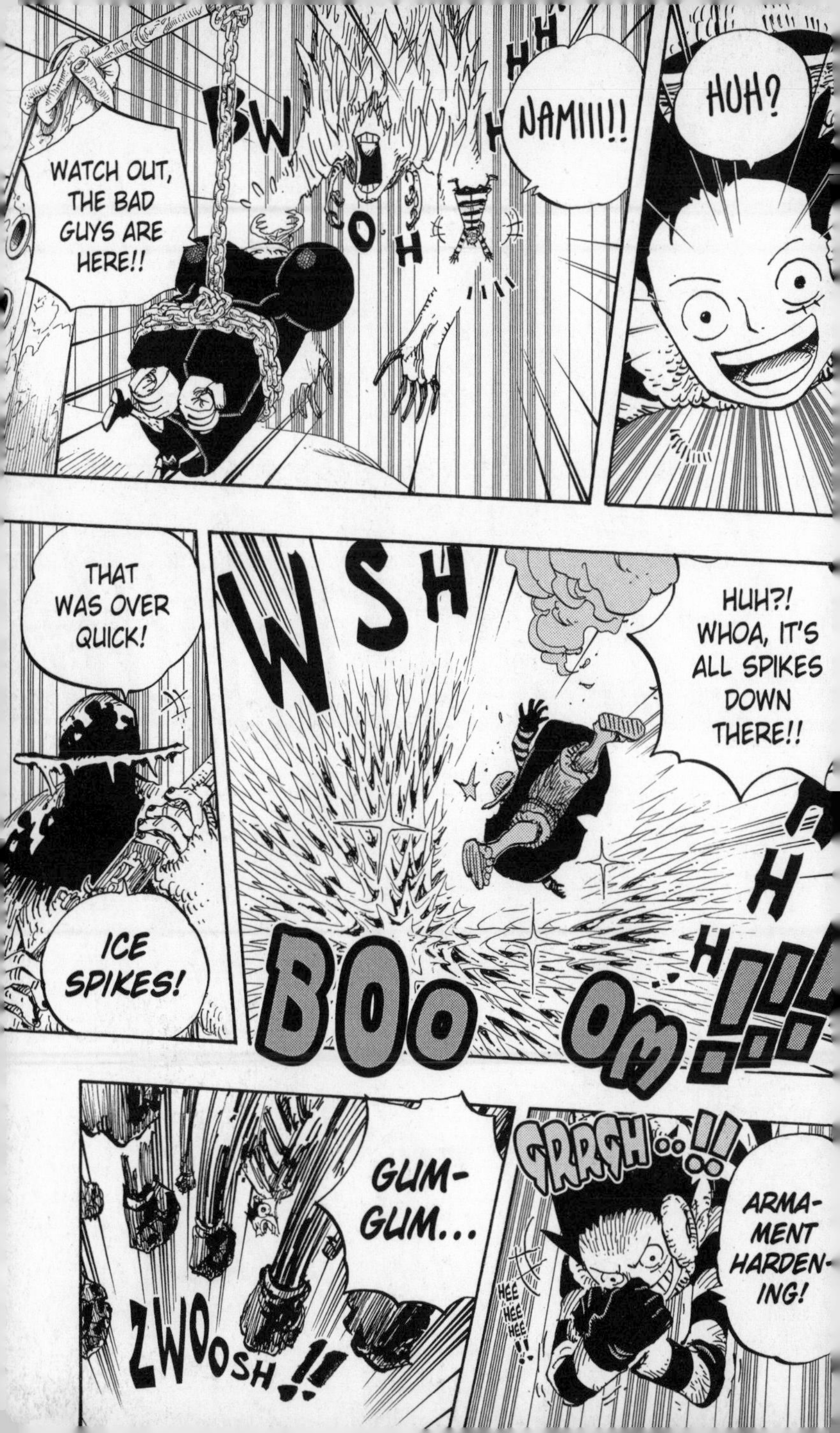
HUH?
NAMIIII!!
BWOHHHH
WATCH OUT, THE BAD GUYS ARE HERE!!
HUH?! WHOA, IT'S ALL SPIKES DOWN THERE!!
HHH
WSH
BOOOM!!!
THAT WAS OVER QUICK!
ICE SPIKES!
ARMA-MENT HARDEN-ING!
GRRGH..!!
HEE HEE HEE!!
GUM-GUM...
ZWOOSH!!

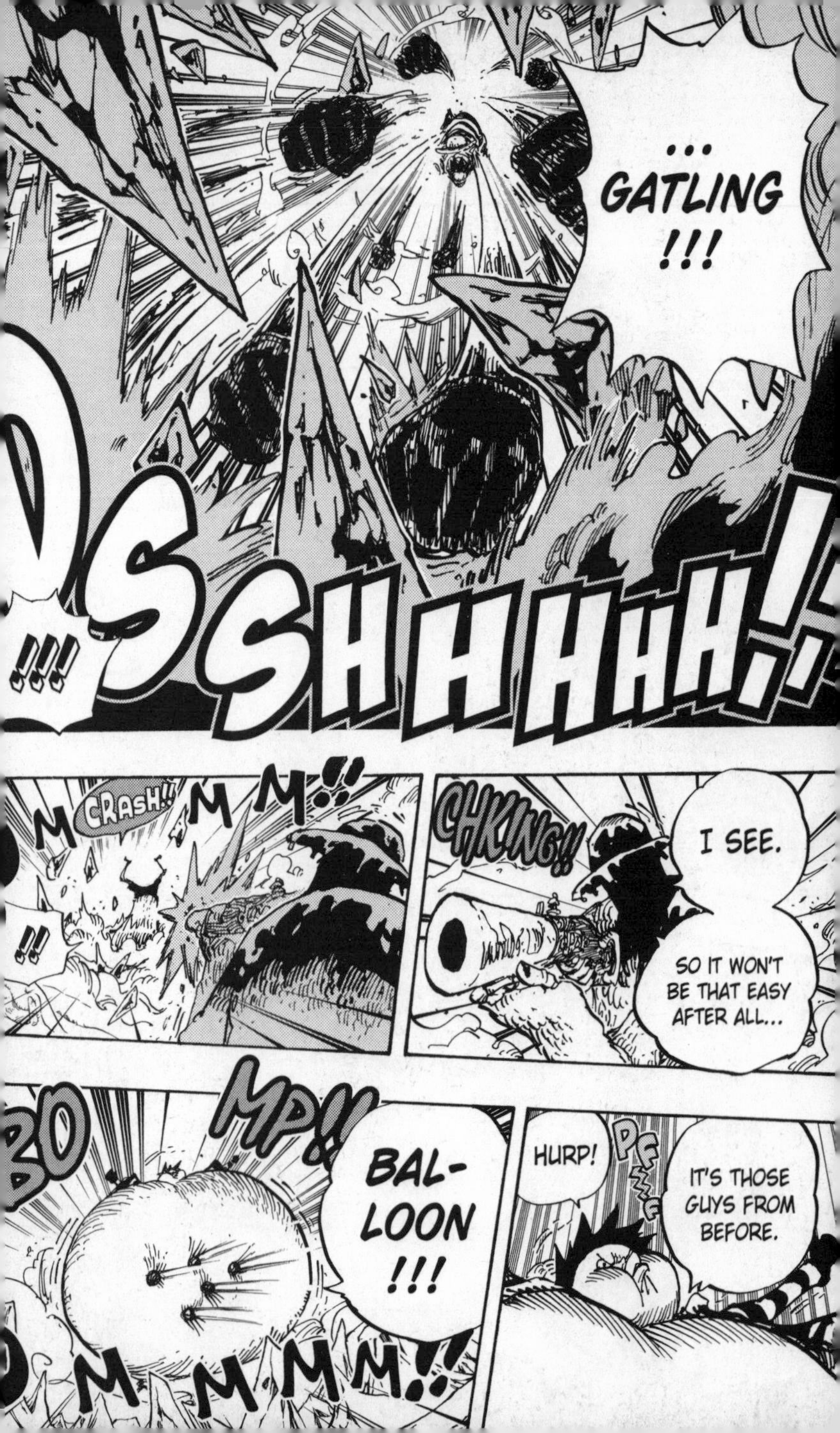

...GATLING !!!
SSHHHHH!!
!!!
CHKING!!
I SEE.
SO IT WON'T BE THAT EASY AFTER ALL...
M M M M!!
CRASH!!
!!
IT'S THOSE GUYS FROM BEFORE.
HURP!
PFFF
BOMP!!
BAL-LOON !!!
MMMM!!

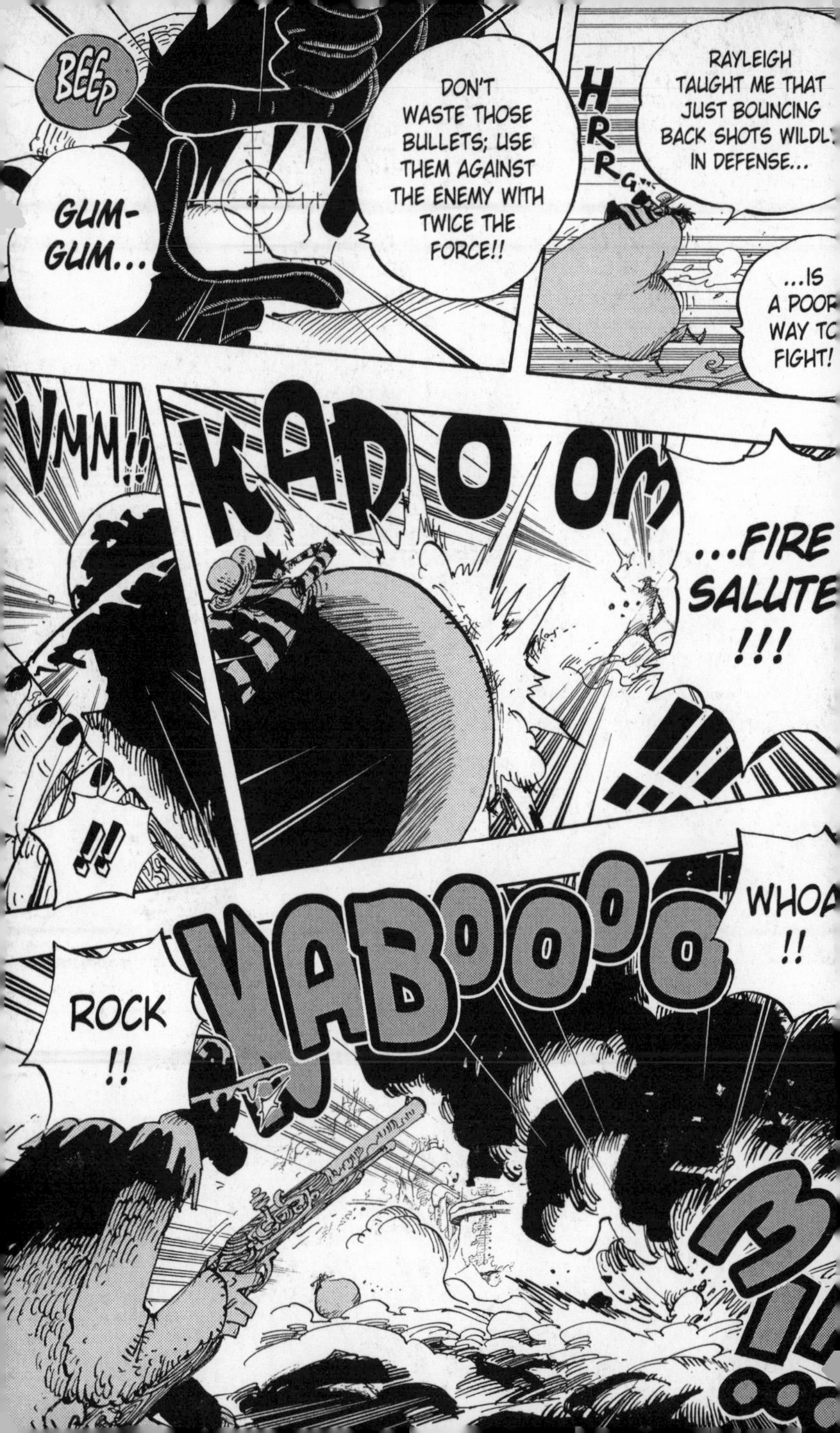
HRRG...
RAYLEIGH TAUGHT ME THAT JUST BOUNCING BACK SHOTS WILDL IN DEFENSE...
...IS A POOR WAY TO FIGHT!
BEEP
DON'T WASTE THOSE BULLETS; USE THEM AGAINST THE ENEMY WITH TWICE THE FORCE!!
GUM-GUM...
KADOOM
...FIRE SALUTE!!!
!!!
VMM!!
!!
WHOA!!
KABOOOOM
ROCK!!

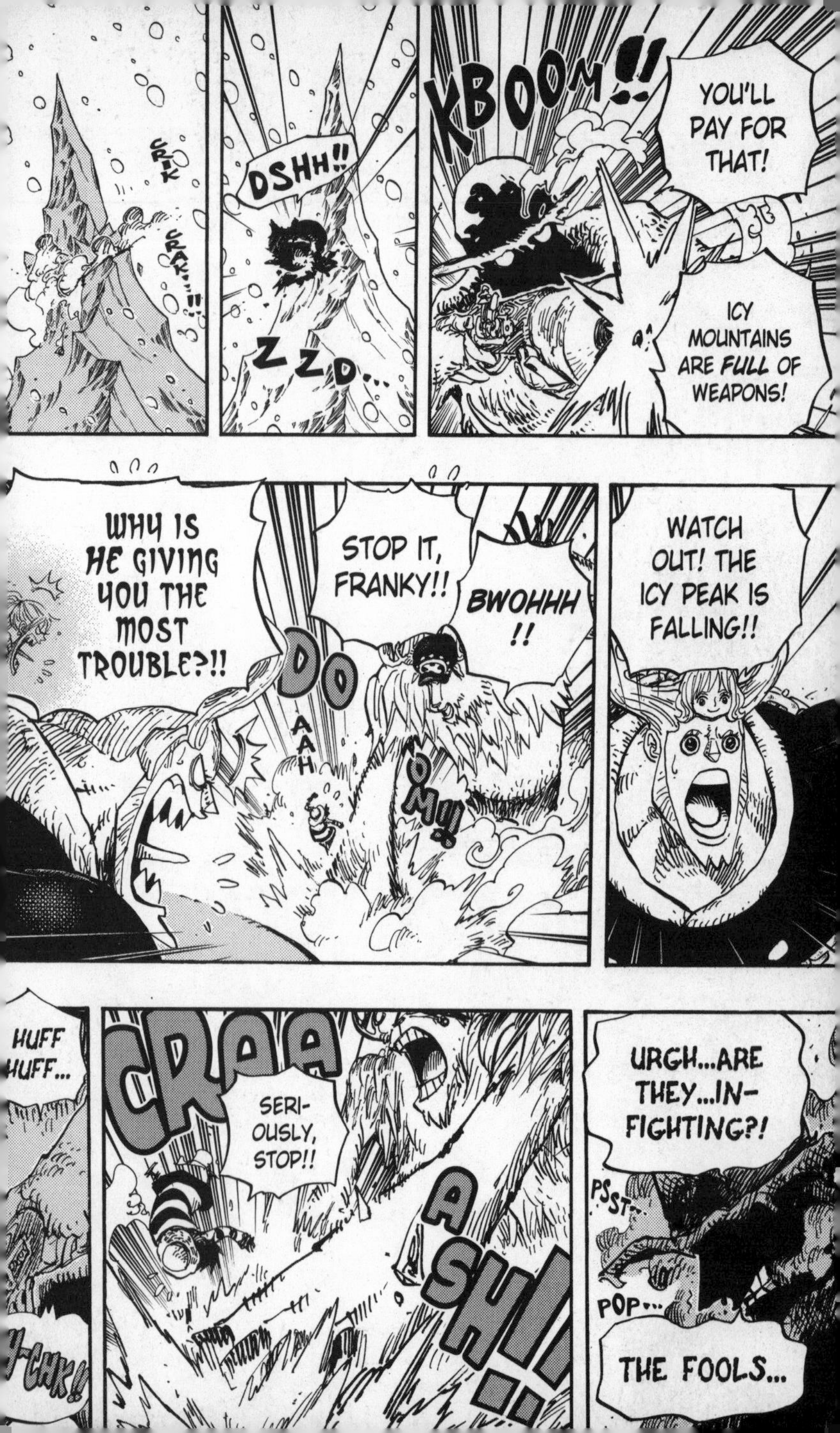
KBOOM!!
YOU'LL PAY FOR THAT!
ICY MOUNTAINS ARE FULL OF WEAPONS!
DSHH!!
ZZZD...
CRIK
CRAK...!!
WATCH OUT! THE ICY PEAK IS FALLING!!
STOP IT, FRANKY!!
BWOHHH!!
WHY IS HE GIVING YOU THE MOST TROUBLE?!!
DOOM!!
AAH
URGH...ARE THEY...IN-FIGHTING?!
PSST...
POP...
THE FOOLS...
CRAASH!!
SERI-OUSLY, STOP!!
HUFF HUFF...

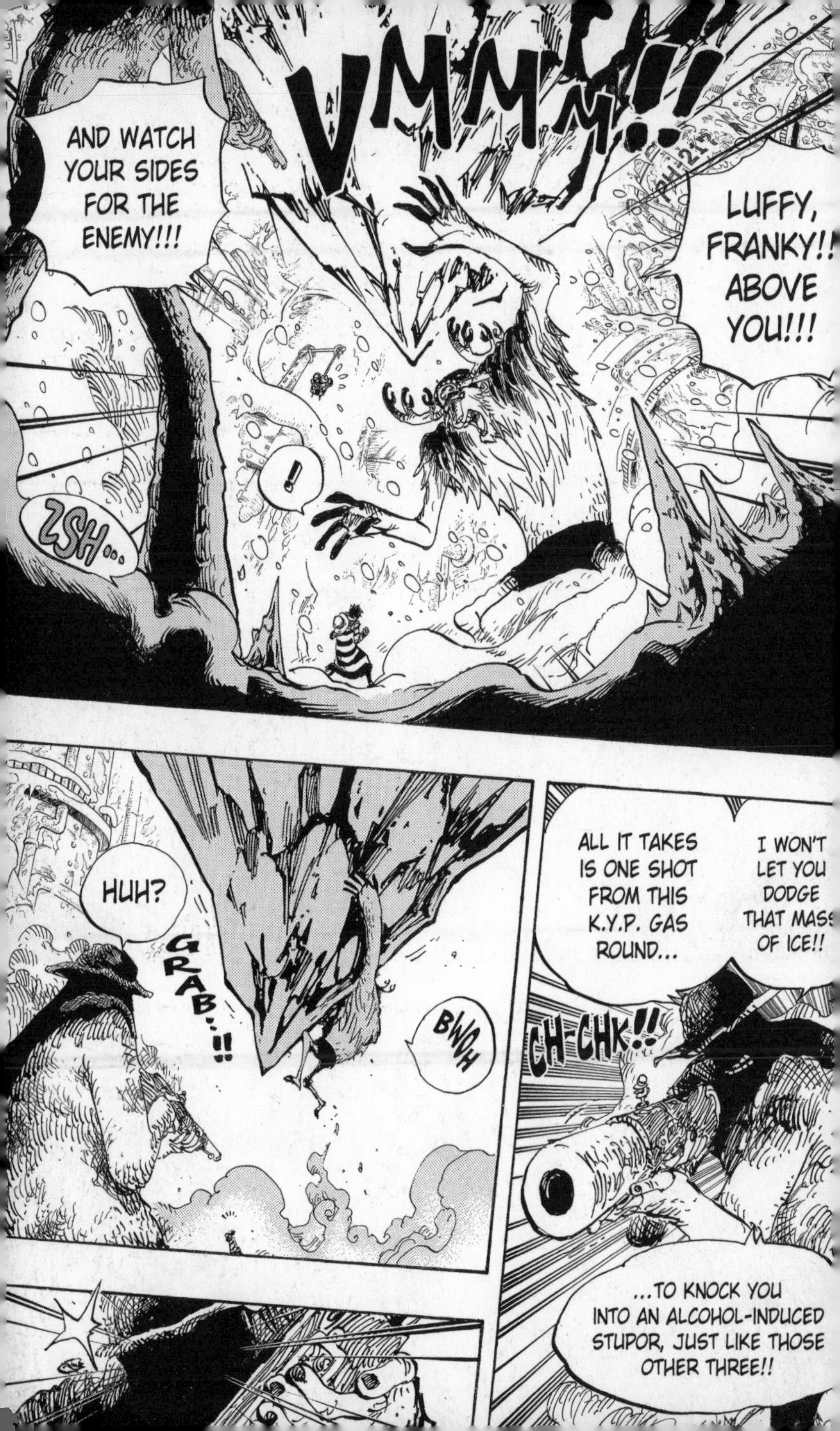
VMMMM!!
LUFFY, FRANKY!! ABOVE YOU!!!
AND WATCH YOUR SIDES FOR THE ENEMY!!!
!
ZSH...
I WON'T LET YOU DODGE THAT MASS OF ICE!!
ALL IT TAKES IS ONE SHOT FROM THIS K.Y.P. GAS ROUND...
CH-CHK!!
...TO KNOCK YOU INTO AN ALCOHOL-INDUCED STUPOR, JUST LIKE THOSE OTHER THREE!!
HUH?
GRAB...!!
BWOH

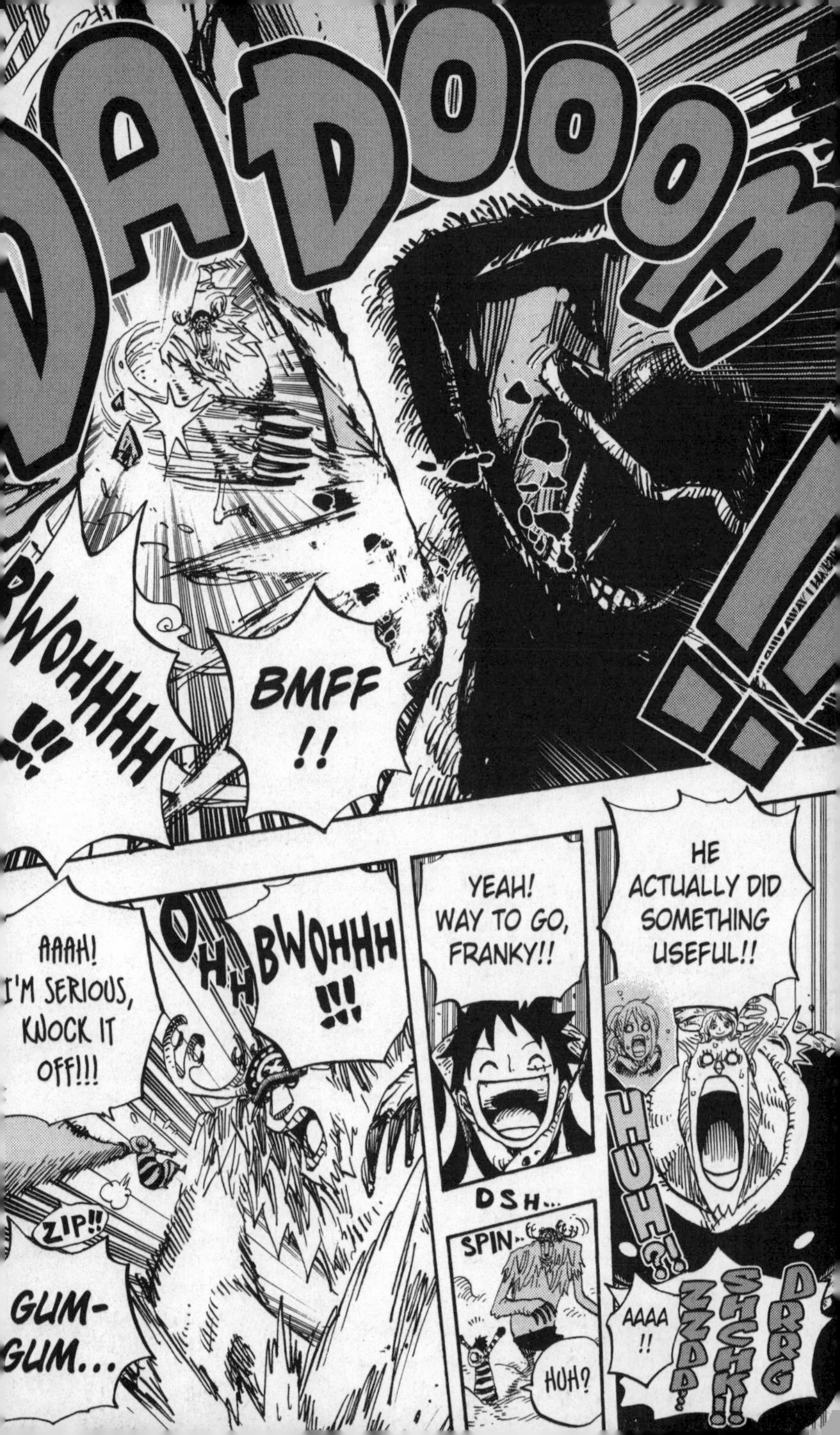
DADOOOM!!
BMFF!!
BWOHHHH!!!
HE ACTUALLY DID SOMETHING USEFUL!!
HUH?!
AAAA!!
DRG DRG
SHCHK!!
ZZDD...
YEAH! WAY TO GO, FRANKY!!
DSH...
SPIN..
HUH?
OHH BWOHHH!!!
AAAH! I'M SERIOUS, KNOCK IT OFF!!!
ZIP!!
GUM-GUM...

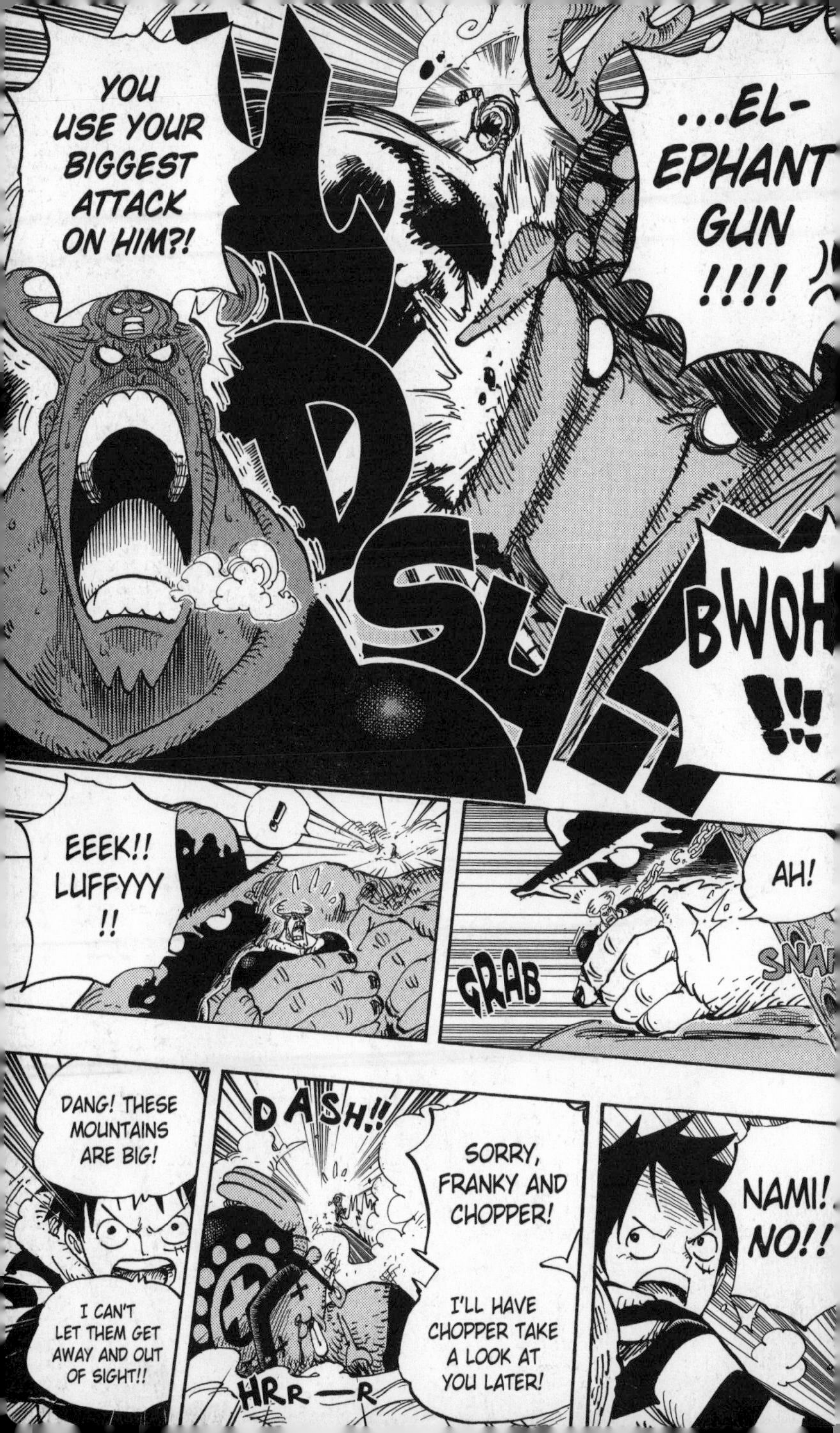
...EL-EPHANT GUN!!!!
BWOH!!!
YOU USE YOUR BIGGEST ATTACK ON HIM?!
AH!
GRAB
!
EEEK!! LUFFYYY!!
NAMI! NO!!
SORRY, FRANKY AND CHOPPER!
DASH!!
I'LL HAVE CHOPPER TAKE A LOOK AT YOU LATER!
HRR—R
DANG! THESE MOUNTAINS ARE BIG!
I CAN'T LET THEM GET AWAY AND OUT OF SIGHT!!

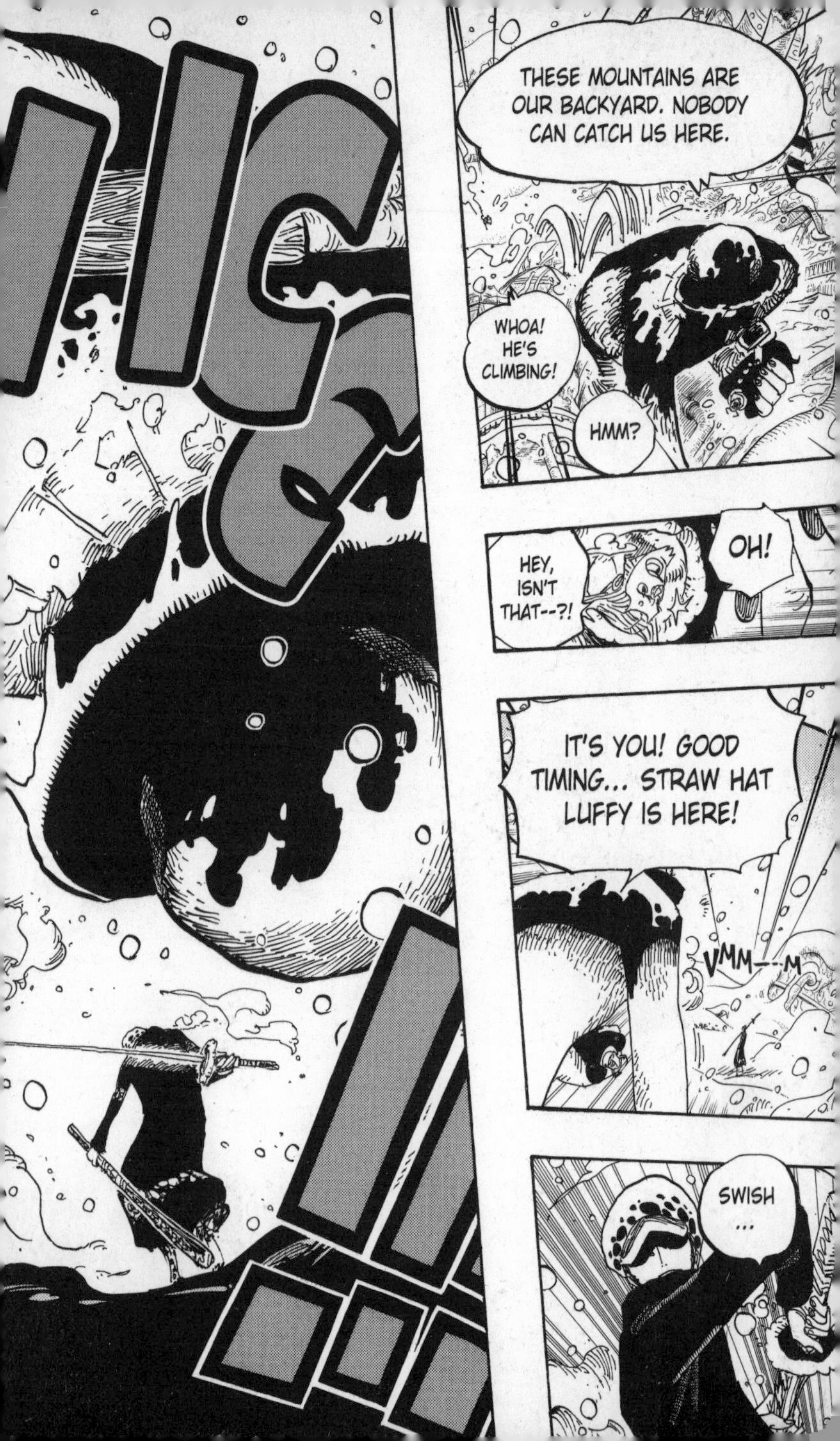

THESE MOUNTAINS ARE OUR BACKYARD. NOBODY CAN CATCH US HERE.
WHOA! HE'S CLIMBING!
HMM?
OH!
HEY, ISN'T THAT--?!
IT'S YOU! GOOD TIMING... STRAW HAT LUFFY IS HERE!
VMM---M
SWISH ...

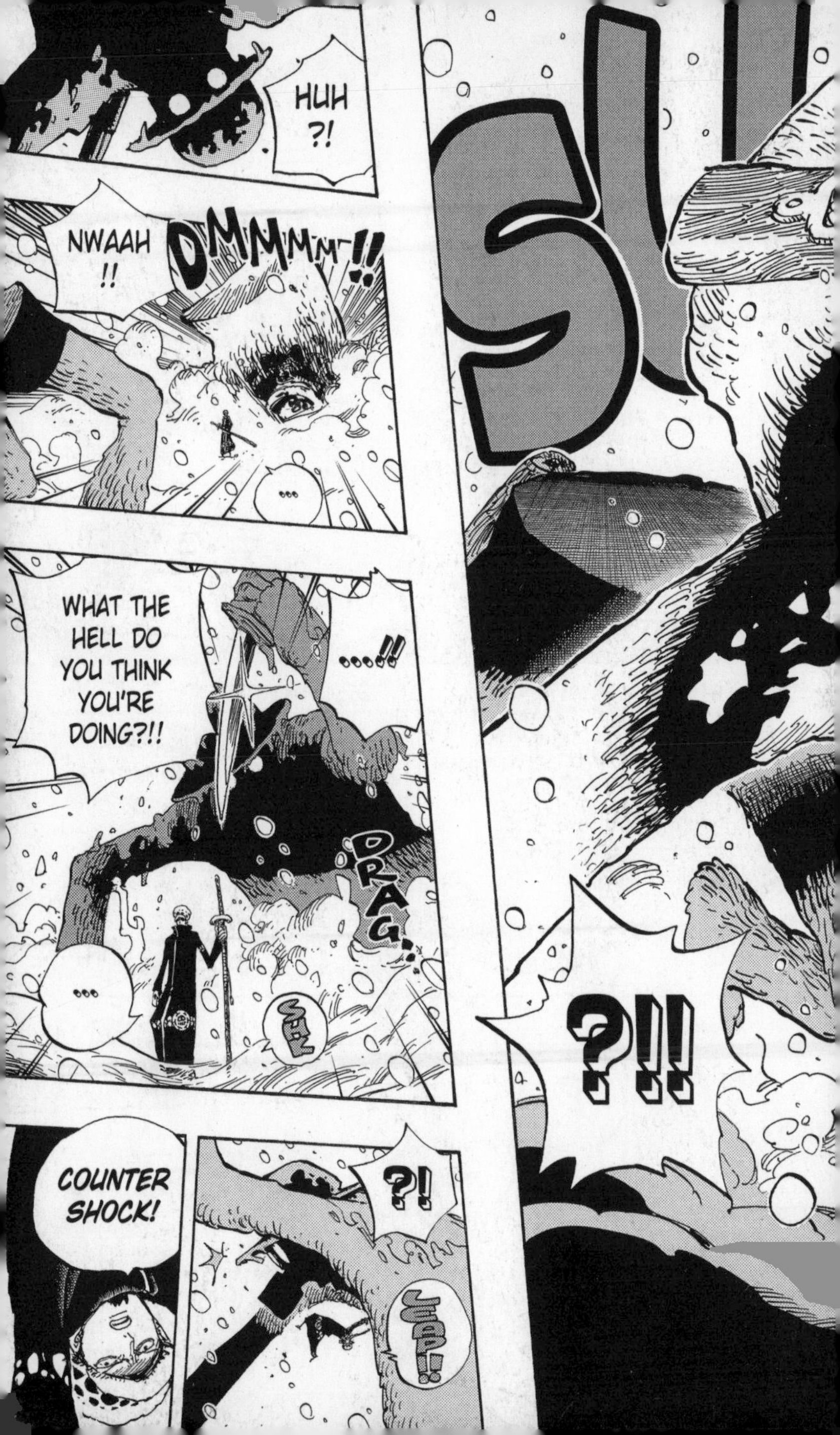
?!!
HUH ?!
NWAAH !!
DMMMM !!
...
WHAT THE HELL DO YOU THINK YOU'RE DOING?!!
...!!
DRAG..
...
?!
COUNTER SHOCK!

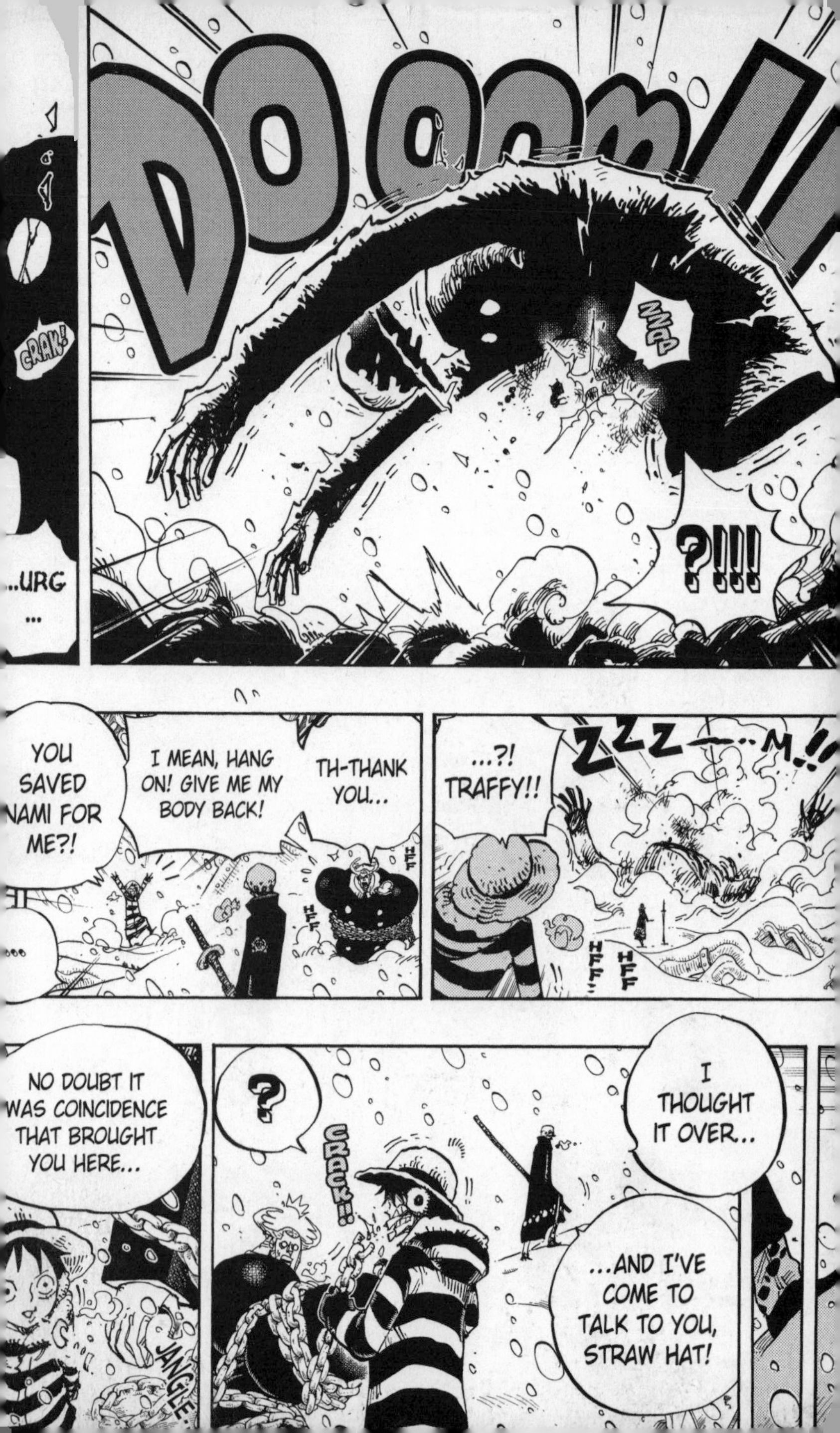
DOOOM!!
ZNAP
?!!!
CRAK!
...URG ...
ZZZ—M!!
...?! TRAFFY!!
HFF
HFF
TH-THANK YOU...
HFF
HFF
I MEAN, HANG ON! GIVE ME MY BODY BACK!
YOU SAVED NAMI FOR ME?!
...
I THOUGHT IT OVER...
...AND I'VE COME TO TALK TO YOU, STRAW HAT!
?
CRACK!!
NO DOUBT IT WAS COINCIDENCE THAT BROUGHT YOU HERE...
JANGLE

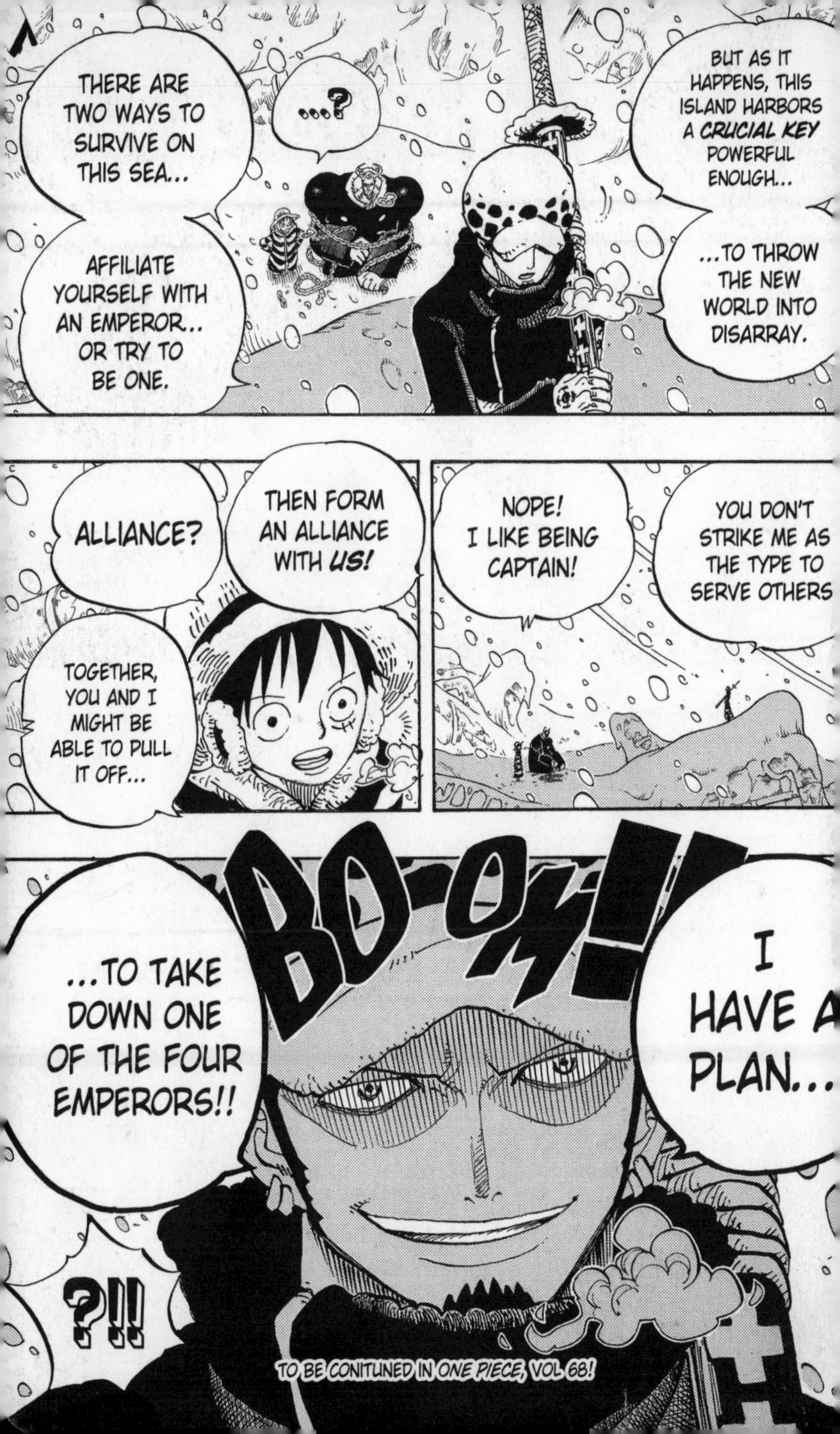
THERE ARE TWO WAYS TO SURVIVE ON THIS SEA...
AFFILIATE YOURSELF WITH AN EMPEROR.. OR TRY TO BE ONE.
...?
BUT AS IT HAPPENS, THIS ISLAND HARBORS A *CRUCIAL KEY* POWERFUL ENOUGH...
...TO THROW THE NEW WORLD INTO DISARRAY.
YOU DON'T STRIKE ME AS THE TYPE TO SERVE OTHERS
NOPE! I LIKE BEING CAPTAIN!
THEN FORM AN ALLIANCE WITH *US!*
ALLIANCE?
TOGETHER, YOU AND I MIGHT BE ABLE TO PULL IT OFF...
BO-OM!!
I HAVE A PLAN...
...TO TAKE DOWN ONE OF THE FOUR EMPERORS!!
?!!
TO BE CONITUNED IN ONE PIECE, VOL 68!

COMING NEXT VOLUME:

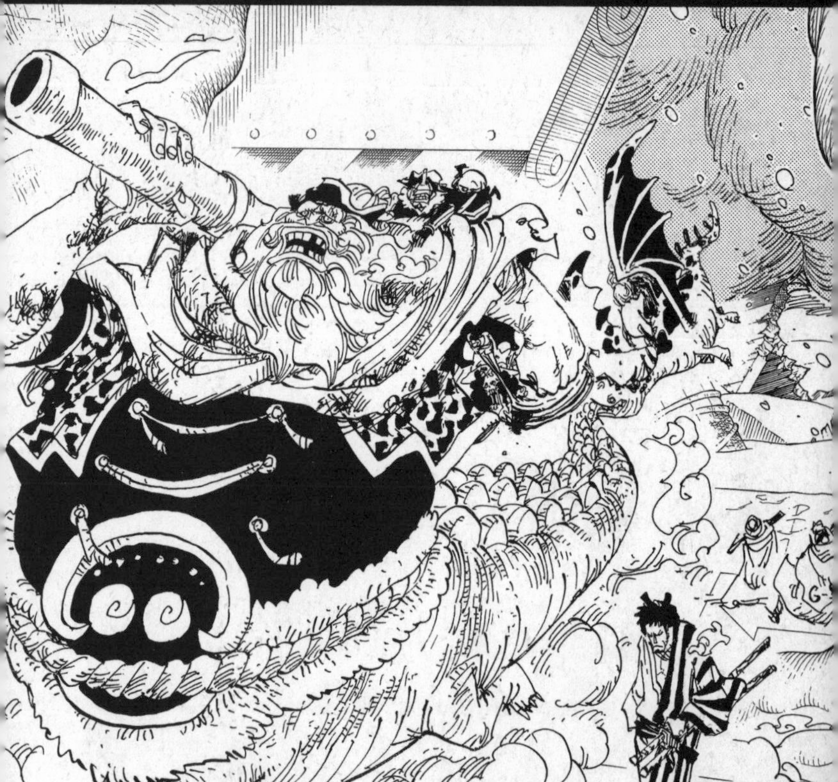

Trafalgar Law makes the shocking offer to form a pirate alliance with the Straw Hats in order to take down one of the four emperors. Will Luffy accept the terms? And what exactly is Law's plan?

ON SALE SEPTEMBER 2013!

BAKUMAN。

STORY BY TSUGUMI OHBA
ART BY TAKESHI OBATA

From the creators of *Death Note*

The mystery behind manga making REVEALED!

Average student Moritaka Mashiro enjoys drawing for fun. When his classmate and aspiring writer Akito Takagi discovers his talent, he begs to team up. But what exactly does it take to make it in the manga-publishing world?

Bakuman。, Vol. 1
ISBN: 978-1-4215-3513-5
$9.99 US / $12.99 CAN *

Manga on sale at store.viz.com
Also available at your local bookstore or comic store

You're Reading in the Wrong Direction!!

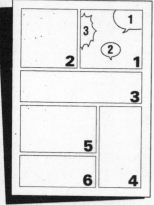

Whoops! Guess what? You're starting at the wrong end of the comic!

...It's true! In keeping with the original Japanese format, **One Piece** is meant to be read from right to left, starting in the upper-right corner.

Unlike English, which is read from left to right, Japanese is read from right to left, meaning that action, sound effects and word-balloon order are completely reversed...something which can make readers unfamiliar with Japanese feel pretty backwards themselves. For this reason, manga or Japanese comics published in the U.S. in English have sometimes been published "flopped"— that is, printed in exact reverse order, as though seen from the other side of a mirror.

By flopping pages, U.S. publishers can avoid confusing readers, but the compromise is not without its downside. For one thing, a character in a flopped manga series who once wore in the original Japanese version a T-shirt emblazoned with "M A Y" (as in "the merry month of") now wears one which reads "Y A M"! Additionally, many manga creators in Japan are themselves unhappy with the process, as some feel the mirror-imaging of their art skews their original intentions.

We are proud to bring you Eiichiro Oda's **One Piece** in the original unflopped format. For now, though, turn to the other side of the book and let the journey begin...!

—Editor